The shadow liabilities of EU member states and the threat they pose to global financial stability

by
Bob Lyddon

www.brugesgroup.com

Published in 2022 by The Bruges Group, 246 Linen Hall, 162-168 Regent Street, London W1B 5TB

Follow us on Twitter @brugesgroup, LinkedIn @brugesgroup, GETTR @brugesgroup

Facebook The Bruges Group, Instagram brugesgroup, YouTube brugesgroup

We are pleased to publish this important contribution to the debate on monetary stability in the Eurozone. I know that Bob Lyddon has devoted a huge amount of time in recent years to understanding the complex issues that arise from the form of monetary union that the European Union has constructed and its ongoing evolution. We also welcome the support he has received and the analysis undertaken by Barney Reynolds and Geoffrey Wood who have immense expertise on this subject.

BARRY LEGG
Chairman of the Bruges Group
February 2023

THE SHADOW LIABILITIES OF EU MEMBER STATES AND THE THREAT THEY POSE TO GLOBAL FINANCIAL STABILITY

Abstract

The EU/Eurozone participate in the rules-based international order, but they break its financial rules in both letter and spirit. The global financial system is a cornerstone of this international order. Rules for its operation have been devised by several global bodies. The bedrock is a proper accounting for the scale of the liabilities of governments and the wider public sector. The EU and the Eurozone member states fail to adequately account for their liabilities, undermining Eurostat's 'General government gross debt' as a reliable figure. The discrepancy consists both of shadow debts and unrecognized contingent liabilities as guarantor. The EU's 'General government gross debt' is understated by 44% if one takes account of the shadow debts, and by 70% if one factors in the contingent liabilities as well. Incomplete accounting masks the degree to which member states are out-of-compliance with the Fiscal Stability Pact. It is a threat to global financial stability where a major set of participants in the system understate their liabilities, because that leads on to the public credit rating agencies over-rating the respective entities' debts, and in turn to other participants in the system setting aside too little capital to account for the risks they are running by doing business with these entities, and/or to other participants – like Central Counterparties running clearing houses for derivatives – requiring too thin a security margin. The Euro currency is structurally weaker than it is made to appear, and both Eurozone and non-Eurozone member states in the EU have higher liabilities than Eurostat reports. Central banks, monetary authorities and investors outside the EU should be pressing for disclosure of detailed information on these liabilities, as well as ensuring that their own financial markets and practices do not replicate the related practices. There are also important implications for the EU's plan to onshore – particularly from London – the clearing of Euro derivatives contracts, because a clearing house should enjoy an adequate collateral margin and the collateral itself ought to be of the highest quality.

Acknowledgments

With thanks to Barnabas Reynolds, Partner, Shearman and Sterling,[1] and Professor Geoffrey Wood, Visiting Lecturer at the University of Buckingham,[2] for their support and guidance during the writing of this book.

---

[1] https://www.shearman.com/People/R/Reynolds-Barnabas accessed on 19 October 2022
[2] https://www.buckingham.ac.uk/directory/professor-geoffrey-wood/ accessed on 19 October 2022

Contents

Contents (cont'd)

List of figures

About the author – Bob Lyddon

Bob has been a major contributor to public debate about the financing mechanisms of the EU and Eurozone. Between 2016 and 2018 Global Britain issued the eight 'Brexit Papers'.[3] In 2021 The Bruges Group issued Bob's paper entitled 'The ECB's Pandemic Emergency Purchase Programme: the undermining of the Eurozone as a free financial market, the epitome of the failure of the Euro project, and a coup d'état by the European Central Bank'. In 2020 Politeia published the book 'Managing Euro Risk', of which Bob was co-author with Barney Reynolds and Professor David Blake.

Bob Lyddon is an experienced management consultant now privately and formerly with PwC.

Recent engagements include:
- Advice to an Electronic Money Institution about options for connecting to the Single Euro Payments Area credit transfer scheme
- Online courses for the accountancy profession on Cash Management, Liquidity Management, Treasury Key Performance Indicators and Anti-Money Laundering/Countering the Financing of Terrorism (AML/CFT)
- Advising Swedish and UK payment institutions on their payments and treasury operations and AML/CFT duties
- Chairing the trade body for the UK's Payment Institutions and lobbying on the issue of their having been cut adrift by the UK's banks
- Expert witness cases on invoice fraud and on international 'cover payments' using the SWIFT MT103 and MT202 COV messages
- Advising a worldwide co-operative for interbank financial telecommunication on opportunities and threats emanating from the establishment of the Payment Systems Regulator, the Payment Strategy Forum and New Payments Architecture

Between 2003 and 2016 Bob ran the central secretariat of the IBOS international banking alliance - www.ibosbanks.com – and expanded it to 70% of global GDP.

With PwC Bob managed several programmes at the time of the initial introduction of the Euro, and prior to that, in a career in international banking spanning 17 years, Bob designed the 'Connector' cash management network – www.connectorbanks.com - for BankBoston, and arranged numerous syndicated loans and derivatives transactions for Chemical Bank/Manufacturers Hanover and for Lloyds Bank International.

Bob Lyddon holds a Bachelor of Arts (First Class) in Modern Languages from the University of Cambridge, gained in 1980, and Master of Arts (Distinction) in History from the Open University, gained in 2022, with dissertation subject 'King's Lynn and the new police, 1830-45'.

---

[3] www.brexitpapers.uk

Setting the scene - why this subject is important

The public authorities of EU and Eurozone have made themselves responsible for much larger amounts of debt and contingent liabilities than are shown in Eurostat, the main statistical database for EU public debt.

Public credit rating agencies consult this database as a mainstay of their analysis, as do other market actors taking risk on EU and Eurozone counterparties. These other market actors also rely heavily on the public credit rating agencies.

Market actors operate risk-management systems which determine the quantum of risk that a particular piece of business with a counterparty presents for them, a process which has results:
- For a bank: the allocation of an amount of capital to support the piece of business;
- For a Central Counterparty such as a derivatives clearing house: the specification of eligible collateral and the security margin applying to that collateral (the so-called 'haircut');
- For institutional investors: the portfolio limit for exposure to that type of business with that counterparty;
- For all the above: the assessment of the liquidity of a financial instrument they hold and at what value it qualifies for inclusion in their obligatory holdings of liquid instruments.

The global financial system is under-weighting its risk on EU and Eurozone public sector business: EU and Eurozone member states are less creditworthy than they appear because they are more indebted. In consequence, dealing with them involves more risk than financial market actors realize. There is therefore, within the global financial system, a sizeable missing amount of regulatory capital, of collateral held within Central Counterparties, and of liquid financial instruments. Were the missing amount present, the global financial system might be as resilient and stable as global financial regulators contend it to be. Its absence is a risk to global financial stability.

It is a risk supplementary to the one explored in 'Managing Euro Risk', which focused on the diminished quality of the euro as a currency because it has no risk-free counterparty backing it.[4] The governments of Eurozone member states are not genuine sovereign borrowers in the way the governments of the USA, UK, Switzerland and Japan are. As a result financial dealings within them should not be accorded a 0% risk-weighting under the BIS methodologies employed in the global financial system for assessing risk.[5] The governments of Eurozone member states are sub-sovereigns, meaning that other public sector borrowers are sub-sub-sovereigns.

It is not the intention of this book to go over this logic again: 'Managing Euro Risk' proved the sub-sovereign status of governments of Eurozone member states, and thereby proved that other types of public sector entity were sub-sub-sovereign, and that none of them should be accorded a 0% risk-weighting under BIS methodologies.

This book proves that the volume of debts is significantly higher than acknowledged.

These two issues are major blindspots in global risk management. Both are individually an area of systemic risk. The combination adds up to significant systemic risk.

Public credit rating agencies appear to be unaware of this significant qualification to the creditworthiness of EU and Eurozone member states. Central banks, monetary authorities and investors outside the EU do not have to share this myopia, and they should be pressing for disclosure of detailed information about the shadow debts and contingent liabilities, as well as ensuring that their own financial markets do not replicate the related practices.

---

[4] Barney Reynolds, Professor David Blake and Bob Lyddon, '*Managing Euro Risk*', Politeia, 2020
[5] The BIS is the Bank for International Settlements, based in Basel, and issues the global frameworks for bank capitalization, leverage and liquidity, which are often referred to as the Basel Accords, or Basel 1, Basel 2 and so on

Setting the scene - what is meant by the term 'sovereign risk'

'Sovereign risk' is the credit risk on a government that:
- Can call upon all the tax-paying entities in its country to help the government meet the capital and interest payments on its debts; and
- Has at its disposal the full powers over the management of its currency, such as setting interest rates.

The backing of all tax-paying entities in the country is sometimes expressed through the phrase 'full faith and credit'.[6]

A classic definition of a sovereign risk loan is simply a loan to a government, the associated risk being expressed as that 'governments always pay their debts'. This definition has been challenged several times over recent decades, and firstly around the currency of a loan.

It is accepted that a government will always be able to meet its capital and interest payments to investors in the government's own currency. This is how a 'risk-free investment' comes to exist. There is no guarantee, though, what those amounts will be worth in a different currency at the time the investor receives them or compared to the value of the loan expressed in a different currency at the time the loan was taken out.

The certainty that 'governments always pay their debts' is seriously undermined not just when a government takes on a debt in a foreign currency, but also when:
- A government adopts a foreign currency as its home currency, such as Ecuador adopting the US$, or the UAE having a currency which is permanently pegged to the US$; or
- Where the government uses a currency as its home currency, but shares control of the policy levers over it, and even surrenders them to a body over which it has tenuous control, such as the euro.

Banks have forever sought the comfort of having public sector support for their lending.

In the wake of the 1970s oil shock, banks played a role in recycling the funds accumulated by oil exporting countries and lending them back to other countries to help them develop their economies. Because these borrowers did not have the highest credit ratings, and because Western governments saw an opportunity to drive down domestic unemployment via export trade, a market developed in export credit lending.

It was based on the concept that sovereigns do not default. It was also based on splitting the credit risk for lending banks between two sovereigns: the borrower sovereign, and the sovereign of the country in which the exporter resided and from which, logically, the goods and services would be exported.

A typical loan would have been this one, provided by Lloyds Bank International, Amsterdam branch, together with a small syndicate of other lenders, in 1982. The borrower was the government of the Federal Republic of Nigeria: Dutch guilders (NLG) 200 million to finance the construction of dry docks in Lagos and Port Harcourt by the Royal Dutch Harbourworks Company N.V., a subsidiary of Hollandsche Beton Groep N.V..

The loan was in two portions and each ranked as a sovereign risk loan:
- A NLG30 million downpayment financing, of 15% of the contract amount, to the Federal Republic of Nigeria. It was to be drawn within 30 days of the loan agreement being signed. It was repayable in 10 equal semi-annual instalments with the first one due thirty months after the loan was drawn, which should have been six months after the dry docks were commissioned;
- A NLG170 million financing, of 85% the contract amount, also made to the Federal Republic of Nigeria and drawn down over the twenty-four months of the construction work. It was repayable in 20 equal semi-annual instalments with the first one due six months after the loan became fully drawn, which should have been six months after the dry docks were commissioned.

Mechanically all the money was paid directly to Royal Dutch Harbourworks Company N.V., NLG30 million against a downpayment receipt, and the remainder against invoices countersigned by the Federal Republic of Nigeria attesting that a given stage had been reached in the construction.

---

[6] https://www.investopedia.com/terms/f/full-faith-credit.asp accessed on 29 September 2022

The key point about the second portion was that 95% of the capital and of a part of the interest on it were insured, for the benefit of the lenders, with the Dutch Credit Insurance Company N.V. (NCM) and reinsured by them with the Dutch Ministry of Finance.

As a result of the credit insurance policy from NCM, the lenders would regard the whole financing as being sovereign risk, albeit some on Nigeria and some on the Netherlands:
- NLG30 million downpayment financing – Nigeria
- 95% of the NLG170 million financing – the Netherlands = NLG161.5 million
- 5% of the NLG170 million financing – Nigeria = NLG8.5 million
- Total country exposure on Nigeria – NLG38.5 million

This business was anchored on the concept that governments always pay their debts, but this was proved to be flawed: in quick succession from the summer of 1983 several countries did default, starting with Mexico, but only on their foreign currency debt. Nigeria defaulted, and so did the above financing.

The response of global regulators was to narrow the definition of countries who were considered immune to default – on debts in their own or in a foreign currency – to members of the Organization for Economic Cooperation and Development or OECD. When the first regime was introduced for how much capital banks needed to hold when they were taking sovereign risk, it was set at 0% for OECD governments.

This regime was issued by the Bank for International Settlements in Basel, hence it became known as Basel 1.

The next regime, Basel 2, permitted banks to substitute a less categorical methodology for assessing risk, under which they could make an assessment of their counterparty and of the piece of business in hand, and combine the two into a risk-weighting: this was the genesis of Risk-Adjusted Return on Capital Models, which are now more commonly known by the epithet of Internal Ratings-Based models or IRB.

These are in global usage in the finance industry and they have generally retained a 0% risk-weighting for business with OECD sovereigns, without insisting on a distinction between where a country does and does not hold the levers of monetary control over the currency in which the liability is denominated. Nigeria at the time had control of the naira; Mexico had control of the Mexican peso. Neither had control of the US dollar or Dutch guilder, which was vested in the governments of the USA and the Netherlands.

The USA has retained that control, but the Netherlands has ceded it to the European Central Bank by adopting the euro. It retains a tenuous, diluted degree of control. Basel methodologies have not addressed this issue of the degree of control: the euro is neither a proper domestic currency nor a fully foreign one for a member state. The member state is represented in the bodies that make decisions about the Eurosystem, but this falls well short of sovereign control. The risk-weighting for a Eurozone member state government should not be the same as for the UK on this basis, assuming a parity of other economic statistics.

The guideline ought to be that, given a parity of economic statistics, a country with control over its currency should be less heavily risk-weighted than one that had only partial control.

Unfortunately the current arrangements do not permit this degree of subtlety. It has become ingrained that Eurozone member states, because they are all OECD members, should enjoy a 0% risk-weighting, and whether the debt is in euro or a foreign currency.

The arrangements are not calibrated to the changing definition of sovereign risk:
- 'Governments always pay their debts' (pre-1983);
- 'Governments always pay their debts as long as they are in the currency they use' (1983-2009);
- 'Governments always pay their debts as long as they are in the currency only they use' (2010-present).

Greece, where private investors had to take a credit loss in 2010, is the example of the flaw in the second definition which gave rise to the insertion of the word 'only' in the third one.

Setting the scene - what is meant by a 'shadow debt'

A 'shadow debt' for the purposes of this book means a public sector debt that is not captured in the EU's main statistical database, Eurostat.[7] The debt may be created via the issuance of a debt security or the contracting of a loan, and it may be taken up from an institutional investor, from a bank or from retail investors.

The key point is that the suppliers of the debt believe – and this will be with justification - that the public sector is responsible for the payment of capital and interest on the debt. The direct borrower of a shadow debt will not be a member state government or any other entity that falls within Eurostat's definition of 'General government'. The direct borrower may even be a private company. Nevertheless the structure of the financing gives the lender or investor an assurance that monies will be forthcoming from the taxpayer in the event that the direct borrower cannot pay the capital and interest.

The financing structures come in a number of forms, which serves to obscure the size of the claim on taxpayers. The debts may be off-balance sheet for parties who are nevertheless on-risk. This type of financing has been growing and will continue to grow because programmes for the recovery from the Pandemic and for the achievement of Net Zero are being mobilized using such financing templates.

The financing templates avoid that any debt taken up from lenders or investors should appear as part of a member state's 'General government gross debt' as captured by Eurostat.

This figure is the numerator in the calculation of Debt-to-GDP for measuring member states' compliance with the Fiscal Stability Pact. This Pact and the Stability & Growth Pact are cornerstones of the euro project and are supposed tokens that the euro is a homogenous currency on the grounds that all its user member states are of the same credit quality, as indicated by consistent measures of economic performance. The main measures are the Debt-to-GDP and the annual fiscal surplus/deficit. Debts contracted by and deficits incurred in entities who fall outside the of Eurostat's definition of 'General government' do not weigh on these measures.

The device of contracting 'shadow debts' outside of Eurostat's scope both exaggerates member states' compliance with the Fiscal Stability Pact and overstates member states' creditworthiness: there is more debt than is shown in the Eurostat figures but no more debt servicing capacity.

---

[7] https://ec.europa.eu/eurostat/ accessed on 31 May 2022

Setting the scene - what is meant by a 'shadow contingent liability'

A 'contingent liability' means an undertaking to pay if a certain circumstance materializes.

A 'shadow contingent liability' for the purposes of this book means a contingent liability of an EU/Eurozone entity that falls within Eurostat's definition of 'General government' but which is not included in Eurostat's table of the contingent liabilities of 'General government'.

The most normal form of contingent liability is a guarantee, such as the member state's guarantee of the EU budget if it should, for example, go into deficit because the EU has had to pay out on one of its guarantees in favour of the European Investment Bank.

Another form of contingent liability arises when a member state has subscribed to the capital of the European Investment Bank, but it has subscribed to part-paid shares. The paid portion may be only 10%. This means that the shareholder has a contingent liability to pay in the remaining 90%.

A further form arises where a shareholder, like a Eurozone national central bank, allows the European Central Bank to engage in very large operations when the European Central Bank has no cushion itself to absorb losses. It can only look to its shareholders to make good the losses. While the Eurozone national central bank has not issued a guarantee or subscribed to part-paid shares so as to irrevocably and unconditionally commit to make good the losses, the integrity of the Euro project dictates that they must, so it is right that a contingent liability be recorded against them.

Setting the scene - presenting a fair picture

Presenting a fair overall picture from a topic as complicated as this one will involve decisions, and those decisions will rightly be open to challenge.

The decisions made and the reasons why are contained in the sections on the related topic, but it will be helpful to highlight here some of the main ones.

Bailout mechanisms

All the loans given out by the European Financial Stabilisation Mechanism, European Financial Stability Facility and the European Stability Mechanism are borrowed by member states and are therefore included in that member state's 'General government gross debt'.

Why, then, are contingent liabilities as guarantor recorded against the other member states as well, for the amounts they might be called upon to pay if the borrowing member state does not? Is that not double-counting?

The reason is that investors in the bonds issued by the bailout mechanisms are relying on the guarantors for repayment, and not the borrowers. The borrowers have already defaulted on their debts, which is why a bailout mechanism was established.

This fact would have been obscured if no contingent liability had been recorded against the guarantor member states, and it is a fact of high importance: risk is transferred through these bailout mechanisms from weaker member states to stronger ones, and that needs to be reflected in the statistics of the guarantors.

The EU Coronavirus Recovery Fund

€80.0 billion was drawn from this fund in 2021. It could have been disbursed as either grants or loans. €390 billion of the fund total of €750 billion is to be disbursed as grants, and €360 billion as loans.

Loans – assuming they were made to an entity falling within 'General government' – would have been subject to the same decision as the bailout funds: recording both the debt and a contingent liability as guarantor would risk an accusation of double-counting.

Grants are simply a debt created by the EU and paid away and should be recorded as a 'shadow debt'.

Because we have no information on (i) what portion of the €80.0 billion was paid out as grants and what as loans, or (ii) whether, even if some was paid out as loans, the borrower fell within 'General government' or outside, we only have the knowledge that the majority of the fund will be paid out as grants.

We have assumed the 2021 amount was all paid out as grants. This avoids the risk of double-counting that exists with loans. It also avoids making either an arbitrary split or a split based on the overall proportions in the programme of 360/750 for loans (i.e. €38.4 billion/€80.0 billion) and 390/750 for grants (i.e. €41.6 billion/€80.0 billion).

The effect of this decision is to raise the 'Debt' portion of member states' liability for the EU's operations as compared to the 'Contingent liability': they already add up to €750 billion because the entire fund has been committed to. In due course €390.0 billion will have moved to the 'Debt' portion, €360 billion remaining as a 'Contingent liability'. The treatment used in this book is merely a small acceleration of this transfer, as against a pro-rata treatment of €56 billion per annum (€390 divided by 7). A possible – but not certain – anomaly of €25 billion seems an acceptable price to pay for avoiding the double-counting issue that arises regarding the bailout funds.

TARGET2 balances

The TARGET2 balances raise three issues.

Firstly the size of the gross balances is opaque. It may be a surprise to some that there are gross balances at all, but there must be, over and above what is in the monthly reports that the ECB issues. Otherwise there would be no need for either the Multilateral Netting Agreement or Article 6 in the TARGET Guideline, whose combined purpose is to permit the ECB to show net balances in its reports, and a net-net liability on its own balance sheet.

The net balances are broadly €1.8 trillion, with €300 billion as the ECB's net-net liability. The amount netted away prior to that has been deduced from the difference between the Eurosystem's business conducted in euro with 'Monetary Financial Institutions' resident in the Eurozone (i) as shown in its Aggregate Balance Sheet, and (ii) as shown in its Consolidated Balance Sheet. The difference between the two is €1.5 trillion. 'Monetary Financial Institutions' includes central banks and commercial banks: both would figure in an Aggregate Balance Sheet but the business between central banks would be eliminated in a Eurosystem Consolidated Balance Sheet. The Eurosystem consists of the ECB and the Eurozone central banks: business in between these entities is excluded upon consolidation. There are no other Eurosystem operations that this difference can relate to. It can therefore be deduced that it relates to the TARGET2 gross balances which are eliminated from view by the netting. They are €1.5 trillion. As a result the original TARGET2 balances, before the netting, are €3.3 trillion.

Secondly why should the gross balances be considered at all when there is a netting system in place?

The TARGET2 netting system is defective; there is a very realistic chance that it would fail to achieve its objectives if tested in a court of law. In that case the participants would have risk on one another for the full unnetted amounts of €3.3 trillion.

Thirdly, surely central banks do not take credit risk, such that where there are loans, they are collateralized and with 'central bank money' assets, primarily bonds issued by Eurozone member state governments that are already reflected in 'General government gross debt'?

Because of the construction of TARGET2, a loan from one central bank to another can be in the form of a deposit, which needs no collateral. The loan can also be in the form of an overdraft, in which case collateral is needed, but it can be any collateral from the ECB's list of eligible collateral. It does not have to be issued by an entity from the same member state as the borrowing central bank. It does not have to be a bond issued by a 'General government' entity in any member state. If the collateral was a bond issued by a public sector entity within the borrowing NCB's member state, there is correlation risk and the credit risk on the borrower is the same as the credit risk on the collateral. Correlation risk means the debt is in reality uncollateralized. In sum, we do not know if any of the TARGET2 debts are collateralized and, even if they are, with what.

Summary

We believe the above examples to represent fair treatment of the situation individually and when taken as a whole. We have made a sincere attempt not to exaggerate the situation, and a token of that is not including any numbers where the backing information is particularly incomplete, such as member state guarantees for securitizations of banks' Non-performing Loans, and the member state exposure under their Bank Deposit Insurance Schemes. This latter exposure arises where banks are put into 'resolution' and the bank has a large portfolio of Non-performing Loans: the member state risks ending up with a permanent addition to its debt at the end of 'resolution' process.

Setting the scene - key findings

The amount of shadow debt is in the region of €6.4 trillion, and the amount of shadow contingent liabilities is in the region of €3.8 trillion.

Eurostat records the EU's General government gross debt as €13.0 trillion, 90% of EU GDP of €14.5 trillion.

EU public sector debt, including the shadow debts, is nearer to €19.3 trillion, or 134% of EU GDP.

EU public sector debt and contingent liabilities are in the region of €23.1 trillion, or 160% of GDP.

Eurostat's Debt-to-GDP Ratio for the EU of 90% understates the situation by 44% if one takes account of the shadow debts, and by 70% if one factors in the shadow contingent liabilities as well.

The situation of the Eurozone member states is considerably worse than that of the non-Eurozone ones: the latter do not participate in several programmes like the European Financial Stability Facility, the European Stability Mechanism, the ECB Asset Purchase Programmes or TARGET2.

Germany as the biggest EU economy and an even bigger one as a proportion of the Eurozone fares worst of all. If 'it all tracks back onto Germany' as financial markets view the debts being incurred by the EU under the Coronavirus Recovery Fund, then financial markets are expecting Germany to be good for the entirety of the extra debts of €6.4 trillion and the contingent liabilities of €3.8 trillion on top of its own existing debt of €2.5 trillion, which is already 69% of its GDP of €3.6 trillion. In other words Germany seems to be regarded as good for extra claims of €10.2 trillion, plus existing ones of €2.5 trillion, meaning a total burden of €12.7 trillion bearing on an economy of €3.6 trillion: that would equate to a Debt-to-GDP Ratio of 353%.

The ballooning of debt separate from General government gross debt is extreme. This is in effect the meaning of a phrase like 'fully mobilize the EIB', that creative schemes can be devised to place the risk on the public exchequer without the accounting showing it.

The public credit ratings of each EU member state are inflated by several notches, because the debts and contingent liabilities bearing down on the member state's debt service capacity are much higher than the figure on which their ratings are based.

The public credit ratings of the EU entity itself and of EU/Eurozone supranationals like the European Stability Mechanism are inflated by several notches, because the credit quality of their backers – the member states – is much lower than it currently appears.

The EU/Eurozone financial system contains a series of gaps caused by this endemic over-rating.

Banks taking risk on EU/Eurozone public sector counterparties have under-provisioned that risk with capital, because the capital currently assigned is based on the under-estimation of EU/Eurozone public sector debt and liabilities.

The Eurosystem contains too little security margin on monetary and payment operations it is conducting because the margin is calculated based on the under-estimation of EU/Eurozone public sector debt and liabilities.

Clearing houses inside and outside the EU, where they accept collateral in the form of EU/Eurozone public sector debt, will be holding too thin a security margin because the amount of collateral has been calculated based on the under-estimation of EU/Eurozone public sector debt and liabilities.

This means that, in effect, the entire global financial system is under-capitalised and trading on too thin a security margin given the true scale of EU/Eurozone public sector debt and liabilities.

Setting the scene - table to support key findings: EU member state Debt-to-GDP Ratios

This table sets out the key findings in terms of the ratio of GGGD (General government gross debt) to GDP of each member state in accordance with Eurostat figures.

The extra debts are then added in to produce the Revised GGGD/GDP ratio.

Then the contingent liabilities (CLs) are added to in to produce the revised GGGD + CLs/GDP ratio.

These figures are worked out using each member state GGGD and GDP as stated in the Eurostat figures, adding to them as per the book's methodology, and then totaling the columns. There are small differences between the results using this methodology and the totals that Eurostat shows, due to rounding differences in Eurostat's figures which then cumulatively create a discrepancy, and due to the issue mentioned in the Disclaimer.

	Eurostat GGGD/ GDP	Revised GGGD/ GDP	Revised GGGD + Extra CLs/GDP
Belgium	108.2%	156.8%	184.6%
Bulgaria	25.1%	67.1%	77.7%
Czech Rep	41.9%	71.7%	79.5%
Denmark	36.7%	55.3%	61.5%
Germany	69.3%	102.8%	130.5%
Estonia	18.1%	59.7%	91.8%
Ireland	56.0%	76.4%	89.2%
Greece	193.3%	298.4%	337.1%
Spain	118.4%	201.3%	233.8%
France	112.9%	147.5%	178.0%
Croatia	79.8%	115.1%	125.0%
Italy	150.8%	222.6%	258.4%
Cyprus	103.6%	141.2%	169.1%
Latvia	44.8%	109.8%	147.2%
Lithuania	44.3%	92.5%	127.3%
Luxembourg	24.4%	43.5%	59.2%
Hungary	76.8%	112.6%	122.2%
Malta	57.0%	91.6%	117.1%
Netherlands	52.1%	83.6%	108.9%
Austria	82.8%	129.0%	156.0%
Poland	53.8%	90.3%	100.8%
Portugal	127.4%	209.6%	242.0%
Romania	48.8%	92.2%	102.9%
Slovenia	74.7%	116.0%	150.2%
Slovakia	63.1%	110.7%	151.0%
Finland	65.8%	95.9%	122.6%
Sweden	36.7%	55.9%	62.0%
Totals	89.7%	133.8%	160.1%

Table 0.1: EU member state debt-to-GDP including shadow debts and contingent liabilities

Setting the scene - methodology

The methodology of the book has been firstly, in Chapter 1, to discuss the Eurostat database, what it shows as the direct debts and contingent liabilities of EU member states, and to start to expose its limitations.

Chapters 2 to 5 plot out the four main phases in which the shadow debts and contingent liabilities have built up, starting, in Chapter 2, with an exposition of the EU itself and the other EU/Eurozone supranational entities.

The debts in these entities can be regarded as the 'status quo ante', because the significant build-up can be charted in three phases:
   i.   The response to the Global Financial Crisis in 2007/8 (Chapter 3);
   ii.   Actions taken to attempt to stabilize the EU banking system and reflate the EU economy after the Global Financial Crisis but before the Pandemic (Chapter 4);
   iii.   The response to the Pandemic (Chapter 5).

The approach has been to initially qualify each source of debt and contingent liabilities in accordance with the timing of its establishment. The respective section covers what entity takes on the debt, what it terms are, and how responsibility for payment of capital and interest comes to be the responsibility of the public sector of a member state.

Chapter 6 contains an interim summary on how the shadow debts and contingent liabilities began and have been added to.

Chapters 7 to 16 work through ten areas where the EU and Eurozone member states have been and are creating shadow debts and contingent liabilities. These range from the more obvious – the creation of debts within the legal entity of the European Union, for which all the EU member states are responsible – to the more obscure – such as member states guaranteeing a portion of the financing when a bank sells off bad debts into a securitzation structure.

The respective chapter recaps how the debt is taken on or how the contingent liability is created and states its amount. Having attempted to quantify the global amount under each heading, the chapter allocates it down to the member state level.

Others may think of further areas of shadow debt or contingent liabilities but these ten appear to us to be the most significant ones.

This task has been complicated first by some areas containing several programmes. A good example of this is the European Union itself. It has several, such as the Balance of Payments Facility, the European Financial Stabilisation Mechanism, and the Coronavirus Recovery Programme,

The second complication is the divergence of the nature of the public support, ranging from explicit guarantees to the ability to call up more capital from member states into a legal entity (such as the European Investment Bank).

The third complication is where responsibility for a debt is either passed from one shadow debtor to another, and/or can reach a member state down more than one pathway but from the same start point. For example the European Investment Bank is the beneficiary of first-loss guarantees from the European Union; if they are called, the EU can in turn call upon the member states for incremental cash contributions. For losses in excess of the guarantee, the EIB has a direct route to the member states through its ability to call up more capital from them.

The fourth complication is that some programmes are backed only by Eurozone member states and some by all EU member states.

The fifth complication is to distinguish correctly between the creation of a shadow debt and the creation of a shadow contingent liability, to both avoid the risk of double-counting, but at the same time to expose where there is a risk transfer between member states.

A risk-transfer occurs where some member states take loans from a bailout mechanism which has borrowed money itself, but the suppliers of the funds borrowed by the bailout mechanism are relying on the member states who guarantee the performance of the bailout mechanism and not on the member states which have borrowed from it. The two constituencies of member states are separate, and the contingent liability of one constituency needs to be recorded as well as the debt liability of the other constituency.

There is a difference between a member state's maximum possible loss under all programmes, and its likely loss given its size relative to the total Eurozone and EU. The maximum possible loss is inflated by all EU member states being liable in full for all debts of the EU. If one allocated this maximum possible loss figure to all 27 EU member states in full, a figure would result which was 26 times as large as the original debt.

It is more realistic to apportion the debts in accordance with a member state's relative size – usually ascertained as each member state's Gross National Income as a proportion of the EU's Gross National Income. That is not completely satisfactory either, because the original loss to be covered would quite plausibly be attributable to a member state being unable to pay its debts. Were that to occur, the defaulting member state would logically be unable to bring forth its share of the guarantee covering the loss. Why would it default on its debt but be able to pay up on its guarantee? Instead the contributions of the other member states would rise in order to cover that of the defaulting member state. The actual liability of each member state is thus dependent on the size of the member state that has defaulted: if a small member state defaulted, the extra contributions of the others would be relatively small, but this would not be the case if a large member state defaulted.

Trying to estimate how an individual member state's liabilities might rise depending upon which other member state or states defaulted and how would have been exceedingly complex, so our calculations have not gone further than what each member state is committed to, and not how that might escalate if other member states defaulted.

Notwithstanding these complications, an effort has been made in each chapter to quantify the maximum possible loss from the area concerned, and then to allocate it down to the member state level. Losses caused by debts and by contingent liabilities are shown separately.

Then there is a collation of the figures derived in every chapter in Chapter 17, firstly of the debts and then of the contingent liabilities, and then the two together. That, then, demonstrates the extent of the problem.

This is followed by the recommendations in Chapter 18 as to what might be done about the problem, both by the European authorities themselves, and then by other financial authorities.

The summary and conclusions follow in Chapter 19.

Setting the scene - disclaimer on disparities in the EU's statistics for Gross National Income and Gross Domestic Product

Despite EU budgetary contributions being calculated according to a member state's Gross National Income (GNI) rather than its Gross National Product (GDP), there is no list issued by a public authority which simply states what each member state's GNI is, alongside its GDP. Eurostat issues statistics for national debt as an absolute figure and as a percentage of GDP, so GDP can be extrapolated from that, and in such a way that the figures for each member state's share of EU GDP add up to 99.96%, introducing a small but tolerable discrepancy.

The available figures around GNI add up to 99.68%, a larger deviation from 100%.

This means that, in the book, where we distribute a debt or liability across the member states based on GNI (because, for example, that is how the debt or liability would be distributed if it went through the mechanism of the EU budget), the addition of the amounts so distributed adds up to less than the original amount. The choice was to use the GNI figures in their raw form, or to try to re-base them in order that they add up to 100%.

Unlike the re-basing of the Capital Keys in the European Central Bank to exclude non-Eurozone member states from meeting claims for losses on Eurosystem monetary and payment operations – an arithmetical exercise - any such alteration of GNI shares risked being arbitrary, so we decided to leave the figures as they were. The differences are noticeable if not genuinely material. The principle that GNI shares do not add to 100% is an absurdity, but a decision had to be made and we have erred on the side of using the raw data rather than amending the data ourselves.

This also leads to a slight understatement of the member state liability when GDP shares and GNI shares are used, with the understatement being larger where GNI is used.

Chapter 1 – Eurostat financial data on EU and Eurozone member states

Chapter introduction

This chapter addresses the anchor point for this book, and for the assessment by global financial markets of the indebtedness of EU and Eurozone member states: the Eurostat database of Government statistics focusing on General government gross debt and the annual fiscal surplus/deficit, both measured as an absolute figure and as a percentage of Gross Domestic Product.

The chapter analyzes the trajectory of the indebtedness, what contingent liabilities of member states Eurostat records, how indebtedness interlocks with member states' annual fiscal surpluses and deficits, and the effect of using the measure of Gross Domestic Product (or GDP) for this database as opposed to using Gross National Income (or GNI), the measure used to calculate member states' contributions to the EU budget.

The database contains the Government deficit and debt figures of the EU and Eurozone member states, as a percentage of GDP and as figure in millions of euro. It is necessary to extrapolate the member state's GDP, as well as its Debt-to-GDP Ratio.

Extrapolating the key measures

It was straightforward to extrapolate the following key measures:
1. The amount of debt in € billions as opposed to € millions, measured as General government gross debt (or GGGD), which 'comprises the subsectors of central government, state government, local government and social security funds'
2. The ratio of Debt, measured as GGGD, to Gross Domestic Product (or GDP) as a percentage lifted directly from the database
3. Each member state's GDP in € billions, being its GGGD divided by its Debt-to-GDP Ratio

The definition of GGGD is important, as it excludes several different types of borrower that might normally be considered as part of the public sector, such as the member state's central bank, nationalized energy and water utilities and transportation undertakings. GGGD also excludes the debt taken on through financing templates where the debt may be borrowed by a private entity but the liability for repayment falls on a public one.

The definition also excludes the debts of European-level entities for which a member state may be ultimately responsible. This includes debts existing within the European System of Central Banks (or Eurosystem). These qualify as being of European-level entities if the European Central Bank is the debtor, or as being at the member state level if a National Central Bank is the debtor.[8] Either way, though, debts within the Eurosystem are excluded from GGGD.

Trajectory of GGGD, the ratio of GGGD to GDP, and of GDP

The trajectory of GGGD, the ratio of GGGD to GDP, and of GDP between 2019 and 2021 has been as per Figure 2.1. The figures across the board deteriorated sharply during the Pandemic in 2020 and recovered slightly in 2021.

According to Eurostat's summary figures, the EU's GGGD at the end of 2021 was €12.7 trillion and its GDP €14.5 trillion, leading to a ratio of GGGD to GDP of just over 88%. The ratio was worse for the Eurozone at 95.6%, with GGGD for the 17 member states of €11.7 trillion and GDP of €12.3 trillion.

There is a small discrepancy between the Eurostat summary figures, and the summation of the individual member state figures. This discrepancy comes to light in the 'Key Findings' section above, and in Chapter 17 – aggregation of the amounts involved, from which the 'Key Findings' are taken. In Chapter 17 we have taken the individual, member state-level figures given in the Eurostat database and totaled them. The outcome is a different figure from Eurostat's total. The differences are not material, but it was felt that an explanation of them was required.

---

[8] The Eurosystem: the collective term used for the European Central Bank and the Eurozone National Central Banks. The Eurosystem is not a legal entity

The Fiscal Stability Pact

Under the Fiscal Stability Pact, member states are supposed to reduce their Debt-to-GDP Ratio to 60% by 2030, or even further if they have substantial age-related social costs materializing up to 2050.[9] Of the eight non-Eurozone member states, all except Croatia (79.8%) and Hungary (76.8%) have ratios that are already compliant. Of the nineteen Eurozone member states, only seven are already compliant: Estonia (18.1%), Ireland (56.0%)[10], Latvia (44.8%), Lithuania (44.3%), Luxembourg (24.4%), Malta (57%), and Netherlands (52.1%). The ratios of Debt-to-GDP deteriorated sharply during the Pandemic, by 13-14% on average between 2019 and 2020, and have recovered by 1½-2% on average between 2020 and 2021.

Seven Eurozone member states have a ratio above 100%: Greece (193.3%), Italy (150.8%), Portugal (127.4%), Spain (1184%), France (112.9%), Belgium (108.2%) and Cyprus (103.6%). This group has a much larger combined GDP than do the seven compliant Eurozone member states, leaving a further five Eurozone member states with a ratio above 60% but below 100%: Germany (69.3%), Austria (82.8%), Slovenia (74.7%), Slovakia (63.1%) and Finland (65.8%).

Given the application of fiscal discipline between 2022 and 2030 the 60% target should be achievable by Germany, Slovenia, Slovakia and Finland but not by Austria: it would require a sustained 2.5% annual fiscal surplus to be achieved in each of the nine remaining years (counting 2022 and 2030) and also applied completely to debt reduction, set against its fiscal deficit of 5.9% of GDP in 2021.

Trajectory of fiscal surpluses/deficits

Figure 2.2 shows the fiscal surpluses/deficits as a percentage of GDP over the same period of 2019 to 2021, noting that a fiscal surplus/deficit is expressed in relation to the GDP of the same year.

Eurozone member states are supposed, under the both the Stability & Growth Pact and the Fiscal Stability Pact, to limit any fiscal deficit to 3% of GDP. These rules were suspended during the Pandemic and one awaits to see in what form they will re-emerge. Only Denmark and Luxembourg achieved a fiscal surplus in 2021. Ten member states ran deficits within the 3% ceiling. The other fifteen had deficits above the ceiling, and they included all of Germany, France, Spain and Italy.

How a fiscal surplus/deficit affects the Debt-to-GDP ratio

A confusing issue is that the Debt-to-GDP ratio does not alter each year by the exact amount of the fiscal surplus/deficit. Figure 2.3 shows the respective data for ten countries to illustrate this point. It cannot be assumed in these statistics that a fiscal surplus automatically reduces General government gross debt, or that a deficit increases it.

One can see that all ten countries featured in Figure 2.3 were in deficit in both years, and that only the Netherlands' 2021 result was within the 3% ceiling. However, the 2020 Debt-to-GDP ratio as recorded by Eurostat was in all cases higher than the figure arrived at by adding the 2020 deficit to the 2019 Debt-to-GDP ratio. Then, in 2021, the Debt-to-GDP ratio actually fell in nine cases where a fiscal deficit was recorded. Only Germany's Debt-to-GDP ratio rose, by 0.6% when its fiscal deficit was 3.7%.

These are meaningful anomalies, although they are not the subject of this book. It defies what, in the author's view, would be the assumption of most finance professionals when, in the case of Belgium, a 2020 Debt-to-GDP ratio of 112.8%, followed by a fiscal deficit in 2021 of 5.5% of GDP, produces a 2021 Debt-to-GDP ratio of 108.2%, 4.6% lower than 2020. The 2021 fiscal deficit, when added to the 2020 ratio of 112.8%, should be expected to produce a 2021 ratio of 118.3%, fully 10.1% different from what Eurostat records.

That has to be parked as a meaningful, unexplained difference. One of its outcomes, though, is to overstate compliance with the Fiscal Stability Pact.

---

[9] The Treaty on Stability, Co-ordination and Governance in the European Monetary Union
[10] Ireland's ratio is in part attributable to its expanding GDP based on its attracting tech and biotech multinationals to establish there for tax purposes, such that their European or even global sales are booked as part of Ireland's GDP

Member states contingent liabilities

Eurostat captures some figures for the contingent liabilities of member states, where these fall outside of the measure of General government gross debt.

Figure 2.4 shows Eurostat's rendition of member states' off-balance sheet liabilities as at year-end 2020, the 2021 figures not yet being available at the time of writing.

The fact that Germany has a figure of zero against its 'Guarantees (contingent liabilities)' proves a main point of this book: Germany has contingent liabilities in respect of the European Union, the European Investment Bank, the European Financial Stability Facility, the European Stability Mechanism and other arrangements. Indeed, the international bond markets have heralded the issuance by the EU of bonds for the Coronavirus Recovery Fund on the grounds that the debt all tracks back onto Germany. This is true from a legal perspective, but not from an EU accounting perspective. Eurostat does not capture them.

It is concerning that two reports are denominated in national currency, such that sizeable figures against the names of Hungary, the Czech Republic, Denmark and Sweden are far smaller when reported in euro.

Each one of the EU supranational entities creates, as will be shown in Chapter 2, a contingent liability for a member state approximately in line with that member state's GDP as a share of EU GDP (approximately because some entities cause risk for Eurozone members only, and because liabilities are calculated according to several formulas).

The failure of the Eurostat database to record member state contingent liabilities proves the weakness of the definitional framework. This adds to the definitional weakness whereby debts of several types of public sector entities are excluded from GGGD: one only has to review the list of borrowers from the EIB or issuers of collateral eligible for ECB operations to discern liabilities of public sector entities whose debts should be counted within any statistics on public sector debt, if the statistics are to be meaningful.[11]

GNI and GDP, and credit ratings applying to different member state ratios

For the purposes of the EU budget the key measure is Gross National Income, not Gross Domestic Product, and this could be worked out from the Eurostat data base of Gross National Income per capita and Eurostat's population figures, both for 2020. The results are shown in Figure 2.5.

Please note again the Disclaimer regarding the figures for GNI and GDP.

61.17% of EU GNI derives from only 4 member states: Germany, France, Italy and Spain. Of these, only Germany carries a AAA public credit rating (expressed as per the Standard and Poor's system). France is rated AA, even with a Debt-to-GDP ratio of 113%. This is a reduction of only two notches of credit rating for a ratio 43% higher than Germany's. Spain, with a ratio of 118% that is higher by only 5% than that France, sits three notches lower than France at A, equivalent to a deterioration of 1.66% in its ratio for each notch of credit rating. Italy ranks a further three notches down at BBB with a ratio of 151% or one notch for each 11% increment to its ratio.

If Debt-to-GDP is a ratio of such pivotal importance as to merit a Pact all to itself, the inconsistency between what a 10% difference in ratio costs a member state in terms of its public credit rating makes no sense. Other factors play a role in a credit rating but this ratio is central, and the differences in the ratio per notch are 21.5% (Germany to France), 1.66% (France to Spain), and 11% (Spain to Italy).

GNI and GDP, and contributions to the EU budget

The final aspect is the difference between GDP and GNI. EU GNI is considerably lower than EU GDP: 92.86%. Eurozone GNI is only 81% of EU GNI, whereas Eurozone GDP is 84.77% of EU GDP.

---

[11] https://www.ecb.europa.eu/paym/coll/assets/html/index.en.html provides a link to the latest list of collateral that is eligible for ECB monetary and payment operations. For the purposes of this book the edition dated 22 May 2022 has been used

An important outcome is that, on average, non-Eurozone member states pay a greater proportion of the EU budget, because the budget is based on GNI shares. Germany is the largest beneficiary of this anomaly, with the Netherlands and Ireland following. Poland and Romania are the main losers. Figure 2.6 lays out the respective figures.

Already at this level there are meaningful anomalies and concerning trends. General government gross debt is high and it is rising. The largest member states have meaningful fiscal deficits and only Germany can plausibly reduce its Debt-to-GDP Ratio to 60% by 2030. This is the picture deriving from what Eurostat reports. As we shall see this is far from the full extent of EU/Eurozone public sector liabilities.

Chapter summary

The Eurostat figures provide a partial picture of the public sector debts of member states, and an inadequate picture of their contingent liabilities. Their contingent liabilities regarding EU-level entities do not register at all.

Even based on what Eurostat does record, the Debt-to-GDP ratios of the EU member states as a whole and the Eurozone ones in particular are well out of compliance with the Fiscal Stability Pact target of 60% by 2030.

No non-compliant member state showed a fiscal surplus in 2021 (although the Debt-to-GDP ratio of several reduced).

Member states that register the majority of GDP are heading in the opposite direction-of-travel than towards compliance. 61.17% of EU GNI derives from only 4 member states: Germany, France, Italy and Spain. Their Debt-to-GDP Ratios are, respectively, 69%, 113%, 151% and 118%. Only Germany can feasibly become compliant.

There are curious anomalies in the Eurostat and EU figures: how GNI is used in some cases and GDP in others, the absence of tables stating member state GNI and GDP and the differences between the two, constituent figures in tables not adding up to the stated totals.

One anomaly deserves special mention: an annual fiscal surplus/deficit does not directly alter the previous year's GGGD into this year's GGGD. There is a possible material understatement of GGGD deriving from this cause.

Figures:

- 2.1: the trajectory of EU member state GGGD, the ratio of GGGD to GDP, and of GDP between 2019 and 2021
- 2.2: Annual fiscal surplus/deficit 2019-2021 from Eurostat Government deficit and debt, in percent of GDP
- 2.3: discrepancies between Debt/GDP Ratio implied by previous year's Debt/GDP Ratio plus the year's fiscal result, and Eurostat Debt/GDP Ratio
- 2.4: Member state off-balance sheet liabilities as at year-end 2020 from Eurostat: Government statistics > Government contingent liabilities and potential obligations
- 2.5: member state Gross National Income and consequential percentage share of the EU budget
- 2.6: EU and EU member state GNI compared to GDP

2.1: the trajectory of EU member state GGGD, the ratio of GGGD to GDP, and of GDP between 2019 and 2021

Country	2019			2020			2021		
	GGGD in €bil	GGGD/ GDP in %	GDP in €bil	GGGD in €bil	GGGD/ GDP in %	GDP in €bil	GGGD in €bil	GGGD/ GDP in %	GDP in €bil
EU – 27 countries	10,856.5	77.5	14,008.4	12,065.7	90.0	13,406.3	12,740.6	88.1	14,461.5
Euro Area – 19 countries	10,045.5	83.8	11,987.5	11,094.7	97.2	11,414.3	11,720.3	95.6	12,259.7
Belgium	467.3	97.7	478.3	515.2	112.8	456.7	548.7	108.2	507.1
Bulgaria	12.3	20.0	61.5	15.1	24.7	61.1	17.0	25.1	67.7
Czech Rep	68.5	30.1	227.6	81.9	37.7	217.2	103.2	41.9	246.3
Denmark	104.1	33.6	309.8	131.8	42.1	313.1	123.4	36.7	336.2
Germany	2,045.7	58.9	3,473.2	2,314.0	68.7	3,368.3	2,475.8	69.3	3,572.6
Estonia	2.4	8.6	27.9	5.1	19.0	26.8	5.5	18.1	30.4
Ireland	204.0	57.2	356.6	217.9	58.4	373.1	235.9	56.0	421.2
Greece	331.1	180.7	183.2	341.1	206.3	165.3	353.4	193.3	182.8
Spain	1,223.4	98.3	1,244.6	1,345.8	120.0	1,121.5	1,427.2	118.4	1,205.4
France	2,375.0	97.4	2,438.4	2,648.1	114.6	2,310.7	2,813.1	112.9	2,491.7
Croatia	39.4	71.1	55.4	43.8	87.3	50.2	45.7	79.8	57.3
Italy	2,410.0	134.1	1,797.2	2,572.7	155.3	1,656.6	2,677.9	150.8	1,775.8
Cyprus	21.0	91.1	23.0	24.8	115.0	21.6	24.3	103.6	23.5
Latvia	11.2	36.7	30.5	12.7	43.3	29.3	14.8	44.8	33.0
Lithuania	17.5	35.9	48.7	23.0	46.6	49.4	24.6	44.3	55.5
Luxembourg	14.0	22.3	62.8	15.9	24.8	64.1	17.9	24.4	73.3
Hungary	94.1	65.5	143.7	105.6	79.6	132.7	114.9	76.8	149.6
Malta	5.7	40.7	14.0	7.0	53.4	13.1	8.3	57.0	14.6
Netherlands	394.6	48.5	813.6	434.8	54.3	800.7	448.1	52.1	860.1
Austria	280.6	70.6	397.5	316.0	83.3	379.4	334.1	82.8	403.5
Poland	245.7	45.6	538.8	293.1	57.1	513.3	306.8	53.8	570.3
Portugal	250.0	116.6	214.4	270.5	135.2	200.0	269.2	127.4	211.3
Romania	78.1	35.3	221.2	102.7	47.2	217.6	116.7	48.8	239.1
Slovenia	31.8	65.6	48.5	37.4	79.8	46.9	38.9	74.7	52.0
Slovakia	45.3	48.1	94.2	55.0	59.7	92.1	61.3	63.1	97.1
Finland	142.9	59.6	239.8	164.2	69.0	238.0	166.4	65.8	252.9
Sweden	168.7	34.9	483.4	197.0	39.6	497.5	192.6	36.7	524.8

Figure 2.1: the trajectory of EU member state GGGD, the ratio of GGGD to GDP, and of GDP between 2019 and 2021

2.2: Annual fiscal surplus/deficit 2019-2021 from Eurostat Government deficit and debt, in percent of GDP

Country	2019	2020	2021
EU – 27 countries	-0.6	-6.8	-4.7
Euro Area – 19 countries	-0.7	-7.1	-5.1
Belgium	-2.0	-9.0	-5.5
Bulgaria	2.1	-4.0	-4.1
Czech Rep	0.3	-5.8	-5.9
Denmark	4.1	-0.2	2.3
Germany	1.5	-4.3	-3.7
Estonia	0.1	-5.6	-2.4
Ireland	0.5	-5.1	-1.9
Greece	1.1	-10.2	-7.4
Spain	-3.1	-10.3	-6.9
France	-3.1	-8.9	-6.5
Croatia	0.2	-7.3	-2.9
Italy	-1.5	-9.6	-7.2
Cyprus	1.3	-5.8	-1.7
Latvia	-0.6	-4.5	-7.3
Lithuania	0.5	-7.3	-1.0
Luxembourg	2.3	-3.4	0.9
Hungary	-2.1	-7.8	-6.8
Malta	0.6	-9.5	-8.0
Netherlands	1.7	-3.7	-2.5
Austria	0.6	-8.0	-5.9
Poland	-0.7	-6.9	-1.9
Portugal	0.1	-5.8	-2.8
Romania	-4.3	-9.3	-7.1
Slovenia	0.4	-7.8	-5.2
Slovakia	-1.3	-5.5	-6.2
Finland	-0.9	-5.5	-2.6
Sweden	0.6	-2.7	-0.2

Figure 2.2: Annual fiscal surplus/deficit 2019-2021 from Eurostat Government deficit and debt, in percent of GDP

2.3: discrepancies between Debt/GDP Ratio implied by previous year's Debt/GDP Ratio plus the year's fiscal result, and Eurostat Debt/GDP Ratio

Country	2019 Debt/GDP	2020 fiscal result as % of GDP	Implied 2020 Debt/GDP	Eurostat 2020 Debt/GDP	2021 fiscal result	Implied 2021 Debt/GDP	Eurostat 2021 Debt/GDP
Belgium	97.7%	-9.0%	106.7%	112.8%	-5.5%	118.3%	108.2%
Germany	58.9%	-4.3%	63.2%	68.7%	-3.7%	72.4%	69.3%
Greece	180.7%	-10.2%	190.9%	206.3%	-7.4%	213.7%	193.3%
Spain	98.3%	-10.3%	108.6%	120.0%	-6.9%	126.9%	118.4%
France	97.4%	-8.9%	106.3%	114.6%	-6.5%	121.1%	112.9%
Italy	134.1%	-9.6%	143.7%	155.3%	-7.2%	162.5%	150.8%
Netherlands	48.5%	-3.7%	52.2%	54.3%	-2.5%	56.8%	52.1%
Austria	70.6%	-8.0%	78.6%	83.3%	-5.9%	89.2%	82.8%
Portugal	116.6%	-5.8%	122.4%	135.2%	-2.8%	138.0%	127.4%
Finland	59.6%	-5.5%	65.1%	69.0%	-2.6%	71.6%	65.8%

Figure 2.3: discrepancies between Debt/GDP Ratio implied by previous year's Debt/GDP Ratio plus the year's fiscal result, and Eurostat Debt/GDP Ratio

2.4: Member state off-balance sheet liabilities as at year-end 2020 according to Eurostat

Country	Guarantees (contingent liabilities)	Liabilities related to private-public partnerships	Liabilities of government controlled entities classified as outside general government	Non-performing loans of government
Measure	€ billions	Billions/national currency	€ billions	Billions/national currency
Belgium	43.9	1.9	0.0	0.2
Bulgaria	0.1	0.0	0.0	0.0
Czech Rep	2.2	0.0	0.0	28.0
Denmark	65.6	4.4	0.0	10.1
Germany	0.0	0.0	0.0	1.4
Estonia	0.5	0.0	0.0	0.0
Ireland	2.3	2.6	0.0	0.7
Greece	0.0	0.3	0.0	0.5
Spain	119.5	3.2	0.0	3.0
France	390.2	0.0	0.0	2.3
Croatia	0.9	0.3	0.0	5.3
Italy	215.7	0.2	0.0	0.1
Cyprus	1.6	0.0	0.0	6.1
Latvia	0.5	0.0	0.0	0.0
Lithuania	0.6	0.0	0.0	0.0
Luxembourg	7.1	0.0	0.0	0.0
Hungary	10.7	517.9	0.0	17.6
Malta	1.2	0.0	0.0	0.0
Netherlands	0.0	0.0	0.0	0.4
Austria	72.5	0.5	0.0	0.2
Poland	11.0	0.0	0.0	2.4
Portugal	12.2	4.6	0.0	3.0
Romania	7.4	0.0	0.0	1.2
Slovenia	3.0	0.0	0.0	1.0
Slovakia	0.1	2.2	0.0	0.2
Finland	86.0	0.0	0.6	0.2
Sweden	54.1	0.0	8.1	29.3

Figure 2.4: Member state off-balance sheet liabilities as at year-end 2020 from Eurostat: Government statistics > Government contingent liabilities and potential obligations

2.5: member state Gross National Income and consequential percentage share of the EU budget

Country	GNI per capita in €	Population in thousands	GNI in € billions	Percentage share of EU budget
EU – 27 countries	29,968	448,089	13,428.3	100.00%
Belgium	36,003	11,560	416.2	3.10%
Bulgaria	16,139	6,915	111.6	0.83%
Czech Rep	26,892	10,706	287.9	2.14%
Denmark	41,852	5,839	244.4	1.82%
Germany	37,756	83,194	3,141.1	23.4%
Estonia	24,991	1,329	33.2	0.25%
Ireland	47,628	4,993	237.8	1.77%
Greece	18,608	10,684	198.8	1.48%
Spain	25,442	47,379	1,205.4	8.98%
France	32,021	68,083	2,180.1	16.24%
Croatia	19,672	4,042	79.5	0.59%
Italy	28,410	59,327	1,685.5	12.55%
Cyprus	24,861	895	22.3	0.17%
Latvia	21,076	1,896	40.0	0.30%
Lithuania	25,288	2,795	70.7	0.53%
Luxembourg	55,683	635	35.4	0.26%
Hungary	21,558	9,741	210.0	1.56%
Malta	26,347	516	13.6	0.10%
Netherlands	36,069	17,470	630.1	4.69%
Austria	37,255	8,931	332.7	2.48%
Poland	21,301	38,308	816.0	6.08%
Portugal	22,529	10,308	232.2	1.73%
Romania	21,123	19,269	407.2	3.03%
Slovenia	26,400	2,110	55.7	0.41%
Slovakia	20,759	5,463	113.4	0.84%
Finland	34,426	5,535	190.5	1.42%
Sweden	38,003	10,379	394.4	2.94%

Figure 2.5: member state Gross National Income and consequential percentage share of the EU budget

2.6: EU and EU member state GNI compared to GDP

Country	GDP in € billions	Percentage share of GDP	GNI in € billions	Percentage share of GNI	Relationship of GNI to GDP
EU – 27 countries	14,461.5	100.00%	13,428.3	100.00%	92.86%
Euro Area – 19 countries	12,259.7	84.77%	10,877.3	81.00%	-3.77%
Belgium	507.1	3.51%	416.2	3.10%	-0.41%
Bulgaria	67.7	0.47%	111.6	0.83%	+0.36%
Czech Rep	246.3	1.70%	287.9	2.14%	+0.44%
Denmark	336.2	2.32%	244.4	1.82%	-0.50%
Germany	3,572.6	24.70%	3,141.1	23.4%	-1.31%
Estonia	30.4	0.21%	33.2	0.25%	+0.04%
Ireland	421.2	2.91%	237.8	1.77%	-1.14%
Greece	182.8	1.26%	198.8	1.48%	+0.22%
Spain	1,205.4	8.34%	1,205.4	8.98%	+0.64%
France	2,491.7	17.23%	2,180.1	16.24%	-0.99%
Croatia	57.3	0.40%	79.5	0.59%	+0.20%
Italy	1,775.8	12.28%	1,685.5	12.55%	+0.27%
Cyprus	23.5	0.16%	22.3	0.17%	+0.00%
Latvia	33.0	0.23%	40.0	0.30%	+0.07%
Lithuania	55.5	0.38%	70.7	0.53%	+0.14%
Luxembourg	73.3	0.51%	35.4	0.26%	-0.24%
Hungary	149.6	1.03%	210.0	1.56%	+0.53%
Malta	14.6	0.10%	13.6	0.10%	+0.00%
Netherlands	860.1	5.95%	630.1	4.69%	-1.26%
Austria	403.5	2.79%	332.7	2.48%	-0.31%
Poland	570.3	3.94%	816.0	6.08%	+2.13%
Portugal	211.3	1.46%	232.2	1.73%	+0.27%
Romania	239.1	1.65%	407.2	3.03%	+1.38%
Slovenia	52.0	0.36%	55.7	0.41%	+0.06%
Slovakia	97.1	0.67%	113.4	0.84%	+0.17%
Finland	252.9	1.75%	190.5	1.42%	-0.33%
Sweden	524.8	3.63%	394.4	2.94%	-0.69%

Figure 2.6: EU and EU member state GNI compared to GDP

Chapter 2 – the EU supranational entities

Chapter introduction

This chapter describes each of the EU supranational entities that existed prior to the Global Financial Crisis of 2007/8. There is an exposition of how the entity creates risk for member states and what the nature of the risk is:

- Capped at a fixed ceiling or on the basis that a member state should pay whatever the entity requires;
- Subject to a maximum share for each member state of a loss, or subject to an initial allocation that can then be revised upwards if other member states are unable to pay their allocation.

The chapter sets out, in this way, the status quo ante of the EU and Eurozone going into the Global Financial Crisis.

What entities existed prior to and at the introduction of the euro

Under a broad-brush history of what is now the European Union, there were originally five supranational entities which undertook financing activities and therefore had borrowings:

- the European Economic Community
- the European Coal and Steel Community
- Euratom
- The European Investment Bank
- The European Investment Fund

Only the European Central Bank (ECB) was added at the point of the introduction of the euro. The ECB is the fulcrum of the management of the euro, but the term 'Eurosystem' does not denote a legal entity. The Eurosystem, or European System of Central Banks, is used as an umbrella term to refer to the ECB and the participating national central banks in the Eurozone, and their arrangements to conduct monetary and payment operations. The Eurosystem cannot contract debts itself, although its members can and do. A main mechanism through which debts are created in the Eurosystem is the TARGET2 payment system. Although it issues its own annual report, TARGET2 is simply the payment system run by and for the Eurosystem participants.

2.1 The European Union

What the European Union is and how its debts are guaranteed

The European Union is the successor entity of the European Economic Community and the European Coal and Steel Community. Euratom still exists as a semi-autonomous entity. Euratom's operations are small compared to those of the EU but its separateness within the same framework is reflected in relevant European Council decisions being termed '(EU, Euratom)'. Despite Euratom's anomalous status, its finances are run to the same template as the EU, and the debts of both entities are jointly-and-severally guaranteed by their members.

This means that the liability of one member state is potentially for the entire debt, if none of the other member states were capable of paying their share. An initial allocation of a debt would be made, based on GNI shares. If one member state failed to pay, the allocations would be reworked by reversing the failing member state's GNI out of EU GNI and running the calculation again: the shares of the residual member states increase.

This poses a problem for the entry of a contingent liability into member state accounts: the maximum possible loss is the whole, but it is not likely that all member states except one would default, leaving 'the last man standing' to pay everything.

The loss to be covered would in the first instance be entered as a debit to the accounts of the EU or Euratom and create a deficit within its budget. Since the member states are obliged to keep the budgets of the EU and Euratom in balance, a claim would be triggered for extra cash from each member state in the normal proportion of its share of the annual EU cash budget.

If the loss occurred in the European Investment Fund, part of it could be passed directly to the EU as one of the EIF's direct shareholders, by the EIF requesting pay-in of its uncalled but subscribed share capital. The EU pays that amount into the EIF budget by debiting its budget, and then, if the EU's budget goes into deficit, a claim is triggered for extra cash form the EU's members in their normal proportion.

We have decided not to include a figure for this particular liability in the overall calculations for several reasons:

1. Complexity compared to materiality: the explanation is long and complex but the amount is quite small, since the uncalled capital from the EU is only €1.75 billion;

2. The EU is not even the EIF's largest shareholder: the EIB has a 59% stake and the EIF's figures are consolidated into those of the EIB: the term 'EIB Group' includes the EIF;

3. Losing sight of the big picture: the EIF has next-to-no capital compared to its business volume. Like the ECB it has become a vehicle for the creation of large financial operations but without its having a meaningful loss-absorption cushion of its own;

4. The EIF's principal loss-absorption cushion is the large direct guarantees (i) that the EU has issued in favour of 'EIB Group' for the InvestEU programme, and (ii) that a subset of member states have issued for the European Guarantee Fund programme (EGF).

How member states' joint-and-several liability for the EU budget and therefore for the EU's debts operates

The joint-and-several liability of member states for the EU's debts is explained in EU Investor presentations, for example the one of July 2015.[12] Pages 7-8 include this feature in 'Credit Strengths'. The document, on p. 2, shows the EU's operations as limited at that time to:

- The European Financial Stabilization Mechanism (only set up in 2010; see below);
- The Balance of Payments Facility, a programme with a ceiling of €50 billion for countries on their convergence path into the euro;
- Macro-Financial Assistance, a facility from which the EU can make contributions to bailouts for non-EU countries that are going through an International Monetary Fund programme.

The EU's current funding system is laid down in 'Council Decision (EU, Euratom) 2020/2053 of 14 December 2020 on the system of own resources of the European Union and repealing Decision 2014/335/EU, Euratom'. This is also explained on the EU's webpage.[13] It is not simple to understand but our interpretation of it is that the EU is entitled to make a cash spend 1.40% of EU GNI per annum during any Multiannual Financial Framework period or MFF, the current one running from 2021 to 2027. Over and above that the EU is entitled to make commitments up to 0.06% of GNI that could lead to the budget being in deficit in the future, the eventuality that would trigger the member state contingent liability referenced above.

A point of particular confusion is the inconsistency with which the term 'own resources' has been used. It can be taken to mean all the money the EU receives via VAT, customs and sugar levies, plastic recycling and the member state cash contributions, or just what it receives via VAT, customs and sugar levies, plastic recycling and any other line items except the member state cash contributions. Council Decision 2020/2053 tends towards the first reading. We have used that reading in this book.

A further point of confusion is that the figure of 1.46% of GNI, termed on the respective webpage as 'Own resources ceiling to cover the annual appropriations for commitments – 1.46% of EU GNI for the period 2021-2027' – does not appear to be cumulative with the figure of 1.40% for the 'appropriation for payments'. Its meaning is taken to be that the EU can engage in funds, facilities and guarantees which could cause it to have to pay out a maximum of 0.06% of EU GNI for any one year. This would occur, for example, where it has borrowed for the purposes of the EFSM, and the country that it on-lent the funds to defaulted. The EU would still have to service its own borrowings. The debt service would push its budget into deficit. The EU has the right to call upon extra money from member states to bring the budget back into balance, up to this ceiling of 0.06% of GNI per annum which, based on 2020 GNI, would be €8.1 billion per annum for the current MFF. That would work out to €56.7 billion over the MFF, if GNI was constant.

We discuss in a later section the amount of €30-40 billion which public credit rating agencies have estimated that the EU can claim from member states over the course of an MFF, and which they quote as a source of credit strength for the EU. The 2021-7 MFF is higher as a percentage of GNI than previous MFFs, and GNI has expanded to some degree since the above estimate was given.

---

[12] EU Investor Presentation, July 2015, by DG Economic and Financial Affairs, European Commission

[13] https://ec.europa.eu/info/strategy/eu-budget/long-term-eu-budget/2021-2027/revenue/revenue-ceilings_en accessed on 15 June 2022

Nevertheless the €30-40 billion quoted by credit rating agencies appears low when measured against this estimate of €56 billion for the 2021-7 MFF, and it is a concern that there should be any difference between the calculations.

Mechanical points about the extent of member state liability for the EU entity

There are three further mechanical points about the extent of member state liability.

Firstly paragraph 23 on p. 4 of Council Decision 2020/2053 lays out how the situation is dealt with when a member state cannot meet a call for money: 'if a Member State fails, in full or in part, to honour a call on time, or if it notifies the Commission that it will not be able to honour a call, the Commission should nevertheless be authorised on a provisional basis to make additional calls on other Member States on a *pro rata* basis'. The usage of the term 'pro rata' means that that the applicable EU GNI shares for the calculation will exclude the GNI of the failing member state. Each remaining member state's share of this re-based GNI is higher than its share of the full EU GNI. This raises the payments. If 26 member states do not honour their call on time, then the reference figure for GNI is the GNI of the sole remaining member state, in which case it pays 100% of the call. This is the basis of the joint-and-several liability or, as it has been put, 'it all tracks back onto Germany'.

The second mechanical point is that a member state becomes liable for EU budget shortfalls under the above mechanism based on the respective operations having been properly contracted within the ceiling applicable to the MFF when the operation began. The member state only ceases to be liable when the operation has expired or been repaid. It is perfectly possible that the EU budget could be pushed into a deficit in excess of €8.1 billion in any one year, if there were simultaneous losses in several programmes. The EU has no control over the potential timing of such losses. As long as the operations causing the losses had been contracted within the terms of the applicable legal instruments and amount limits at inception, the claim on member states is triggered. This implies that the liability of member states is cumulative over different MFFs: it does not expire at the end of the MFF if the underlying operation still exists. If this is the case, a guarantee issued during the 2014-20 MFF for a loan of 15 years' duration and of final maturity 2030, can cause a budget deficit right through the 2021-7 MFF and into the 2028-34 MFF. If a call is made, it is still marked against member state liabilities under the 2014-20 MFF, when the guarantee was enacted, without this diminishing the member states' liability for operations put on during later MFFs. The principle is that the member state liability only lapses when the underlying operation lapses. The implication of this is that the total member state liability is not the 0.06% of EU GNI during the current MFF, but potentially that indicator accumulating over several MFFs, limited by the size, nature and duration of the operations that the EU engaged in during that MFF. Under this reading the €30-40 billion which public credit rating agencies have estimated that the EU can claim from member states over the course of an MFF seems even further adrift. The measure is not 'over the course of an MFF' but 'per MFF', in addition to the amount being understated.

The third mechanical point is that Council Decision 2020/2053 allows an extra 0.6% of GNI to be borrowed and relayed during the 2021-7 MFF in the form of the Coronavirus Recovery Fund, whose ceiling is €750 billion. The 0.6% is added both to the payments that can be made and the 'annual appropriations for commitments', meaning that the cash can be disbursed under the first and borrowed and marked against the member state liability to keep the future budget in balance under the second. It must be hoped that the reference GNI rises by 2027 because, as of 2020, €750 billion is €107 billion per annum and €37 billion higher than 0.6% of 2020 EU GNI. This issue would also point to the backloading of the disbursements from the Fund, undermining credibility that the disbursements really were related to Coronavirus. This also shows how the member state liability is created in the MFF when the fund, facility or guarantee itself is created, and survives until the fund, facility or guarantee has expired or been repaid. The member state liability for this fund is cumulative with those under all other funds, facilities or guarantees validly created and still outstanding.

Quantifying a member state's liability for the EU and Euratom debts

Quantifying the liability of each member state begins with capturing the EU's total possible claim on member states under all its funds, facilities and guarantees that have not expired or been repaid. The next issue is to determine the allocation to each member state of that amount.

A member state might legitimately enter its liability as the EU's debts and guarantees multiplied by its normal percentage allocation of the EU budget.

This overlooks the fact that the deficit in the EU's budget might come about because of a default by a member state on its obligations towards the EU, and if that member state had defaulted on its direct obligation, it is unlikely that it would be able to meet the EU's cash claim to cover the deficit emanating from its own default.

As a result, a member state ought to recognize that, if a cash claim was made by the EU, it was bound to be larger than the member state's normal share. However, this gives little clue as to how much the excess would be. It would seem over-dramatic to record a contingent liability for the whole amount, even if that is what the legal position is. An attempt to solve the question of the raising of the contributions of solvent member states and indeed to address the issue of borrowers from an EU entity also being the guarantors of the entity's debts can be seen in both of the autonomous Eurozone bailout mechanisms, the European Financial Stability Facility (EFSF) and the European Stability Mechanism (ESM).

2.2 The European Investment Bank Group comprising the European Investment Bank and the European Investment Fund

What the European Investment Bank and the European Investment Fund do

The EIB Group – consisting of the EIB and EIF – is the EU's development bank. It provides long-term debt funding through the EIB, and equity and quasi-equity funding through the EIF.

A typical EIB loan will be of 17-18 years' final maturity, with a period of 2-3 years after loan signature for the loan to be drawn down, and then repayment in 30 equal semi-annual instalments. The loans generally carry a fixed rate of interest, a feature that borrowers could not achieve in their own right.

The EIF enables, rather than provides, equity and quasi-equity financing. It might subscribe to shares in a project which were part-paid: the difference acts as a form of guarantee fund for the project. The EIF might guarantee money injected by another financier, on the basis that the financier had the cash to invest but did not wish to take the level of risk implied by injecting the money either on an unsecured basis or on a basis where their claim on the project's assets was subordinated to the claims of other creditors.

EIB Group operations before the euro

It would be wrong to view the days before the euro as the halcyon days of the EU but, with the benefit of hindsight, one can state that the operations being undertaken were limited in both purpose and volume. The EIB was the most active EU supranational entity pursuing its three lines of business:

1. Development loans outside the EU always to a sovereign borrower or under a sovereign guarantee;
2. Project and development loans inside the EU with a strong emphasis on public sector borrowers who, because of the EIB's mandate, would fall in the main outside 'General government' as defined by Eurostat;
3. Loans to Small and Medium Enterprises within the EU under programmes where the EIB's credit risk lay with a bank, which on-lent the funds borrowed from the EIB to a portfolio of SMEs.

The second activity is the bedrock of the EIB's purpose, and the preponderance of the borrowers are entities outside 'General government'. It is not a hard-and-fast rule that the EIB was not permitted to lend to EU entities within 'General government'; it was rather that the activities and projects falling within the EIB's terms-of-reference would tend to be pursued by an autonomous entity, such as Autopistas de Catalunya for a toll motorway or Canal Isabel II for water supply in Madrid. The EIB's complete list of projects financed since its establishment is in the public domain.[14] For the period 1980-2 one can see loans such as to:

- Pacific Forum Line in Fiji and Tonga, under the envelope for loans outside the EU;
- Port Autonome de Rouen, France
- The Faro Motorway Bridges NIC, Portugal
- Italgas Piemonte-Liguria NIC2 Italy

Even from this short list one can observe a mixture in the purposes of the loans between upgrading existing facilities and new build: Rouen had been a port for centuries but there had been no motorway bridge, or motorway, at Faro. The EIB was performing the classic function of a development bank: supplying long-term

---

[14] https://www.eib.org/en/projects/loans/index.htm accessed on 24 May 2022

funding to infrastructure projects on the basis that these projects would enable economic growth in the private sector, which in turn would deliver the taxes and levies needed to repay the debt.

We will see later that it has become questionable whether the EIB is still performing this function or whether there is a sense in which it is financing projects for the sake of giving the appearance of GDP growth (because the spending of the loan money in the short term boosts GDP), and in which its loans aimed at Net Zero are for a like-for-like replacement of existing capacity and are not aimed at fostering economic growth in the private sector.

How the debts of the European Investment Bank and the European Investment Fund are covered

The European Investment Bank and the European Investment Fund operate under the principle of part-paid shares. A shareholder subscribes to a block of shares and pays in a portion. The unpaid portion functions like a guarantee. The shareholder's risk is on a several-but-not-joint basis: it cannot be asked to pay in any amounts subscribed by other shareholders who then fail to pay. The issue is in the size of the unpaid portion and who has to pay it.

In the case of the European Investment Bank this obligation falls directly on the member states, and it is very large: €226 billion.

In the case of the European Investment Fund this obligation falls indirectly on the member states through the EIB and the EU, and it is small: €1.75 billion can be called up from the EU and €3.4 billion from the EIB.

The EIB has a majority stake in the EIF, would pay in the extra capital and then, if it was financially embarrassed thereby, could call upon the member states to pay in extra capital in itself.

The EU has a substantial minority stake in the EIF and if it had to pay in extra capital, this claim would fall on the member states on a joint-and-several basis like any other deficit in the EU budget. The EU would debit the EIF's claim to its own budget, putting it into deficit, and then have the member states increase their cash contributions so that the EU budget came out of deficit.

Private financial institutions own a small minority of the EIF's shares, and their shares are in effect fully paid-in; they have pre-deposited a 'share premium' amount that matches their subscribed-but-not-paid amount. A loss would be applied to them by the writing-down of the value of their shares.

To put things in perspective, the EIB's subscribed capital is large but the EIF's is small. Both have engaged in financial operations on a large scale. In fact the size of the operations enabled by the EIF may even be larger than the EIB's balance sheet. The EIF's uncalled capital is far too small to act as a meaningful loss-absorption cushion for a portfolio of that size: the loss cushion is the guarantees that 'EIB Group' has received from other EU supranationals and of which the EIF is a beneficiary by dint of being majority-owned by the EIB.

EU guarantees in EIB's favour for certain EIB lending programmes

'EIB Group' benefits from a series of first-loss guarantees issued by the EU in its favour.

This applies to the first line of business described above: EIB lending outside the EU. A new guarantee is issued for each Multiannual Financial Framework, and to cover the EIB for losses up to the guaranteed amount, as long as the loan in question was signed during the Multiannual Financial Framework. The loan did not have to be drawn during that period in order to be marked against the guarantee for the period. If the losses exceed the guaranteed amount, they diminish the EIB's capital and reserves. If the losses are severe enough, the EIB could call up more capital from the member states.

The third line of business in the list above has been substantially ceded by the EIB to the EIF under the InvestEU programme and, latterly, under the European Guarantee Facility, both of which are discussed more fully later chapters.

The EU has issued guarantees in respect of InvestEU. These guarantees are in favour of both EIB and EIF – the 'EIB Group' - and are on a first-loss basis. The EIB Group is permitted to put its 'own resources at risk' within the InvestEU programme, up to a certain ceiling over and above the EU guarantee amount. What that phrase means is also discussed in a later chapter. The upshot is that the EIB and EIF together have taken risks within the InvestEU programme that are larger than the amounts of the EU guarantees.

For this chapter it is necessary only to appreciate that if, for example, the InvestEU programme resulted in a total book of business for EIB Group of €50 billion and the EU first-loss guarantee was €20 billion, the first €20 billion that EIB Group lost on InvestEU – whether it was lost in the EIB or EIF – could be reclaimed directly from the EU and, through the EU budget, the member states.

If the residual €30 billion was lost, though, there would be a different pathway to reclaiming it from member states depending upon which entity lost it:
- If the EIB lost it: call-up of share capital from member states
- If the EIF lost it:
  i. call-up into the EIF of share capital from the EIB; and
  ii. EIB then calls up share capital from member states if it needs to;
  iii. call-up into the EIF of share capital from the EU; and
  iv. the EU debits the call-up to its budget and triggers a supplementary call on member states; and
  v. write-off of share capital of the financial institutions who own about 10% of the EIF.

There are thus a series of convoluted pathways for shifting the risk onto member states from the EIB Group. This does not amount to member states guaranteeing the payment of capital and interest on all the borrowings EIB Group has made, but it does amount to a major safety net for any bank or investor lending to EIB Group. The value of EIB Group's book of business would have to fall by 50% or more in order for the safety net to be broken through, such that banks or investors would be having to look to EIB Group's remaining assets in order to obtain payment of capital and interest.

Overlap between EIB lending, GGGD and entities falling within the definition of 'General government'

There is no fixed exclusion for EIB's loans counting as 'General government gross debt'. It might be possible, though extremely challenging, for an outsider to work out the figures for direct borrowings from the EIB by entities falling within 'General government'. The EIB project lists do not give the name of the borrower. One would have to ascertain the name of the project sponsor, obtain its annual report, try to identify the respective EIB financing in it and who the borrower was, and then work out whether the borrowing entity fell within 'General government'.

From our research into the EIB database our view is that this approach would fail to draw robust conclusions. Instead we can permit ourselves to moot that 95%+ of the EIB's project and development loans within the EU are made to borrowers outside the scope of 'General government', and that these borrowers sit both within the public sector and the private one in terms of who their owners are. Where the borrower is in the private sector, this cannot be taken to mean that the EIB is taking private sector risk.

Risk-transfer into 'General government' or the public sector

There is another form of overlap with 'General government gross debt' that is important. It is the degree to which the credit risk on an EIB loan is taken over:
- By an entity within 'General government' when the borrower is a public sector entity sitting outside 'General government';
- By a public sector entity sitting outside 'General government' when the borrower is also a public sector entity sitting outside 'General government', but the guarantor sits higher up the pyramid of public sector entities;
- By an entity within 'General government' when the borrower is in the private sector;
- By a public sector entity sitting outside 'General government' when the borrower is in the private sector.

This would not mean that the debt ought then to be added to 'General government gross debt': the obligation of the entity within 'General government' is a contingent liability, not a direct debt.

Methods of creating contingent liabilities

The forms in which such a contingent liability may be cast and the take-over of the responsibility for payment of capital and interest be brought about can be many and various, and may exist in combination with one another, such as:
1. Explicit guarantee;
2. Letter of Knowledge and Consent;
3. Direct share ownership, with a covenant not to reduce the percentage, or not to reduce below a majority ownership;
4. A golden share owned in the borrower;
5. The writing of an option to buy shares in the borrower;
6. Indirect share ownership, possibly through a development agency;
7. A commercial contract with the borrower for the offtake of the project;
8. A guarantee or other credit support behind a commercial contract between the borrower and a public sector entity outside 'General government'.

There are many ways and structures, but the objective for the lender is always the same:
- to get stronger support, moving up from warranties to covenants and from covenants to guarantees;
- to get the support from entities higher and higher up the pyramid, from public sector entities outside 'General government', to public sector entities inside 'General government', to agencies of central government to the central government itself.

The EIB's efforts in this regard would not differ from those of a commercial bank, and indeed EIB has frequently been a co-financier of projects i.e. lending under the same framework of guarantees, warranties and so on as commercials banks lending into the same project, and differing in the longer final maturity of its loans and its ability to offer a fixed rate of interest.

For the purposes of this book this issue bears on the question of a discrepancy: between the borrower view as expressed by Eurostat figures for the total volume of debts that 'General government' believes it is responsible for, and the investor view of the total volume of debts that all investors view as tracking back onto the EU public sector, whoever the direct borrower is, and however the path of recourse is constructed, and whether the path ends at an entity within the scope of 'General government' or in the remainder of the public sector.
The contention is that many more financings are viewed by their suppliers as 'EU/Eurozone public sector risk' than are contained in the Eurostat figures.

Investor risk assessment

This in turns leads to a point about bank capitalization under the Basel Accords.[15] Banks risk-weight their loans and calculate their requirement for capital in accordance with where they believe their risk on payment of the capital and interest lies.[16] In the Eurozone the risk-weighting is too low when applied to obligations of Eurozone member state government given the nature of the euro.[17] There is also the trickle-down effect: once obligations of the government are risk-weighted at 0%, it follows that the risk-weightings applied to government agencies, other entities within 'General government', and other public sector entities are too low as well. This extends to obligations of privately-owned companies where the financial structure produces recourse to a public sector entity. The upshot is not only that the banking system holds a large volume of obligations that they deem to be 'government-backed' in the widest sense which the respective government does not necessarily know that it is backing, but also that the capital held by the banking system in respect of these obligations is too low.

---

[15] The Basel Accords are explained in detail in the section about EU/Eurozone banks optimizing their methodologies for calculating capital as a response to the Eurozone sovereign debt crisis

[16] The requirement is most frequently expressed in terms of a need for Common Equity Tier 1 ('CET1') to be at least a given percentage of the bank's Risk-Weighted Assets, which the bank has calculated through a methodology of the type explained in a later chapter. The need for CET1 normally lies in the range of 8-10% of the bank's Risk-Weighted Assets, depending upon the importance of the bank to the national and global financial system, and upon occasional premia imposed by financial regulator from time to time

[17] 'Managing Euro Risk' pp. 23-6

Loans by other investors into the same borrowers who have EIB loans

EIB's loan book inside the EU demonstrates the existence of a sector of 'other public sector entities' outside General government. There are many such entities and they have borrowing powers. EIB will not be a monopoly supplier of finance to this sector. EIB frequently co-funds with other investors under a common security package: the borrower then has debts both to the EIB and other lenders.

On top of that there will be a block of debt in which EIB is not involved at all, taken on from private financiers – as both loans and bonds – by the same public sector entities outside of General government. All the debts and contingent liabilities of such public sector entities fall outside Eurostat figures. An attempt, not wholly successful, has been made in a later chapter to estimate the extent of those debts, and a methodology proposed for verifying who all these borrowers are and how much they owe.

2.3 The Eurosystem of the European Central Bank and the Eurozone National Central Banks

The introduction of the euro in 1999 was a bigger watershed than it may have appeared at the time, in that the European Central Bank (ECB) seamlessly appeared out of the European Monetary Institute, the European System of Central Banks emerged out of the European Monetary System, and the euro itself was in a sense not a creation but a redenomination of the European Currency Unit or ECU: the irrevocably fixed exchange rate between the ECU and the euro was 1:1.

Only one new supranational legal entity emerged: the ECB. All EU member states are shareholders in it, through their national central banks (NCBs). It has a very small capital base. The shareholdings of Eurozone NCBs are fully paid in, while those of non-Eurozone NCBs are part-paid. This is a trivial point in practice because the ECB's capital base is so small: calling in the balance of the subscribed capital of the non-Eurozone NCBs would raise a very small proportion of the size of the ECB's operations. The main line of recourse for the ECB if it need to be recapitalized is to the NCBs of the Eurozone member states.

The ECB is the coordinating point of the Eurosystem or European System of Central Banks, but the Eurosystem is not a legal entity. It is simply a term referring to the collective of the ECB and NCBs of the Eurozone member states acting in line with the relevant EU treaties: the NCBs of the non-Eurozone member states may be shareholders in the ECB, and may participate in the TARGET2 payment system but they are not part of the Eurosystem and do not take part in Eurosystem monetary operations.

How the Eurosystem works and the importance of eligible collateral

The agreements around the operation of the euro oblige Eurozone NCBs to participate in ECB monetary and payment operations, and, in doing so, to accept the collateral and with the valuations as specified in the ECB's list of eligible collateral. Eurosystem members should not take on credit risk, either in the dealings with the commercial banks whom they sponsor into the Eurosystem arrangements, or with one another, or with the ECB. The contents of the list of eligible collateral and the valuations are themes that will recur in this book. When an NCB accepts eligible collateral from a counterparty and with a security margin at or superior to that stated in the ECB list against the respective security (the so-called 'haircut'), then the NCB is deemed not to be taking credit risk on its counterparty.

This tends to obscure the facts that the NCB is taking credit risk on the issuer of the security, and is taking market risk on the performance of the security – which is a fixed-rate bond or money market instrument. A deterioration in the credit risk of the issuer or a rise in absolute interest rates (and also more technical movements in the structure of the interest rates prevailing for different maturities) will cause the market price of the security to fall: the haircut exists in order to allow for a fall before the value of the security ceases to be sufficient to cover the loan. The question is whether the haircuts are large enough given that the credit risk component of a haircut is calculated using the same premises as banks apply when risk-weighting an obligation of the same counterparty. A loan by a major Eurozone bank to, for example, La Poste in France will be risk-weighted using a similar methodology as the ECB would use when calculating the haircut on a bond issued by La Poste. The methodologies behind the Basel Accords permeate the Eurosystem and can be considered to be a 'super-spreader' of the basic fault in the euro: there is no genuine 'sovereign risk' counterparty backing it that merits a 0% risk-weighting.

Who bears the losses from Eurosystem operations

In the first instance it is the Eurozone NCBs that bear the risks in Eurosystem operations. The ECB having scant resources of its own, it is the NCBs who carry out the Eurosystem operations, under an agreement whereby profits and losses on those operations are allocated back to the ECB when they have been realized.

If a loss occurs, the NCB that incurred it passes it back to the ECB. The ECB then splits the loss amongst all the NCBs – including the one that incurred it – by debiting a portion of the loss to the capital account of each NCB in accordance with their ECB Capital Key.[18] This diminishes the ECB's capital, as well as diminishing the value of each NCB's shares.

The ECB can make a request for extra capital from the NCBs but its furnishing is not automatic: the shares of Eurozone NCBs are fully paid-in. A global call for a new amount of capital would go through the ECB governance process and, once approved, be allocated out amongst the NCBs according to each one's ECB Capital Key.

It has to be stressed again that the Eurosystem is not a legal entity but a contractual arrangement between the ECB and the NCBs, there is no Eurozone government, and the term 'Eurozone government bond' is a misnomer. The term should be 'Eurozone member state government bond'.

The architecture of TARGET2

The partially-centralized architecture of the Eurosystem is reflected in its payment system, called TARGET, standing for Transnational Automated Real-time Gross-settlement Express Transfer system. The bedrock of TARGET remains the national Real-time Gross-Settlement (RTGS) payment systems in existence obligatorily in every Eurozone member state and, at the option of each non-Eurozone member state, a euro RTGS running alongside their national-currency RTGS. Five such euro RTGS of non-Eurozone member states are now part of TARGET. All of these national-level RTGS are run by the respective NCB: all payments flow through an NCB. TARGET is coordinated by the ECB but this does not mean that all payments flow through it; in fact very few do.

The original TARGET was an arrangement based on the principles of correspondent banking. Payments with both endpoints in a single member state were cleared and settled within the national RTGS and through its NCB: only that NCB was involved. Payments with endpoints in different member states were transmitted by the sending NCB to the receiving NCB over the 'TARGET Interlinking', which really meant the SWIFT network. These cross-border TARGET payments cleared and settled through the current accounts held by the respective NCBs with one another. These are referred to as 'nostros' and 'vostros'. An account held by the Bundesbank at the Banque de France is a 'nostro' (our account in another bank's books) in the Bundesbank's view and a 'vostro' in the view of the Banque de France (another bank's account in our books). Every NCB held an account with every other NCB, and they each also held a 'nostro' account at the ECB and ran a 'vostro' account in their own books for the ECB.

How cross-border payments were cleared, and the build-up of the TARGET debts

Payments with endpoints in different member states – cross-border TARGET payments – were debited first to the sending bank by its NCB within the national RTGS. That NCB credited the 'vostro' of the receiving NCB in its books, and sent a payment message over the SWIFT network to the receiving NCB. The receiving NCB debited the sending NCB's 'nostro' in its books, and credited the receiving bank within the national RTGS. This was a very antiquated correspondent banking system, because it required two amounts of money: the amount credited by the sending NCB onto the receiving NCB's 'vostro' account, and a balance on the sending NCB's 'nostro' at the receiving NCB. The receiving NCB was not allowed to view the amount in its account at the sending NCB as good funds to pay away against, because those funds represented a credit risk on the sending NCB. Only the funds on the sending NCB's 'nostro' could be regarded as good funds and risk-free, because they were already lying in the books of the receiving NCB.

---

[18] These Capital Keys are arrived at by weighting a member state's GNI and its population against those of the Eurozone as a whole, a different formula than for EU cash contributions but in the same vein.

If the sending NCB did not have sufficient funds on its 'nostro' but held collateral at the receiving NCB, then the collateral was allowed to serve in place of sufficient funds and the payment could be completed by the sending NCB's 'nostro' account going into overdraft. Indeed, the collateral did not have to be pledged at the receiving NCB: it could be held at any NCB in the Eurosystem or at the ECB and charged in favour of the receiving NCB under the terms of the CCBM: the Correspondent Central Banking Model.

This construction explains the build-up of debts within the TARGET system: NCBs did not have to clear their accounts with one another and with the ECB to zero at the end of each business day as was the normal practice in other RTGS systems. Instead the balances came to reflect the money flows around the Eurosystem and, with Germany running large Balance of Payments surpluses against other Eurozone countries, the latter countries began to run into deficit and Germany into credit.

TARGET2 construction and the imbalances

This remains the logical construction of the current system, TARGET2. TARGET2 has a centralized IT platform that performs many of the tasks for which NCBs originally had to build their own IT applications. SWIFT messages are still used but in many cases these are transmitted within the centralized IT platform and do not pass over the SWIFT communications network.

TARGET2 is at best partially centralized. NCBs can opt out of certain modules on the centralized IT platform and continue to run the IT applications for the respective functions themselves. The centralized IT platform operates in three data centres in three countries: Germany, France and Italy. The roles of production site and warm standby site are rotated: the hot standby site is always within the environment of the data centre that is the production site at the time.

Even with the centralized IT platform, NCBs can both run up overdraft positions during the business day on their accounts with one another, and not clear them off at the close-of-business.

How other RTGS systems enable participants to have enough money to get their payments made

The UK's RTGS (CHAPS) does not allow participant banks to go into overdraft on their Settlement Accounts at all, even during the business day[19]: instead the Bank of England enables the participants to sell eligible securities to it with an agreed buy-back price and time, known as a Repurchase Agreement or 'repo'. The participant sells the securities for cash, the cash ends up on their Settlement Account, and payments debiting their Settlement Account will continue to clear. The 'repo' may be intraday, and the cash be re-debited to the Settlement Account at end-of-day, by which time the participant should have received all its scheduled payments and be in credit anyway: the residual credit balance, after the re-debiting of the 'repo' transaction, is then automatically moved into the participant's Reserve Account overnight, leaving the Settlement Account with a zero balance.

The US's Fedwire RTGS permits participants to go into overdraft during the day without entering into a repo, and without pledging collateral if the overdraft remains below a certain figure. However, an excess overdraft above that figure must be collateralized: the type of collateral that the Bank of England would demand to be the subject of a 'repo' is analogous to the type of collateral that the Federal Reserve would require to be pledged to it, but in US$. Fedwire participants must bring down the balance of their account by end-of-day or else the Federal Reserve has the right to seize the pledged collateral and sell it to cover the overdraft.

The Federal Reserve and the Bank of England use differing techniques to arrive at the same place, but TARGET2's approach is different in nature: account balances at end-of-day are subjected to a legal reinterpretation whereby each NCB is supposed to have just one net residual claim on or liability to the ECB. This is the way in which the ECB accounts for the situation but what the debits and credits are that go over on the original accounts to operationalize this (if any) is unclear.

---

[19] A bank's CHAPS Settlement Account is the one from which all its CHAPS payments are debited and into which all its CHAPS receipts are credited; the equivalent type of account in TARGET2 is called an RTGS Account

Trajectory of the TARGET balances

The balances of the NCBs to and from the ECB are now very large, and have been interpreted by commentators as loans by NCBs to one another. The December 2020 report showed figures only from 2009 onwards, and then only at year-end. Now the ECB issues a report every month, for the balances on the final day of the month. Here is a snapshot of the trajectory of the year-end position, every two years from 2009 to 2019:

€ billions	End of 2009	End of 2011	End of 2013	End of 2015	End of 2017	End of 2019
ECB	+4.0	+42.2	-6.7	-83.8	-222.8	-236.1
Belgium	-42.5	-52.9	-15.5	-7.7	-36.1	-63.7
Germany	+177.7	+463.1	+510.2	+584.2	+906.9	+895.2
Estonia	0.0	+0.6	+1.8	+2.8	+0.9	+0.6
Ireland	-53.5	-120.4	-55.1	-3.0	+1.9	+35.4
Greece	-49.0	-104.8	-51.1	-94.4	-59.4	-25.7
Spain	41.1	-175.0	-213.7	-254.1	-373.7	-392.4
France	-62.0	-77.4	-16.2	-29.2	+30.0	+28.5
Italy	+54.8	-191.4	-229.1	-248.9	-439.0	-439.4
Cyprus	-7.1	-7.9	-6.8	+2.4	+7.4	+8.5
Latvia	0.0	0.0	0.0	-1.3	-6.3	-3.8
Lithuania	0.0	0.0	0.0	+0.2	-4.0	-0.9
Luxembourg	+52.5	+109.4	+103.7	+147.6	+192.1	+192.4
Malta	-0.8	-0.4	-0.7	-0.9	+4.3	+5.6
Netherlands	+15.4	+152.8	+46.1	+54.7	+71.0	+46.4
Austria	-19.6	-34.6	-39.2	-29.2	-45.9	-46.6
Portugal	-23.4	-60.9	-59.6	-61.7	-81.2	-77.0
Slovenia	-3.3	-2.7	-1.0	+0.2	-1.4	+3.4
Slovakia	-14.5	-13.6	+2.7	+0.5	+9.0	+9.3
Finland	+9.5	+66.0	+22.2	+20.1	+40.4	+57.1
Non-Eurozone[20]	+3.2	+7.9	+8.0	+1.5	+6.1	+3.3

Table 2.1: development of the TARGET balances

It can be seen that the major expansions occurred between 2009 and 2011, and again between 2015 and 2017. These were not the timings of the Eurozone debt crisis. The ECB's figure is the balancing item, and this went from being insignificant between 2009 and 2015, to the ECB being a major creditor of the system in an amount in a multiple of its own capital: it would only be able to repay the creditor NCBs if the debtor NCBs repay.

The nature and size of the TARGET2 balances are themselves an area of shadow debt, and are not included in the Eurostat figures, either on a net or gross basis, as an NCB is not within the scope of 'General government', and as 'gross' balances existing at the end of the processing day are netted off before the ECB issues its monthly reports.

TARGET, while not a discreet institution, is a distinct mechanism and has the capacity to act as a borrower and a lender, even if that should not be the purpose of a payment system and even though it was not performing this function in meaningful size at the time.

Chapter summary

The EU and the EU/Eurozone supranationals create risk for which the member states are responsible. In the case of the EU's operations their risk is for the total amounts that the supranational engages; in the case of the EIB Group there is a limited legal liability. This legal limitation is compromised where the EIB Group has received EU first-loss guarantees: the first losses are passed to member states through the EU budget and are subject to no limitation other than their own size. The EIB Group can, on top of that, call up capital from the member states for further losses.

---

[20] The NCBs of Bulgaria, Croatia, Denmark, Poland and Romania: they are not permitted to run overdraft balances

The situation with the Eurosystem is less clear-cut: losses on Eurosystem operations would first be booked by an NCB, and then passed up to the ECB. The ECB can make a call on the NCBs for extra capital through the ECB governance process. There are more steps to be gone through than in the case of the EIB Group: the ECB cannot simply call up the unpaid portion of subscribed capital as the EIB can do.

TARGET2 has emerged as a major and contentious source of debt creation in its own right. These are debts of NCBs, not of member states, and they do not themselves feature in Eurostat GGGD. There may or may not be on offset if the TARGET2 debts are collateralized with debt securities that already fall within GGGD, and this issue is dealt with further below.

An NCB normally has a reinsurance arrangement with the finance ministry of its country so that a call for more capital by the ECB can be funded by new debt issuance by the member state, but the exact mechanisms for achieving this differ from one member state to another.

Global financial markets would be aghast if they were confronted with a situation where either the ECB refused to take over a loss from an NCB on a Eurosystem operation, or where the NCBs blocked the ECB's mechanisms for asking NCBs to subscribe to new capital in order to make good a loss, or where a finance ministry refused to furnish its NCB with the necessary funds to meet an ECB capital call.

Here we have another situation where the global financial system believes that the EU and Eurozone mechanisms are watertight, and that EU/Eurozone supranationals are and will be backed by member states, whatever are the exact mechanisms for bringing that about.

It is a matter of speculation whether member states believe they have the power, either in law or in practice, not to back the EU/Eurozone supranationals. All of the EIB, EIF and ECB can theoretically go bankrupt, but that would undermine the EU and Eurozone projects. The best one can say is that member states would back these supranationals if they are able to: the credit risk lies on the member states themselves. These supranationals have limited loss cushions of their own – they are look-throughs to the creditworthiness of the member states, but without all the debts, for which member states are responsible, appearing in the Eurostat database.

This, then, was the array of EU supranational institutions up until the Global Financial Crisis of 2007-8 and the Eurozone debt crisis of 2010-3, the latter of which began with the situations of Portugal and Ireland.

Chapter 3 – responses to the Global Financial Crisis of 2007/8

Chapter introduction

The EU authorities undertook a series of responses to the Global Financial Crisis of 2007/8 and to the Eurozone debt crisis of 2010-2013:

- European Financial Stabilisation Mechanism
- European Financial Stability Facility
- European Stability Mechanism
- ECB Asset Purchase Programmes
- Expansion of the ECB's list of collateral eligible for Eurosystem monetary and payment operations
- Bank Deposit Insurance Schemes

That amounts to two new mechanisms (the European Financial Stability Facility and the European Stability Mechanism), three expansions of the remit of existing mechanisms (the European Financial Stabilisation Mechanism, the ECB Asset Purchase Programmes, and the expansion of the ECB's list of collateral eligible), and one completely new piece of legislation (the Bank Deposit Insurance Schemes).

The addition of six responses into a pre-existing framework has greatly complicated the understanding of the whole, as well as significantly increased the member states' risks.

Where certain mechanisms raise funds to relay to member state governments (whether by the making of a loan or the buying of debt securities), the funds so relayed do feature in the member state's and the EU's GGGD. However, the risk, as far as the original suppliers of the funds are concerned, lies not with the member state to whom the funds have been relayed, but with the member states who are guaranteeing the good operation of the mechanism.

3.1 European Financial Stabilisation Mechanism (EFSM)

The first new mechanism was the EFSM. It was the first bailout mechanism established in 2010 pursuant to Council Regulation (EU) No 407/2010.[21] The beneficiaries of loans from this fund were Ireland and Portugal. The EFSM involved all EU Member States and was an EU fund, meaning that the funds were borrowed by the EU and on-lent to Ireland or Portugal. Were Ireland or Portugal to default, the debt service for the EU's borrowings would be debited to the EU budget and result in increased member state cash contributions. This invokes the joint-and-several liability of member states for the EU's borrowings: the EU budget cannot be allowed to remain in deficit.

The EFSM ceiling is €60 billion; €46.8 billion were lent to Ireland and Portugal under the series of loans, the most long-dated of which matures in 2042. Ireland currently owes €15.6 billion and Portugal €14.25 billion. €30.15 billion remains nominally available. Greece was permitted to take bridge financing from the EFSM in 2015 but that has been repaid.

Member states ought to record a contingent liability in respect of the whole €60 billion. Regarding the €29.85 billion owed by Ireland and Portugal, the other member states will have to replenish the EU budget so that the EU can service the bonds it has issued if these member states fail again. Ireland's and Portugal's debts to the EFSM will be included in their own 'General government gross debt'. They should not hold a contingent liability as well for their own debt, but they should consider that they would be liable to replenish the EU budget in the case that the other failed, so some provision for that would be prudent. The balance of the fund - €30.15 billion – remains redrawable so the situation that exists now with Ireland and Portugal could be replicated for other member states, or indeed for Ireland or Portugal again.

---

[21] https://ec.europa.eu/info/business-economy-euro/economic-and-fiscal-policy-coordination/financial-assistance-eu/funding-mechanisms-and-facilities/european-financial-stabilisation-mechanism-efsm_en accessed on 24 May 2022

3.2 European Financial Stability Facility (EFSF)

The EFSF was the second Eurozone bailout mechanism, also agreed in 2010 but involving only the Eurozone member states.[22] It had loans out under three programmes, all fully drawn, as at 30 December 2020 as follows: Ireland €18.6 billion with final maturity 2042; Portugal €25.5 billion with final maturity 2040; Greece €141.0 billion with final maturity 2070; total €186.1 billion.[23]

The EFSF is a Luxembourg-incorporated special purpose company. Its capital is in the form of fully-paid shares owned by the Eurozone countries. Unlike the EIB, there is no subscribed-but-not-called amount of capital. Member state backing for the EFSF is in the form of guarantees.

No new programmes can draw on the EFSF, and no existing borrowers can draw more. The European Stability Mechanism (ESM) administers the EFSF, meaning receiving capital repayments and interest on its loans, paying out on the bonds issued to finance the loans, and calling the member state guarantees if needed.

The capital of the EFSF amounts to €28 million, which is miniscule. All Eurozone member states are shareholders except Latvia and Lithuania who were not in the Eurozone at the time.[24]

Debt securities and the guarantee behind them

As of 31st December 2020 the EFSF had €191 billion of debt securities in issue. With loans at €186 billion, it can be seen that the EFSF borrows almost all the funds it relays. Investors are willing to supply those funds to the EFSF, not due to the creditworthiness of the EFSF's borrowers, but because their investments 'are backed by irrevocable and unconditional guarantees of the euro area member states'.[25]

This is the main source of strength in the EFSF and the guarantees are on a several-but-not-joint basis, and are in line with the member states' Capital Keys in the ECB, with the Capital Keys of Latvia and Lithuania backed out along with the Capital Keys of the non-Eurozone member states.[26] The base Capital Keys are visible in the ECB Annual Accounts, and we have re-based them to take account of the above-mentioned exceptions.[27]

Initially, under these programmes, all issued debt was backed by an over-guarantee of 120% from the Guarantee countries (Guarantors) and by cash retentions from the proceeds of the issued bonds. The cash retentions were calculated in a way that the guarantees from AAA-rated countries (on the Standard and Poor's rating scale) and the cash retained would be sufficient to cover all of the associated debt service if the underlying loan was not paid in full (see below). These credit enhancements were designed to support a AAA rating for the EFSF as an issuer itself.[28]

On 24 June 2011, the Eurozone Heads of State or Government agreed to increase the EFSF's scope of activity and raised its guarantee commitments to €780 billion from €440 billion. This included an over-guarantee of up to 165%, which corresponded to a lending capacity of €440 billion on the one hand and ensuring the highest possible credit rating for the EFSF on the other, bearing in mind which guarantors were still AAA-rated at the time.[29]

Weaknesses in the EFSF template

The EFSF, under this template, could borrow and on-lend €440 billion, as long as guarantees of at least €726 billion were from AAA-rated member states and as long as no member states were borrowers. This was not the case even in 2011, even had there been no borrowers. The guarantee size of €780 billion was theoretical given that not all guarantors were AAA-rated, meaning that the lending ceiling of €440 billion was also theoretical.

---

[22] https://www.esm.europa.eu/about-us/efsf/before-the-esm accessed on 24 May 2022
[23] EFSF Annual Report 2020 p. 39
[24] EFSF Annual Report 2020 p. 17
[25] EFSF Annual Report 2020 p. 54
[26] https://www.investopedia.com/terms/e/european-financial-stability-facility.asp accessed on 24 May 2022
[27] 2021 ECB Annual Accounts p. 57
[28] EFSF Annual Report 2020 p. 25
[29] EFSF Annual Report 2020 p. 24

The result as from the new 2011 agreement is shown in Figure 3.1, in terms of the guarantee share of each member state. The construction caters for what are known as 'Stepping-Out' guarantors. This recognizes that a member state that borrows from the EFSF, because it is in financial trouble, cannot be relied upon to meet a call on its guarantee. The guarantee allocations of borrowing member states are backed out of the available guarantee amount. Thus the capacity of the fund, being a portion of the guarantee amount, has to be diminished in line with the diminution of the guarantee.

Furthermore, with only Germany, Luxembourg and the Netherlands now having AAA credit ratings, the EFSF was unable to both retain a meaningful size and enjoy a AAA rating. Instead its rating is now AA.

Each member state has a maximum guarantee liability of the overall guarantee size multiplied by its rebased ECB Capital Key out of 100%, after Latvia and Lithuania have been reversed out. That results in the 'Allocation from €780 billion', the theoretical total amount of guarantees to which the total borrowing and lending would be linked.

Then the amounts allocated to 'Stepping-Out' guarantors are deducted from the guarantee amount: the amounts are not reallocated to the other guarantors. The EFSF annual reports state that 'the Republic of Ireland, the Portuguese Republic and the Hellenic Republic had become Stepping-Out Guarantors. The Republic of Cyprus became a Stepping-Out Guarantor as of 29 April 2013'. The guarantee ceiling falls to €745.0 billion.

Finally we have the residual member states that hold a AAA-rating: their guarantees amount to €246 billion. This factor means that it was unviable for the EFSF to maintain its firepower with the 'over-guarantee' margin of 165% and retain its own AAA-rating. The bonds and the lending would have to have been reduced from €190 billion to €150 billion (to €246 billion divided by 165%) in order to achieve that. This was not possible when the outstanding loans had scheduled capital and interest payments attached, upon which the borrowers were not in default, and when the bonds had no early repayment clause without the payment of a penalty.

Instead the EFSF had to give up its AAA-rating, recognize that the firepower capacity between €190 billion and €440 billion could not be mobilized, and close itself to new operations.

EFSF as an example of circularity and theoretical firepower

This is another example of the circularity already referred to above that causes the difficulty in a member state calculating its maximum and likely exposure under such arrangements, when the allocations on paper include ones to a member state whose default was the cause of an allocation being called upon.

It also an example of how firepower can be created in an EU-level institution based on the credit ratings of member states and causing them to be exposed to risks created in an EU-level institution. But it is also an example of how the firepower becomes diminished when the backers lose their own ratings, and when some become borrowers. The reductions in the ratings of member states have occurred after the EFSF made its loans. Even after the 'Stepping-Out' of borrowing guarantors, the guarantee was still meaningful at €745 billion and is 169% of the lending ceiling of €440 billion and 390% of outstanding loans. However, the firepower could only exist if the vast majority of the guarantees were from member states rated at AAA or AA+. That has ceased to be the case, leaving the firepower theoretical rather than real.

Member state accounting for the EFSF

The borrowing member states will have their loans from the EFSF included within their 'General government gross debt'.

Guarantor member states ought to record a contingent liability in the amount of their guarantee, albeit that they can argue that their cumulative guarantees exceed the total of bonds being guaranteed and that their contingent liability should be regarded as smaller. This argument has merit in that the guarantees are several-but-not-joint in this case. However, they have a face value, and they add to up to far more than the bonds outstanding. One should consider the situation where a guarantor, who was not a borrower, defaulted on a guarantee call. If each guarantor's liability is expressed as 'x% of any guarantee call up to a limit of y', then a guarantor might argue that they were not liable to pay more than this x% of the call.

On the other hand, if stress was instead laid on the limit amount of y and a call of z amount came in, and if one or more guarantors could not pay, there would be an argument that the solvent guarantors might be liable to pay right up to the amounts of their guarantees. The guarantors might not be liable for the whole debt amount, but nor are they for sure liable only for the guarantee call amount multiplied by their re-based ECB Capital Key.

Following that logic chain, there is a dependency of guarantors on whether it is a large fellow guarantor, or a small one, that ceases to be good for its guarantee. In the former case, the amounts called from other guarantors would escalate substantially; in the latter case they would escalate by a smaller amount.

To simplify matters we have remained with the concept that a guarantor member state's contingent liability is the total of EFSF bonds in issue multiplied by the guarantor member state's ECB Capital Key. Nevertheless it should be noted that there are plausible circumstances where a member state's liability might escalate. The EFSF thus presents a subset of Eurozone member states with a contingent liability of €191 billion, the amount of its debt securities in issue.

3.3 European Stability Mechanism

The European Stability Mechanism (ESM) was the third Eurozone bailout mechanism, also agreed in 2010 and again involving only the Eurozone members.[30] The ESM is the now main Eurozone bailout fund should further members be unable to access capital markets directly: the ESM would finance the member state, as they have done for their five existing debtors, who are Spain, Greece, Portugal, Ireland and Cyprus.[31] The ESM has a maximum lending capacity of €500 billion.

The ESM is a Luxembourg-incorporated special purpose company. Its capital follows the pattern of EIB Group, being in the form of part-paid shares owned by the Eurozone countries, with the subscribed-but-uncalled capital callable on a several-but-not-joint basis.

Capital amount and lending ceiling

The total subscribed capital is €705 billion, 141% of the maximum lending capacity of €500 billion. The same problem emerges here as with the EFSF: can Spain, Greece, Portugal, Ireland and Cyprus be relied upon the pay in their subscribed-but-not-called capital, if they are borrowers from the fund and when a need to call up new capital would be caused by one of the fund's borrowers defaulting? If not, then the 'guarantee fund' (which is what the subscribed-but-not-called capital amounts to) should be diminished by their subscribed-but-not-called capital, and the lending capacity diminished by the guarantee amounts so eliminated divided by 141%.

The consequent problem with the ESM is that it does not have the headroom to deal with a new Eurozone debt crisis if a major member needed to borrow from it.

Current ESM loan volumes

Current loan outstandings to ESM debtor members and the start of their run-off are:
- Spain €24 billion running off from 2022
- Greece €131 billion running off from 2022
- Portugal €25 billion running off from 2025
- Ireland €18 billion running off from 2029
- Cyprus €6 billion running off from 2025

These outstandings total €204 billion, as against a maximum lending cap of €500 billion, ostensibly leaving headroom at present of €296 billion for new loans.

The ESM balance sheet totals €829 billion, also inferring ample resources.

---

[30] https://www.esm.europa.eu/ accessed on 22 May 2022
[31] www.esm.europa.eu, accessed on 02 April 2022

However the ESM's balance sheet is inflated by €624 billion.[32] The ESM has subscribed capital of €705 billion, subscribed by the Eurozone member states on a several-but-not-joint basis.[33] €81 billion of this is paid-in. The remaining €624 billion is a 'guarantee fund' to be called up if one or more of the debtors default and the ESM is unable to repay the bonds it has issued in order to raise funds to lend.

Faulty ESM accounting for and presentation of its assets

The ESM balance sheet wrongly carries the full €705 billion of capital on the liabilities side, and the unpaid portion of €624 billion on the asset side, when it is not an asset but a contingent claim. It has no place on a balance sheet. The EIB, whose capital structure is similar, correctly nets its unpaid capital of €227 billion off against its subscribed capital of €247 billion on the liabilities side of its balance sheet without claiming the existence of any related asset.[34] The ESM balance sheet footing ought instead to be lower by this €624 billion and be on a level with the outstandings to the debtor members: the ESM has no other assets of any substance.

There is a second significant accounting legerdemain in that the ESM balance sheet carries €58 billion under the heading of 'Cash in hand, with central banks and post office banks' and a further €11 billion under the heading of 'Loans and advances to credit institutions'.

These treatments infer that the captioned assets are separate from the bailout programmes, that they are of higher quality and liquidity than bailout programme assets, and that they are free resources available to be mobilized for new bailout programmes.

In reality they are part and parcel of the existing bailout programmes for the five debtor members and are of the same quality and liquidity as 'Loans and advances to euro area member states' (€90 billion) and 'Debt securities' (€44 billion).

These four balance sheet positions totaled €203 billion and equated to the outstandings as they were at the end of 2020.[35] The ESM has no banking assets outside of its bailout programmes, contrary to what the presentation of its accounts infers.

ESM liabilities and capital structure

The ESM had €118 billion of bonds in issue at the end of 2020.[36] That amount, together with the €81 billion of paid-in capital, formed 98% of the refinancing for its loans: €199 billion out of €203 billion. There were €4-5 billion of miscellaneous liabilities to make up the balance sheet footing as it should have been stated.

The ESM's capital is structured similarly to the EIB's in that there is recourse to members for extra money if a debtor defaults, but there are meaningful differences: only the 19 Eurozone countries are ESM members, the ESM's assets are concentrated into five ESM members, and these members have been in or near default in the recent past. The ESM loan book cannot therefore exceed the paid-in capital plus the subscribed-but-not-paid capital of non-debtor members, reduced by the application of the 141% over-guarantee. This severely limits the ESM's actual firepower compared to the resources inferred by its 2020 balance sheet footing.

Firepower calculation must deduct back the unpaid capital of debtor members

Although the reserve fund is €624 billion on a gross basis now, one has to deduct back the €116 billion of unpaid subscriptions of the debtor members:
Spain: €73 billion
Greece: €17 billion
Portugal: €15 billion
Ireland: €10 billion

---

[32] ESM 2020 Annual Report p. 68
[33] Each subscriber is responsible only for their own allocated portion. They do not have to pay more if other subscribers fail to pay in their respective allocated portion
[34] EIB 2020 Financial Report p. 39
[35] ESM 2020 Annual Report p. 68
[36] ESM 2020 Annual Report p. 68

Cyprus: €1 billion

One might argue that it is unfair to discount the entire subscribed-but-not-paid capital of €73 billion of Spain, when they have only borrowed €24 billion, but that is the logic of the set-up, and it threatens to rebound on the European authorities.

The amount to be deducted back from the reserve fund is €116 billion, which reduces its effective size from €624 billion to the €508 billion that can be called in from non-debtor members. Together with the paid-in capital of €81 billion, the ESM has reference resources of €589 billion behind its supposed lending cap of €500 billion.

The margin of 141% then needs to be factored in. If the ESM has reference resources of €589 billion, then its lending cap is not €500 billion but €417 billion (€589 billion divided by 141%).

With €203 billion of loans already made, the ESM's headroom for new operations is just €214 billion.

Inadequate firepower to bail out an Italy or a France

The lending headroom now, at €214 billion, is not large compared to the 'General government gross debt' of these two member states at the end of 2020: Italy's at €2,573 billion and France's at €2,649 billion.[37] Nor does the ESM have major run-offs in the near future that will create re-drawable capacity.

The additional problem is that, if either of these member states needed to become debtors to the ESM, their subscribed-but-not-paid capital would have to be deducted back from the current reference resources to determine the actual headroom for new ESM lending. Italy and France, being large members, account for significant shares of the ESM's subscribed-but-not-paid capital.

Once the deductions have taken placed and the reference resources diminished as a consequence – and account is taken of the existing loans – the ESM only has firepower in the order of 5.28% of Italy's GGGD and 4.34% of France's. Its firepower is less than 1% of the combined GGGD of these two member states.

The ESM does not measure up to the challenge. A need for either Italy or France to tap the ESM would increase the outstandings markedly if the ESM's intervention were to be material in terms of the size of Italy's or France's debts, but the structure of the ESM inhibits its intervening in new cases of a material scale. It could not take on the level of share of the GGGD of these members that it owns of Greece's (38%) or of Cyprus' (25%).[38]

The ostensible 'over-capitalization' of the ESM, achieved by its having subscribed capital of €705 billion and a lending cap of €500 billion, only works so long as the larger members do not become debtors.

While this has not been explicitly admitted to by the European authorities, it is a possible explanation for their establishment, in July 2022, of the so-called 'Transmission Protection Mechanism'. This appears to have the characteristics of a bailout fund, as its purpose is to allow the Eurosystem to buy member state government bonds. The claimed rationale is to avoid the yield differences between the government bonds of different member states that are not objectively justified. It has no stated ceiling. The mechanism is discussed in a later chapter.

Member state accounting for the ESM

All of the ESM's loans should already be counted within the 'General government gross debt' of the borrower country, even the ones to Spain which were for the purposes of bank recapitalization. The ESM's respective webpage states that the loans were 'to Spain', which infers that the borrower was the Kingdom of Spain.[39]

The non-borrower member states should be showing a contingent liability for a portion of their subscribed-but-not-paid capital.

---

[37] https://ec.europa.eu/eurostat/databrowser/view/sdg_17_40/default/table?lang=en, accessed on 1 April 2022
[38] €131 billion out of Eurostat's €341 billion for Greece and €6 billion out of €24 billion for Cyprus
[39] https://www.esm.europa.eu/assistance/spain accessed on 24 May 2022

The borrower countries should in theory do this as well, as they are liable in the case that different borrower countries default, although in practice not if they default themselves: this is the same problem, that a guarantor will not pay if they are themselves the debtor under the debt so guaranteed.

Having to pay in their subscribed-but-not-paid capital in case a different borrower defaults does not relieve them of the necessity of continuing to service their loan from the ESM. It would bear some debate as to what would be the correct level of contingent liability to recognize, but it is not correct to fail to record this issue at all.

An outcome is needed, however, and our conclusion is that the non-borrowing member states could find themselves liable to pay in uncalled capital (i) for the €118 billion of bonds in issue (the ESM's current funding over and above the called-up capital), and (ii) for funding new programmes with capital just as €81 billion was called to fund the current programmes, and (iii) in respect of the balance of new programmes that are funded by bonds.

The total amount of this contingent liability cannot exceed the €417 billion ceiling on loans that the ESM can give out, less the €81 billion of capital already paid in: the difference is €332 billion. This is the same as the bonds already in issue of €118 billion plus the headroom of €214 billion.

The ESM thus presents a subset of Eurozone member states with a contingent liability of €332 billion.

3.4 ECB Asset Purchase Programmes

In common with many other central banks, the ECB injected liquidity into the financial system by buying existing financial assets for cash. This policy goes globally by the name of Quantitative Easing or QE, whereas the ECB have named it their Asset Purchase Programmes or APP. The Eurosystem did already own a portfolio of securities before the Global Financial Crisis and the bonds in the portfolio had to be on the ECB list of eligible collateral. However, APP was of a different order of magnitude entirely.

Whilst there have been sub-programmes within the APP envelope that have opened and then closed, the main one has existed throughout – the Public Sector Purchase Programme or PSPP. The PSPP, like the other sub-programmes, is meant to buy assets that are seasoned, and which are traded in the secondary market not the primary market. This is so as to avoid 'direct monetary financing' of member states i.e. buying up new issues of member states or of entities within 'General government'. It was contended that this was outside the ECB's powers.

The programmes are operated by the NCBs but at the ECB's behest, and the make-up of the overall portfolio must accord to the Capital Keys of the Eurozone member state NCBs in the ECB, re-based to 100%. The programme assets sit on the balance sheets of the NCBs, and on the Eurosystem aggregate and consolidated balance sheets, but not on the ECB's individual balance sheet.

As of 8th April 2022 the holdings in the APP programmes totaled €3.2 trillion, of which €4.1 billion were in run-off mode from 'Closed APP programmes'.

Of the remainder held in active programmes. 79% or €2.5 trillion of the APP was represented by the Public sector purchase programme or PSPP. This does not mean that all the holdings qualify within 'General government gross debt', although of course the largest borrower in each member state is the government itself and for that reason alone it is likely that the PSPP contains a majority of bonds that sit within 'General government gross debt' and a minority that do not.

The other balances totaled €657 billion, spread across Covered bonds, Asset-backed securities, and Corporate securities.

The Pandemic Emergency Purchase Programme, or PEPP, is an asset purchase programme in the widest sense, and is often referred to as an ECB APP. However, it was only started up in 2020 and, although it undertakes similar operations, it obeys meaningfully different rules. It is dealt with in a later chapter. Where we use the term 'APP', we mean the programmes started up before the Pandemic.

The new Transmission Protection Mechanism will also be an asset purchase programme in the widest sense, but obeying different rules from the APP and from the PEPP.

3.5 Expansion of the ECB's list of collateral eligible for Eurosystem monetary and payment operations

The ECB has always had a list of the collateral eligible for securing its monetary and payment operations. Purchases into all of the APP, the PEPP and the TPM must be of bonds on this list.

At the time of the introduction of the euro there were two lists: the A list which was eligible for pledging at any NCB, and the B list which was eligible only for borrowers from the NCB in the member state in which the borrower was located. Typically, then, a bank such as Societe Generale, operating in several Eurozone countries, would hold A list collateral which it could pledge to several NCBs and borrow from them. A Credit Mutuel operating only in France would have A list collateral and B list collateral, and it would logically use either to borrow from the Banque de France, it having no reason to borrow from other NCBs or account relationships through which to borrow.

The contents of both lists were public sector entities, with a stress on member state governments and their agencies. Member state government bonds were on the A list. B lists might contain, apocryphally, unused Paris metro tickets and unfranked French postage stamps, because these were liabilities of a French government entity. They could be pledged to the Banque de France by financial institutions for whom the Banque de France was their sponsor into the Eurosystem, but they could not be pledged at the Bundesbank or Central Bank of Ireland. It could reasonably be claimed that all the assets on the A and B lists were 'central bank money': obligations of governments that could be exchanged between one another 'at par' i.e. without a discount on account of credit risk. The three classic forms of 'central bank money' were:
1. A balance on an account at the central bank;
2. Cash;
3. Government securities of the country in question.

Unused Paris metro tickets and unfranked French postage stamps could be classified as government securities, as they were stores-of-value for the repayment or discharge of which the French government was responsible.

No 'haircut' is needed on 'central bank money' assets to take account of credit risk, because they fulfill the criteria of a risk-free investment if they are denominated in the currency of the country of the central bank, and if that central bank exercises full sovereign power over the currency. No 'haircut' is needed because there is no risk of the obligor being unable to pay out on it.

A 'haircut' is needed on classic 'central bank money' assets only to take account of market risk: the risk that a fixed-rate government security may decline in value due to a rise in interest rates, as is explained further below.

Current extent of ECB list and related 'haircuts'

Even setting aside the issue that the euro has no 'central bank money' at all in the classic sense, the current ECB list has degenerated to the point where numerous securities appear on it that cannot by any stretch of the imagination be classed as euro 'central bank money'.

The list has nearly 26,000 bonds on it, and it ranges across banks, corporates, securitization vehicles, and public sector entities of all types. Each bond is entered on the list with its International Securities Identification Number (ISIN), its particulars, and the applicable haircut, but not its amount.

The Eurosystem trades on much thinner 'haircuts' for its monetary and policy operations than the European Banking Authority imposes on commercial banks when they present the same assets as proof of their institution's liquidity.

The haircut exists to protect the Eurosystem from loss, in the case that it has to attach and sell the collateral.[40]

The haircut acknowledges firstly that the collateral may fall in value during the timelag between the occurrence of the event triggering the attachment of the collateral and its sale.

---

[40] 'Attach' means going through the process of converting legal documentation giving the Eurosystem member a security interest in the collateral into the necessary papers to have the Eurosystem member replace the defaulting institution as the beneficial owner of the collateral, and to move the collateral from the securities custody account of the defaulting institution into the account of the Eurosystem member

It secondly acknowledges that a piece of collateral might lose its credit quality and have to be replaced: the haircut needs to be sufficient to cover the timelag between this happening, the collateral not being replaced, the loan therefore defaulting, and the Eurosystem attaching and selling the collateral. This second eventuality might involve a longer timelag because there are more steps in it, so the haircut should cover the longer period and be conservative.

It is not possible from the information in the public domain to determine the way in which the Eurosystem haircuts take account of credit risk and market risk, except that the resulting haircuts appear thin. As an example we can take the bond with ISIN DE000NLB2TD7 issued by Norddeutsche Landesbank with an A3 Moody's rating and a coupon of ¾%, maturing in January 2028. Its haircut is 2.8%. Were bond market yields to rise by ½% in the 5½ year maturity, the bond's price would fall by 2.8%, leaving the Eurosystem with no security margin. Bank bonds are more liquid than corporate bonds, but with a rating of only A3 this is not a top-quality bond and there should be some haircut incorporated for credit risk, and for the measure that is a combination of credit and market risk: liquidity risk. Liquidity risk is a reflection of the situation that, the lower the credit rating, the thinner will be the secondary market of buyers willing to buy the bond. Furthermore, in stressed market conditions, there may be no buyers at all for medium- and low-quality bonds. The haircut on this bond has scant coverage for market risk, and little if any cover for credit and liquidity risk.

'Central bank money' and the Eurosystem's divergence from it

Central banks classically inoculate themselves from credit risk by having eligible collateral lists consisting exclusively of 'central bank money' assets. Being free of credit risk, they should be free of liquidity risk (other than in a situation of market collapse). The central flaw in the euro is that it has no 'central bank money' in the classic definition: the core problem addressed in 'Managing Euro Risk'. Far from acknowledging this the Eurosystem has gone further than other central banking systems in accepting assets that fall outside any plausible definition of 'central bank money'. Others have done this, like the Bank of England, but the UK firstly does have genuine 'central bank money' assets and secondly the scope of other eligible assets does not stray as far from the reservation as the Eurosystem's.[41] The requirements of the Bank of England are summed up in Figure 3.5.

Bank of England requirements compared to those of the Eurosystem

No bond rated lower than A- is eligible at the Bank of England, whereas the ECB list now permits bonds rated BB, as long as they were rated BBB- in April 2020.

In order to be eligible, the Bank of England sets a narrow limit on the securities clearing and settlement organisations through which collateral must be delivered: the 'Eligible OMO Collateral as at 12 July 2022' quotes only six securities depositories through which collateral operations with the Bank of England can be undertaken: CREST, Euroclear, Clearstream, the Eurosystem Correspondent Central Banking Model or 'CCBM', Bank of Canada and the Federal Reserve Bank of New York. This indicates that the collateral list is limited to high-quality securities for which the market is global.

By contrast the ECB quotes a lengthy list of securities clearing and settlement organisations.[42] This indicates that, while some of the securities on the Eurosystem list are high-quality with a global market, others have a much more limited market, possibly just one member state, and can be of lower credit quality, and – consequentially to both points – less liquid.

As regards 'haircuts', the Bank of England has issued its 'Summary tables of haircuts for bank lending operations'. Importantly they include base haircuts and uplifts applying to the lending facilities where it is possible to borrow in a different currency from the collateral. The ECB only has one haircut per bond. All its lending is in euro, whereas some collateral is not in euro.

The Bank of England base haircuts, to which the uplifts would be added, range from 0.5% for Level A collateral which has a short maturity date and which as a consequence will show less price volatility, up to 42% for long-term corporate bonds. Additional uplifts are possible in given circumstances, for instance where there has been

---

[41] https://www.bankofengland.co.uk/markets/eligible-collateral accessed on 13 July 2022
[42] htttps://www.ecb.europa.eu/paym/coll/coll/eligiblesss/html/index.en.html accessed on 20 September 2022

no recent trading, or where portfolios are not deemed to be sufficiently diversified. The uplifts can be cumulative.

The Eurosystem haircuts are not structured as a base with uplifts to be added under certain circumstances. There are no tests such as where there has been no recent trading, or where portfolios are not deemed to be sufficiently diversified. The Eurosystem haircuts look very thin compared to the Bank of England's, and to lack responsiveness to characteristics of specific bonds.

The Eurosystem can be said to be taking much more risk than the Bank of England on ostensibly identical operations.

Basel III Liquidity Coverage Ratio for measuring banks' liquidity

Under the Basel III Liquidity Coverage Ratio, banks must prove to their financial regulator that their bank has the resources to meet its liabilities as they fall due, over a period of time and in stressed market conditions.

Liquidity metrics such as Basel III Liquidity Coverage Ratio are part of the same global financial regulatory framework as Internal Ratings-Based Methodologies, and are issued by the BIS.[43]

BIS' BCBS 238 publication of January 2013 entitled 'Basel III: The Liquidity Coverage Ratio and liquidity risk monitoring tools' sets out the regime for Liquidity Coverage Ratio.

There are anomalies in national implementation around the time period and the degree of market stress, but the base is universal: banks must demonstrate that they own High-Quality Liquid Assets which they can sell for cash if they have to, and these resources must exceed what can be withdrawn from the bank over the related time period.

These High-Quality Liquid Assets are accorded a haircut depending on their category. Their face value less the haircut is then inserted into the bank's calculation of its available assets. Liabilities maturing over the same time period go into the calculation at their full face value. Available assets – with their values reduced by the haircuts - must nevertheless exceed liabilities falling due.

Bonds must be rated Investment Grade and show a maximum 20% price fall over a 30-day period in order to be ranked as High-Quality Liquid Assets at all.

If they do pass the qualification tests, they are then ranked into Level 1, Level 2A and Level 2B. The respective haircuts rise, with Level 2B attracting the highest.

60% or more of a bank's High-Quality Liquid Assets must be of Level 1. In fact a bank is entitled to carry all of its High-Quality Liquid Assets in the form of Level 1 assets if it wishes to. Of the 40% that can be Level 2, no more than 15% can come from Level 2B: 25%+ must be Level 2A.[44]

Level 2B assets are thus seen as a make-weight, in effect a third line of defence, by the BIS. In the Eurosystem they are mainstream. For the purpose of this exercise we concentrate on Level 2 Assets, how they feature in the ECB eligible collateral, and how Level 2B is allowed to feature with haircuts well below those foreseen by the BIS.

Focus on Level 2 High-Quality Liquid Assets

This is an extract drawn from the definition of Level 2 Assets in the BCBS 238 paras 51-54:

'Level 2A with a haircut of 15% includes 'Corporate debt securities (including commercial paper) and covered bond' satisfying all of a series of criteria including:
- either (i) have a long-term credit rating from a recognized external credit assessment institution (ECAI) of at least AA- or in the absence of a long-term rating, a short-term rating equivalent in quality to the

---

[43] Internal Ratings-Based methodology – the proprietary methodology allowed to banks under the Basel regime whereby they convert every piece of risk-bearing business into an equivalent Risk-Weighted Asset
[44] BCBS 238 paras 46-8

long-term rating; or (ii) do not have a credit assessment by a recognized ECAI but are internally rated as having a probability of default (PD) corresponding to a credit rating of at least AA-;

- are traded in large, deep and active repo or cash markets characterized by a low level of concentration; and
- have a proven record as a reliable source of liquidity in the markets (repo or sale) even during stressed market conditions: ie maximum decline of price or increase in haircut over a 30-day period during a relevant period of significant liquidity stress not exceeding 10%.

Level 2B assets include Residential Mortgage-Backed Securities with a haircut of 25% if they have a public credit rating of at least AA.

Level 2B assets with a haircut of 50% include 'Corporate debt securities (including commercial paper) and covered bond' satisfying all of a series of criteria which parallel those governing Level 2A corporate debt securities except:
- ECAI or internal rating of between A+ and BBB- (i.e. within Investment Grade)
- a maximum decline of price or increase in haircut over a 30-day period not exceeding 20%'

The points of importance from this wording are:
- Assets must be rated in Investment Grade to qualify at all: that means rated BBB- or above
- Level 2A assets must be rated AA- or better
- In that case a 15% haircut applies
- The haircut for Level 2B assets is 50%, and their rating will be between A+ and BBB-
- Residential mortgage-backed securities enjoy a special regime
- They qualify only as Level 2B assets but enjoy a haircut of 25% if they are rated AA or above
- They attract a 50% haircut their rating is between AA- and BBB-
- This recognizes their reliable quality if they are well-rated, but limits how much of a bank's portfolio they can make up, given that Level 2B assets cannot make up more than 15% of the whole
- All bonds must meet tests for the depth of the secondary market in them

Comparison of Bank of England list with that of the Eurosystem

One can state with confidence that all of the bonds on the Bank of England list would qualify as High-Quality Liquid Assets for the purposes of the Basel III Liquidity Coverage Ratio, and the haircuts specified by the Bank of England are within the range of those given in the Basel III Liquidity Coverage Ratio requirements for the same bonds.

The Eurosystem's list contains many bonds which would not qualify as Level 1 High-Quality Liquid Assets, and many others which might well not qualify as High-Quality Liquid Assets at all.

The Eurosystem's haircuts are far away from the ones that are imposed under Basel III Liquidity Coverage Ratio. This is demonstrated below with reference to corporate bonds and Figure 3.6.

Usage of corporate securities in the Eurosystem

Many corporate securities appear on the ECB list of eligible collateral.

Corporate securities are notoriously illiquid but they can still be counted into the Basel III Liquidity Coverage Ratio if they meet rating and price decline tests, only with a much larger haircuts than securities that have better credit ratings and proof of deep secondary markets.

It is extremely difficult to believe that any corporate bond would meet the BIS' tests of liquidity to count as a Level 2A HQLA, even if it were well enough rated. The BIS' liquidity test for a ranking of Level 2B is far less demanding; indeed, if the bond is illiquid, it may not have traded at all in the preceding month, thereby passing the test by default.

This means that the default haircut for corporate bonds should be 50%. 15% would apply only if the bond was rated AA- or better and could be proven to be liquid.

Examination of 27 corporate bonds on the ECB list

We can compare the Liquidity Coverage Ratio haircuts with those for a selection of 27 corporate bonds on the ECB list, all fixed-rate bonds issued in 2020 and with a five-year maturity.[45] They are subject to all of credit risk, liquidity risk and market risk.

The comparison is in Figure 3.6.

We have obtained the public credit rating for each bond, where one exists, from Moody's, Standard & Poor's, Fitch and DBRS. DBRS has only rated one issuer – Daimler AG, now renamed Mercedes-Benz Group AG.

We have taken it that the portfolios of CA Immobilien Anlagen AG and Deutsche Wohnen SE are commercial property and not residential mortgages. This is supported by the Moody's statements of both issuer's Peer Group as being 'REITs and Other Commercial Real Estate Firms'. Neither issue is well enough rated to rank as a Level 2A HQLA, so they both attract a 50% haircut for LCR, whereas the haircut would have been 25% if either had been a residential mortgage-backed security.

Were a bank to present these securities to their supervisor as High-Quality Liquid Assets, none would qualify as Level 1.

Only two issues might possibly qualify as Level 2A: those of SANOFI and of SNCF, and based only on their ratings of AA and AA- respectively, not on their liquidity. The haircut for all the others would be 50%, assuming they met the test of a maximum price fall of 20% over 30 days.

In our professional experience neither the SANOFI nor the SNCF bond would meet the BIS tests of secondary market liquidity. Corporate bonds do not actively trade after their pay-in date, whatever their credit rating, and could not be proven to:
- '[have been] traded in large, deep and active repo or cash markets characterized by a low level of concentration; and
- have a proven record as a reliable source of liquidity in the markets (repo or sale) even during stressed market conditions: ie maximum decline of price or increase in haircut over a 30-day period during a relevant period of significant liquidity stress not exceeding 10%.'

Nevertheless, lacking definitive evidence on that point, we have ascribed a Level 2A ranking to them in the table based on their credit rating.

All 27 bonds qualify for the ECB list and with one of seven haircut values: 1.6%, 2.4%, 8.0%, 9.6%, 13.2%, 18% and 19.2%. That there are only seven values suggests a system that is inflexible:

Haircut value	Number of issues
1.6%	5
2.4%	3
8.0%	1
9.6%	7
13.2%	8
18.0%	1
19.2%	2

Table 3.1: ECB haircut values on sample of 27 corporate bonds

The only instance where the ECB haircut is higher than the LCR haircut is in the case of SNCF. SNCF is the best-rated issuer individually at AA, meriting a 15% haircut for LCR if the bond proves to be liquid, but the bond attracts an 18% Eurosystem haircut because it is denominated in USD.

Schaeffler AG should arguably not be on the list at all any longer: it has lost its sole Investment Grade rating (BBB- from Fitch) since the bond was issued.

---

[45] ECB Eligible Collateral list dated 22 May 2022

The majority of the ECB haircuts – 24 out of 27 - are lower than the 15% which would apply to Level 2A HQLAs in the Liquidity Coverage Ratio, except that the majority – and possibly all – of the bonds themselves are Level 2B HQLAs at best.

The Eurosystem's haircuts are far lower than those applied for LCR on the same bonds. In fact many are wafer-thin.

This serves to demonstrate the high level of commercial credit risk that the Eurosystem is running, as well as to belie the delusion that the Eurosystem will ever try to re-sell these assets if it owns them, or indeed that it expects to ever have to execute on any collateral it holds. For the Eurosystem to make a loan to a commercial bank of €1 million based on collateral of €1.132 million issued by a Ryanair or an MTU Aero Engines indicates a high, and probably misplaced, confidence that the loan cannot go bad.

Explanation of why Eurosystem haircuts are thin

An explanation is needed as to why the Eurosystem haircuts are so thin. Perhaps one can only answer that this is a further aspect of the under-rating of risk endemic within the Eurosystem.

Quite plausibly the Eurosystem is running its own Internal-Ratings Based methodology, borrowed from commercial banks.

The section below about the Pandemic Emergency Purchase Programme and the relaxation of credit standards describes how public credit ratings and Internal-Ratings Based methodologies have become interchangeable and intertwined, when they should be independent and contrarian, and the ECB list could be an example of that phenomenon.

3.5 Bank Deposit Insurance Schemes

Finally amongst the actions taken after the Global Financial Crisis we have the one taken to reassure small depositors of the safety of their bank balances, called the Bank Recovery and Resolution Directive 2014/59. The headline provision was that there would be an insurance scheme whereby up to €100,000 per qualifying depositor in a qualifying institution would be backed by the member state government. The backing would be through a fund but that did not have to mean that the fund had assets. A member state was at liberty to arrange it in that way, but in the main the fund would be a device to link the depositor to the exchequer of the member state, who would pay out up to the ceiling of €100,000 per qualifying claim, within a few weeks of the bank involved having gone into 'resolution'.

The 'resolution' process would be invoked upon the occurrence of one or more negative triggers of financial performance, not necessarily involving the bank going into administration. In fact the objective was to stop a bank falling into a disorderly and inflexible process as happened in the case of Lehman Brothers, where conversely all the creditors were eventually paid out: the institution was not bankrupt, but its fall into bankruptcy proceedings due to illiquidity nearly brought down the global financial system.

The triggers for putting a bank into 'resolution' would be a shortfall of capital or liquidity compared to official thresholds. The thresholds would be set at a conservative level so that a breach of them would leave for the authorities both a period of time and a remaining cushion, so they could intervene and put the bank onto a new footing, without depositors – or themselves – having to meet a loss. The presumption is and was that the bank supervisory regime is capable of identifying that the bank was likely to fail, and of stepping in before it did so.

How a 'resolution' would be enacted

The 'resolution', orchestrated by the bank supervisors, would see the bank's erstwhile capital expunged. This means its Common Equity Tier 1, its 'other Tier 1' capital and its Tier 2 capital: that includes any and all 'capital-like instruments' sitting within either 'other Tier 1' or Tier 2 capital. These might be bonds convertible at the bank's election, subordinated debt and so on. The owners of these 'capital-like instruments' would by definition be junior creditors of the old bank, and they would lose their investments.

There would also be residual senior creditors of the old bank. They would be 'residual' because their claims would be ineligible for reimbursement from the deposit insurance scheme (i) because of their own identity as a financial institution or similarly excluded depositor type; (ii) because they held an ineligible liability type; (iii) because their holding exceeded the €100,000 limit: they would receive €100,000 in compensation but the excess over that would remain as an amount still owing. Together these form the ineligible senior liabilities of the old bank.

The ineligible senior liabilities become the capital of the new bank: these liabilities – based on deposits or loans or bonds – are 'bailed in': they are exchanged for capital-like instruments in the new bank The ineligible senior creditors of the old bank become the shareholders in the new bank.

However, there are no applicable rules that a bank must have an amount of ineligible senior liabilities that, once bailed-in, would form a capital cushion in the new bank at least large enough for the new bank to meet its regulatory requirements. It is theoretically possible that the failed bank has no ineligible liabilities at all, so that there is no amount to be bailed-in, and no capital in the new bank.

Despite the absence of such a control, one has to accept it as likely that there is some amount of ineligible senior liabilities to be bailed-in. Once the owners of these liabilities in the old bank had become the owners of the new bank, there would be one senior creditor only in the new bank: the deposit insurance fund itself, which is the member state in essence, probably acting through the guise of an intermediary legal entity. Having paid out €100,000 on each eligible claim, this legal entity becomes subrogated into those claims and becomes the main depositor in and senior creditor of the new bank.

How the compensation claim is paid out and the implications for the member state

This brings us on to the issue of significance for this paper. The €100,000 claims are paid out by the member state government's exchequer by its issuing new debt itself, debt that becomes part of 'General government gross debt'. The member state government's exchequer obtains in exchange, through the intermediary of the deposit insurance scheme, an asset in the nominal amount of the claims.

If the bank supervisor has done its job, this has all happened before the bank has become bankrupt, where its liabilities exceed its assets. If, however, the assets of the bank contained many doubtful items, one cannot rely on the valuations on its balance sheet. This has become an issue when the banking systems of certain member states have generated large amounts of Non-Performing Loans or NPLs. Given that banks generally show a relationship of 20:1 between total assets and capital, it is a problem if over 5% of assets are NPLs.[46] Of course having a loan classed as an NPL does not mean there will be no recovery: its value is impaired and the question is how badly impaired, and at what value should it be held in the bank's balance sheet.

The customary answer, in the EU/Eurozone, is that their value in the bank's books is higher than their recoverable value.

How NPLs have been treated and what happens to them in a 'resolution'

As a matter of good banking practice NPLs should either be written down from their nominal value to a lower 'carrying value', or a provision should be created that has the same effect. The result is an asset that is held at its recoverable value.

However, where a bank has as much as 20% of its total assets on NPL status, then it cannot write them down to such a low 'carrying value' (or create such a large loan loss provision) that the bank fails to meet its regulatory capital threshold, whatever they are really worth. Writing them down aggressively would trigger resolution.

Let's say a bank has 22.2 nominal of NPLs and it is holding them at a 'carrying value' of 90% of their nominal value on average, meaning at 20. Then it is put into resolution.

---

[46] This is the maximum relationship between on-balance sheet assets and capital under the Basel 3 Leverage Ratio

Here is a before-and-after picture of what might happen if the bank went into 'resolution':

Old bank		New bank	
Assets	**Liabilities**	**Assets**	**Liabilities**
Loans – 65	Insured senior – 85	Loans – 65	Government – 85
NPLs – 20	Residual senior - 7	NPLs – 12	Capital – 7
Other assets - 15	Junior – 3	Other assets - 15	
	Capital – 5		
100	100	92	92

Table 3.2: example of a bank's skeleton balance of sheet before and after 'resolution'

The capital and junior debts of the old bank, totaling 8, are expunged: the balance sheet shortens by 8.

The old bank's residual senior creditors have their investments of 7 converted into the capital of the new bank. The bank has 1 less capital and 8 less assets: its leverage has increased from 12.5-to-1 to 13.1-to-1.

The shortening of the balance sheet by 8 enables the NPLs to be written down by a further 8, from 20 to 12. They are now held at a 'carrying value' of 54% of their face value (12/22.2). This does not mean they are worth this amount: it just so happens that the resolution has enabled their writing-down from one arbitrary value to another. This policy of discretionary valuation can continue until an event occurs whose result is that an NPL can no longer be held at a value decided upon by the bank.

For example, a borrower dies and, when their estate is wound up, it yields only 20% of the loan's face value. The bank is no longer master of its own destiny as far as the valuation of its NPLs is concerned. If that happens across the board NPLs turn out to be worth 20% of their face value, in which case they are only worth 4.44 in our example and not 12: another 7.56 must be deducted both from the asset and the liability sides of the balance sheet. This expunges the entirety of the new bank's capital. The new bank is now not just in breach of its regulatory capital ratios, it is bankrupt. The government is now the full owner with an asset worth 84.44, less than its liability of 85 – the debt it took on to pay out the insured depositors in the old bank.

This may seem a highly esoteric point, but there is a chance of a gap in the member state's national accounts because the asset it will have acquired is worth less than the liability it took on to buy it.

How this can work through into a permanent addition to member state debt

The public sector liability caused by the 'resolution' of a bank would be significant on a gross basis: the member state would have to issue new debt in respect of the entirety of an institution's deposits that were covered by the scheme.

The intention would be to re-float the bank with the ineligible senior creditors now acting as the new shareholders, and with enough money deployed so that the new bank met its capital and liquidity obligations. The member state would then hope to be able to pay off the new debt it had contracted, once the re-launched bank attracted deposits of its own or sold off assets, because those incoming monies would revert to the member state.

The member state ought to be left with no residual net liability from this operation. The assets of the new bank ought to be larger than the payout from the Deposit Insurance Scheme. This is because the banking regulators ought to have been in a position to step in before the old bank had gone into a downward spiral: the triggers for invoking resolution ought to have been that the bank breached buffers that were set at a conservative level.

However, if it turns out that the buffers were only optically set at a conservative level, and actually the margins that the old bank was trading on were much thinner, then there is a problem. This could occur thanks to 'risk-weighting': a capital buffer of 8-10% of 'Risk-Weighted Assets' sounds conservative, but this will be undermined if the process of 'risk-weighting' is aggressive i.e. if the bank has been allowed to diminish the face value of its business by a large percentage in order to determine its supposed 'risk-weighted' equivalent.

This links to the core problem in the EU/Eurozone of the endemic under-assessment of the risks being taken, starting with risk taken on member states. Its result is capital buffers being too thin. 'Conservative' buffers turn out not to be conservative when the assumptions upon which they are calculated turn out to be overly lax.

It is perfectly possible that Non-Performing Loans in particular, and risk-bearing assets in general, are over-valued by the old bank. Risk-weighting can create a picture of comfortable compliance with regulatory buffers. This will lead to the old bank breaching its buffers later than it should have done. In turn this leads to the triggers for 'resolution' being met at too late a stage, and the banking regulators stepping in when the financial downward spiral has begun.

There turns out to be considerably less value in the old bank than its regulatory capital ratios infer.

In that case the working-through of the 'resolution' does not produce sufficient cash for the member state to pay off all the debt it took on to fund the compensation for eligible depositors. Instead the 'resolution' process adds a block of debt permanently to the member state's GGGD.

Chapter summary

The pattern of how shadow debt and contingent liabilities have been created outside of the Eurostat figures should start to become discernible from the EU/Eurozone's immediate responses to the Global Financial Crisis.

The EFSM is the bailout programme mounted through the person of the EU. The EFSF and ESM are stand-alone mechanisms created each with its own support mechanism from the member states but both working to the same template: the creation of an apparently large facility which, as soon as some member states start to borrow and others have their public credit ratings reduced, has inadequate firepower to face a major challenge. The EFSF is now closed for this reason, and the ESM is a dead letter: it lacks the capacity to make a meaningful contribution to any bailout of a member state on the scale of Italy or France, and for sure not both of them.

This recognition could be a reason why, in July 2022, the European authorities established the so-called 'Transmission Protection Mechanism'.

The ECB has made sure that member states were not short of liquidity in the meantime, so that the lack of firepower within the bailout mechanisms did not become apparent. It has bought €2.5 trillion of public sector bonds into its APP scheme as well as €657 billion of other bonds. In addition it runs a collateral system far less arduous and far larger than that of the Bank of England, meaning that a much higher percentage of total bonds in issuance in euro are eligible to be borrowed against from the Eurosystem than is the case for bonds in issuance in UK pounds, and a higher percentage of each bond's value can be borrowed.

In addition a potentially huge public sector liability has been created through the Bank Deposit Insurance Schemes as it has been in the UK but with one difference: UK banks do not have large blocks of Non-Performing Loans. As EU/Eurozone institutions do have such NPLs and as such NPLs and indeed other assets may be held at too benevolent values, there is chance that the 'resolution' of bank would lead to a permanent addition to the respective member state's GGGD.

Figures:
- 3.1: guarantees of member states behind the EFSF and impact of 'Stepping-out' guarantors and loss of AAA credit ratings with amounts in € billions
- 3.2 capital of the ESM as at 31 December 2020 in € billions.
- 3.3: ESM's lack of firepower to support Italy or France as debtors
- 3.4: balances in the ECB's APP programmes as of 8 April 2022
- 3.5: Bank of England table of eligible collateral
- 3.6: Eurosystem haircuts, Liquidity Coverage Ratio haircuts, and credit ratings for 27 selected corporate bonds

3.1: guarantees of member states behind the EFSF and impact of 'Stepping-out' guarantors and loss of AAA credit ratings with amounts in € billions:

Country	Capital Key out of 100%	Without Latvia and Lithuania	Rebased to 100% w/o LV/LT	Allocation from €780 billion	After 'Stepping-Out' of Guarantors	Credit Rating now[47]	AAA Guarantors
Belgium	2.9630	2.9630	3.6789	€28.7	€28.7	AA	0
Germany	21.4394	21.4394	26.6192	€207.6	€207.6	AAA	€207.6
Estonia	0.2291	0.2291	0.2845	€2.2	€2.2	AA-	0
Ireland	1.3772	1.3772	1.7099	€13.3	0	AA-	0
Greece	2.0117	2.0117	2.4977	€19.5	0	BB+	0
Spain	9.6981	9.6981	12.0412	€93.9	€93.9	A	0
France	16.6108	16.6108	20.6240	€160.9	€160.9	AA	0
Italy	13.8165	13.8165	17.1546	€133.8	€133.8	BBB	0
Cyprus	0.1750	0.1750	0.2173	€1.7	0	BBB-	0
Latvia	0.3169	--	--	0	0	A+	0
Lithuania	0.4707	--	--	0	0	A+	0
Luxembourg	0.2679	0.2679	0.3327	€2.6	€2.6	AAA	€2.6
Malta	0.0853	0.0853	0.1059	€0.8	€0.8	A-	0
Netherlands	4.7662	4.7662	5.9177	€46.2	€46.2	AAA	€46.2
Austria	2.3804	2.3804	2.9555	€23.1	€23.1	AA+	0
Portugal	1.9035	1.9035	2.3634	€18.4	0	BBB	0
Slovenia	0.3916	0.3916	0.4862	€3.8	€3.8	AA-	0
Slovakia	0.9314	0.9314	1.1564	€9.0	€9.0	A+	0
Finland	1.4939	1.4939	1.8548	€14.5	€14.5	AA+	0
Total	81.3286	80.5410	100.00	€780.0	€745.0	--	€256.0

Figure 3.1: guarantees of member states behind the EFSF and impact of 'Stepping-out' guarantors and loss of AAA credit ratings

3.2 capital of the ESM as at 31 December 2020 in € billions.

Country	ESM Key	Shares	Subscribed	Paid-in	Callable
Belgium	3.4513%	243,244	€24.3	€2.8	€21.5
Germany	26.9449%	1,899,071	€189.9	€21.7	€168.2
Estonia	0.1847%	13,020	€1.3	€0.1	€1.2
Ireland	1.5804%	111,383	€11.1	€1.3	€9.8
Greece	2.7957%	197,044	€19.7	€2.3	€17.4
Spain	11.8153%	832,743	€83.3	€9.5	€73.8
France	20.2346%	1,426,131	€142.6	€16.3	€126.3
Italy	17.7807%	1,253,184	€125.5	€14.3	€111.0
Cyprus	0.1948%	13,729	€1.4	€0.2	€1.2
Latvia	0.2746%	19,353	€1.9	€0.2	€1.7
Lithuania	0.4063%	28,634	€2.9	€0.3	€2.6
Luxembourg	0.2486%	17,519	€1.8	€0.2	€1.6
Malta	0.0899%	6,338	€0.6	€0.1	€0.5
Netherlands	5.6746%	399,945	€40.0	€4.6	€35.4
Austria	2.7627%	194,718	€19.5	€2.2	€17.3
Portugal	2.4906%	175,534	€17.6	€2.0	€15.6
Slovenia	0.4678%	32,973	€3.3	€0.4	€2.9
Slovakia	0.8184%	57,680	€5.8	€0.7	€5.1
Finland	1.7841%	125,744	€12.6	€1.4	€11.2
Total	100.0000%	7,047,987	€704.8	€80.5	€624.3

Figure 3.2: capital of the ESM as at 31 December 2020 in € billion.

---

[47] From the Standard and Poor's Rating system accessed on 24 May 2022

Figure 3.3: ESM's lack of firepower to support Italy or France as debtors

In € billions	Italy becomes a debtor	France becomes a debtor	Italy and France become debtors
ESM reference resources now	589	589	589
ESM lending ceiling now	417	417	417
ESM loans now	203	203	203
ESM headroom now	214	214	214
Debtor subscribed-but-not-paid capital	111	126	237
New references resources[48]	478	463	352
New lending ceiling	339	328	249
ESM loans now	203	203	203
Revised, lower headroom[49]	136	115	46
Revised headroom as a percentage of debtor GGGD[50]	5.28%	4.34%	0.88%

Figure 3.3: ESM's lack of firepower to support Italy or France as debtors

Figure 3.4: balances in the ECB's APP programmes as of 8 April 2022

Programme	Amount
Closed APP programmes	€4.1 billion
Covered bonds purchase programme 3	€296.8 billion
Asset-backed securities purchase programme	€27.2 billion
Public sector purchase programme	€2,535.8 billion
Corporate sector purchase programme	€332.8 billion
Total	€3,196.7 billion

Figure 3.4: balances in the ECB's APP programmes as of 8 April 2022[51]

---

[48] Reference resources now less Debtor subscribed-but-not-paid capital
[49] New references resources less Current outstandings
[50] 2020 'General government gross debt'
[51] https://www.ecb.europa.eu/mopo/implement/omo/html/index.en.html accessed on 17 April 2022

Figure 3.5: Bank of England table of eligible collateral

Level	Description	Rating/Comments
A	'Sterling, euro, US dollar and Canadian dollar denominated securities (including associated strips) issued by the governments and central banks of the UK, Canada, France, Germany, the Netherlands and the United States'	• Central bank money - government securities of a limited number of countries in their own currency • France, Germany and Netherlands are included despite their not having a sovereign currency • Central banks are by inference considered part of central government, whereas neither Eurostat nor the BIS define them as such • Rated AAA or AA
B	• Government and central bank debt of a series of other EU member states plus Australia, Japan, New Zealand and Switzerland • Bonds of major supranationals • Bonds of G-10 countries' government agencies • UK government debt in currencies other than GBP • Bonds of US home loan agencies like FreddieMac and FannieMae • Asset-backed securities, based on residential mortgages, car loans, credit card receivables, student and consumer loans	• Expansion to 'central bank money' of a limited list of further countries • Limitation by currency of issuance to domestic currency, GBP, euro, USD and CAD • Expansion to supranationals and government agencies, including the US home loan agencies • Bonds must carry AAA-rating or be of a quality 'broadly equivalent' to AAA • Asset-backed securities must also be of that quality, meaning that the most senior tranches only will qualify
C	• The same types of Asset-backed securities quoted as Level B, plus ones backed by corporate loans, SME loans, commercial mortgages, corporate bond, commercial paper • Corporate bonds pledged directly • Includes Level C Loan Collateral: 'Portfolios of residential mortgage, consumer, commercial real estate or corporate loans to a non-bank where the borrower is domiciled in the UK, or in the case of a corporate, the UK is its centre of main interest'	• A- long-term rating, or A1+ short-term • Diversified asset pool • Level C Loan Collateral is subject to a further set of limiting conditions

Figure 3.5: Bank of England table of eligible collateral

Figure 3.6: Eurosystem haircuts, Liquidity Coverage Ratio haircuts, and credit ratings for 27 selected corporate bonds

ISIN	Coupon %	Issuer Name	Eurosystem Haircut %	LCR Haircut %	LCR Level	Public Long-term Credit Ratings			
						Moody's	S&P	Fitch	DBRS
XS2248827771	1	CA Immobilien Anlagen AG	13.2	50	2B	Baa3	--	--	--
DE000A289Q91	2.75	Schaeffler AG	19.2	50	2B	Ba1	BB+	BBB+	--
XS2232027727	1.625	KION GROUP AG	13.2	50	2B	--	BB+	BBB	--
XS2228260043	2.875	Ryanair DAC	13.2	50	2B	--	BBB-	BBB	--
XS2197673747	3	MTU Aero Engines AG	13.2	50	2B	Baa3	--	BBB	--
XS2192431380	0.25	Italgas S.P.A.	13.2	50	2B	Baa2	--	BBB+	--
FR0013519048	0.625	CAP GEMINI	13.2	50	2B	--	BBB	--	--
XS2189592616	1.375	ACS, Act.de Constr.y Serv. SA	19.2	50	2B	--	BBB	--	--
FR0013518156	0.86	SOCIETE NATIONALE SNCF	18	15	2A	Aa3	AA-	A+	--
XS2182067350	2.25	Scania CV AB	13.2	50	2B	--	BBB	--	--
DE000A289NX4	0.625	Evonik Industries AG	13.2	50	2B	Baa2	BBB+	--	--
XS2171759256	2.375	Nokia Oyj	9.6	50	2B	Ba2	BB+	BBB-	--
DE000A289NE4	1	Deutsche Wohnen SE	1.6	50	2B	A3	BBB+	--	--
XS2163320679	0.75	SODEXO SA	9.6	50	2B	Baa1	BBB+	BBB+	--
XS2154441120	0.875	Red Electrica Corporacion S.A.	9.6	50	2B	--	A-	A-	--
XS2153405118	0.875	Iberdrola Finanzas S.A.	2.4	50	2B	Baa1	BBB+	BBB+	--
FR0013506813	2.125	UNIBAIL RODAMCO SE	9.6	50	2B	Baa2	BBB+	BBB+	--
XS2152899584	1	E.ON SE	2.4	50	2B	Baa2	BBB	BBB+	--
FR0013506508	0.75	LVMH Moët Henn. Vuitton SE	1.6	50	2B	A1	A+	BBB	--
DE000A289RN6	2.625	Daimler AG	8.0	50	2B	A3	A-	BBB+	A (Low)
FR0013506524	1.125	Pernod-Ricard S.A.	9.6	50	2B	Baa1	BBB+	BBB+	--
XS2147977479	1.625	Heineken N.V.	9.6	50	2B	Baa1	BBB+	--	--
XS2149368529	1.375	Koninklijke Philips N.V.	9.6	50	2B	Baa1	BBB+	--	--
FR0013505104	1	SANOFI SA	1.6	15	2A	A1	AA	A+	--
FR0013504644	1.375	ENGIE	1.6	50	2B	Baa1	BBB+	A-	--
XS2133390521	0.05	Vattenfall AB	2.4	50	2B	A3	BBB+	--	--
XS2104915033	0.19	National Grid Electr.Trans.PLC	1.6	50	2B	Baa1	BBB+	BBB+	--

Figure 3.6: Eurosystem haircuts, Liquidity Coverage Ratio haircuts, and credit ratings for 27 selected corporate bonds

Chapter 4 - further measures in the wake of the Eurozone debt crisis and before the Pandemic

Chapter introduction

Further measures were undertaken in the wake of the Eurozone debt crisis and before the Pandemic. The EU and Eurozone economies were not growing at an acceptable rate, and inflation was falling short of the ECB's long-term target of 2%. TARGET2 balances expanded considerably between 2015 and 2017. The banking system required further 'stabilization'.

'Stabilization' meant, in some countries, to cleanse banks' balances sheets of their Non-Performing Loans. In all countries it meant bringing the majority of the banking system – the 'systemically-important' institutions – within a single framework of banking supervision. The objectives of this were two-fold. Firstly to try to forestall a bank going into 'resolution' by imposing tough minimum standards for the bank's capital and liquidity, and to test these levels under scenarios of economic stress. Secondly, to formalize that failure to pass tests of capital and liquidity would act as the triggers for banking regulators to put an institution into 'resolution' before it legally failed.

These minimum standards were enshrined in (i) further editions of Basel capital adequacy standards to ensure that banks had adequate amounts of capital to absorb losses (known as 'capital cushions' or 'capital buffers'); and (ii) Basel III Liquidity Coverage Ratio to ensure that banks could meet all their obligations as they fell due, which was dealt with in the previous chapter.

The standards to do with capital adequacy have been alluded to in previous chapters but are explored in depth in this one. They are the Basel Internal-Ratings Based methodologies for calculating the 'risk-weighted' equivalent of every piece of risk-bearing business that a bank has undertaken. The outcome of the calculation is the bank's 'Risk-Weighted Assets', and it is against this figure that the bank must hold a loss-absorption cushion of 8-10%. The leading point is not whether 8-10% is conservative, but whether the 'risk-weighting' adjustments to the original, face value of a bank's business are conservative.

The key developments over this period were:
- 'Full mobilization of the EIB'
- The European Fund for Strategic Investments now called InvestEU
- ECB Targeted Longer Term Refinancing Operations
- Securitization of banks' Non-Performing Loans (NPLs)
- Basel Internal-Ratings Based methodologies (IRB)
- Impact of the combination of NPL securitization and of Advanced IRB on member state liability for their Bank Deposit Insurance Scheme

4.1 'Full mobilization of the EIB'

Because the EIB has been used since 2012 as the fulcrum of a number of creative financing schemes, we have placed the main analysis of its financials here, rather than in the chapter about what happened prior to the GFC and the Eurozone sovereign debt crisis.

In 2012 Angela Merkel and Francois Hollande agreed to fully mobilize the potential of the EIB for engaging in counter-cyclical public spending, also known as Keynsian economics.

'German Chancellor Angela Merkel added her voice on Saturday to calls to bolster the European Investment Bank (EIB) and to use EU infrastructure funds more flexibly to help spur economic growth in Europe. Her comments are part of a new German emphasis on growth-boosting measures to complement painful tax hikes and spending cuts that have triggered a political and popular backlash against austerity across the Eurozone.'[52]

The Preface section of the EIB 2014 Annual Financial Report confirmed this:
- '2014 was the second year of implementation of incremental lending associated with the €10 billion capital increase.'

---

[52] http://uk.reuters.com/article/uk-germany-merkel-idUKBRE83R02120120428 accessed in August 2014

- 'During the challenges of 2008-2011, the EIB provided exceptional support to the European economy to help soften the impact of the crisis. The bank is again on course to do so by additional lending volumes for the period 2013-2015, facilitated by the €10 billion capital increase. Over 2015-2018 the EIB is expected to shoulder additional responsibilities to support sustainable long-term growth and employment in Europe, bolstered by EU guarantees.'[53]

EIB capital structure

The EIB's shareholders is owned by the EU member states. The EIB has a subscribed capital of €248.8 billion but only €22.2 billion of this has been paid in. The remaining €226.6 billion acts as a guarantee fund and as a credit enhancement for bond investors.

The above amounts of uncalled capital should be recorded as contingent liabilities of member states, since the commitment to pay in the extra capital is a 'sovereign risk' claim.

Shareholdings by member state are shown in Figure 4.1. They are not precisely calibrated to either GDP or GNI in all cases, although the shares of smaller shareholders are differentiated from one another more greatly than the shareholdings of the larger member states. 78% of the uncalled capital is due from just six countries: Germany, France and Italy (all €42.5 billion), Spain (€25.5 billion), and Netherlands and Belgium (each €11.8 billion).

EIB loans in total and within special schemes

Before this policy of 'full mobilization' was agreed upon, the EIB 2012 Annual Financial Report p. 3 showed a loan book outstanding at year-end of €413 billion with loans to be disbursed of €81 billion. The EIB 2021 Annual Financial Report p. 4 shows a loan book outstanding at year-end of €433 billion with loans to be disbursed of €123 billion. This is more like a reduction in real terms than the type of major increase implied by the term 'full mobilization'.

However, the size of the main EIB balance sheet masks the implications for the EIB Group of the mantle for SME financing having passed from the EIB to the InvestEU programme and the European Guarantee Fund programme, in both of which the European Investment Fund (EIF) is the main actor.[54] EIB itself makes loans under its normal terms and conditions into InvestEU/European Guarantee Fund (EGF) projects subject to given ceilings. This ceiling was €40 billion within the initial InvestEU programme size of €315 billion, or 12.7% of the programme size.

InvestEU appears to have reached a total size of about €471 billion at the end of 2020. InvestEU and the EGF combined appear to have reached a total size of €612 billion at the end of 2021. The breakdown between InvestEU and EGF of the €141 billion of financing put on in 2021 is unclear. For ease of understanding we have attributed all of it to EGF, with no drawing of EGF in 2020 and the balance of the EGF of around €60 billion being put on in 2022. Given the same proportions for the EIB's normal loans as prevailed for the first phase of InvestEU, its normal loans into these structures would have been €59.8 billion out of the €471 billion total at the end of 2020 and €77.7 billion out of the €612 billion total at the end of 2021, or about 18% of EIB's total loans.[55]

---

[53] EIB 2014 Annual Financial Report p. 4

[54] European Guarantee Fund was a response to the Pandemic and is discussed in the next chapter. It follows the InvestEU template. It was substantially drawn during 2021, appearing to replace InvestEU for that year, InvestEU having begun to expand again in 2022

[55] It is worth noting that EIB Group has a permission from the EU, under the legal instrument establishing InvestEU, to put a given 'amount of its own resources at risk', over an above the amount of the EU's first-loss guarantee in respect of InvestEU. This amount is far smaller than the amount of normal loans that the EIB has made into InvestEU projects, so the logical conclusion of that is that the EIB's making normal loans into InvestEU projects does not count as 'putting its own resources at risk'. Instead, 'putting its own resources at risk' must mean taking the kind of equity or equity-style position in a financing that the European Investment Fund takes, noting that the permission to do this is addressed to 'EIB Group', of which the EIF is a part, whereas it is the EIB that extends normal loan financing

Terming EIB's loans into such projects as 'normal' only applies to their maturity and interest rate. The EIB's loans are inserted into the project at a level that ranks inferior to some of the other debts taken on. The EIF's position then invariably ranks even lower that of the EIB. The positions taken by 'EIB Group' low down the order of priority enables large amounts of more senior debt to be taken on: 'EIB Group' acts as a loss cushion for the loans made into the same projects by other lenders. These loans will not be secured with tangible collateral: one can be sure that any tangible security on offer will be hypothecated in favour of the senior creditors.

The relationship of the 'EIB Group' involvement to the involvement of other financiers is rendered by the terms 'mobilization' and 'leverage', which appear frequently in the EIB Group documentation about InvestEU/EGF projects. Typical statements might be that (i) the 'engagements of €17 billion by the EIB Group were leveraged nearly 5 times' and (ii) the 'engagements of €17 billion by the EIB Group mobilized an amount of €100 billion'.

The financing of such a project might work like this for a project needing €100 billion: the 'mobilized' amount.

There is a miniscule layer of equity.

The EIF issues €7 billion of guarantees to induce suppliers of capital-like finance to inject cash at a level ranking below the junior debt, mezzanine debt and senior debt.[56]

The EIB lends €10 billion as junior debt, which ranks below the mezzanine debt and senior debt.

Other financiers lend €83 billion as a combination of mezzanine debt and senior debt.

The project raises €90 billion of third-party funding: the €7 billion of 'capital-like finance' against the EIF's guarantee, and the €83 billion of mezzanine and senior debt. The EIB's junior debt loan of €10 billion makes up the €100 billion of cash.

The contribution of 'EIB Group' is €17 billion: €7 billion of guarantees and €10 billion of loans. This €17 billion is 'leveraged' 4.88 times (€83 billion divided by €17 billion). EIB Group's €17 billion 'mobilizes' €100 billion.

EIB lending into the EU and source of funding

The EIB's lending to EU borrowers was €385.4 billion at the end of 2021, or 89% of its total lending of €433 billion. The balance – 11% of the total and an amount of €47.6 billion - was made to borrowers outside the EU and was covered by an EU first-loss guarantee.

EIB's lending within the EU includes all of its lending within the context of InvestEU/EGF.[57] If, as surmised, this was €77.7 billion at the end of 2021, EIB's book of loans to EU borrowers outside the context of InvestEU/EGF was €307.7 billion.

'Loans and advances to credit institutions' are taken to be part of its lending programmes, and not deposits by EIB's Treasury department for liquidity management purposes. This is the same point as was noted above regarding the ESM: the ESM records part of its bailout programmes in such a way as to infer that they are Treasury deposits.

The EIB's funding taken from capital markets was €440 billion, only €7 billion different from its loan book of €433 billion. With capital and reserves (which it calls 'Own Funds') of €76.1 billion, and miscellaneous other liabilities of €50 billion, this €440 billion makes up the liabilities side of the balance sheet to €565.5 billion.

Clearly the debts to capital markets are not direct liabilities of member states, nor is the EIB an entity within 'General government'. The issue for member states is the EIB's ability to call up the subscribed-but-not-paid-in capital.

---

[56] See below for an explanation of the EIF's two types of engagement, a guarantee and an 'equity commitment', on the back of which the project takes on third-party finance. The finance could be equity, or one level about equity in a project where the equity is very low indeed

[57] EIB 2021 Financial Report p. 5

EIB's off-balance sheet business and its usage of an Internal Ratings-Based Methodologies

The EIB states that it has €22.6 billion of 'Contingent liabilities and guarantees'.[58] This does not include the contingent liabilities of its subsidiary, the EIF, such as its guarantees and 'equity commitments' in the context of InvestEU or the EGF.

However, under 'Other items' in its off-balance sheet business, it has derivative, futures and options contracts with a total nominal amount of €1,111.6 billion, meaning that its total nominal amount of off-balance sheet business was €1,134.2 billion. This is 200% of its on-balance sheet assets of €565.5 billion.

EIB thus has a total of risk-bearing positions of €1,699.7 billion, as against Own Funds, or capital, of €76.1 billion.[59]

We take 'Own Funds' and CET1 to be synonymous in EIB's case. We have refrained here from investigating the differences between the EIB's Own Funds as it states them, and what it has as capital according to definitions issued by bank regulators. These definitions describe a bank's core capital as its Common Equity Tier 1 or CET1, with add-ons of 'other Tier 1' capital and of Tier 2 capital. These types of capital feature in the balance sheets of commercial banks and are explained in the section below about Internal Ratings-Based methodologies (IRB).

EIB claims that it has a so-called CET1 Ratio of 32.3%. This means its Own Funds are 32.3% of its Risk-Weighted Assets, a very favorable CET1 Ratio compared with those prevailing in the banking industry, where the minimum is in the range 8-10% and anything over 12% would be viewed as a surplus.

EIB's Risk-Weighted Assets figure is the result of each of the risk-bearing positions within the total of €1,699.7 billion being put through its IRB methodology. Each position – on or off-balance sheet – is thereby converted individually into a Risk-Weighted Asset, and then all are totaled to ascertain EIB's Risk-Weighted Assets. This total of Risk-Weighted Assets is the denominator in the CET1 Ratio, where the EIB's CET1 amount is the numerator.

Working backwards from the CET1 amount of €76.1 billion and applying the CET1 Ratio of 32.3%, we can calculate that EIB's total Risk-Weighted Assets are €235.6 billion, a discount to their nominal value of 86%. Put another way, EIB's Risk-Weighted Assets are 14% of the nominal value of EIB's risk-bearing business.

Adverse Facility Weighting of EIB's loans but favorable Risk-Weighted Assets

Risk-weighting a loan is customarily the product of multiplying a Counterparty Weighting – an assessment of the borrower – by a Facility Weighting – the characteristics of the loan itself. The product of this calculation – the Credit Conversion Factor - is then multiplied by the face value of the loan to produce its Risk-Weighted Asset equivalent.

EIB's loans have a long final maturity, as much as 18 years: a 3-year period to draw the loan down and 15 years to repay it. This long maturity would cost the loan 2 or 3 notches in a commercial bank's risk-weighting system on a scale of 1 to 20. They are also unsecured, which might not be an issue for EIB's loans outside InvestEU/EGF, on which the EIB's ranking ought to be the same as that of other creditors. This status would be rendered by the term 'pari passu'.

This long maturity would worsen the Facility Weighting and serve to expand the face value of the loan: the result of that is a larger Risk-Weighted Asset equivalent and a drag on the CET1 Ratio.

A similar impact would be caused, within the InvestEU and EGF programmes, by the EIB making loans that ranked lower down the order of priority and were subordinated to the claims of other creditors. The EIB's position would be further weakened if tangible security had been hypothecated in favour of other creditors, as that would increase the EIB's risk-of-loss. That eventuality would need to be noted and the Facility Weighting worsened accordingly, further increasing the loan's Risk-Weighted Asset equivalent.

---

[58] EIB 2021 Financial Report p. 46
[59] EIB 2021 Financial Report p. 5

In EIB's case, and despite its having loans inside and outside InvestEU/EGF whose characteristics would tend to expand its Risk-Weighted Assets and drag down the CET1 Ratio, its Risk-Weighted Assets are very low and the CET1 Ratio is extremely favorable.

EIB's high CET1 Ratio comforts its shareholders

The favorable picture of EIB's CET1 ratio will comfort EIB's creditors, but its principle audience is EIB's shareholders, to assure them that the EIB's business is extremely low-risk, and that there is a consequentially low chance that the unpaid capital will be called up. We need to enquire why that is.

If the audience were EIB's creditors, the low-risk nature of the creditors' lending to the EIB would be attributable to several factors:
- Its loan book to borrowers outside the EU being covered by a series of first-loss guarantees from the EU, not so as to cover the whole amount but at least to provide a cushion;
- Its loan book in the context of InvestEU and the EGF programme being covered by first-loss guarantees from the EU and further guarantees from the member states participating in the EGF, again not so as to cover EIB's whole exposure because of the limited amount and because the guarantees are shared with the EIF, but at least to provide a cushion;
- €226.6 billion of capital being callable from the EU member states, its shareholders, if there are losses in excess of the guarantees on loans outside the EU and InvestEU/EGF, or losses on the residual portfolio to EU borrowers.

These levels of comfort for EIB's creditors are the opposite of what would comfort the member states, as they show that losses can track back to them in several ways.

The comfort for shareholders would derive from the underlying business being low-risk, even where, in InvestEU/EGF, the EIB ranks as a junior creditor, where loans are long-term and where other creditors may be enjoying tangible security - all those factors that would increase the Facility Weighting.

Why EIB's Risk-Weighted Assets are so low

The answer to why the EIB's CET1 is so favorable when elements in the Facility Weighting of its loans are adverse is that the Counterparty Weighting or other elements in the Facility Weighting more than make up for them.

The Counterparty Weighting is low on two sectors in the loan book where its borrowers are public sector entities:
- To sovereign or sovereign-backed borrowers outside the EU;
- To public sector entities within the EU in its main, direct loan book;

Within the third sector of its loan book – loans into InvestEU/EGF – the Facility Weighting will end up as favorable because the debt service is based on claims on EU public sector entities, even with the negative elements and a direct borrower with no substance.

The EIB' shareholders could then view the lending risk that the EIB is taking within the EU as a risk on itself: the EIB's shareholders sit at the top of the public sector pyramid in each member state, and a major portion of the EIB's loan book is to public sector entities further down the pyramid in the same member states. If there are losses on the direct loans into the lower levels of the pyramid, EIB can get its money back from the entities at the top of the pyramid, or else it can negotiate with its shareholders for them to bail out the defaulting entity themselves, such that EIB's borrower does not default. Either way the EIB gets made whole.

The EIB would have embedded into its IRB methodology that all EU member states merit a 0% risk-weighting, and it would have implemented the trickle-down whereby its other public sector counterparties are assigned low-risk weightings because of their ultimate connection to a member state.

The high CET1 Ratio derives from EIB's business being conducted substantially with public sector entities. This gives comfort to the shareholders that the losses deriving from EIB's book of business will be low, meaning the likelihood of a new call upon the unpaid capital is low.

EIB's loans and General government gross debt

EIB's €307.7 billion of loans to EU public sector borrowers fall mainly outside the scope of 'General government gross debt'. EIB's €77.7 billion of loans to EU private sector borrowers within InvestEU/EGF certainly fall outside the scope of 'General government gross debt' and of public sector direct debt, but that does not mean that they do not depend for their debt service on the EU public sector. That issue is developed in the sections on InvestEU and EGF.

The EIB is thus a device enabling borrowings by public sector entities held at a distance from inclusion in 'General government gross debt', but supported on the back of the creation of contingent liabilities for the core element in 'General government': the member states. The member states support EIB through their liability to pay in the callable capital, and their liability to bring the EU budget into balance in case any of the EU's guarantees in EIB's favour had to pay out.

4.2 The European Fund for Strategic Investments now called InvestEU

The failure of the EIB loan book to increase in a way that reflects a 'full mobilization' obscures an area of rapid increase. This is the European Fund for Strategic Investments or EFSI and now called InvestEU and its operation is described in detail in 'Managing Euro Risk' Annex 3 pp. 111-6. InvestEU has also been called 'The Juncker Plan', then 'the Investment Fund for Europe'.

Usage of accepted structured finance templates

These transactions are based around a standard 'structured finance' concept whereby a project is mobilized through a special-purpose company. The finance is taken on by the special-purpose company in tranches at different levels of seniority: senior debt, mezzanine debt, junior debt, and equity. These tranches represent different levels of risk and therefore attract different levels of reward. A securitization of Italian bank non-performing loans is structured on the same basis. The equity, junior and mezzanine levels act as a loss cushion for the investors in the senior debt: project operating losses and declines in the value of project assets eat through these tranches first, before the senior debt makes a loss.

The equity layer is invariably thin, possibly no more than 2-3% of the project cost, such that it is the junior and mezzanine tranches – which are more substantial – that carry the highest risk, if risk is measured as a combination of a likelihood of loss and its impact if it does occur. The equity layer has the highest likelihood of loss, but a relatively low impact if it does, because it is so small. The provider of the equity may also have made commercial supplies to the project or else be retained as a manager of the project, the profit margin and fees on which may be higher than the equity injection. In that case they may have earned back their equity and can easily withstand its loss. The suppliers of finance as 'capital-like instruments' or as junior debt have a slightly lower risk of a loss occurring, but a much higher impact if it does, because they represent 8-20% of the entire financing. Of the two, the 'capital-like instruments', ranking below the junior debt, has the higher risk of less. The thicker the tranche of 'capital-like instruments', the easier it is to attract the junior debt tranche. The thicker are these two tranches combined, the easier it is to attract the mezzanine and senior debt tranches.

How the InvestEU project has been mounted

InvestEU is primarily mounted through the European Investment Fund or EIF, by its issuing either guarantees or 'equity commitments' in favour of private-sector financiers of InvestEU projects.[60] These private-sector financiers are ostensibly taking on high-risk tranches of the project's financing, but then the EIF inoculates them against that level of risk. Once this inoculation from the EIF is in place, the EIB is willing to insert a tranche of its normal loan financing ranking superior to the EIF-guaranteed tranche. Because the financing has two or three levels of loss-absorption cushion in place, other financiers are willing to inject funds at the level above the EIB's normal loans – the mezzanine and senior levels.

The levels of loss-absorption cushion below the senior debt may be as many as four:
1. Equity;
2. Capital-like instruments (supported by EIF guarantees and 'equity commitments');
3. Junior debt (EIB loans);

---

[60] 'Equity commitments' are also termed 'equity signatures'

4. Mezzanine debt.

There may not be as many levels in every financing, and the EIF's engagements might range across all of the levels of Equity, Capital-like instruments and Junior debt, but this is the broad template for the scheme.

The concept is that, by the EIF enabling the insertion of and the EIB actually inserting tranches of funds at a low level in a project, it enables large volumes of private-sector financing to be unlocked and inserted at a higher level, and for the project to proceed. The EIF-enabled tranches and the EIB's lent tranches, inserted at the low levels of seniority, serve to 'mobilize' a much larger total volume of money, the vast majority being senior to the positions taken by the EIB and EIF. The EIB and EIF positions get leveraged so as to produce the entire amount of finance required.

Calculation of the 'mobilized amount'

When the European authorities announce that InvestEU has 'mobilized' a given amount of money, the figure includes the tranche that the EIF has guaranteed or the EIF's equity commitment, and the tranche that the EIB has lent. The pattern is that the EIF issues either a guarantee or an equity commitment per project but not both. There appear to be one or two exceptions but this is the overriding pattern.

What operations the EIF undertakes

An EIF guarantee is created when a third-party financier has committed funds into a project but the EIF takes over the credit risk.

The nature and structure of an EIF equity commitment are less clear. It is possible that there is no funding against the 'equity commitment' when it is made: in that case there might be a class of shares in a project which were authorized but not issued, and the EIF had entered into a commitment to buy them when issued. However it seems more likely that there is funding made by third-parties into the project at the outset, and that the meaning of the EIF's 'equity commitment' would be to allow existing shareholders to exit, either by their being able to sell their shares to the EIF at a fixed price, or by the enterprise cancelling shares of exiting shareholders and replacing the money either with new shares that the EIF buys, or by a calling-in of the unpaid portion of shares that the EIF already subscribed to. However it works mechanically, it is assumed that an EIF 'equity commitment' causes a private financier to make a cash investment in the enterprise at the start, which counts into the total of finance 'mobilized' by InvestEU. If the 'equity commitment' is called, the EIF pays in cash and the cash is used to take the existing shareholders out of the picture.

Significance of the EIB/EIF tranches and the 'missing private investor'

The supply (by the EIB) or the support (by the EIF) of the highest-risk tranches act as the key to unlocking the financing of the whole, and providers of these tranches are in the shortest supply. The tranches carry the highest risk of loss because a loss is both quite likely and is also very substantial if it does occur, added to which the tranches either pay a fee (to the EIF) or carry a return based on an interest rate (to the EIB), albeit with a higher interest margin added on than applies to mezzanine and senior debt. These tranches do not carry an equity-style return: unlimited profit potential in the case of success. This is a poor mix of risk and return, which explains why the private investor is missing. It is also the basis of the rationale for the EIB and EIF getting involved.

The unwillingness of private investors to accept the offered mix of risk and return is regarded by the EU authorities as unwarranted given the importance of the projects to the public interest. A statement of a policy priority can always be quoted for why the project must proceed. It is therefore deemed to be against the public interest for the policy priority to remain unfulfilled due to the absence of private investors. This stance on the part of the private market is the justification for public authorities to mobilize programmes in which a public financing entity – in this case the EIB Group – takes over the unattractive mix of risk and return on offer for the capital-like instruments and junior debt tranches.

The EIB Group's operations through EIF do not require an injection of cash. EIF, under both its guarantees and its 'equity commitments', takes on risk without injecting cash. EIF inoculates other entities from risk, who then invest their cash. EIF's engagements are all in the form of contingent liabilities, so they do not feature on the EIF's individual balance sheet, or on the EIB Group's.

Disturbingly the EIF does not even show the nominal amounts of its guarantees or its 'equity commitments' as contingent liabilities in its accounts. They are therefore not consolidated into the contingent liabilities of EIB Group, and thus do not figure in the EIB's calculations of its Risk-Weighted Assets or CET1 Ratio.

The third-party finance taken on by the project against the EIF's commitment does not figure on the balance sheets of the EIF or the EIB Group either.

Only the direct loan made by the EIB into the project figures on the EIB Group balance sheet, and is duly converted into a Risk-Weighted Asset and impacts the EIB's CET1 Ratio.

All the debt of course sits on the liabilities side of the balance sheet of the project's Special Purpose Company.

InvestEU is an extremely efficient way of the EU supranationals engaging high risk business and in big amounts but with minimal balance sheet impact, and no impact at all on General government gross debt. It is highly questionable that the EIF does not show the nominal amounts of its guarantees or its 'equity commitments' as contingent liabilities in its accounts. It is highly convenient that the EIF, not being a bank, does not have to calculate and report its own Risk-Weighted Assets or CET1 Ratio. It is then highly convenient, but also questionable, that the EIB Group does not consolidate the EIF's contingent liabilities with its own, despite its being the majority owner, and that the EIB consequently excludes them from its computations of its Risk-Weighted Assets and its CET1 Ratio.

The upshot of all of this is that EIB Group manages to exclude a large portfolio of high-risk business from its Risk-Weighted Assets and CET1 Ratio – by making a majority-owned, non-bank subsidiary undertake the business, in which case the business can be excluded from EIB's computations. The EIB's computations would not be as favorable if these contingent liabilities had been consolidated into the EIB's accounts, and if EIB Group had been compelled to hold a Risk-Weighted Asset on account of them.

Even if this treatment is defensible because the EIF is not a bank, it is not defensible that EIF fails to record contingent liabilities which it has in its own accounts, and that EIB does not add them to its own upon consolidation. The EIF's contingent liabilities are not accounted for anywhere at their nominal amount.

It cannot be a correct treatment that EIB Group fails to account for a large amount of high-risk business, and brings about that this business yields no Risk-Weighted Asset and fails to impact its CET1 Ratio.

Who is the borrower under these schemes, and under the UK's 'Private Finance Initiative'?

The next question is what entity is the project's Special Purpose Company. It will not fall within 'General government', or be an 'other public sector entity', because the project's equity is owned by the project's sponsor. The Special Purpose Company is a privately-owned entity, even if the project equity is 2% of the project cost or less. The project in which it is engaged is by definition in the public interest, or else it would be ineligible for the respective financing scheme. The conclusion is that we are looking at an EU-wide version (and possibly wider) of what in the UK would be known as Private Finance Initiative or PFI.

PFI was introduced by the Conservative government under John Major as a way of tapping private sources of finance for public projects but its heyday was under Gordon Brown and the Labour government, when it was used as a major channel for investment in assets to be used by the public, but without the accompanying debt figuring in the UK's 'General government gross debt'. Despite falling into disuse in England, Wales and Northern Ireland after 2010, it continued to be used actively by the Scottish National Party to make – or to attempt to make – new schools, roads and hospitals appear via the magic touch of Scottish nationalism.

The basic template is that an asset is built by a project company using privately borrowed money, and the asset, once built to the specifications of and accepted by the end-user, is rented by the end-user for a rental amount and term as will ensure the payment of all the debt service and dividends, although the project sponsor may not need to count on project dividends, there being ample ways for them to gain remuneration through other channels in the commercial structure. Like aircraft leases, the commercial contracts between the sponsor entity and the end-user can have various degrees of 'wetness', ranging from a full outsourcing of operation (such as of a university hall of residence) to just building maintenance (such as where a hospital has all care performed by the National Health Service).

Risk transfer onto a public sector entity

The principle of the project being in the public interest normally translates into the comfort for investors that rentals will be paid because they are coming out of public budgets. This can be because the end-user is a government ministry or, like the National Health Service, acts through a trust whose income is guaranteed by the government. An NHS Trust is an 'other public sector entity' itself, but its paymaster sits within 'General government'.

The point is that these structures create financial liabilities for the public sector as the rentals are calculated to meet debt service obligations. Because, however, the rentals are within a commercial contract and not within a financing agreement, the end-user does not have to record the debt as a liability and the finance object (hospital, hall of residence) as an asset. This is different from a finance lease for an aircraft where an airline does have to record an asset and a liability. These structures keep the asset and the liability off the public balance sheet at the levels of both 'General government' and 'other public sector entities', but nevertheless there is a binding obligation to pay, and the amount of the obligation is calculated with reference to a principal amount and an interest rate.

The investor's risk lies on the ability of 'General government' and 'other public sector entities' to meet their financial liabilities. It would be an error to imagine that the investors run any risk on the project sponsoring entity: all payments from the end-user will be made to an escrow or trust agent who will allocate them in accordance with the terms of the financing agreements, in the exact way that the agent does this on an Italian bank securitization of non-performing loans. It would be an error also to imagine that the end-user can withhold payments if one or other service is not performed; it has normally proven to be the case that the project sponsor entity need perform either few services and/or to a modest level after the asset has been commissioned, and it rather falls upon the end-user to pay more either for services that were not specified in the service agreement or so that a usable service is made available as opposed to the low-level one specified in the agreement.

PFI structures have proved to be legally watertight for the investors: they thought they were obtaining a UK 'sovereign risk' asset albeit at one or two steps removed, and receiving a far higher return than that on UK government bonds for doing so. This proved to be the case, and it is important to note the investor view: the investor believed they were taking public sector credit risk, and, where they were banks, they would have calibrated their Internal Ratings-Based assessment of the risk that they were running accordingly.

Key issue: debt service depends on a public sector entity but the debt is borrowed by a private sector one

The key is that the servicing of the debt taken on by the project company enjoys levels of credit support from public entities, but it is far from easy to determine what all these levels are and how large in any particular instance. Both the ownership structures and the terms of debt financing enjoy considerable levels of opacity.

Since EIB Group has named itself 'The EU Climate Bank', projects connected with Net Zero and renewables are in abundance within its portfolio and pipeline. If the UK wind farm industry is any guideline, the industry enjoys considerable government subsidies, and the generating companies have unrestricted access to the national grid. They are permitted to sell as much as they produce into the national grid without the government, the UK electricity distribution intermediaries or the business or private consumers having the right to stop them, and therefore to stop their access to the buyer, or else make their access to the buyer at the buyer's decision, or subject to a buyer decision on whether the price is acceptable. The wind farm generators can foist their offtake onto the buyers in unlimited volume and at a guaranteed minimum price that is favorable to themselves.

This is akin to a tax-raising power. The existence of this power justifies the financiers of the project in assessing their risk as on 'General government'. An industry has been manufactured in order to achieve public policy objectives and the industry is able to obtain a major level of public financial support: in effect its debts are liabilities of the 'General government' but without the debts featuring in 'General government gross debt'.

What risk EIF and EIB are taking

The next step is to assess what risk EIF and EIB are taking within InvestEU.

EIB's normal loans into InvestEU projects (and indeed into EGF projects) are subordinated to other creditors, who may also enjoy tangible security. This is out-of-line with the EIB's traditional policy.

As will be seen, the EIF on its own has made engagements that are much larger than the EU guarantees that EIB Group received. The EIF seems also to have used up the permission for the EIB Group to 'put its own resources at risk', leaving EIB both without guarantee cover, and in a subordinated position on its InvestEU/EGF loans that run out as far as 18 years. These loans do not translate into substantial Risk-Weighted Assets.

The working assumption is that the EIB's borrowers under InvestEU and EGF financings enjoy strong levels of public sector support, even if the direct borrower is not a public sector entity. The credit risk will not fall on the public sector via an explicit guarantee, but rather thanks to a series of undertakings, agreements to buy and use, or similar. The support may not be total from a legal point of view, but may rather be substantively total, such as in a price support agreement, or in a facility to sell unlimited amounts of project offtake at a known price. It will not be possible to capture the instances in a simple template. The acid test is whether a supplier of funds believes that their ultimate credit risk is on the public sector, and the proof of this would be in their internal papers for assessing the risk and obtaining credit approval to supply funds into the transaction.

For suppliers of loan funds, a credit application has to be drawn up which will quote – in the analysis of the Facility Weighting - the many lines of public support for the project cashflows, even where the Counterparty Weighting on the project entity is high and were there are other elements in the Facility Weighting that pull in the other direction.

The loan or debt investment will end up with a favorable Credit Conversion Factor based on a low Facility Weighting, thanks to public sector support. In the Eurozone the Facility Weighting will be even more favorable than it should be because of the endemic over-rating of Eurozone sovereigns and the consequential over-rating – due to trickle-down – of all public sector entities and liabilities than depend on public sector entities.

The acid test, then, is the Credit Conversion Factor that the suppliers of money assign to their loans into the project entities.

EIB Group Internal Ratings-Based methodology

EIB should publish its Counterparty Weighting and Facility Weighting sheets for its InvestEU and EGF loans. These sheets would identify the borrower, its financial strength, and all the particulars of the transaction that act as a credit support, notably any and all levels of guarantee, shareholding, contractual commitments, commercial agreements from public sector entities – inside or outside the perimeter of General government – that result in the transaction gaining a favorable Credit Conversion Factor.

EIB has a very favorable CET1 Ratio, and we inferred above that this derived from its having so much EU public sector risk in its portfolio. Now we need to see how much of that public sector risk is contained in its portfolio of structured financing.

Where EIB Group is not the only institution involved in a particular financing, the Customer Weighting and Facility Weighting sheets need to be obtained on a non-attributable basis from one of the other lenders or investors that is committing money into the scheme, and which runs an IRB methodology. IRB methodologies being so similar from one bank to another, we can take it that the approaches of EIB and private lenders are interchangeable.

Obtaining the investor/lender view of the degree of risk they are taking

The upshot of this work will be to demonstrate what the providers of finance think is the risk, and how they grade it. This is the acid test, as stated before. If it is their opinion that the principal comfort that debt service will be paid is the roles and commitments of public sector entities in the financing, then the debt ought to be recorded as a debt of the EU public sector. It is not possible that the public sector react to that by pretending that it is not their responsibility if investors choose to construe their credit risk as being public sector risk. If the credit risk is justifiably construed as falling on the public sector, then public sector entities will have signed undertakings that have been authorized through their own approval processes and on which they will have taken legal advice. There can be no second version such as that investors believe they have public sector risk but the public sector does not. We already have two versions: investors and the public sector know they have created liabilities for the public sector but these liabilities are not accounted for as debt liabilities. The liabilities are therefore invisible. They now need to be made visible.

InvestEU target market and borrowers

The EIF's target market is supposed to be Small and Medium-sized Enterprises (SMEs) as defined in EU recommendation 2003/361.[61] To fall within this definition, staff levels must be above 10 but below 250, and turnover must be between €2 million and €50 million, or else the balance sheet must total between €2 million and €43 million.

The list of beneficiaries of EIF guarantees and of projects towards which the EIF has made 'equity commitments' in 2021 includes the following taken at random from the overall list.[62]

Guarantees:
- Alpha bank - EGF – CDG
- DSK Bank - EGF – CDG
- Privredna Banka Zagreb - EGF – CDG
- UAB ORION LEASING – EGF – CDG
- Banque Populaire du Sud - FOSTER-Languedoc Roussillon ERDF
- Banca del Mezzogiorno - Mediocredito Centrale - EGF – UDG
- Intesa Sanpaolo - (ex Mediocredito Italiano) - IFSMEG (COVID)

Equity commitments:
- Everwood Renewables Fund V
- Mirova Energy Transition V Fund
- BPM Mezzanine Fund II
- Atlantic Bridge IV
- SMERemediumCap
- CIS Medecins du Monde AiLSi
- LAUNCHub Fund II Cooperatief U.A.
- Simpact 2.0

The guarantees are all towards financial institutions; it is to be assumed that the guarantees do not back individual 'senior debt' loans to SMEs, but rather back portfolios of low-ranking loans to or capital-like instruments in SMEs. The loans/capital-like instruments may well be granted by a fund run by the guarantee's beneficiary.

The 'equity commitments' appear to be all towards funds, which in turn can be assumed to be taking up capital-like instruments or equity stakes in SMEs.

InvestEU transactions cannot be for SMEs directly

The amounts mobilized under InvestEU do not match a pattern where the transactions are for SMEs directly: there are far too few of them listed in the EIF Annual Reports. Clearly the guarantee beneficiaries and equity commitment beneficiaries are financial institutions or funds that have the role of multipliers: they engage in numerous transactions with SMEs on the back of one deal with the EIF. If the InvestEU programme and the EGF programme have now 'mobilized' €612 billion of financing for these SMEs, then that amounts to a very large number of individual transactions (14,209) between the financial institutions and funds on the one side and SMEs on the other, if the maximum financing is €43 million (the entire liability side of an SME's balance sheet, beyond which it ceases to be an SME).

2021 was EIF's most active year, in which it committed €30.5 billion itself and enabled €110.6 billion, over approximately 400 transactions listed in pp. 62-72 of its annual report. The total of finance 'mobilized' was therefore €141.1 billion, implying an average transaction size of €352.7 million, which is far in excess of the balance sheet total of an individual SME. It defies credibility that the EIF has performed analysis on the individual transactions between the financial institutions and funds on the one side and SMEs on the other, and yet that must be where EIF's risk lies as the taker of the highest-risk tranches.

---

[61] https://ec.europa.eu/growth/smes/sme-definition_en accessed on 26 May 2022
[62] EIF 2021 Annual Report pp. 62-72

Structure of the EIF's capital

The EIF has a very small capital base: €7.3 billion of which only €1.46 billion is paid-in.

Its structure is laid out on p. 81 of the EIF 2021 Annual Report. The subscribed capital was raised in 2021 by 64%:

	31.12.21	31.12.20
Called capital	€1.46 bn	€0.90 bn
Uncalled capital	€5.84 bn	€3.60 bn
Subscribed capital	€7.30 bn	€4.50 bn

Subscribers	31.12.21	31.12.20	Percent
EIB	€4.34 bn	€2.65 bn	59.4
European Union	€2.19 bn	€1.34 bn	30.0
Financial institutions	€0.77 bn	€0.51 bn	10.6

31.12.21	Called capital	Uncalled capital	Subscribed capital
EIB	€0.87 bn	€3.47 bn	€4.34 bn
European Union	€0.44 bn	€1.75 bn	€2.19 bn
Financial institutions	€0.77 bn	€0.0 bn	€0.77 bn

Table 4.1: EIF capital

Financial institutions own the 10.6% not owned by European institutions. The shareholdings of these financial institutions are fully paid-in in the sense that the institutions have pre-deposited an amount of 'share premium' that accords to their unpaid amount. The shareholdings of the EIB and EU are part-paid, and their unpaid portions are only €3.47 billion for EIB and €1.75 billion for the EU. Even with this enlarged capital base, the EIF is spinning a very large wheel on a very small axle.

InvestEU programme size and the EU's guarantees

The initial aim of InvestEU was to 'mobilize' €315 billion of financing, and this was later raised to €500 billion, to be achieved by the end of 2020, which was at the same time the end of the EU's budget period or Multiannual Financial Framework (MFF) for 2014-2020.

To assist the EIF and EIB in reaching this target the EU issued a guarantee of €16 billion, for direct coverage of losses on InvestEU, applying to projects agreed to during the MFF: the losses did not have to materialize during the MFF but (i) before a loan from the EIB was repaid; or (ii) before a guarantee from the EIF expired; or (iii) when an EIF 'equity commitment' was called and the shares the EIF thereby acquired were worth less than the purchase price specified in the 'equity commitment'.

This EU guarantee would naturally be called upon by the EIF before it had recourse to the unpaid portion of its subscribed capital from the EIB and EU.

The EU guarantee would similarly be called upon by the EIB before it had recourse to the unpaid portion of its subscribed capital from the EU member states.

Calls upon the EU guarantee would be debited to the EU budget, which would then go into deficit. Supplementary calls for member state cash contributions would be made to stop the EU budget being in deficit, the liability for eliminating the deficit being a joint-and-several one between the member states.

The EU guarantee does not specify an allocation of its amount between the EIF and EIB: it is to cover the first losses either institution makes and if the EIF and EIB in combination lost more than that, there would have to be an agreement struck as to how much of the guarantee proceeds would be allocated to each institution.

InvestEU's overall size was supposedly limited, as is explained in 'Managing Euro Risk', by a ceiling on (i) the nominal amount the EIF can commit; and (ii) the relationship between the EIF's commitment and the EIB's lending; and (iii) the relationship between the combination of EIF's commitment plus the EIB's lending on the one hand, and the amount of private financing the projects take up on the other hand. The sum of the EIF's commitment and the EIB's lending can exceed the EU guarantees, but only by the amount they can 'put at risk'.

The amounts that might be lost by the EIB and EIF under InvestEU are considerable, and the likelihood of a loss is much higher than on the EIB's normal loans: the EIB and EIF have accepted a lower position of seniority for their claims. The maximum leverage of total project funding to the EIF's position is 15:1; the maximum leverage of total project funding to the EIB's and EIF's combined position is 5.2:1.

We have calculated that EIB's loans into InvestEU and EGF were €77.7 billion out of a total loan book of €433 billion at the end of 2021. We have also calculated that the EIF's engagements at the same date were €76 billion, but deriving from all of its programmes.

Difficulties in determining the amount at risk

For the purposes of the remainder of this section we do not differentiate between InvestEU and EGF. The risk of a loss occurring in the EIF does not differ between the two programmes: the difference is in the guarantees that would be called to make good the loss.

It is not straightforward, even from the EIF's Annual Reports, to ascertain the face amounts of the guarantees and equity commitments it has made. The amounts have to be derived from the information that the EIF does divulge.

The question of how much the EIF has become exposed via its guarantees and 'equity commitments' is not specifically stated: it is off-balance sheet for the EIF, as well as for the EIB and EU. For the purposes of 'Managing Euro Risk' a methodology was developed to use the information that was there, its results being on pp. 106-8 and covering the period 2009-18. The same methodology has been used to incorporate the period 2019-21, as a result of which the data begins in 2012.

The total nominal amount of guarantees issued has not been given since the 2010 annual report where, on p. 43, it was stated as €14.7 bn. What we are given instead is an on-balance sheet provision for the likelihood of losses under guarantees (only €47,370 in the 2018 annual report) and a statement of the 'exposure at risk'. This is determined through the EIF's Internal Ratings-Based model, which presumably will bear great similarity to the EIB's one. There is a chance that the amount stated as possible losses under guarantees has no relationship to InvestEU, in which case only the nominal amount of guarantees issued since 2010 is a relevant figure.

The base information available for 2019 was less than was made available in 2018, being only a breakdown of new commitments via guarantee and 'venture capital' for five activity segments. At least there was a breakdown for each segment in terms of the commitment and the leveraged amount, which could be married back to the overall statement of commitments (€10.2 billion) and the leveraged amount (€58.7 billion).

In 2020 and 2021 even this level of transparency had been withdrawn. Instead we were only able to ascertain the overall statements of commitments and the leveraged amounts, and we have allocated them between guarantees and equity commitments in the same proportion as occurred in 2019. For 2020 the overall statement for commitments was €12.9 billion and the leveraged amount was €66.8 billion. For 2021 the overall statement for commitments was €30.5 billion and the leveraged amount was €110.6 billion.

It does seem to be questionable that the EIF does not clearly state:
- The total nominal values of their guarantees issued and their maturity dates;
- The account party of each guarantee, meaning the party that counter-indemnifies the EIF and must reimburse the EIF if the guarantee is called by its beneficiary: the beneficiary is disclosed but not the account party;[63]
- The total nominal values of their 'equity commitments' and their duration;
- What enterprises they have agreed to buy equity in and at what price;
- What asset the EIF will be left with if their commitment is called.

---

[63] To give an analogy, if a bank is asked to issue a rent guarantee for a tenant to their landlord, it is an alternative to the tenant placing a cash deposit; the tenant is the 'account party' and the landlord is the 'beneficiary'. The account party will be asked to sign a counterindemnity in the bank's favour so that, if the landlord makes a claim under the guarantee, the account party is obliged to reimburse the bank. There are no lists of account parties for EIF's guarantees issued as part of InvestEU

Basic financial information replaced by questionable statements

This is the basic financial information about EIF and InvestEU and it is submerged. There is a pattern of transparency being reduced as volume and risk increase. Instead of the amount of guarantees, we are shown EIF's calculation of the Value-at-Risk, arrived at via an Internal Ratings-Based methodology. The problem with such methodologies in understating risk is one of the other topics in this chapter. If the EIF's total book of guarantees is €56.9 billion as we have calculated, and if the Value-at-Risk of this portfolio is only €10.8 billion, then each unit of nominal value is accorded a risk-weighting of only 19%. This is implausible if the guarantees are in respect of high-risk tranches of financing to private sector entities. For a commercial bank a weighting of 19% would in turn mean that the bank only required CET1 of around 1.3% of the nominal value (7% of the risk-weighted value). The EIF, not being a bank, does not have to run such a methodology but it does, and comes up with altogether benevolent weightings.

This is a concern because it means that the EIF may have misunderstood the degree of risk it is taking by issuing guarantees to other parties whose claims rank low down the 'creditor ladder' and where the enterprise involved is highly leveraged. When the EIF pays out on its guarantee, it becomes subrogated into the same claims, and this will be at a time when the enterprise is in financial trouble. A loss of some kind is certain if this eventuality arises, so why is the chance of the eventuality arising regarded as so low? It can only be because the enterprise enjoys some form of public sector backing, such that the EIF can regard its guarantee as giving onto a claim on itself in the widest sense, because the EIF is backed by the member state governments who sit at the apex of the pyramid of public sector entities in their member state. If the transaction that the EIF's guarantee is serving is backed by an entity in the same pyramid, then it might be justified in regarding its risk of loss as low, because it will get its money from the same ultimate source (the member state), whether it comes via the EU/EIB or through the enterprise it is helping finance. The open question would be how this second line of recourse works: what is the claim the EIF has on a public sector entity through the enterprise it is helping finance?

Amount of EIF portfolio of guarantees

Figure 4.2 tracks the EIF's portfolio of guarantees from 2012 to 2021. The volume of new issuance has increased sharply, and so, possibly, has the average maturity – the percentage of guarantees of maturity over five years was 17.49% in 2014 but had risen to 85.03% in 2019. It then dropped sharply in 2020 before rising again in 2021. The increments to the 'exposure at risk' figure are unlikely to correlate to the rising volume of new business. Such sudden changes may point to an alteration of the methodology used to derive the figures from the nominal values: it is unlikely that a very large portion of the portfolio is due to run off in 2024, such that it still had over 5 years to run in 2019 but less than 5 years in 2020. The guarantees are linked to medium-term funding and have been added in rising increments. It is not credible that the percentage with over 5 years to run should drop sharply as a natural run-off. On the other hand this 'exposure at risk' figure may have nothing to do with InvestEU.

We assume that the beneficiary of the EIF guarantee has taken on a borrowing against it, and that it makes further borrowings from banks and from the EIB. We take these further borrowings to be the 'leveraged amount' stated by the EIF in its annual reports and that the total amount of finance enabled is known as the 'mobilized amount' and is the sum of the 'leveraged amount' plus the EIF's guarantee.

Our extrapolation of the current total size of the guarantees book - based on nine years of the average of new nominal written amount to take some account of the increase in scope and maturity since 2015 - is €56.9 billion, nearly quadruple the last amount stated in an EIF annual report in 2010.

This book of EIF guarantees mobilizes €257 billion, based on the average annual total finance enabled (€22.6 billion), multiplied by nine years to take account of the expansionary trajectory.

Amount of EIF portfolio of 'equity commitments'

As regards the so-called 'equity commitments', the type of operation involved is not explained in detail, and there are other categories like 'Securitization' and 'Alternative debt' which sound like the same thing. The EIF supposedly commits to buy equity - in funds and not directly in projects - but the nominal amounts it commits are a large multiple of the equity investments that appear in the EIF balance sheet.

One explanation of this is that the EIF may be using the technique favoured by itself, the EIB, ECB and ESM: the EIF buys part-paid shares, in which the paid portion is very low. The EIF commits very little cash, but the subscribed-but-not-called portion of its shares acts as a reserve fund for the fund the shares are in. Another explanation is that while some transactions operate on the part-paid model, in others the EIF has committed to buy existing shares with a form of put option for exiting shareholders, or that it has committed to buy new shares at a price that will enable the existing shares of exiting shareholders to be redeemed.

At any rate the EIF has committed to become a shareholder, and in circumstances that can only be adverse when it happens. As a shareholder the EIF takes the highest slice of risk and makes the first loss. Again, it can claim these amounts back through a capital call of its own, or through a call by the EIB on the EU's InvestEU guarantee – as long as the EIB has not exhausted the guarantee with claims of its own.

Once again, we assume that the fund that has issued the shares (which the EIF has committed to buy, one way or another) can take on money against or as a result of the EIF's 'equity commitment', and that it can make borrowings as well at a more senior level from banks and from the EIB. We take these further borrowings to be the 'leveraged amount' stated by the EIF in its annual reports and that the total amount of finance enabled is known as the 'mobilized amount' and is the sum of the 'leveraged amount' plus the EIF's 'equity commitment'.

We have extrapolated the development of the book, the part-paid percentage and the callable amounts from the EIF's 2009–2018 annual reports in Figure 4.3.

This portion of the EIF's book is even more highly leveraged than the guarantees: equity commitments of €19.1 billion enabled total finance of €354.6 billion to be mobilized.

Total of financing amount enabled by EIF

Totalling the EIF's guarantees and equities books and the totals of finance mobilized by both results in:

Overall estimate total of EIF book – aggregate of estimated total of EIF guarantees and equity books											76,002
Estimated total book of finance mobilized – aggregate of estimated books of finance mobilized by EIF guarantees and equity books											611,964

Table 4.2: EIF book of commitments and total finance enabled by them

This is as per the end of 2021. The total book of finance exceeds the €500 billion which was the target for InvestEU by the end of the 2014-20 Multiannual Financial Framework. It was reported that InvestEU had reached its initial target of €315 billion by mid-2018, and will have expanded further by year-end.

These figures are plausible if InvestEU was targeting a volume of €500 billion by the end of 2020, and had reached €471 billion by then, and if EIF put on an extra €141 billion in 2021, to reach €612 billion.

The only problem is reconciling these amounts back to the EU guarantees. There is a difference of €156 billion between the initial ceiling of InvestEU of €315 billion and the €471 billion it had apparently reached by the end of the 2014-20 MFF, but no new guarantee beyond the one for €16 billion and no new permission to put further of EIB Group's funds at risk beyond €5 billion. This €21 billion, when leveraged by the permitted multiple of 15:1, delivers the initial InvestEU programme ceiling of €315 billion.

A new guarantee has been issued for the 2021-7 MFF, and we have €141 billion of new business put through EIF in 2021, but we also have the European Guarantee Fund (EGF), a new 'envelope' with a ceiling of €200 billion, a guarantee of €24.4 billion, no apparent permission to put EIB Group funds at risk beyond the guarantee, and an apparent leverage multiple of 8.2:1.

Little if any of the €471 billion put on by the end of 2020 could have been done through EGF because of when it was established and the lead time to have business committed and drawn down. That leaves the €156 billion mentioned above uncovered. EIF then put on €141 billion in 2021 and it is plausible to imagine that all of this was done under EGF, with the EGF balance of €60 billion being put on in 2022. By then the new EU guarantee for InvestEU for the 2021-7 MFF was in place and further business could be transacted under that 'envelope'.

Lack of guarantee cover and tracking utilization of InvestEU, EGF and other schemes

Without more guarantee cover than €16 billion, EIB Group appears to be taking far more risk in InvestEU than was originally envisaged. InvestEU had a mobilized amount of €471 billion by the end of 2020 which remained more or less static until sometime in 2022. EIF had about €55 billion of guarantees and 'equity commitments' in issue at the end of 2020, €24 billion more than its permissions under the initial phase of InvestEU. The amount issued rose by €20 billion in 2021, about 83% the EGF 'envelope', a figure that tallies with other evidence.

We are left with this discrepancy of €24 billion. It may relate to other programmes, but none are mentioned in the EIF's annual report that are of that magnitude. The EIF Annual Report for 2021 tags new business with 'EGF' in many cases, but there are also a good number tagged with 'EFSI' (which is how EIF tags InvestEU transactions) and also a number tagged with neither. This latter outcome indicates the existence of a certain block of transactions that are structured exactly like ones coming under the InvestEU and EGF envelopes, but which are conducted under separate 'envelopes' whose ceiling is not as transparent as the ceilings for InvestEU and EGF.

It behoves the EU authorities, rather than the author, to identify each transaction to the programme it was put on under, and then to creates totals per programme that reconcile to the programme ceilings. The furthest that this subject can be taken is in the global figures at 2020 and 2021 year-end, the statement of the identifiable programmes and their ceilings.

Trajectory of the volume of EIF's business

Whatever the detail, the overall trajectory of InvestEU is clear – rapid expansion, with the member states bearing the first loss either through the EU's InvestEU guarantee of €16 billion during the 2014-20 budget period, or the EGF, or the new EU first-loss guarantee of €26.2 billion issued for the 2021-7 MFF.

The degree of risk being taken is opaque because we do not know who the account parties of the guarantees are, and we do not know what projects the 'equity commitments' are supporting: the EIF annual report lists the funds and companies in which shares have been bought but provides no clues about what projects the funds have invested in. As a shareholder, the EIF presumably has no recourse to any party involved in the project if the project fails.

Summary on InvestEU and EGF

A prime objective of InvestEU and EGF is to complement the efforts of the EIB to reflate the Eurozone economy after 2011-13, and it has now become a main enabler for the attempt to reach Net Zero. The InvestEU/EGF structure, to which the EIF is central, enables more debt to be raised and spent on public sector work, without the debts counting into the Eurostat figures. Nor do the debts greatly impinge upon the balance sheets of the EU, EIB or EIF.

The liabilities of these entities are all contingent ones, predominantly off-balance sheet. Both the guarantees and the 'equity commitments' are off-balance sheet for the EIF, except for the funded private equity investments and for the provision for guarantee liabilities. Indeed they are so far off the EIF's balance sheet that their nominal amount is not given at all.

The EU's liabilities - under €16 billion and €26.2 billion InvestEU guarantees - should be marked against the Commitments Appropriation of the EU Budget for the respective MFF. The status of the EGF in this regard is uncertain.[64]

---

[64] It has to be regarded as uncertain how the EGF fits in with the 2021-7 Multiannual Financial Framework given that five member states have stepped out of the structure and the EGF is not formally an EU guarantee. It seems improbable that the 22 participating member states would all allow the EGF – and therefore InvestEU – to be incremental to the MFF ceilings agreed with some difficulty for the period 2021-7

The supposition is that InvestEU and EGF together had created up to €612 billion of new liabilities for the EU public sector up to the end of 2021, of which €77.7 billion are on the balance sheet of the EIB, and the rest of which appear nowhere in any EU public sector balance sheet.

The liabilities are not debts but commercial obligations within rental or supply contracts, which do not have to be capitalized and placed as a liability on a balance sheet. Because the obligations are not debts, they need not be included in 'General government gross debt' even if the direct debts of the respective contract counterparty do fall within in. They need not go onto the balance sheets of public sector entities that fall outside 'General government': the debt burden on the EU public is triply hidden in this case.

4.3 ECB Targeted Longer Term Refinancing Operations

Refinancing operations have always been part of the ECB's policy toolbox, both what they term 'Main refinancing operations' (MRO) and 'Longer term refinancing operations' (LTRO). Both represent loans to banks, with MRO being short-term and LTRO being of 2-4 years' duration. The loans are extended by the NCBs, not the ECB, even though these are ECB programmes. The borrowers are the universe of Eurozone banks that the NCBs have sponsored into the Eurosystem, mainly by admitting them as participants in the national RTGS and therefore TARGET2. Non-Eurozone NCBs do not participate in either MRO or LTRO, and as a result the banks in their countries do not borrow under these programmes.

Interplay between MRO/LTRO and TARGET2

There is a close interplay between MRO, LTRO and the TARGET2 **system**. A loan to a bank under MRO is furnished in the form of an overdraft on the RTGS account that the bank runs with its NCB within the national RTGS system, which is the national component in TARGET2. A loan to a bank under LTRO is created in a loan account in the books of the bank's NCB, and the proceeds are paid onto the bank's RTGS account.

It is unclear, though, what the interplay is between MRO/LTRO and the TARGET2 **balances**. The Bundesbank (see below) explains that the TARGET2 balances have arisen entirely because of cross-border payments. On the other hand the accumulated overdraft positions of all the RTGS accounts that an NCB runs for banks in its country would cause the NCB to be substantially in deficit itself, and, within the closed circle of TARGET2, there are only two places where the NCB can fund the overdraft from:
1. Other NCBs; or
2. The minimum reserve balances that its banks must hold with it.

Option (2) would be a round trip: minimum reserves are recycled as MRO or LTRO to the same universe of banks. Option (1) contradicts the explanation given by the Bundesbank.

At any rate here is the development of MRO and LTRO balances since 2010, taken from the year-end Consolidated Balance Sheet of the Eurosystem, which is normally included with the ECB's Annual Report:

€ billions	2010	2011	2012	2013	2014	2015	2016	2017	2018	2019	2020	2021
MRO	227.9	144.8	89.7	168.7	156.1	89.0	39.1	3.4	9.6	7.9	0.5	0.4
LTRO	298.2	703.9	1,035.8	583.3	473.3	469.5	556.6	760.6	723.8	616.2	1,792.6	2,201.5
Total RO	526.1	848.7	1,125.5	752.0	629.4	558.5	595.7	727.2	733.4	624.1	1,793.1	2,201.9
BS Footing	2,002.2	2,733.2	2,962.8	2,273.3	2,208.3	2,780.5	3,662.9	4,467.6	4,702.4	4,671.4	6,979.3	8,556.4
RO/BS	26.3%	31.1%	38.0%	33.1%	28.5%	20.1%	16.3%	16.3%	15.6%	13.4%	25.7%	25.7%

Table 4.3: trajectory of ECB Refinancing Operations 2010-21

The notable developments are:
- MRO/LTRO made up a high portion of the Eurosystem balance sheet from 2010 to 2014, to a level only reached again in 2020 and 2021;
- The virtual elimination of MRO over the period to a point where it is well below 1% of the whole;
- The tripling of LTRO between 2020 and 2021.

Towards the latter end of the period LTRO became concentrated into so-called 'Targeted LTRO' or TLTRO. There have been three series, and Series 1 and 2 have been paid off, albeit that maturities under Series 2 which fell due between March and December 2020 were paid off out of a new facility called the Bridge LTRO. The same amounts were then refinanced out of operations in Series 3, the Bridge LTRO reverting to having a nil balance. TLTRO Series 3 was already underway when the Pandemic struck, and one of the ECB's actions (see below) was to add a number of operations to the schedule, and also greatly increase the amount.

4.4 Securitization of banks' Non-Performing Loans

Eurozone banks generated large volumes of bad loans in the run-up to the Eurozone debt crisis. A technique was developed in Italy, which was named 'market-based', for banks to sell off these loans into securitization structures. The implementation of this technique at Banca Popolare di Bari was examined in detail in Brexit Paper No. 8, published by Global Britain in 2017 and written by the author and Gordon Kerr, an experienced capital markets and structured finance specialist.[65]

What is a securitization

A classic securitization is an arm's-length, commercial transaction, whereby a bank sells performing loans into a special-purpose company or SPC. The SPC is also known as the 'securitization vehicle'. The normal purpose of the transaction is for the bank to free up its capital in order to make new loans. The SPC itself is debt-funded, with very low capital and indeed the capital may be owned by a trust or charity, because the essence is that the assets and liabilities of the SPC should not be consolidated into the accounts of either the selling bank or any of the investors providing the funding to the SPC with which it buys the loans.

The loans are sold to the SPC by the bank, and the SPC needs to raise the finance for the purchase. The normal pattern is for there to be three tranches of bonds issued, and these are a senior debt tranche, a mezzanine debt tranche, and a junior debt tranche. The returns for investors on the tranches start low for the senior debt, and rise through to the junior debt, because the risk rises in line with the lowering of the level of seniority. The legal papers allocate the proceeds of the SPC's book of loan assets in order to realize the risk/return profile that the investors in each tranche have agreed to.

The transaction as circled in this way must meet accounting tests for the loans to move off the bank's balance sheet, and thus to release the capital for the bank to re-use. This is normal business whereby banks may sell off residential mortgage loans, car loans or credit card loans. However it is unusual for bad loans, or 'Non-Performing Loans' (NPLs), to be securitized.

How EU accounting rules help banks understate what loans are bad

Under current EU accounting rules a loan is classified as an NPL if it either shows specific indicators of non-payment (like that the borrower has filed for bankruptcy) or if it is 90 days since the borrower was due to make a debt service payment and failed to, and has not cured their failure in the meantime.[66] The loan must then be classified into one of the categories defined by banking regulators according to the degree of delinquency:
- Past Due and Non-Performing
- Unlikely to Pay
- Bad Exposures

Please note for this purpose the normally accepted definitions of 'Past Due' and 'Non-performing':

Past due	a loan payment that has not been made as of its due date. A borrower who is past due may be subject to late fees, unless the borrower is still within a grace period
Non-performing	the sum of borrowed money upon which the debtor has not made his scheduled payments for at least 90 days. A nonperforming loan is either in default or close to being in default

Table 4.4: definitions of 'Past Due' and 'Non-performing' loans

The first NPL category 'Past Due and Non-Performing' need not include loans that are 'Past Due' but not yet by 90 days. Only then do they become classed as 'Non-Performing' as well and register as an NPL.

The volume of loans that are 'Past Due' is thus disguised, and this problem is exacerbated by two further techniques permitted by financial regulators:
- Restructuring – normally adding unpaid interest to the principal amount, and/or accepting supplementary collateral;
- Forbearance – normally permitting an extensive grace period for the borrower to cure the delinquency.

---

[65] 'The true cost of EU membership' by Bob Lyddon and Gordon Kerr, accessible via www.brexitpapers.uk
[66] https://www.bankingsupervision.europa.eu/about/ssmexplained/html/npl.en.html accessed on 28 May 2022

The application of either of these techniques will prevent a loan from going 'Past Due' at all, or will return it from 'Past Due and Non-Performing' to simply 'Past Due', or will return it from 'Past Due' to 'Performing' or may even return it from 'Past Due and Non-Performing' to 'Performing'.

These techniques improve reported figures for bad loans, without the borrower needing to make any debt service payments.

Rules on NPL classification allow interest to continue to be accrued

The next major issue is how the bank should handle the interest. The bank's objective is to maximize the booking of the interest that was scheduled to be received, even if the borrower does not pay it. Where interest is capitalized, it can still be booked as 'Interest Received', albeit not received from the borrower. The interest on the 'restructured' loan can be accrued as the interest on a normal performing loan can be, as can interest on 'Past due' loans.

Only the loans classified as 'Past due and Non-Performing' need to be put onto 'non-accrual', whereby the scheduled interest cannot be automatically credited to 'Interest Received'. The interest is still calculated in line with the loan agreement, and delay interest on top of the regular interest, and charges and so on, but it cannot then be booked into the bank's 'Interest Received' line and serve to improve its Profit&Loss Account. The loan agreement will state an order in which the bank will apply any debt service payments received from the borrower, and these will start with costs, charges, delay interest, ordinary interest, and finally the principal amount.

Notwithstanding proper treatment once a loan has been classified as 'Past due and Non-Performing', the waiver to banks from putting 'Past due' loans immediately onto non-accrual, as well as the techniques of 'restructuring' and 'forbearance', enable interest to be calculated on the loan and put into the bank's Profit&Loss Account where the borrower has not paid the interest.

This inflates the bank's profits.

How NPLs should be managed and valued

NPLs will normally be managed, not in the department that generated the loan, but in a central department going by a name such as 'Special Credit Department' or 'Impaired Loans Administration'. This should happen at the latest when a loan is classified as 'Past Due and Non-Performing'. It may well be left to the original loan production department to operate remedies like restructuring and forbearance, and so to conceal the degree of delinquency in their departmental portfolio.

When the delinquency can no longer be concealed, the loan has to be passed to the central department.

The first task is to alter the Business Unit Code attached to the loan, from that of the original loan production department. This distinguishes delinquent loans from Performing loans because they then roll up through a different path in the bank's internal account chart and therefore into a different line on the Asset side of the balance sheet.

The next task of the central department is to determine the likelihood of a recovery on the principal amount, assuming that some or all of the interest and charges are recovered. This determination will be influenced by the time needed and likelihood of the bank successfully attaching any security, such as repossessing any real estate through the respective legal process, becoming its owner, and then putting it up for sale. Having made an assessment both of the likelihood of the borrower curing the loan's delinquency in whole or in part, and the time-to-attach/realizability/value of any security, the department will assign the NPL to its correct category. The category should then directly drive the value in the bank's accounts at which the NPL is held, a value that reflects the lower end – not the higher end – of the bank's expectations for the likely recovery of the principal amount.

The result will inevitably be a diminution of the loan's nominal value, and this is classically achieved in one of two ways:

1. The loan's value is maintained in the Asset side and a Loan Loss Provision for the write-down is created on the Liabilities side. It is created through a debit to the Profit&Loss account so the write-down of the loan causes the bank's profit to reduce or push it into loss;
2. The loan's value is reduced on the Asset side without anything appearing on the Liabilities side. The nominal value of the loan is reduced to a lower 'carrying value'. The write-down between the nominal value and carrying value is a debit to the Profit&Loss account so it causes the bank's profit to reduce or push it into loss.

EU/Eurozone banks have tended to employ the second method, but without necessarily drawing the obvious conclusions about how big the write-down should be if the loan is categorized as 'Unlikely to Pay' or 'Bad Exposures' and without ensuring that the resulting valuation is at the lower end of the bank's expectations for what will be recovered.

'Unlikely to Pay' loans should not be valued at above 50% of face value. 'Bad Exposures' should be valued at 0%. Eurozone banks in Italy, Greece and Cyprus had such large portfolios of NPLs that these treatments might not have made the bank bankrupt, but they would for sure have caused the bank to breach its regulatory capital ratios, and triggered a 'resolution' event. This would have caused the national Deposit Insurance Scheme to pay out depositors, and in turn obligated the respective member state government to issue more debt.

This situation gave rise to the 'market-based' securitzation template, which has been employed extensively in Italy, and which has been deployed also in Greece and Cyprus. Its aim is to back NPLs out of bank balance sheets, without the banks thereby falling into resolution.

Amounts of NPLs in different banking systems – Greece

The governor of the Greek central bank revealed a figure of €75 billion of NPLs in the Greek banking sector as of mid-2019, equivalent to 43.6% of all loans.[67] Even this figure was lower than it had been: 'Over the past three years to mid-2019, the absolute stock of NPLs fell by about €30 billion, largely through write-offs and sales'.[68] In other words hardly any borrowers had cured their delinquency by paying, there were some sales, but the larger part of the €30 billion reduction was due to write-downs on loans still owned by Greek banks.

Ambitious targets for NPL reduction were agreed between the four largest banks and the ECB/Single Supervisory Mechanism, and under a similar framework by the Bank of Greece for smaller banks: NPL ratios were to fall to 35% by the end of 2019, and to 20% by the end of 2021.[69] Even so, they would still at that point be five times the average for the euro area.[70]. To this end a programme to securitize the €75 billion nominal of NPLs in the Greek banking system – 'Project Hercules' - was approved by the European Commission.[71]

Hercules II was launched in 2021.[72] Reuters reported that Hercules I had only enabled Greek banks to offload €30 billion nominal of NPLs. Hercules II would assist banks in further reducing non-performing loans by €32 billion and 'bring NPL ratios down to single digits by the end of 2022, close to EU averages'. NPLs had been reduced by 'about €59 billion from a peak of be €106 billion in March 2016…the banking system's overall NPL ratio of 36% at the end of September remains far above a euro zone average of 2.9%'.

Clearly these statement and statistics do not allow a full reconciliation of where NPLs levels began, what they are now, or what was either restructured/foregone or securitized each year. Nevertheless one can conclude that NPLs are high and much larger than the banks' capital. Nevertheless the respective banks are still trading.

---

[67] https://www.keeptalkinggreece.com/2019/09/23/greece-banks-recapitalization-project-hercules/ accessed on 31 May 2022
[68] https://www.bis.org/review/r190910b.pdf accessed on 31 May 2022
[69] NPL Ratio – the ratio of the carrying value of Non-Performing Loans to the face value of Performing Loans
[70] from BIS Bank of Greece governor speech 05sep19
[71] https://europa.eu/rapid/press-release_IP-19-6058_en.htm accessed on 22.10.19
[72] https://www.reuters.com/article/us-greece-banks-loans/greece-to-extend-hercules-bad-loan-reduction-scheme-minister-says-idUSKBN2AO2J1 accessed on 31 May 2022

As regards Cyprus, it was reported by the Cyprus Business Mail in July 2018 that NPLs in the Cypriot banking system had fallen in March 2018 by almost €2.1 billion to €19.9 billion compared to February 2018's figure, and that this was the lowest figure for NPLs since December 2014. The figures were attributed to the Central Bank of Cyprus (CBC).[73] The NPLs ratio in the system fell in March 2018 to 43% from 45.3% in February 2018 and 46% in March 2017. That still meant that 43% of all loans extended by Cyprus' banks were NPLs.

Cyprus' banks were and are locked into a form of continuous bailout in this mode with rolling lines of credit from CBC and the other Eurozone central banks, until every now and again a bank does go down, as Cyprus CoOperative Bank did, in which case another Cyprus bank (in that case Hellenic) was lined up to acquire its deposits and its Performing loans, and the Cyprus taxpayer was awarded the NPLs.

CBC relayed that the implementation of international financial reporting standard (IFRS) 9 in January 2018 had led to an increase in banks' NPLs, but now a new classification methodology was in place which 'provides for a minimum 12-month probation period for restructured facilities'.

In other words when an NPL has been 'restructured', it returns to 'Performing' status and cannot fall back into NPLs whatever happens for a year. That means that Cyprus' banks could enjoy a reduction in NPLs that would last at least a year by not enforcing the loan conditions on the borrower.

CBC's further statements reinforced this unease: 'The downward trend in NPFs (non-performing facilities) can be attributed to write-offs, increased restructurings successfully completed by the end of the observance period and reclassified as performing facilities, repayments as well as settlement of debt through swaps with immovable property that is expected to be sold with the aim of a faster cash collection'.

The point about 'immovable property' is that any hope of the loan being repaid via the borrower's cashflow is replaced by reliance on mortgage security. The loan can then be classified back into 'Performing' status. CBC admitted that loan restructurings did involve write-offs but added, emolliently, that the write-offs were 'amounts that already form part of credit institutions' loan loss provisions,' which fell by €2.2 billion in a month to €9.7 billion in March.

It may well be that Cyprus' banks had either built up a Loan Loss Provision on the liability side of their balance sheets to account for the impairment of the value of these loans on the Asset side, or that they had written off part of the value of the asset by taking a charge through the Profit&Loss Account, and were now valuing the loans at a 'carrying value' below face value.

It seems far-fetched to imagine that Cyprus' banks could afford to put new write-offs through their Profit&Loss Account, or that their loan loss provisions were already adequate to cushion the realization of losses on the 43% of their loan book that had gone bad. It is more plausible that the main factors that had reduced NPLs were restructurings involving forbearance techniques and the pledging of mortgage security of whatever quality.

The factor that normally reduces NPLs is not even mentioned: the ability of borrowers to meet their commitments when they could not do so before.

NPLs in the Cyprus banking system were reduced thanks to accounting policies and the watering-down of borrowers' commitments, not thanks to a recovery of the economy or of the creditworthiness of borrowers.

That this should have been recorded as some form of success is measure of the depth of the difficulties in which the Cyprus banking system remained mired. As it is there are now two main banks – Hellenic and Bank of Cyprus – and neither has been put into resolution. These two banks must now survive: they have been used in the past to acquire failed banks until, at this point, these are the sole remaining banks of substance. CBC has just one card it can still play: merge them.

---

[73] https://cyprus-mail.com/2018/07/29/shocked-by-co-ops-fate-other-banks-may-now-act/ accessed on 31 May 2022

The securitization template used in Greece and Cyprus was pioneered in Italy[74] and used, inter alia, by Intesa SanPaolo when it agreed to rescue two domestic banks as an alternative to their having to be put into resolution.[75]

It is in relation to Italy that we will go into the greatest depth, examining securitization as one of the ways in which Unicredit S.p.A. was kept afloat.

Typical transaction structure using tranching, and associated terms

Under a typical structure a bank is holding a portfolio of defaulted loans in its books and at a certain 'carrying value'.

The bank then sells the portfolio off to a special-purpose securitization company (SPC). The SPC has scarcely any equity. To raise the money to buy the portfolio, the SPC issues three or four tranches of bonds, with the largest one being also the most senior one in order of priority. If the collections from the portfolio are adequate, each tranche will be paid its interest, but it is the most senior tranche that is paid down first.[76]

The financing template is similar to an InvestEU one.

A typical deal with three tranches would have outline terms as follows:

Tranche	Ranking	Percentage	Interest	Repayment
A	Senior	85%	3-month Euribor plus ¼%	As soon as collections allow
B	Mezzanine	12%	3-month Euribor plus 8%	Once collections allow and Tranche A has been fully repaid
C	Junior	3%	3-month Euribor plus 10%	30 years after issuance and if collections allow it

Table 4.5: typical tranching of a securitization financing and associated interest margins

It is the Mezzanine tranche that is of the highest risk: it is much larger than the Junior tranche, meaning that a loss has a high likelihood of occurring and a high impact if it does.

The size of the B and C tranches – acting as second- and first-loss cushions respectively - should allow the A tranche to achieve public credit ratings of its own. In the Italian scheme under a law known as the 'GACS', the Republic of Italy will add its guarantee to the A tranche (but never to the B or C tranches) if certain conditions are met.

The terms of the A tranche when issued will include 'Guarantee pending', as the bonds must first be issued and go through the public rating process before they become eligible for the Republic guarantee. They must receive an 'Investment Grade' rating from two of the four agencies recognized by the EU as a precondition of the Republic guarantee being issued.

---

[74] It was used notably by Intesa SanPaolo during its takeover of Veneto Banca and Banca Popolare di Vicenza after the ECB/SSM determined that these two regional banks were unsound – https://www.bankingsupervision.europa.eu/press/pr/date/2017/html/ssm.pr170623.en.html, accessed on 22.10.19

[75] The Republic of Italy agreed to provide €12 billion of guarantees to assist with securitisation of NPLs - see "Italy: liquidation of Veneto Banca and Banca Popolare di Vicenza", by BNPParibas

[76] It is worth noting as an aside that the primary destination of the collections made on NPLs is the set of lawyers and agents appointing to press and realise the unpaid claims. An examination of a ratings update on Unicredit's Fino 1 securitisation indicated that a portfolio sold off by the bank for €770 million was planned to yield €1.6 billion, but that almost €400 million of this amount was not needed to pay the principal and interest on the €770 million borrowed, but rather to realise to the unpaid claims.

Unicredit's 'Project Fino'

One of the highest-profile users of NPL securitization has been Unicredit, for example in the context of a project known as 'Fino' executed at the same time as it undertook a major rights issue in early 2017, and as it executed a project called 'Porto'. 'Fino' was the securitization of NPLs whilst 'Porto' was the write-down in the carrying value of the NPLs that Unicredit was planning to retain.

'Fino' was aggressive and public, because the survival of a bank was involved that was important both in Italy, in many Central and Eastern European countries, and globally. Unicredit had acquired both Hypovereinsbank of Germany and Creditanstalt-Bankverein of Austria, both of which invested heavily in Central and Eastern European countries post-1989. Unicredit is 'systemically-important' to the national financial environment in Germany and Austria as well as in Italy, and is known there as an 'Other systemically-important institution' or O-SII. On top of this the global Financial Stability Board includes Unicredit as a globally systemically-important financial institution, or GSIFI.[77]

These statuses impose on the bank an obligation to maintain a CET1 Ratio that is higher than is incumbent upon banks that are not seen as systemically-important.[78]

Project Fino within the context of the sanitization of Unicredit

In mid-2016 the CEO of Unicredit Group, Jean-Pierre Mustier, made it known that radical action was needed to repair the bank's balance sheet and particularly that of the Italian bank, Unicredit S.p.A..

Appendix 1 goes into more detail about the scope of the plan, the rights issue associated with it, and the development of Unicredit's capital through the process.

We are focusing here on Unicredit's substantial NPLs, concentrated in the Italian bank and group parent, and the two projects to sanitize this bank:
1. Project Fino: a substantial block of NPLs on the books of Unicredit S.p.A. would be sold off into a 'market-based securitization'
2. Project Porto: the carrying value of the residual NPLs left on the books of Unicredit S.p.A. would be substantially written down

Unicredit proposed to make €12.2 billion of provisions to 'improve the quality of its assets', which meant writing off a portion of their value. €8.1 billion was to be devoted to the 'Porto' and 'Fino' projects and the remaining €4.1 billion to right-valuing other assets.

The actions were carried through by March 2017 with a number of provisos as pointed out in our paper of the time entitled 'The recapitalisation of Unicredit S.p.A.: an examination of (i) the accounting of its 13-for-5 rights issue (ii) its level of provisioning for Bad and Doubtful Debts and (iii) the accounting of its investments in its banking subsidiaries and sub-subsidiaries'.[79]

Unicredit's NPLs before 'Fino' and 'Porto'

Unicredit S.p.A.'s loan loss figures were quite confusing in the detail as they referred at length to adjustments made thanks to policy notes from the European and Italian banking supervisors.

Nonetheless the chart on p. 30 of the 2015 Unconsolidated Annual Report of Unicredit S.p.A. was enlightening, and it is included as Figure 4.4.

---

[77] https://www.fsb.org/2021/11/2021-list-of-global-systemically-important-banks-g-sibs/
[78] There is an anomaly in the system for determining the correct CET1 Ratio because, where a bank is an O-SII in several countries, it falls to the national regulators to determine the incremental CET1 percentage for the subsidiary bank in their country, and it is both possible that this may not be the same in all countries, and that it may be higher than the Financial Stability Board determines for the group. The Financial Stability Board has categorized Unicredit as a Tier 1 GSIFI requiring a CET1 ratio higher by an extra 1%: this is well within the range of what national regulators might impose on an O-SII on a subsidiary bank. This issue is discussed at greater length in 'Managing Euro Risk' Annex 4 'EBA Stress Tests' pp. 117-26 and Annex 5 'ECB Supervoisory Report and Evaluation Process (SREP) 2019 Outcome' pp. 127-9.
[79] Available through Research Papers on www.lyddonconsulting.com

22.61% of all loans were on NPL status, a level far in excess of the bank's capital. 14.88% of all loans were classified as 'Bad Exposures'. 'Bad Exposures' had been written down to a 'carrying value' of 37.49%. 'Unlikely to pay' had only been written down to a 'carrying value' of 66.5%, which indicated they were likely, rather than unlikely, to pay. The write-down on 'Unlikely to pay' was only 3.83% higher than on 'Past Due and Non-Performing'.

In terms of gradation of seriousness, the author's experience would indicate that the levels of write-down were not prudent levels, and a comparison is given in Figure 4.5.

By these measures of the gravity of the situation, the loans were under-provisioned in the 2015 Annual Report by €16.4 billion. These figures would be improved by €12.2 billion through the extra 'coverage' afforded by the 'Porto' and 'Fino' projects as long as the other €4.1 billion of provisions were also devoted for this purpose. That would have reduced the under-provisioning to €4.2 billion. If the other €4.1 billion provisions were not devoted to reducing the 'carrying value' of NPLs, then the under-provisioning would remain at €8.3 billion.

Substance of the 'Fino' transaction and application of provisions

The 'Fino Project' involved Unicredit selling off a certain face value of loans to special-purpose companies, which in turn would issue bonds to finance the purchase. The special-purpose companies would try to make a recovery on the loans so as to meet the debt service on the bonds. Whether they did or not should have no financial impact on Unicredit.

The restructuring plan acknowledged that the write-downs of €29.1 billion on NPLs as a whole up to late 2016 had not been adequate to write the loans down far enough (i) for their 'carrying value' to equate to the likely recovery on the loans Unicredit retained under 'Porto', and (ii) for the investors to have been willing to take the ones Unicredit wished to sell under 'Fino'.

A further write-down of at least €8.1 billion was needed in order to close up those two gaps between the 'carrying value' of the loans in Unicredit's books and their recoverable value: Unicredit would attempt to recover the 'Porto' loans itself, and it would act as collecting agent to recover the 'Fino' loans for the benefit of the investors who put up the finance to buy them.

We do know that €4.0 billion of the €8.1 billion was eventually devoted to 'Fino', and the remaining €4.1 billion to 'Porto'. We do not know explicitly how the €8.1 billion was distributed across the 'Bad exposures' and 'Unlikely to pay' categories of NPL. Nor do we know how the residual €4.1 billion of the €12.2 billion of provisions was allocated.

However we can make certain presumptions:
- All the 'Bad exposures' were written down and substantially;
- As the 'Fino' portfolio was being sold off into a structure that included third-party financiers, the portfolio had to be written down to a 'market-tested' level, and this was expected to be in the range of 10% of nominal value;
- On the other hand the papers that later emerged on 'Fino' infer that the value agreed by the third-party financiers was 13% of nominal value, or at least for a portion of the portfolio, and that the nominal value of the 'Fino' portfolio was €17.7 billion;
- If this is the case, the 'Fino' provision of €4.0 billion, being 22.6% of the nominal, reduced the 'carrying value' of the portfolio from 35.6% of nominal to 13%, or from €6.3 billion to €2.3 billion;
- This means that the 'Fino' portfolio was being held, prior to the application of the provision, with a write-down of 64.5%, as opposed to the average for 'Bad exposures' of 62.51%;
- The 'Fino' portfolio was thus on average worse in quality than the average of 'Bad exposures'.

Details of the Fino transaction

The 'Fino' securitization transaction involved an SPC being established to buy the 'Fino' portfolio of nominal value €17.7 billion for 13% of that, or €2.3 billion.

The SPC itself will have been thinly capitalized. Unicredit would continue to act as the SPC's agent to discharge some of the work needed to make a recovery on the loans, but other agents would be employed by the SPC, for undertaking legal proceedings against delinquent borrowers, for attaching and selling collateral, and for managing the monies recovered from these actions and applying them to meet the claims of the financiers who have put up the €2.3 billion.

We have an extensive paper on the transaction entitled 'Project FINO: defining a framework to understand market prices and analyzing the main drivers', dated June 2017 from the Banca d'Italia, we have a rating report dated 23 November 2017 from Moody's Investors Service, and we have two ratings bulletins, one from Moody's and one from DBRS, these both being amongst the group of public credit rating agencies approved by the EU.[80]

The oddity is that only one SPC is in the public domain, under the name of 'Fino 1 Securitization S.r.l'. It only took on a portion of the 'Fino' portfolio. This infers that there may have been an intermediary SPC that took on the entire portfolio, and then parceled off a portion of it to this one, retaining other parcels to sell off to a 'Fino 2 Securitization S.r.l' or a 'Fino 3 Securitization S.r.l', were they to be launched, which they have not been.

We have a ratings bulleting from Moody's for the debts of Fino 1 Securitization S.r.l:

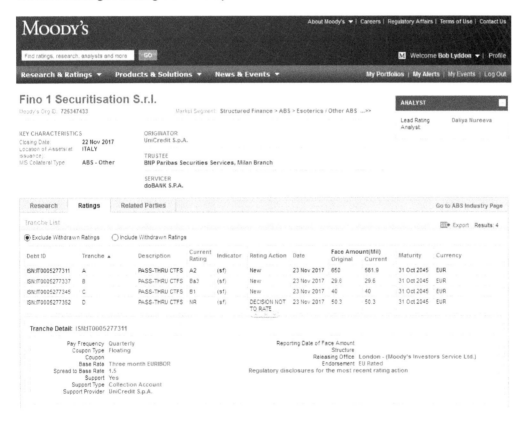

Table 4.6: Moody's ratings bulletin on Fino 1 Securitization S.r.l

---

[80] The other regulated agencies are Fitch Ratings and Standard and Poor's Global Ratings, normally abbreviated to S&P Global Ratings or simply S&P

We also have a ratings bulleting from DBRS for the debts of Fino 1 Securitization S.r.l:

Table 4.7: DRBS ratings bulletin on Fino 1 Securitization S.r.l

The bulletins confirm the expectation that there would be subsequent 'Fino' transactions. The first transaction had its SPC issue several tranches of bonds in a typical arrangement as follows:

Tranche name	Tranche amount	DBRS rating	Moody's rating	Moody's banding	Moody's credit risk
A	€650.0 million	BBB (high)	A2	Investment	Low
B	€29.6 million	BB (high)	Ba3	Speculative	Substantial
C	€40.0 million	BB	B1	Speculative	High
D	€50.3 million	Not mentioned	Not rated	n/a	n/a
	€769.9 million				

Table 4.8: tranching arrangement in Fino 1 securitization

How the tranching operates

All the bonds are on a floating interest rate with the base rate being re-set quarterly, and a pre-specified margin added on, in order to determine the interest applicable to each tranche for the next-following period. The holders of tranche A receive the lowest rate, the holders of tranche D the highest. Monies coming in are applied firstly to meet the SPC's costs in making the recovery, and the residue is allocated to each tranche so as to meet delay interest first, then normal interest, then principal. The tranche-holders should not incur any costs or charges that they can reclaim from the SPC: it is the SPC that incurs these.

The principles at work will be familiar ones, except that in this case the size of the A tranche is 84.4% of the entire financing, and that 'Fino 1' refinances only 33.5% of the cost of the 'Fino' portfolio (€769.9 million out of €2.3 billion), whilst the nominal value of the NPLs behind 'Fino 1' is 30.5% of the whole (€5.4 billion out of €17.7 billion).

On the face of it the refinancing of 'Fino 1' has realized a higher ratio of written-down value/nominal value than Unicredit achieved in selling the entire 'Fino' portfolio: 14.3% compared to 13%. However 'Fino 1' has an extra tranche of €50.3 million, which acts like an equity cushion in the SPC. Its impact vis a vis the holders of the Tranche A, B and C bonds is to provide them with an extra loss cushion. Its presence might indicate that these investors believed the 'Fino' portfolio was over-valued at 14.3% of nominal, so the insertion of this extra €50.3 million cushion within 'Fino 1' has the same effect on the other tranche holders as a reduction in the written-down value/nominal value back to 13.3%, more or less the same as on the original sale out of Unicredit.

The Moody's rating report states that 'Fino 1' is supported by €5.4 billion nominal of NPLs, of which the total of tranches A, B and C of €719.6 million represents 13.3%.

Who owns the tranches and where the Republic of Italy guarantee fits in

The question, then, is who the holders of these other tranches are. Page 4 of the Banca d'Italia paper states that 'FINO involves a disposal to third party investors', but this is only part of the story. Venture capital and hedge funds were regularly discussed in the press as suppliers of the Tranche B and C financings – the mezzanine and junior tranches totaling €69.6 million.

The essence of the scheme from the point of view of the Republic of Italy is that they would add their guarantee to the A tranche as long as it obtained Investment Grade ratings from two of the four regulated credit agencies. It would gain these ratings on the strength (i) of the portfolio of NPLs; and (ii) of the size of the loss-cushions represented by the other tranches. It could be that it was the combination of the criteria of the Republic of Italy and of the rating agencies that caused the need for Tranche D to be inserted.

As it was the Tranche A benefited from an explicit Investment Grade rating of A2 from Moody's. DBRS gave the tranche a rating of 'BBB (high)' on what it would term a 'pass-through instrument', meaning that it is at the superior end of 'adequate quality'.[81] This rating would appear to equate to BBB+ from S&P and thus to have been rated Investment Grade, triggering the addition of the Republic's guarantee. The limit of Investment Grade is BBB- on the S&P scale and Baa3 on Moody's.

For ease of reference we have used the S&P scale to compare the ratings that the 'Fino' tranches achieved from DBRS and Moody's:

Tranche name	Tranche amount	DBRS rating	S&P equivalent	Moody's rating	S&P equivalent
A	€650.0 million	BBB (high)	BBB+	A2	A
B	€29.6 million	BB (high)	BB+	Ba3	BB-
C	€40.0 million	BB	BB	B1	B+
D	€50.3 million	Not mentioned	Not rated	Not rated	n/a
	€769.9 million				

Table 4.9: S&P equivalents to the ratings assigned by Moody's and DBRS on Fino 1 tranches

The notable points are:
- DBRS rated the A tranche two notches below Moody's;
- DBRS rated the B tranche two notches above Moody's;
- DBRS rated the C tranche two notches above Moody's.

However, the addition of the Republic of Italy guarantee would not have improved the bond's rating by either DBRS or Moody's, given that Italy is rated Baa3 by Moody's and BBB by S&P. Was the guarantee pointless? What was going on?

---

[81] DBRS Rating Scale For Pass Through Instruments 01apr21

What is the objective of the Republic of Italy guarantee

The answer lies in the fact that Unicredit bought the A tranche, and indeed the D tranche, and in fact owned 49% of the SPC as well. Unicredit was forced to insert the extra loss cushion in the form of the D tranche in order to induce the investors in the B and C tranches to commit, and in order to obtain the Investment Grade ratings and Republic of Italy guarantee on the A tranche.

Unicredit's owning the A and D tranches and 49% of the SPC defy the definition of 'Fino 1' as a sale to third-party investors. The deal should have failed the tests of deconsolidation from Unicredit's balance sheet. However, these tests were measured by Italian banking regulators where the alternative was a resolution in which depositors would have been paid from the Deposit Insurance Scheme, and the Republic of Italy would have had to issue new debt itself, thereby becoming the senior creditor in the resolved bank.

Knowing that Unicredit's NPLs were both extensive and overvalued, the Italian state would have found itself in the position described elsewhere in the book: owning a resolved bank whose assets were worth less than they had paid out to depositors, as well as having added tens of billions of euro to their 'General government gross debt'.

Instead it was deemed expedient to disguise the problem in securitizations that can only be described as 'market-based' to the very limited extent that (i) they involve public credit rating agencies and (ii) that venture capital and hedge funds have contributed about 10% of the funding (the B and C tranches).

Impact on Unicredit: substantially the same asset but tying up much less Common Equity Tier 1

The main effect is a 'round trip': Unicredit manages to deconsolidate €2.3 billion nominal of NPLs into a structure of which it is the main financier. In return it receives a note guaranteed by the Republic of Italy which, despite its carrying a rating towards the low end of Investment Grade and one worse than the A tranche bonds merit without it, can be risk-weighted at 0% in Unicredit's books because it counts as sovereign risk. Unicredit also has to take on the D tranche and that is unrated and relatively high risk.

This is the legerdemain of the 'Fino' transaction, and of the Italian NPL securitization industry as a whole. The selling bank has to write the NPLs down to their 'market-based' carrying value of 10-15% before they are sold to an SPC. These NPLs should have been risk-weighted at a minimum of 400% through the bank's IRB model, reflecting a high risk of loss. €1 billion of carrying value would translate into a risk-weighted value of €4 billion. The bank would need to hold CET1 of 8% of that figure as a GSIFI: €1 billion of carrying value has to be supported by Unicredit with €320 million of CET1, reflecting the realistic chance of the bank losing 33% of the carrying value.

€1 billion nominal of Tranche A bonds needs no CET1 at all to support it. Unicredit, under 'Fino 1', needed to take on €50.3 million of Tranche D bonds, in a relationship of 1:13 to Tranche A. This means it would hold €77 million nominal of Tranche D bonds for every €1 billion nominal of Tranche A bonds. As Tranche D bonds represent high risk, they might well be risk-weighted at 400%, and assigned a risk-weighted value of €308 million, thus needing to be supported with 8% CET1 or €24.6 million.

Prior to 'Fino' Unicredit had €320 million of CET1 tied up by these NPLs for every €1 billion of carrying value. So, on a carrying value of €2.3 billion, it had CET1 of €736 million tied up. After 'Fino' it would have €24.6 million tied up by Tranche D and none tied up by Tranche A. 'Fino' freed up €711.4 million of scarce CET1.

That is a tremendous outcome for the bank but also for the Republic of Italy: banks recapitalized via a sleight of hand without impacting 'General government gross debt'.

'Fino' project not fully completed

The only problem is that there has been no 'Fino 2' or 'Fino 3', or at least no bonds issued and rated by Moody's and DBRS in the way they were for 'Fino 1'. Unicredit announced that 'Fino' as a whole had been completed, but does that mean that Unicredit failed to obtain ratings for it, or that it could not line up investors for the B and C tranches, and so it failed to obtain the Republic of Italy guarantee? We do not know.

Nevertheless the switching of an asset that was attracting a high risk-weighting for one attracting a 0% risk-weighting ranks as an outrageous example of arbitraging the BIS rules.

Logic flaws in the credit ratings

It is absurd and should not be permitted that the gaming of the regulatory regime described earlier should occur. Defaulted loans consuming considerable CET1 are repackaged, with the selling bank then buying back a majority of the financing instruments issued by the securitization SPC, but being able to assign almost no CET1 behind these instruments thanks to the Republic guarantee, even though the Republic is rated BBB.

It is a further logic flaw that it can be possible for any bonds backed by defaulted loans to obtain an Investment Grade rating on their own account, when it is a matter of speculation whether there will be any collections on the underlying loans. The A tranche should be rated as BB+ - the highest notch in Speculative Grade – as an absolute maximum, with the more junior tranches being assigned lower ratings based on the subsidiarity of their claims to the A tranche. This question should be put to the credit rating agencies. The according of such ratings is of great benefit to the bank, and to the member state in which the bank is located, as it spares the member state an expensive intervention. Whether the ratings genuinely represent the application of absolute and impartial standards is another matter.

Nevertheless, setting aside these logic flaws as we must, the scheme has been used in significant size and these 'principles' have been socialized and accepted as normal terms-of-trade in the business of massaging NPLs off the balance sheets of Eurozone banks.

Scope Ratings and Italy

Scope Ratings issued an update in November 2020 of all the Italian NPL-based bonds where they themselves had issued ratings.[82] This is not necessarily the entire market but the update's Appendix gives a figure of €76 billion for the gross book value of all the securitization deals that Scope have rated. They have not issued a summary of the current outstanding amount of all the tranches to which the Republic of Italy has attached its guarantee, and nor has any other source.

Summary on NPLs - supposedly massaged away by securitization and other techniques

The handling of NPLs was a major topic in between the Eurozone debt crisis and the onset of the Pandemic. The problem has been massaged away from view via a combination of five techniques:
- Precluding that a loan be classed as an NPL until a debt service payment is 90 days past due, rather than as soon as a debt service payment is missed;
- 'Restructuring' and 'Forbearance' actions that return an NPL to 'Performing' status, and also return a 'Past due' loan to 'Performing' status before it is ever classed as 'Past due and non-performing' and therefore as an NPL;[83]
- The progressive writing-down of the carrying value in the bank's books, limited by the amount of capital that the bank has and the consequential need for the bank not to fall below the threshold for its minimum regulatory capital;
- Securitization, based on the bank swapping NPLs for sovereign-guaranteed bonds which, thanks to an anomaly that any EU sovereign obligation is 0% risk-weighted regardless of the sovereign's public credit rating, releases the bank from holding regulatory capital against what is tantamount to the same asset;
- Having the banks implement a very aggressive methodology for assessing the risks of losses on their portfolio of business, known as Advanced IRB, and applying this both to Performing loans and to the 'carrying value' of NPLs (see below).

---

[82] Scope Ratings_Italian NPL securitisation monthly collections update_2020 Nov
[83] It must be regarded as improbable that a loan which had already gone through 'Past due and non-performing' status and into 'Unlikely to pay' could be brought back to 'Performing' via 'Restructuring' or 'Forbearance'; rather it is probably that the loan only goes into 'Unlikely to pay' when these techniques have either been mooted or tried, and been found impractical or have failed in that instance

We will see whether the NPL issue re-emerges after the Pandemic. The fact that Project Hercules has had to be re-launched in Greece indicates that it may do. On the one hand the economic situation is unfavorable; on the other hand the ECB's low interest rate policy has triggered inflation in the value of real estate. This could deliver a windfall to banks trying to sell real estate security in order to make recoveries on NPLs.

4.5 Basel Internal-Ratings Based methodologies (IRB)

The last in our list of official responses to the Eurozone debt crisis is the imposition on banks of the BIS regulatory capital regime in a paradoxical manner: demanding impressive capital ratios based on restrictive definitions of the numerator, whilst permitting lax standards to be applied in determining the ratio's denominator.

The numerator is the bank's capital, the denominator is its calculation of Risk-Weighted Assets, calculated through its own IRB methodology.

The lower the denominator, the more resilient the bank appears. The regime has been reverse-engineered so as to accept the banks' pre-existing, fixed and low amount of capital as the numerator, and invent a methodology to compress banks' high, expanding and risk-laden volumes of business into a small denominator.

How the IRB regime works

Although we have alluded to this several times before, it is worth repeating the key elements in the regime.

The base documents are issued by the Bank for International Settlements, or BIS, in Basel: the shareholders in this bank are the world's central banks, and it is through the BIS that the central banks have agreed and promulgated the regime, which is often referred to as the Basel Accords. There have been four versions so far, but the currently-implemented one is Basel 3. Albeit that the official go-live deadline in the EU is 2025, major banks are already operating in line with its requirements, at least in the area of the IRB regime, since it is so favorable to them.[84]

The Basel versions are incremental attempts to capture all the types of risk-bearing business that banks may engage in, and to assign a quotient of capital that the bank must have against each piece of business, whether it sits on its balance sheet (like a loan), or off its balance sheet (like a guarantee), or is an operational piece of business that is open to mistakes and consequent operational losses (like processing payments).

The Basel Accords and sovereign risk

'Sovereign risk' is regarded as the lowest possible credit risk in a particular country because it entails dealing with the entity that has the strongest revenue-raising powers and on the widest number of citizens and businesses.

'Sovereign risk' acts as the baseline for the Basel Accords. Where the 'sovereign' involved is a member of the OECD, Basel treats business with it as risk-free, and meriting a 0% risk-weighting.

'Sovereign risk' lending is thus attractive to banks from the risk point of view, but can pose challenges when it comes to revenues. The yields on the 'sovereign risk' assets of a given country would normally be lower than the cost of bank deposits. A bank could not borrow in the interbank market, invest in 'sovereign risk' assets and expect to make a profit. If, however, a bank was able to make an interest margin on a transaction that involved taking 'sovereign risk', the transaction would appear to be highly profitable. A Risk-Adjusted Return on Capital model would assess the risk of loss as low, assign a very small amount of capital to support the transaction, so any interest margin, however thin, would deliver a high Return on Capital.

The section near the start of the book gives an example of a transaction from the early 1980s. This transaction was genuinely profitable (until Nigeria defaulted). It incorporated sovereign risk in two forms: a loan to the Nigerian government with partial credit insurance from the Dutch government.

---

[84] https://finadium.com/european-commission-releases-basel-iii-package-for-go-live-in-2025/ accessed on 2 June 2022

The section also describes how the definition of sovereign risk links to a currency, and how the definition of sovereign risk has been challenged by governments like Mexico – which defaulted but only on its foreign currency obligations – and Greece – which defaulted on its obligations in its domestic currency the euro of which it was not sole user and over which it did not holds the levers of sovereign control.

The Basel Accords have taken some note of the different risk of default by a government on its foreign currency obligations compared to ones in its domestic currency, but they have not touched the issue of the difference between a sovereign domestic currency (like the USD or GBP) and a quasi-sovereign one, like the euro, over which none of its user countries holds the levers of sovereign control.

The trajectory of the Basel Accords has gone instead into other areas, still important but leaving this issue unresolved.

How much capital is needed and what does the capital consists of

The quotient of capital is commonly understood to sit within a range of 8-10% of the bank's Risk-Weighted Assets (RWAs), RWAs being the denominator in all the capital ratios. This 8-10% refers to the strongest type of capital – Common Equity Tier 1. Confusion is bound to arise because there are three ratios and because they vary from one bank to another.

Three ratios are calculated:
- Common Equity Tier 1 ratio
- Tier 1 capital ratio
- Total capital ratio

The regulatory thresholds applied to an individual bank will appear as a progression such as:
- Common Equity Tier 1 ratio – 7.5%
- Tier 1 capital ratio – 8.5%
- Total capital ratio – 10.5%

The numerators of the three ratios progressively add different categories of capital:
- Common Equity Tier 1
- Common Equity Tier 1 plus 'other Tier 1 capital'
- Common Equity Tier 1 plus 'other Tier 1 capital' plus Tier 2 capital

These different types of capital need to be considered like rock strata, with the very strongest at the base - Common Equity Tier 1 – with a strong layer directly above it – 'other Tier 1 capital' – and a slightly less strong layer above that – Tier 2 capital.

The difference between these different types of capital is a very big subject in itself, and it is not the intention to critique it in detail but rather to simplify and bring out the main points.

These main points are arithmetical:
      a.   how is the range of the capital between 8-10% arrived at?
      b.   what balance sheet postings can be counted within each type of capital?
      c.   what is the cost of the capital?
      d.   how is the denominator of the ratio - Risk-Weighted Assets or 'RWAs' - arrived at?

The range of the capital

The BIS explains the requirement for capital, but there is a difference of general understanding of whether a range of 8-10% means a variation in the Common Equity Tier 1 ratio between different banks, or refers to the progression of the different ratios at the same bank.

The version used in this book is the former: we concentrate on the Common Equity Tier 1 ratio and show how it differs between different banks. It differs because there is a common base but then variable additional buffers on top.

The purpose of capital is to absorb losses, before the bank's liabilities exceed its assets and it is bankrupt. The buffers are also referred to as 'loss absorption buffers' and 'loss absorption cushions'. The strong base must be held as Common Equity Tier 1 (CET1) and are an accumulation of:

- A minimum capital requirement of 4.5% of RWAs;[85]
- An obligatory Capital Conservation Buffer of 2.5% of RWAs;[86]
- Meaning an obligatory, common minimum base of 7% of RWAs;
- With premia as applicable for:
  - The Countercyclical Buffer, an extra percentage of RWAs imposed by a banking regulator across all the banks it supervises from time to time in phases of rapid credit growth;
  - The Globally Systemically Important Financial Institution premium of between 1% for a Tier 1 GSIFI and 2½% for a Tier 4 GSIFI;[87]
  - The Other Systemically Important Institution premium, subject to an offset of this O-SII premium against the GSIFI premium.[88]

Make-up of the capital of Monte dei Paschi di Siena Group

As an illustration, Monte dei Paschi di Siena Group, on p. 59 of its Consolidated Interim Report as at 31 March 2021, gives a statement of the requirements incumbent upon it.[89] We can overlook the references to Pillar 1 and Pillar 2, which are expressions used in the BIS documentation but which add little to understanding. The bank states that it has been required to maintain the following ratios as a minimum:

- CET1 Ratio of 8.74%;
- Tier 1 Capital Ratio of 10.75%;
- Total Capital Ratio of 13.44%.

These ratios are noted as including:

- The Capital Conservation Buffer of 2.5%;
- A Countercyclical Buffer of 0.19%;
- An O-SII premium of 0.002%.

It appears that the banking regulator has added a discretionary 1.55% of CET1 above the obligatory, common minimum base of 7%: 8.55% plus the Countercyclical Buffer of 0.19% adds up to 8.74%. The bank is not a GSIFI and merits a miniscule premium for its status as an O-SII, yet its target of 8.55% excluding the Countercyclical Buffer is on a level with a GSIFI.

The banking regulator is also, in effect, ordering the bank to hold another 2% of 'Other Tier 1 capital' and, on top of that, a further 2.7% of Tier 2 capital. In theory the additional 'Other Tier 1 capital' could be in the form of CET1, and the additional Tier 2 capital could also be in the form of CET1 or 'Other Tier 1 capital'. In practice this is unrealistic since it is CET1 that is in such short supply.

The bank's 'Other Tier 1 capital' and its 'Tier 2' capital will be in the form of certain types of reserves, and of interest-bearing bonds which have 'capital-like' attributes.

Justification of the simplification that banks require capital of 8-10% of their Risk-Weighted Assets

The reader will additionally note that the bank's Tier 1 Ratio and the Total Capital Ratio are higher than the range of 8-10% that has frequently been used in this book. The reason is that both (i) 'other Tier 1 capital' that is not Common Equity Tier 1, and (ii) Tier 2 capital, are a less strong base. This point comes over more clearly in the definitions below. From our experience of how banks evaluate one another's strength, we conclude that bankers appreciate the lower reliability of types of capital beyond CET1, and that they focus on the CET1 Ratio as the main token of a bank's strength: CET1 is an amount of money that is definitely equity and never a form of debt, and is not subject to arbitrary decision-making as applies to something like a Revaluation Reserve.

---

[85] https://www.federalreserve.gov/publications/large-bank-capital-requirements-20210805.htm accessed on 2 June 2022
[86] https://www.bis.org/fsi/fsisummaries/b3_capital.htm accessed on 4 June 2022
[87] There is only 1 Tier 4 GSIFI – JPMorgan Chase – and Tier 5 is empty; Tier 5 would attract an extra 3½%
[88] See Annex 4 of 'Managing Euro Risk' pp. 117-126 for an explanation of the interplay between the statuses of GSIFI and O-SII
[89] Monte dei Paschi di Siena Group - Consolidated Interim Report - as at 31 March 2021

In addition a bank's target CET1 Ratio includes all of its buffers added at the discretion of financial regulators. The common minimum CET1 is 7%, and this will be increased, where applied, by (i) a GSIFI buffer of 1-2.5%, (ii) an O-SII buffer, and (iii) a Countercyclical Buffer of 0.1-1% from time to time (it being assumed that this buffer, specified by a national banking regulator, would only apply to a portion of a GSIFI).[90]

For these reasons we believe that the range 8-10% accords with how the financial market assesses banks, and reflects that few significant banks will not at all times be subject to a buffer that is either counter-cyclical or due to the bank being systemically important (either in one or a small number of countries, or globally).

Concentrating on CET1 inoculates against discretion applied by the bank, its auditors and financial regulators.

In the case of Monte dei Paschi one must be forgiven for taking the view that whatever the bank considers it has as 'other Tier 1 capital' beyond its CET1, or as Tier 2 capital, is open to considerable skepticism, even if its auditors have signed their accounts and even if banking regulators have not objected to them.

This simplified view also serves to counteract the confusion introduced by the different types of capital referred to and the different ratios applicable to them.

Balance sheet postings that count within these different measures of 'capital'

These definitions set out the balance sheet postings that count within these different measures of 'capital' – the denominators of the three ratios. The measures represent a hierarchy of quality of capital, with CET1 being at the top.

Investopedia defines 'Common Equity Tier 1' (CET1) as comprising 'a bank's core capital and includes common shares, stock surpluses resulting from the issue of common shares, retained earnings, common shares issued by subsidiaries and held by third parties, and accumulated other comprehensive income (AOCI)'.[91]

Investopedia defines 'other Tier 1' capital as 'instruments that are not common equity but are eligible for inclusion in this tier. An example … is a contingent convertible or hybrid security, which has a perpetual term and can be converted into equity when a trigger event occurs'.

Investopedia defines Tier 2 capital as second or supplementary layer of a bank's capital and is composed of items such as revaluation reserves, hybrid instruments, and subordinated term debt.[92]

Two items deserve special mention. Revaluation reserves only sit in Tier 2 capital, even though they might be included in a statement of 'Capital and reserves', which might be thought to be the same as CET1. Accumulated other comprehensive income' will not include unappropriated profit: a year's profits should eventually be counted within CET1, but not before the accounts have been audited and adopted through the bank's governance process.

Investopedia quotes 'hybrid securities/instruments' as potentially sitting in either 'other Tier 1' or Tier 2 capital, but not in CET1. This gives an inkling of the contentious issues around types of financial instrument that are not deposits or senior debt, and which would sit below them in seniority but above share capital and Profit&Loss reserves. They are instruments that attract a premium interest margin over a base rate, but which are subordinated and/or might be convertible into shares in certain circumstances.

The attraction for the bank of such instruments is that the interest rate on them is linked to the same base rate – such as LIBOR historically – as many of the bank's assets are linked to.[93] This facilitates Asset and Liability Management because it moderates any mismatch between the interest basis of the two. The interest margin is higher than on deposits and senior debt, but the all-in cost is viewed as being lower than capital.

---

[90] We have skated over how an O-SII buffer is dealt with when the bank in question is part of a international group to which a GSIFI buffer applies

[91] https://www.investopedia.com/terms/c/common-equity-tier-1-cet1.asp accessed on 2 June 2022

[92] https://www.investopedia.com/terms/t/tier2capital.asp accessed on 2 June 2022

[93] LIBOR – London Interbank Offered Rate; the interest rate at which prime banks in the London market would offer deposits to one another in the standard lot size for the currency for 1, 2, 3 or 6 month maturities in unstressed market conditions and during normal business hours

Banking regulators, however, have brought into question whether such instruments can be counted as capital at all, and, even if they are, Basel 3 has forced such instruments into the lower categories of capital, and severely limited the proportion they can take on as a total of the bank's capital.

For the reasons laid out above, it is the CET1 Ratio that can be concentrated on, and this has to be a minimum of 7% of Risk-Weighted Assets, with fixed and variable premia added on, meaning a working minimum of 8% but rarely exceeding 10%.

How the cost of 'other Tier 1' and Tier 2 capital are dealt with

This links to the issue of the cost of capital. As 'other Tier 1 capital' and Tier 2 capital are interest-bearing instruments attracting a higher interest margin than the bank's senior liabilities, the higher margin can be dealt with by the central Finance Department simply as an uplift to a single 'cost of capital' that is charged to the internal business units that use capital.

If these instruments constitute 1% of the balance sheet, and the interest margin on them is 4% over the interbank rate, and the CET1 is 4% of the balance sheet, the additional cost of 4% on 1% of the balance sheet can be converted into a 1% additional cost on 4% of the balance sheet. The premium interest margin on 'other Tier 1' and Tier 2 capital is thus converted into a premium of 1% on the cost the CET1 capital. The 'other Tier 1' and Tier 2 capital instruments can then be considered as liabilities costing the interbank rate of interest. If the cost of CET1 is 20%, then the premium for 'other Tier 1' and Tier 2 capital raises this to 21%. This feeds through into the 'return on capital' targets communicated to internal business units for different types of business, without them having to concern themselves with either the existence or cost of 'other Tier 1 capital' or Tier 2 capital.

The 'cost of capital' issue can then be focused on the cost of Common Equity Tier 1 which, after all, is share capital and the accumulated Profit&Loss reserves that belong to shareholders.

The cost of CET1

Firstly the cost of CET1 is an annual percentage rate not an interest base rate plus a margin.

Secondly the cost of CET1 capital is viewed in line with a formula that emerged in the 1980s and has generally not been adapted since. It is that share investors – who are taking the highest risk of loss – need to receive a high return and one commensurate with their level of risk-taking. This was determined to be a return 10% higher than senior debt investors. At the time when LIBOR in US$ was in the range of 10-15%, it then became a mantra that the cost of capital was 20-25%: investors needed to earn, and the bank needed to deliver, a return in this range in order to attract capital.

Adding in the premium for 'other Tier 1' and Tier 2 capital, you have an all-in target of 21-26%.

The curious thing of course is that the 21-26% 'return on equity' target has remained an article of faith even when interest rates have fallen below 1%.

At any rate the concept has stuck that capital is expensive, so it must be carefully husbanded and only deployed where high returns are possible. The question is how does the bank assess different types of business and fix their target for the return on them. The answer is in the methodology that determines how much capital needs to be held behind different pieces of business, and what interest margin, fee, bid/offer spread or whatever delivers the 21-26% 'return on equity' on that piece of business.

How the denominator of the capital ratios - Risk-Weighted Assets – is arrived at

This is the fourth issue referred to above.

There has been a progression towards the IRB regime under Basel 3, and it has gone through the Basel 1 regime and then through Risk-Adjusted Return on Capital (RAROC) and Basel 2, which formalized RAROC.

The Basel 1 regime permitted a series of dispensations from the norm, the norm being that the bank needed to have capital of 8-10% of the nominal value of the piece of business. Dispensations to reduce the nominal value of a piece of business before the 8-10% capital quotient was applied were granted on the following:

- Where the counterparty was an OECD government – a 100% dispensation;[94]
- Where the counterparty was an OECD bank – an 80% dispensation;
- Where there was mortgage security - a 50% dispensation;
- Where the transaction was a trade Letter of Credit under which the bank had title to the goods – an 80% dispensation

Derivative transactions, being in their infancy, escaped the net completely.

Major banks, led by the US banks, found this regime commercially restrictive in that it forced them to treat all corporate customers in the same way, whether it was a AAA-rated multinational or an SME. Their solution was to run, in parallel, the Basel 1 regime at the head office level to fulfill the requirements of banking regulators, but to allow the individual business units to run a 'Risk-adjusted return on capital' model – or RAROC. RAROC is the genesis of IRB, or Internal Ratings-Based methodology – the approach common in major banks under Basel 3.

RAROC permitted a bank's business unit to apply two weightings to the nominal amount of a piece of business, in order to ascertain its risk-adjusted amount. The capital assigned to the piece of business was then 8-10% of the risk-adjusted amount, and the return needed to be 20-25% of the capital.

The weightings could be higher than 100%, if the business merited it. It is a common misconception that 100% is the ceiling. A risk-weighting of 100% on a transaction with a nominal value of 100 requires 8 of capital in a bank whose capital threshold is set at 8%. A risk-weighting of 100% on a piece of business means there is an 8% chance of a loss. If there was a 50% risk of loss on the transaction then the capital assigned to it should be 50. In that case the combined risk-weightings should inflate the nominal amount from 100 to 625 so that 8% of that is 50. In other words the transaction's risk-weighting should be 625%.

The two RAROC weightings were the following:
1. Counterparty Weighting, on a scale of 1-20, to take account of the creditworthiness of the borrower;
2. Facility Weighting, on a scale of 1-20, to take account of the characteristics of the piece of business.[95]

The weightings were multiplied together to reach the Credit Conversion Factor, or 'CCF'. The CCF was multiplied by the nominal amount to determine the transaction's risk-adjusted amount, which was in turn multiplied by the bank's capital threshold to determine the amount of capital required.

Worked example of risk-weighting for a lending transaction under RAROC

Here is a worked example of a piece of business undertaken by Manufacturers Hanover Trust Company of New York (MHT) in the early 1990s, for an Irish leasing company called Guinness Peat Aviation (GPA), which was based in the Shannon airport zone.

The business was a series of loans to special purpose companies established in the USA through which to construct the tax-leveraged leasing of new Airbus A-320 aircraft. These aircraft would be purchased by the special purpose companies from Airbus for their fair market value, using the loan proceeds and the equity injection from a US multinational that was using the investment to generate depreciation allowances on the cost of the aircraft, with which it would be able to reduce its US tax bill.

The aircraft would first be leased by the special purpose companies to a single GPA-controlled new entity under a series of long-term leases, and then that entity would sub-lease them to a series of US airlines under operating leases, normally of shorter duration. The aircraft cost about US$24 million each and there were to be eight of them, and eight special purpose companies.

---

[94] OECD – Organization for Economic Cooperation and Development, an association of the capitalist economies, as opposed to Comecon for the Soviet-backed association of nations
[95] This approach was common to Manufacturers Hanover Trust Company, Chemical Bank and BankBoston in the period 1989-1997

The GPA parent – GPA plc – would guarantee the lease rentals owed by their GPA-controlled new entity to the special purpose companies, and these would be set at a level sufficient to meet the debt service owed by the special purpose companies to the MHT. This enabled MHT to carry out the Counterparty credit assessment on GPA plc itself, and not on the special purpose companies, which had no substance.

Counterparty Weighting

The major factors influencing the Counterparty Weighting on GPA plc were:

Positives	Negatives
• GPA had an A long-term rating from S&P	• Quite highly leveraged
• Largest operating lease company for aircraft in the world	• Owned equity in a series of associated companies, joint ventures that were also highly leveraged, meaning that the GPA capital base was being leveraged twice over
• Good track record of repossessing aircraft when a lease went into default, and finding a substitute lessee	• On a major expansion path, ordering many new aircraft and buying purchase options on further ones
• Ownership included several large banks and players in aircraft finance, such as Long-Term Credit Bank of Japan, and Mitsubishi Trust	• Not massively profitable given its big fleet and market share
• Modern fleet, supplied by all of Boeing, Airbus and McDonnell Douglas	• Susceptible to rises in interest rates, and to a downturn in the aviation market generally

Table 4.10: GPA – factors influencing Counterparty Weighting

The upshot was that, on the scale of 1-20, GPA plc was graded as a 7 by the MHT Aircraft Financing Unit and this was confirmed by the Credit Unit. A grading of 1 would be sovereign risk, whilst 17-18 would be the different stages of a default, 19 would be in liquidation, and 20 would be a write-off.

A grading of 7 meant that the Counterparty Weighting was about 100%: the nominal amount was the same as the amount risk-adjusted for the quality of the counterparty.

Facility Weighting

The major factors influencing the Facility Weighting on this transaction were:

Positives	Negatives
• First priority mortgage over the aircraft	• Long term – 15-year final maturity, albeit with repayments in the meantime
• A low loan-to-value of 70%, due to the optimization calculations on the US lease, and a consequential low loan amount after 15 years compared to the projected residual value of the aircraft	• Structured finance, which always contains legal risks, including that several of the aircraft were subject to a 'double dips': another tax lease on top of the US one out of Japan, Hong Kong and Sweden, whereby the supposed owner in that jurisdiction had to meet a test of ownership of the aircraft to be able to claim depreciation allowances on it, and the legal papers warranting that ownership might conflict with the papers warranting that the special companies owned the aircraft and could therefore grant MHT a first priority mortgage over them
• GPA had undertaken on a best-efforts basis to replace the bank's financing with long-term, fixed rate financing from US insurance companies, and it was confirmed by market enquiry that this was an active market and that GPA were putting the proposition to the main names active in it	• The engines, a new type from Rolls-Royce, were not the standard ones fitted to an Airbus A-320 (which were those manufactured by Pratt&Whitney or General Electric), a factor which could limit the marketplace of airlines willing to lease the aircraft

Facility Weighting factors (cont'd):

Positives	Negatives
• The interest on the loan started at 1.625% over LIBOR and would escalate in increments of ½% every six months if GPA were unsuccessful in these attempts, and could go as high as 4.625% over LIBOR	• Being financed under an American tax lease, the aircraft had to either be flown by US carriers, or by carriers who flew them regularly into the USA. Because of the range of the A-320 this meant that the market for them was limited to US, Canadian, Mexican, Central American and Caribbean carriers
• GPA would place a security deposit of a rising portion of the loan, starting six months from pay-out, going up to 20% of the loan after two years	• This was GPA's first major attempt to penetrate the US market, where several domestic competitors were already well established, including a sister company of MHT itself

Table 4.11: GPA – factors influencing Facility Weighting

On the scale of 1-20, this piece of business was graded as a 5 by the MHT Aircraft Financing Unit and this was confirmed by the Credit Unit, largely on the basis of the adequate security package, backed up by the knowledge that the financing papers were being prepared by Simpson, Thacher and Bartlett, a major external New York law firm and MHT's main adviser, at which the MHT CEO John McGillicuddy had been a partner.

Combined risk-weighting, capital required and earnings target

A grading of 5 for the Facility Weighting caused the business' risk-adjusted value to be lower than its nominal value, by about 30%.

The resulting overall weighting, or 'Credit Conversion Factor' (CCF) in Basel 2 terminology, was 70% and drove the capital required as follows:

Loan amount	Counterparty Weighting	Amount risk-adjusted for Counterparty	Facility Weighting	Credit Conversion Factor	Amount risk-adjusted for Counterparty and Facility Weightings	Capital quotient	Capital required
US$187 mil	100%	US$187 mil	70%	70%	US$130.9 mil	8%	US$10.5 mil

Table 4.12: GPA - Credit Conversion Factor and capital required

The final step was calculating the earnings target:

Capital required	Return on capital target	Annual earnings needed to hit target	Earnings as a percentage of loan amount
US$10.5 mil	25%	US$2.63 mil	1.41%

Table 4:13: GPA – return on capital target and earnings needed to meet it

A minimum interest margin of 1.41% was required for MHT to hit its Return on Capital target on this transaction, and indeed the loan margin started at 1.625%, with the potential for it to rise to 4.625%, albeit that both the Counterparty and Facility Weighting had to be confirmed each year in an annual review process: the risk-adjusted amount and therefore the capital required and the return on capital target might alter on an annual basis, whilst the terms and conditions of the loan were fixed.

Reassessment of risk-weighting over time

In the event the combined the risk-weighting remained static at around 70%, causing the capital assigned to the transaction to remain static at US$10.5 million.

This was not because either the Counterparty Weighting or Facility Weighting remained static individually: both changed significantly but in a way that the one offset the other. The bottom fell out of GPA's market after the 1991 Gulf War.[96] It made a disastrous mistake in attempting a public share listing soon afterwards.[97] This reduced its Counterparty Weighting upon annual review. As regards the transaction itself, GPA failed to place the aircraft with a reliable airline, but only with the latest version of Braniff, which went into Chapter 11 bankruptcy shortly after some of the aircraft had been delivered and before others had been. All parties were committed by that stage, including Braniff to take the aircraft on lease. Braniff being incorporated in Florida, the state bankruptcy court regarded the airline's right to lease the aircraft as an asset that belonged to the bankruptcy estate, even if Braniff could neither pay the deposit nor the rentals. It subjected the aircraft to an order-of-stay against GPA from even attempting to find an alternative lessee until Braniff had either been rescued or liquidated. The aircraft remained grounded for some time. GPA were unable to secure long-term financing from insurance companies.

For that reason MHT's loan margin increased and GPA had to pay in the cash deposit: this caused MHT's security package to increase such that MHT would only lose if the aircraft value dropped to 50% of its purchase price. The Facility Weighting fell as the Counterparty Weighting increased. In consequence the risk-adjusted value of the loan remained at about 70% of nominal, and the increasing interest margin caused the 'Risk-Adjusted Return on Capital' figures to rise as follows:

Margin	1.625%	2.625%	3.625%	4.625%
Annual earnings	US$3.04 mil	US$4.91 mil	US$6.78 mil	US$8.65 mil
Capital	US$10.5 mil	US$10.5 mil	US$10.5 mil	US$10.5 mil
Return on Capital	28.9%	46.75%	64.56%	82.37%

Table 4.14: GPA – return on capital as the deal progressed

This deal, given also its large size, was later said to be the single most profitable piece of lending business that MHT had transacted in its entire history.

It is also a good example of a RAROC methodology operating within a bank in parallel to Basel 1, the official methodology. It can be seen that in this example the risk-weighted amount and the nominal amount were not radically different. The key to running RAROC and Basel 1 in parallel was to direct business units to aim to generate new loans that would fall in a risk-weighting range of 65-120%, and for the central finance unit to manage the portfolio mix. What had to be avoided was a large build-up of business in the risk-weighting range 1-64%, unless it was with OECD sovereigns or OECD banks, or was backed with mortgage security.

Basel 2 – including the incorporation of RAROC

Under Basel 2, two methodologies were permitted:
- Standard – the same as the Basel 1 methodology;
- Risk-Adjusted – the already-existing RAROC, as above.

Derivatives now fell within scope, and a Fractional Exposure amount of the nominal amount as the first step in calculating the capital required to support each type of derivative.

Major banks adopted Basel 2 Risk-Adjusted because it enabled them to hold less capital as a function of the nominal amount in large lines of business in which they were engaged:
- Business with sovereign and public sector counterparties
- Business with major corporates
- Mortgage-backed business
- Derivatives

Here were the seeds of the Global Financial Crisis and the Eurozone sovereign debt crisis: the incentive for mortgage-backed and derivatives business built into the regulatory capital regime.

---

[96] https://en-academic.com/dic.nsf/enwiki/484917 accessed on 2 June 2022
[97] https://www.irishtimes.com/business/ambitious-gpa-forced-to-abort-flotation-in-a-few-short-hours-1.1087945 accessed on 2 June 2022

How Basel 2 Risk-Adjusted was operationalized for loan officers

Bank loan officers were supplied with a simple grid of the 'RAROC Hurdle': the interest margin required on a loan in order for the loan to meet the 'return on capital' target. Loan officers were not invited to concern themselves with the capital quotient, different types of capital, or the 'return on capital target'. The grid was a simple list of loan margins to be requested in accordance with the results of the risk-weighting process:

Facility Weighting ▶ Counterparty Weighting ▼	1	2	..	19	20
1	0.01%	0.02%	..	0.44%	0.45%
2	0.04%	0.08%	..	7.52%	9.62%
...	..	..	..	..	..
19	5.28%	6.71%	..	1,070.00%	1,180.00%
20	10.00%	15.00%	..	1,180.00%	1,250.00%

Table 4.15: example extract from a RAROC Grid for loan officers

The loan officer simply has to read off the minimum margin for the piece of business from the grid and try to elicit that from the borrower.

Of course no new business was done where either of the grades was 17 or higher. The meaning of a loan margin of over 1,000% is that the loan must yield almost its own value in loan interest in the first year. If the capital quotient is 8% and the loan margin 1,250%, one year's interest is the exact loan value. This is because, on a loan with a combined risk-weighting of 20, it had to be regarded as a certainty that the entire loan principal was at risk: a 1-for-1 provision for the loss needed to be created straight away, out of the loan interest. As stated earlier, it is a common misconception that 100% is the maximum risk-weighting: 1,250% is the maximum, because capital is just 8% of the loan nominal amount when a risk-weighting of 100% has been applied.

How Basel 2 Risk-Adjusted was operationalized for derivatives

Derivatives came formally within Basel's scope. They were first subjected to a calculation model to determine how much the bank might lose if the counterparty did not fulfil its side of the contract, whoever the counterparty was. This model was invariably based on the principles of a Black-Scholes pricing model,[98] and a Monte Carlo simulation.[99] Under Basel 3 it would be known as a Value-at-Risk model or 'VaR'.

Under Basel 2 it output what was known as a Fractional Exposure amount: that fraction of the nominal amount which was estimated to be the maximum that the bank could lose, and its time-horizon was until the maturity of the contract. The Relationship Manager and the Credit Department then had to gain authorization of a Fractional Exposure Limit – in the same way in which they had to gain authorization for a loan – in order for the bank to take on the transaction. If the transaction went bad, the Relationship Management Business Unit would reimburse the loss to the Derivatives Business Unit up to the amount of the Fractional Exposure limit.

The capital required to support the Fractional Exposure limit was calculated using the same methodology as for lending, except that the amount input was not the nominal amount, but the already-reduced Fractional Exposure amount.

The amount against which capital needed to be held was Fractional Exposure amount x Counterparty Weighting x Facility Weighting. The product of this calculation was the Credit Conversion Factor for the nominal amount of the transaction.

The Counterparty Weighting would be the same for that counterparty whether the underlying business was a loan, a guarantee, derivatives or whatever.

---

[98] https://www.investopedia.com/terms/b/blackscholes.asp accessed on 16 October 2022
[99] https://www.investopedia.com/terms/m/montecarlosimulation.asp accessed on 16 October 2022

The Facility Weighting at this time played a minor role because:
- The maturity of the transaction was already reflected in the Fractional Exposure amount;
- Derivatives were normally transacted on an unsecured basis, meaning without either tangible security or a guarantee.

The Facility Weighting was therefore neutral, meaning it was placed at 100%: it neither increased nor diminished the product of the calculation.

Long-dated derivatives and especially exotic ones delivered substantial Fractional Exposure amounts, but this did not necessarily tie up large amounts of capital. The largest Fractional Exposure amount might be 30% of the nominal, and this would frequently be diminished by a favorable Counterparty Weighting. If the Counterparty Weighting was 40%, then a capital allocation of 8% of the 'at-risk' amount is worked out through the following formula:

Nominal x Fractional Exposure x Counterparty Weighting x Facility Weighting x 8%

This is the same as Nominal x Credit Conversion Factor x 8%, since the Credit Conversion Factor is Fractional Exposure x Counterparty Weighting x Facility Weighting.

Even for an exotic derivative contract and a Counterparty Weighting of 40% the result of the calculation would be:

100 x 30% x 40% x 100% x 8% = 1%

Or, using just the Credit Conversion Factor:

100 x 12% x 8% = 1%

Capital of only 1% of the nominal amount is a very thin loss cushion, as was proven during the Global Financial Crisis. Each step in the weighting has the effect of diminishing – never raising – the nominal on the way to establishing its risk-adjusted value.

That was the cushion for an exotic derivative with a high Fractional Exposure at 30% and a 40% Counterparty Weighting. For shorter-dated and unexotic derivatives with the same Counterparty the Fractional Exposure might be 10%. Then the capital required was:

100 x 10% x 40% x 100% x 8% = 0.33%

40% as a Counterparty Weighting is not particularly low. Globally Systemically Important Financial Institutions might have merited a weighting lower than that, with a consequent diminution of the loss cushion.

Of course, if the counterparty was a Eurozone government or supranational and merited a 0% Counterparty Weighting, there would be no need for a loss cushion at all, however large the Fractional Exposure was.

Basel 3 – a further opportunity for banks to understate their risks

Basel 3, brought in after the Global Financial Crisis to supposedly strengthen bank capitalization, allows three methodologies:
- Standard – which is Basel 1
- Standard Internal Ratings-Based – which is RAROC or Basel 2/Risk-Adjusted
- Advanced Internal Ratings-Based

All the methodologies are aimed at determining the Risk-Weighted Asset equivalent of each piece of a bank's risk-bearing business, but the flexibility permitted rises sharply though the three methodologies.

Always the calculation is Nominal x Credit Conversion Factor = Risk-Weighted Asset.

Then Risk-Weighted Asset x 8-10% = capital required (i.e. CET1 required).

The steps in determining the Credit Conversion Factor do not differ from Basel 2. However the weightings themselves can decline sharply under Advanced IRB if a bank has long a series of data proving its excellence at risk management, the unlikelihood of a default occurring, and the low impact if it did. This is where one of the current problems emanates from. Advanced IRB allows a bank to hold even less capital as a function of its book of risk-bearing business than RAROC Basel 1 did.

For lending, leases and guarantees the Counterparty Weighting and Facility Weighting – and therefore the resultant Credit Conversion Factor – are permitted to be lower than they were for the same bank under Basel 2.

There is also a particular problem with derivatives as described below, because a large proportion of them have a Credit Conversion Factor of 0%.

Admittedly Basel 3 disallows certain types of interest-bearing bond from a bank's calculation of its capital. This restriction was discussed above but it pales into insignificance compared to the advantage of Advanced IRB over RAROC and Basel 2 Risk-Adjusted in reducing risk-weightings and making banks appear to have adequate capital, indeed surplus capital, compared to the risks they are running.

The ECB, and indeed the Bank of England, now regularly boast of banks' resilience, of their strong capital positions compared to before the Global Financial Crisis, and of their surplus CET1. They are boasting about the results of their 'Stress Tests' whereby IRB grades are subjected to adverse economic scenarios, such that IRB grades are reduced, and Risk-Weighted Assets correspondingly increased. The re-running of the calculations shows that the bank, notwithstanding the increase in Risk-Weighted Assets, still meets its minimum CET1 threshold.[100]

EU/Eurozone adoption of AIRB

AIRB grades in Eurozone banks – and this trickles across into non-Eurozone EU banks – suffer from inflation: because a Eurozone sovereign is 0% risk-weighted when it should not be, the grading pyramid starts at too benevolent a level. Below that the counterparties are graded relative to their peers and superiors, and all end up receiving inflated grades. The Stress Tests accept these inflated grades as their start point: the adverse economic scenarios do not unwind this error made at source. The Stress Test results do not prove that the banks are resilient or that their loan book will not go bad in adverse economic scenarios.

A harmonized and misleading deployment of AIRB has been promulgated from the banking regulators and harmonized across the EU:
- Through the European Banking Authority and the Single Supervisory Mechanism, and their Stress Tests
- Aided by national banking regulators who conduct benchmarking studies so as to surface when banks are not all doing it the same, approved way
- Underpinned by the Big Four accounting firms being both the implementers of the methodology and its auditors
- Further underpinned by benchmarking studies carried out amongst their clientele by the Big Four where the clientele are distributed across different countries

The result is a missing amount of capital, and a divergence from the market's acid test of a bank's capitalization: the bank's market-to-book ratio. This ratio compares the bank's market value on the one hand – the number of shares in issue x the share price – with the bank's capital as stated on its balance sheet – its 'book value'. It is not uncommon for European banks to have a market-to-book ratio of 25% or lower.

---

[100] See Annex 4 of 'Managing Euro Risk' pp. 117-126 for an explanation of Stress Tests

Derivatives under Basel 3

The term 'Fractional Exposure' under Basel 2 has been replaced by 'Value-at-Risk' or VaR under Basel 3, but the calculation models are the same.

The main change after the Global Financial Crisis globally was that the authorities dictated that unexotic contracts should be transferred to a 'Central Counterparty' or 'CCP' for clearing and settlement. In other words, the original counterparties would cease to have a contract with one another, but would have separate contracts with a derivatives clearing house, the CCP.

Each party would then place collateral with the CCP, known as 'margin', in a fraction of the contract's nominal amount. The CCP would regularly revalue the contract and update the margin. If the value of a contract declined from one valuation to the next, there would be a 'margin call': the party would have to send more cash or bonds of the required type to the CCP by a fixed deadline to bring their 'margin' up to the correct level.

Exotic contracts would remain in place between the original counterparties but they should also be 'margined' under a similar process.

In the context of AIRB this radically reduced both the VaR and the Risk-Weighted Asset, and therefore the capital held:
- The time horizon for the VaR calculation was not the final maturity of the contract, but the period between one valuation, and the point after the next-following valuation when the counterparty had been asked to top up the margin and failed to do so;
- The time horizon reduced from months or years to hours or at most a day;
- This factor on its own could reduce a VaR from 10% to 3%;
- The Facility Weighting becomes of much greater importance, because the contract's VaR is collateralized with cash or bonds;
- In the case of cash, or of bonds issued by a 0% risk-weighted counterparty, the Facility Weighting goes to 0%;
- In that case the Credit Conversion Factor also goes to 0%, whatever the VaR and the Counterparty Weighting components of it were.

So the Risk-Weighted Asset equivalent of the derivatives contract under Basel 3 is:

Nominal x VaR x Counterparty Weighting x Facility Weighting = RWA

Where a contract with a Counterparty Weighting of 40% is margined through a CCP and the margin is held in the form of UK government bonds, the RWA of a contract with a VaR of 3% is:

100 x 3% x 40% x 0% = 0

Or, in shorter form:

Nominal x Credit Conversion Factor = RWA

100 x 0% = 0

Thus, under a very large proportion of derivatives contracts, the post-2008 arrangements yield no Risk-Weighted Asset at all. The contracts require no capital to be allocated behind them at all by a bank. The margin serves as the sole loss cushion.

Under exotic derivatives where the contract stays between the original trading parties and is not transferred to a CCP, a margin arrangement is also in place. If the assets placed as margin merit it in the IRB system, the Risk-Weighted Asset equivalent of the contract is again zero.

In all cases the margin serves in place of a Risk-Weighted Asset. The assumption is that the bank's loss on the contract's value cannot exceed the margin amount, therefore there can be no net loss. This is the presumption of the post-GFC arrangements, and they hinge on the accuracy of the VaR models and on the quality and nature of the collateral posted as margin.

Non-rebuilding of bank capital bases since the GFC

Thanks to AIRB and VaR an appearance is held out that banks have rebuilt their capital bases since the GFC, but this appearance belies what has happened in the three channels through which banks normally obtain new capital:
- Corporate restructurings like a spin-off, an acquisition or a merger
- Profits
- New share issuance

New share issuance has only occurred in distress situations like Unicredit. Corporate restructurings have been rescues: Intesa SanPaolo of Veneto Banca and Banca Popolare di Vicenza, Santander of Banco Popular Espanol, Hellenic Bank of the Cyprus Cooperative Bank, and so on. Banks have not been making substantial profits, and certainly not the ones who have high NPL ratios.

Banks' capital bases have been optically strengthened firstly through a harmonized and aggressive implementation of Advanced IRB. Advanced IRB has been used to drive down the Risk-Weighted Asset equivalent of banking business by reliance on spurious proof that the risks are low, when the evidence of the past 22 years is that the risks are meaningful and that banks are good neither at assessing how large they are in quantum terms, how likely they are to materialize, nor how to mitigate them when they do occur. In the real world the banking industry has lurched from one crisis to another, and from one blow-up to another.

The impact of off-balance sheet business on a bank's RWAs has been radically reduced by the combination of VaR, margining, and the transfer of unexotic derivatives contracts to CCPs. The working assumption is that contracts transferred to a CCP for clearing and settlement generate no RWA at all. The knock-on inference is that a bank's RWAs for derivatives relate to exotic transactions which have not been transferred to a CCP.

It is not uncommon for the RWAs of a bank to be less than 30% of on-balance sheet assets. Without a statement of the nominal value of a bank's off-balance sheet business and its related RWA, it is not possible to deduce the discount factor applied to the on-balance sheet assets to extrapolate their RWA.

One is then left to speculate on all of the total nominal value of off-balance sheet business, the subset of that which has been transferred to CCPs, the RWA equivalent – if any – of this portion of the business, the nominal value of the portfolio of contracts not transferred to CCPs, and its RWA equivalent. Without this information it is not possible to see what discount factor has been applied to any of the bank's business to deliver its RWA equivalent.

As it is, EU and Eurozone banks' business is subject to steep discounts to determine its RWA equivalent. It is always a discount, not a premium. It is almost as if EU and Eurozone banks share the misconception, discussed above, that the maximum risk-weighting is 100%, and not 1,250%, for a bank whose CET1 quotient is 8%.

Risk-weighting at Monte dei Paschi di Siena

A case in point is the Monte dei Paschi di Siena Group, to which we return.

Monte dei Paschi's consolidated interim report of 31st March 2021 showed on p. 59 that it had CET1 of €5.96 billion, when, on p. 5, its nominal assets were €146.66 billion.[101] This is a Leverage Ratio of 24.6-to-1, well outside the maximum of 20-to-1. However, its RWAs were shown on p. 59 as only €48.90 billion. Of this figure €34.58 billion was ascribed to 'Credit and Counterparty Risk' and a further €0.46 billion to 'Credit valuation adjustment'. The first of these will include credit risk in off-balance sheet business, as well as in on-balance sheet business. The third component – Market Risk – of €2.70 billion will apply to both on- and off-balance sheet business e.g. on holdings of fixed-rate securities as well as on derivatives. Finally there is €11.16 billion of RWAs attributable to Operational Risk.

This is yet another way of blurring what is going on between on- and off-balance sheet business.

---

[101] Monte dei Paschi di Siena Group - Consolidated Interim Report - as at 31 March 2021

The following are not disclosed:
- The total nominal value of all off-balance sheet business;
- The RWAs that equate solely to on-balance sheet assets or, put another way, the portion of €35.04 billion (the aggregate of 'Credit and Counterparty Risk' and 'Credit valuation adjustment') that pertains to loans rather than to counterparty risk on derivatives and other off-balance sheet business;
- What portion of Market Risk pertains to on-balance sheet business and what portion pertains to off-balance sheet business.

All that one can say for certain is that the RWAs pertaining to on- and off-balance sheet business add up to €37.74 billion, which is 25.73% of the bank's on-balance sheet assets, or a discount of 74.26% on the nominal value of assets. This calculation holds only if the off-balance sheet business delivers an RWA equivalent of zero. When that has been ascertained and factored in, the RWAs pertaining to on-balance sheet business will be correspondingly lower, and their discount vis a vis their nominal value correspondingly higher.

To illustrate that point we simply have to infer numbers for the off-balance sheet business:
- That the portion of 'Credit and Counterparty Risk' attributable to off-balance sheet business was €5.0 billion and the portion attributable to on-balance sheet business €29.58 billion;
- That all of the €0.46 billion 'Credit valuation adjustment' was attributable to on-balance sheet business;
- That the portion of 'Market Risk' attributable to off-balance sheet business was €1.7 billion and the portion attributable to on-balance sheet business €1.0 billion;
- That, as a result, the total RWAs attributable to on-balance sheet business were €31.04 billion and those attributable to off-balance sheet business were €6.7 billion.

Based on this simulation, the RWAs of the on-balance sheet business were 21.16% of their nominal value, a discount factor of 78.83%. To re-iterate, we cannot perform the same simulation for off-balance sheet business because we are not told its nominal value.

Monte dei Paschi capital ratios

Based on its stated RWAs, Monte dei Paschi claimed a CET1 ratio on p. 7 of 12.2%, a healthy surplus over the 8.75% target imposed by its regulator, which was nearly 2% higher than its minimum of 7% plus its combined premia of 0.19%.

The CET1 ratio is meaningless, of course, in the face of the bank's having applied such an enormous discount to the face value of its business in order to state its Risk-Weighted Assets.

This analysis was originally undertaken in September 2021 when it was strongly mooted that the bank would be taken over by Unicredit. The Italian government had previously given support to the bank and, in order to appease the EU, had agreed that it would sell off its 64% shareholding by 31 December 2021. At that time the bank's share price was €1.15. Share capital was €9.15 billion, of which the bank owned 3% itself as 'treasury shares' (p. 17). However, 'Group net equity' (meaning balance-sheet capital) was only €6.0 billion, after the reversing-out of these treasury shares (€261 million) and of negative Reserves (€3.42 billion), whilst adding in the Valuation reserve (€368 million) and the profit for the period (€119 billion).

It is noteworthy that 'Group net equity' at €6.0 billion was almost identical to CET1 at €5.96 billion, whereas the bank's total capital - shown on p. 59 - was €7.76 billion. This means it had €1.80 billion of liabilities, beyond its balance-sheet capital, which it was able to count as capital in its regulatory returns but not on its balance sheet. These liabilities will instead be sitting in 'Direct funding: (b) Securities issued' as part of the €11.93 billion under that heading on p. 48.

With €6.0 billion of balance-sheet capital ('Group net equity'), the 'book value' of the bank was €6 billion: €6 per share with 1 billion shares quoted (p. 48). The share price was €1.15 meaning the bank had a market capitalization of €1.15 billion. That is a market-to-book ratio of 19.2%, or a discount of 80.8% to the balance-sheet capital.

Given that CET1 was given at €5.96 billion, it means that the bank traded at a market-to-CET1 ratio of 19.3%, or a discount of 80.7%. The market was thereby expressing an opinion that over 80% of the bank's CET1 did not exist because its assets were over-valued.

Monte dei Paschi throws up a curious situation around its market capitalization:
- 0.78% of total assets;
- 2.35% of RWAs;
- 19.3% of its CET1

At the same time the bank claims it has surplus CET1 at 12.2% and surplus total capital at 14.1%.

Disconnect between capital ratios – calculated internally – and market capitalization

The market-to-CET1 ratio of 19.3% is quite close to our simulation of the relationship of the RWAs to their face value of 21.16%. RWAs shrink the risk-bearing business without shrinking the capital. Market-to-CET1 shrinks both and paints a true picture of the bank's capitalization, whilst RWAs paint a fictional one.

There is a complete disconnect between the real value of the enterprise on the one hand and, on the other, all of the published accounts, the RWAs, and the bank's Stress Test results. The bank shows indicators that ought to put it into resolution, but instead the RWAs are so aggressive that even the most adverse Stress Test scenarios do not eliminate its capital. This is sheer delusion, but necessary in order that the Republic of Italy is not forced to pay out depositors of anything up to €87 billion, issue new debt itself in order to raise the cash to do this, and then be faced with the likelihood that the assets upon which it has become a senior creditor are worth less than that amount.

Monte dei Paschi is an object lesson in the necessity of Advanced IRB delivering a very low RWA figure in order to keep a bank alive: its shareholders do not want to, or cannot, inject more capital, so the only method of improving its apparent performance is to diminish its RWAs. The only indication that anything is wrong is the share price: it is the only place where the dream world of the bank's Advanced IRB and the real-world meet.

Summary on Advanced IRB

Advanced IRB has permitted a superficial recapitalization of the global banking system in total and that of the EU/Eurozone in particular. The situation in the Eurozone is made the more acute by the lack of a sovereign counterparties who merit a 0% risk-weighting. None exist in the Eurozone. The false allocation of a 0% risk-weighting to Eurozone member state governments has led to the overly benevolent risk-weighting of entities placed above Eurozone member state governments – the EU/Eurozone supranationals – and below them: the array of EU/Eurozone public sector entities and the private sector entities whose debt service depends on public sector entities.

Advanced IRB has caused a routine shrinkage of the face value of banking business – on- and off-balance sheet – into its risk-weighted equivalent, almost to the point that the banking regulators and banks themselves firstly cannot conceive that a piece of business may have a risk-weighted equivalent of itself or greater than itself, and secondly have forgotten that the bank's capital is only a small fraction of its Risk-Weighted Assets. The result is that a Risk-Weighted Asset is almost never as large as the asset's face value, resulting a maximum of 8-10% of its face value being held as capital and usually far less.

Non-Performing Loans in particular should have a Risk-Weighted Asset equivalent of 400% of their face value or more, such that the bank would need to have 32%+ of their face value as capital. That would be a more accurate estimation of the amount the bank could lose. Instead the 'carrying value' of NPL is treated as a Performing loan, and again might be backed with 8-10% of its 'carrying value' as capital.

Derivatives now have much lower VaRs under the model where they are margined – either at CCPs or bilaterally – for which the time horizon for revaluation is hours or a day, not months or years. The form in which CCPs demand that the margin be held brings the Facility Weighting into play to a greater extent than was the case under Basel 2. Where margin is held in cash or in the form of bonds issued by 0% risk-weighted counterparties, a bank need hold no further loss cushion itself. There is an argument in favour of that model but it does mean that banks can state next-to-no RWA against that portion of their derivatives business which is cleared and settled through a CCP.

4.6 Impact of the combination of NPL securitization and of Advanced IRB on member state liability for their Bank Deposit Insurance Scheme

This final area is not a deliberate action by the European authorities, but an involuntary knock-on impact on one of their actions by two others: NPL securitization and Advanced IRB combine to exacerbate member states' risks under the Bank Deposit Insurance Schemes.

NPL securitization, as in the case of 'Fino', games the regulatory capital rules and exchanges an asset with a high Credit Conversion Factor for one with 0%. It also falsely deconsolidates the asset.

NPLs retained by the selling bank, as in 'Porto', remain over-valued. The write-down is what the bank has been able to afford, rather than the amount needed to bring the asset down to a realistic value. The written-down value is then subjected to a further shrinkage – it is accorded a Credit Conversion Factor under Advanced IRB. The 'carrying value' is treated in the Advanced IRB system as if it were a Performing Loan, not a Non-Performing Loan. Or at least it is treated as Partially Performing – performing on the 'carrying value' rather than on its original nominal value.

With a Credit Conversion Factor of 100%, the bank only has to carry capital of 8-10% of the 'carrying value'. If the NPL is a 'Bad exposure', and for a bank with an 8% capital threshold, the Credit Conversion Factor should be 1,250%, so that that 'carrying value' x 1,250% x 8% = the 'carrying value'.

It is hard not to imagine that many central and commercial bankers believe that a risk-weighting of 100% is the absolute maximum, when, for a bank with a CET1 threshold of 8%, the absolute maximum risk-weighting is 1,250%. By way of illustration, the Bank for International Settlements recently recommended that a risk-weighting of 1,250% be applied to banks' holdings of cryptocurrencies like Ethereum or Bitcoin.[102]

Why the resolution process may cause the reconsolidation of securitized NPLs

If such a bank goes into resolution, the member state – now the senior creditor – will find that the assets contain considerable retained NPLs, as well as bonds that are claims on the pool of NPLs that was securitized and deconsolidated. The economic scenario causing the bank to go into resolution will affect the retained and securitized NPLs equally: there is in essence no difference between the two portfolios, and they should be valued using the same metrics.

This is not possible if one set of NPLs is held on-balance sheet and the other is held at arm's-length in a securitization structure that games the regulatory capital regime thanks to a guarantee from the new bank's sole senior creditor – the member state. The member state will want to find out what its risk really is, and make sure a consistent methodology is being applied for valuing its component parts. Collapsing the securitization structure would be a way of achieving that, bringing the related assets and liabilities back onto the bank's balance sheet. The liabilities would not be extensive – the B and C tranches in the Fino 1 transaction or 10% of the whole – because the bank would already have funding in place against the bonds it owns – the A and D tranches in Fino 1 or 90% of the whole.

The member state may also feel itself compelled to do this if the A tranche bonds issued by the securitization vehicle company were to default: the member state would be called upon to pay out on its guarantee, effectively to itself. It would have to issue new debt to do that, and for 87% of the whole. It would surely be preferable for the member state to have the bank buy out third-party investors (e.g. the owners of the B and C tranches in Fino 1) because they are a much smaller amount. The member state can then stop the bank from calling the guarantee on the A tranche against the member state. The member state can instead prevail upon the interested parties to collapse the securitization structure, take the pool of NPLs back onto the Asset side of the new bank's balance sheet and the third-party debts onto the Liabilities side.

---

[102] https://www.wsj.com/articles/bitcoin-other-crypto-assets-targeted-for-stiff-banking-regulation-11623324990 accessed on 12 June 2021

How the reconsolidation of NPLs affects the new bank's capital

Both the retained and the reconsolidated NPLs need to be realistically and consistently valued in the new bank's accounts.

If the NPLs coming back from the securitization structure really have been market-tested – and it would be difficult for the member state now to argue that they had not been – then they act as the baseline for the valuation of the retained NPLs. As we saw in the analysis of 'Fino' and 'Porto', the 'Fino' NPLs were written down more aggressively, and the 'Bad exposures' were written down more aggressively than the 'Unlikely to pay'.

With a firm baseline of market-tested valuations at around 13% on the 'Bad exposures' coming back from the securitization, it will not be possible to value the retained 'Bad exposures' at more than 16-17%. Then it will not be possible to value 'Unlikely to pay' much above 40%.

The process will result in significant write-downs to consistent, lower 'carrying values', with the 'carrying values' needing to be accorded an appropriate Credit Conversion Factor. It is possible that the lower 'carrying values' may consume more capital than the higher 'carrying values' were doing before, if the Credit Conversion Factor is now conservative.

The upshot is that RWAs expand, actual capital reduces, and the new bank's regulatory capital thresholds come under pressure.

How AIRB is found wanting under the same circumstances

The economic conditions that caused the old bank to go into resolution now have their effect through AIRB. At each annual review loans and other facilities have to be marked down. RWAs expand for this reason as well, putting the new bank's regulatory capital thresholds under pressure further pressure.

What happens to the new bank

The processes put in train by the resolution and the economic situation that precipitated it conspire to create a new bank which breaches its regulatory capital thresholds and its Leverage Ratio as well. Indeed, it may even be bankrupt, given that the capital of the new bank is the amount of ineligible depositors in the old bank, to which no metrics apply.

The new bank should go into resolution again but now with no capital. The capital-like instruments owned by the new shareholders (i.e. by the ineligible depositors of the old bank) are expunged and there are no ineligible depositors in the new bank to be bailed in.

The second new bank contains one party only on the liability side of its balance sheet - the member state – and assets on the other side that are now less than this liability, because they are now realistically valued.

There is a shortfall between the assets and the liabilities. This shortfall is the difference between the debt the member state took on in order to pay out the eligible depositors in the old bank, and the real value of the assets of the old bank.

The shortfall corresponds to a permanent addition to the member state's General government gross debt. This was mooted in the previous chapter but the combination of NPL securitization and AIRB have made it worse, primarily by allowing a bank to continue in business through financial engineering – bogus deconsolidation of bad assets and spurious under-weighting of risk.

Without NPL securitization and AIRB a bank could still have gone into resolution and revealed a shortfall that translated into a permanent addition to member state debt. With NPL securitization and AIRB the bank will continue in business far longer and without engaging any of the triggers for resolution.

This means that, when it does go into resolution and the dream world is shattered, the difference between the bank's real value and its regulatory returns will be all the greater, as will the permanent addition to member state debt.

This is the meaning of a 'zombie bank': a bank that has a shortfall of value but where it serves the interests of its controllers to keep it existent, albeit in suspended animation, because the bank's resolution would cause the shortfall to be allocated to the controllers, the member states.

Worked example - reconsolidation of NPLs

The securitization structure is collapsed and the pool of NPLs is reconsolidated. This involves the take-over of the third-party funding contracted by the special purpose company (SPC), none of which would qualify as Tier 1 or Tier 2 capital.

In the example the bank had deconsolidated a 'carrying value of 10 of NPLs. It now owns 8 of A tranche bonds, which it holds within its Loans. The SPC took on 2 of B and C tranche bonds. The bank also has retained NPLs to a 'carrying value' of 10. The bank's balance sheet before and after would be as follows:

Before reconsolidation	
Assets	**Liabilities**
Loans – 94	Insured senior – 83
NPLs – 10	Residual senior - 27
Other assets - 15	Junior – 3
	Capital – 6
119	119

After reconsolidation	
Assets	**Liabilities**
Loans – 86	Insured senior – 83
NPLs – 10	Residual senior - 27
Reconsol. NPLs - 10	NPL-linked debt - 2
Other assets - 15	Junior – 3
	Capital – 6
121	121

Table 4.16: skeleton bank balance sheet if NPL securitization is reversed

Loans drop by 8 but there is a new asset of 10 – the reconsolidated NPLs. There is a new liability of 2: the NPL-linked debt. The 8 of funding that previously supported the A tranche bonds is assumed to remain in place.

The balance sheet still balances, it is longer by 2, and the so-called Leverage Ratio has deteriorated to 4.95%, below the regulatory minimum of 5%.

The main issue is that the quality of the assets has reverted to what it was before the NPLs were securitized, and the CET1 ratio will be coming under strain. In short, the bank ends up with more assets but no more capital, and the reconsolidated assets are of low quality. Being of low quality they attract a high risk-weighting and consume a large block of CET1.

This bank now touches the triggers for resolution.

Situation without the reconsolidation of NPLs and reversion to other Basel methodologies

The situation before reconsolidation of the NPLs would look even worse if the bank was compelled to run a Standard IRB methodology under Basel 3, and almost impossible if it had to run the Standard approach – the legacy of Basel 1 with no shrinkage possible from risk-weighting business with corporates and consumers.

Let us first see how the situation would look if the bank moved from Advanced IRB to Standard IRB without the reconsolidation of NPLs.

The benevolent risk-weightings under AIRB should be noted, with no part of the portfolio having a CCF of above 40%. The 'carrying value' of NPLs is 40%, meaning a loss cushion of 3.2% of the 'carrying value' in a bank with an 8% CET1 Ratio.

The result is a bank with a very comfortable, surplus CET1 Ratio. This surplus evaporates under Standard IRB in which the CCFs are 15% higher across the board:

Advanced IRB				Standard IRB		
Nominal	Risk-Weighting	RWAs		Nominal	Risk-Weighting	RWAs
Loans – 94	27%	25.4		Loans – 94	42%	39.5
NPLs – 10	40%	4.0		NPLs – 10	55%	5.5
Other assets - 15	35%	5.3		Other assets - 15	50%	7.5
Off-b/s - 85	10%	8.5		Off-b/s - 85	25%	21.3
Total RWAs		43.2		Total RWAs		73.8
Capital		6.0		Capital		6.0
Capital ratio		13.9%		Capital ratio		8.1%

Table 4.17: bank RWAs and Capital Ratio under AIRB and Standard IRB, before NPL securitization is reversed

The transition to Standard IRB moves the bank from having surplus capital to its capital being adequate as long no extra buffers are applied.

Then we can combine the application of Standard IRB with the reconsolidation of NPLs, the 'carrying value' of the reconsolidated ones being risk-weighted at 100%:

Standard IRB		
Nominal	Risk-Weighting	RWAs
Loans – 86	42%	36.1
NPLs – 10	55%	5.5
Reconsol. NPLs - 10	100%	10.0
Other assets - 15	50%	7.5
Off-b/s - 85	25%	21.3
Total RWAs		80.4
Capital		6.0
Capital ratio		7.5%

Table 4.18: bank RWAs and Capital Ratio under Standard IRB, after NPL securitization is reversed

Now the bank would fail its the Basel 3 minimum capital test if any buffers of substance were added to the 7% minimum, and the risk-weighting of Retained NPLs is out-of-line with the risk-weighting of Reconsolidated ones.

Risk-weighting of NPLs

A bank, reconsolidating NPLs as per Table 4.17, might argue that reconsolidated NPLs should not be risk-weighted at 100%, when they might have been written down to 15% or less to enable their securitization, and when this value had been 'market-tested.

However, we know, as was the case of Unicredit's 'Fino' transaction, that it was the worst of the 'Bad exposures' that were securitized; there is little value there. We also know that retained NPLs have subjected to arbitrary write-downs, aimed at not breaching regulatory capital thresholds, meaning their 'carrying values' might be inflated and should carry a higher risk-weighting.

Arguing between a 55% or a 100% CCF for the 'carrying value' of NPLs steers discussion away from basic principles: the 'carrying value' of any NPL should be risk-weighted at well over 100%, if the bank only holds CET1 of 8% of the resultant RWA. 'Bad exposures' should be risk-weighted at 1,000% or more, however small the 'carrying value' is compared to the nominal. 'Unlikely to Pay' must have a 'carrying value' below 40%, and the 'carrying value' should be risk-weighted at 400%. 'Past due and Non-performing' should have a 'carrying value' below 80%, and the 'carrying value' should be risk-weighted at 400%.

This would result in defensible and conservative valuations, with a likelihood of recoveries in the future, at which point the proceeds of an NPL might exceed its 'carrying value' and allow a windfall profit to be booked.

As it is, NPLs remain over-valued on EU/Eurozone balance sheets and under-weighted for the risk of loss.

Realism on 'carrying values' and risk-weighting causes the bank to fail

The next-following steps would be to subject the picture of a Standard IRB treatment with the NPLs reconsolidated to two further scenarios:

1. application of the Basel 3 Standard approach, with no IRB
2. risk-weighting the 'carrying values' of NPLs at 400% within Standard IRB

Firstly we have how the picture might look if the bank was running the Basel 3 Standard approach, with some loan business qualifying for dispensations, but with off-balance sheet business now captured as it was not by Basel 1, and the 'carrying values' of NPLs risk-weighted the same as performing loans because the borrowers will be corporates and consumers:

Standard		
Nominal	**Weighting**	**RWAs**
Loans – 86	90%	77.4
NPLs – 10	100%	10.0
Reconsol. NPLs - 10	100%	10.0
Other assets - 15	100%	15.0
Off-b/s - 85	25%	21.3
Total RWAs		133.7
Capital		6.0
Capital ratio		4.5%

Table 4.19: bank RWAs and Capital Ratio under Basel 3 'Standard' approach, after NPL securitization is reversed

The capital ratio is only 4.5%, well below the minimum, and the 'carrying values' of NPLs are risk-weighted at 100%, like any other loan to a corporate or a consumer.

Secondly there is the picture where the bank is still running Basel 3 Standard IRB but now the 'carrying values' of all NPLs – including those of 'Bad exposures' that might merit an even higher CCF - are risk-weighted at 400%:

Standard IRB		
Nominal	**Risk-Weighting**	**RWAs**
Loans – 86	42%	36.1
NPLs – 10	400%	40.0
Reconsol. NPLs - 10	400%	40.0
Other assets - 15	50%	7.5
Off-b/s - 85	25%	21.3
Total RWAs		144.9
Capital		6.0
Capital ratio		4.1%

Table 4.20: bank RWAs and Capital Ratio under Standard IRB, with NPLs risk-weighted at 400%

The banks fails its capital adequacy threshold by some distance.

How this final picture accords to the true situation at banks with historically high NPLs

Table 4.20 is probably the most accurate scenario of the true level of capitalization of a bank like Monte dei Paschi. It underweights its performing loans, its other assets and its off-balance sheet business through its Advanced IRB model. It has securitized NPLs into structures where it is the main provider of funds. The securitization fails normal tests for deconsolidation, and the NPLs should be reconsolidated.

Once reconsolidated their 'carrying value' should be risk-weighted at 400% at least (and more if there is a large measure of 'Bad exposures'). Likewise the 'carrying value' of the rest of the portfolio of NPLs should be risk-weighted at least at 400%. That still only causes the bank to hold capital in the amount of 32% of the carrying value (4 times the 7% minimum plus 1% to take account of any extra buffers).

With those adjustments made the bank's capital ratios sink from a healthy surplus to nowhere near to being adequate. The bank should be put into resolution.

Summary on NPL securitization and Advanced IRB

The EU/Eurozone banking systems have fixed and low levels of capital. The normal sources of addition to capital – profits, new share issuance, and corporate restructurings – have not been occurring. The business volume has nevertheless grown and with risk levels in line with the economic performance of the EU/Eurozone.

NPL securitization and Advanced IRB are the techniques used to justify the capital back to the business volume and risk profile. The need for capital is not extrapolated from the business volume and risk profile: instead methodologies and techniques are invented to link the two ends of the sum, and make the low amount of capital of EU/Eurozone banks appear adequate to the business they have on their books.

This was the already strained situation of the EU/Eurozone at the end of 2019, with the banking system having too many bad loans and using an AIRB methodology aggressively to make itself look better capitalized than it was. Greece and Cyprus could be presented as weathering their defaults in the earlier part of the decade, and Ireland and Portugal as fully out of bailout, which was not to be taken to mean that they had repaid the bailout funds. The efforts through the APP, EIB and InvestEU to reflate the EU and Eurozone economies had not been manifestly successful up to then.

Chapter summary

Despite the announcement by the French and German governments, a 'full mobilization' of the EIB has not subsequently occurred if one understands by that a sharp increase in the volume of loans into the EU from the EIB.

Instead there has been a sharp increase in finance enabled by EIB Group and off-balance sheet for both the EIB and the EIF, which has been the main entity through which extra risk has been taken on. The result has been an enablement of €612 billion of financing up the end of 2021 through two schemes: InvestEU and the EGF. The latter scheme was the one used for deals signed in 2021, the former for deals up to the end of 2020 and after the latter was closed in 2022.

Both schemes result in new financial obligations but not in new debts for public sector entities and certainly not new debts for General government.

The ECB has kept banks liquid by supplying €2.2 trillion of unsecured 3-year financing through Targeted Longer-Term Refinancing Operations.

Banking regulators have in parallel endorsed a sham recapitalization of the EU/Eurozone banking system, firstly by permitting banks to deconsolidate Non-Performing Loans into securitizations for which the selling bank provides the majority of the finance.

Secondly banking regulators have permitted the same banks to arbitrage the Basel capital adequacy regime, where the government of a member state adds a guarantee to a large portion of the financing of the securitization. The guarantee is commercially worthless because the bonds so issued have achieved a higher credit rating on their own than that of the guarantor. But the guarantor is a Eurozone member state government, risk-weighted at 0%. The seller of the NPLs, buying back the bonds that financed the majority of the sale, need hold no capital at all against bonds that sit on top of the exact same portfolio of bad loans

Thirdly banking regulators have endorsed the EU/Eurozone-wide application of the most aggressive manifestation of the Basel capital adequacy regime: Advanced IRB. Banks are permitted to shrink their risk-bearing business to a fraction of its face value. Banks' low capital can thus be declared adequate to their 'Risk-Weighted Assets', a feat of both herculean reverse engineering and self-delusion.

NPL securitizations and Advanced IRB have enabled banks to avoid hitting the triggers that would result in bank resolutions, the better to avoid member states having to fund the resolution in the first instance. That is vital, because, in resolution, the fool's paradise would end. Banks would be shown to have over-valued their assets, understated their risks, and to present a major deficit compared to both the capital in the old bank and the in the new one. The true value of the bank would eat through both the capital of the old bank and of the new one (which are the ineligible deposits of the old bank).

This double resolution process would bail in the member state government: it would be the sole creditor of a bank whose assets were less than its liabilities. The difference between the two would be a permanent addition would occur to the member state's General government gross debt.

Instead of risking that, it is preferable to keep these 'zombie banks' afloat with liquidity through Targeted Longer-Term Refinancing Operations, and apparently solvent through NPL securitizations and Advanced IRB.

Figures:

- 4.1: EIB capital structure as at 31 December 2021 in € billions
- 4.2: EIF portfolio of guarantees from 2012 to 2021
- 4.3: EIF Part-Paid Percentage and Callable Amounts
- 4.4: Unicredit S.p.A. Non-Performing Loans at the end of 2015
- 4.5: comparison of level of write-down for NPLs held in portfolio on a prudent basis and in Unicredit S.p.A.

Figure 4.1: EIB capital structure as at 31 December 2021 in € billions

Nr	Country	Subscribed capital	Called capital	Uncalled capital
1	Germany	€46.7	€4.2	€42.5
2	France	€46.7	€4.2	€42.5
3	Italy	€46.7	€4.2	€42.5
4	Spain	€28.0	€2.5	€25.5
5	Netherlands	€12.9	€1.1	€11.8
6	Belgium	€12.9	€1.1	€11.8
7	Poland	€11.4	€1.0	€10.4
8	Sweden	€8.6	€0.8	€7.8
9	Denmark	€6.6	€0.6	€6.0
10	Austria	€6.4	€0.6	€5.8
11	Finland	€3.7	€0.3	€3.4
12	Greece	€3.5	€0.3	€3.2
13	Portugal	€2.3	€0.2	€2.1
14	Czech Republic	€2.2	€0.2	€2.0
15	Hungary	€2.1	€0.2	€1.9
16	Ireland	€1.6	€0.1	€1.5
17	Romania	€1.6	€0.1	€1.5
18	Croatia	€1.0	€0.1	€0.9
19	Slovakia	€0.8	€0.1	€0.7
20	Slovenia	€0.7	<€0.1	€0.7
21	Bulgaria	€0.5	<€0.1	€0.5
22	Lithuania	€0.4	<€0.1	€0.4
23	Luxembourg	€0.3	<€0.1	€0.3
24	Cyprus	€0.3	<€0.1	€0.3
25	Latvia	€0.2	<€0.1	€0.2
26	Estonia	€0.2	<€0.1	€0.2
27	Malta	€0.1	<€0.1	€0.1
	Total	€248.8	€22.2	€226.6

Figure 4.1: EIB capital structure as at 31 December 2021 in € billions

Figure 4.2: EIF portfolio of guarantees from 2012 to 2021

Guarantees – with run-off – in Euro millions											
	2012	2013	2014	2015	2016	2017	2018	2019	2020	2021	Average
New nominal written	1,180	1,844	1,616	4,697	6,153	5,905	6,500	6,700	8,514	20,130	6,324
Balance sheet provision	175	177	146	82	29	15	0	11	11	11	66
"Exposure at Risk" on entire portfolio	4,696	3,281	3,121	3,511	5,959	6,712	8,537	10,724	5,528	10,872	6,294
Percentage with life over 5 years	25.81%	17.61%	17.49%	81.03%	67.18%	75.19%	80.89%	85.03%	32.60%	69.85%	55.27%
Cumulative new nominal written	3,108	4,952	6,568	11,265	17,418	23,323	29,823	36,523	45,037	65,167	n/a
Increment to "Exposure at Risk"	324	-1,415	-160	390	2,448	753	1,825	2,187	-5,196	5,344	n/a
Leveraged amount	5,111	8,611	5,574	16,628	23,587	18,995	23,900	22,800	28,973	68,502	22,268
Total finance enabled	6,291	10,455	7,190	21,325	29,740	24,900	30,400	29,500	37,487	88,632	28,592
Estimated total of EIF guarantees book – 9 years of the average of new nominal written											56,915
Estimated book of finance enabled – average of Total of finance enabled multiplied by 9 years											257,328

Figure 4.2: EIF portfolio of guarantees from 2012 to 2021

Figure 4.3: EIF equity commitments

Equity Commitments – without run-off other than via sale or failure – in Euro millions											
	2012	2013	2014	2015	2016	2017	2018	2019	2020	2021	Average
New nominal written	1,350	1,468	1,650	2,180	3,171	3,324	3,500	3,500	4,386	10,370	3,490
Book value at end of year	243	270	315	346	387	466	570	776	982	1,539	589
Book value at start of year	212	243	270	315	346	387	466	570	776	982	457
Change in book value during year	31	27	45	31	41	79	104	206	206	557	133
Estimated part-paid amount	31	27	45	31	41	79	104	206	206	557	133
Estimated callable amount	1,319	1,441	1,605	2,149	3,130	3,245	3,396	3,294	4,180	9,813	3,357
Percentage of part-paid to nominal	2.30%	1.84%	2.73%	1.42%	1.29%	2.38%	2.97%	5.89%	4.70%	5.37%	3.09%
Percentage of callable to nominal	97.70%	98.16%	97.27%	98.58%	98.71%	97.62%	97.03%	94.11%	95.30%	94.63%	96.91%
Leveraged amount	7,078	7,147	8,200	9,841	18,507	15,727	19,000	36,100	37,827	42,098	20,152
Total finance enabled	8,428	8,615	9,850	12,021	21,678	19,051	22,500	39,600	42,213	52,468	23,642
Estimated total of EIF equity book – average book value at end of year divided by average part-paid to nominal											19,087
Estimated book of finance enabled – average of total finance enabled multiplied by 15 years due to no run-off											354,636

Figure 4.3: EIF equity commitments

Figure 4.4: Unicredit S.p.A. Non-Performing Loans at the end of 2015

As at 31/12/15 in €millions	Bad Exposures	Unlikely to pay	Non-performing & past due	Total Non-performing	Performing loans	Total loans
Gross exposure	36,523	17,411	1,554	55,488	189,898	245,386
As % of total loans	14.88%	7.1%	0.63%	22.61%	77.39%	-
Writedowns	22,831	5,832	461	29,124	1,087	30,211
As % of face value	62.51%	33.50%	29.67%	52.49%	0.57%	-
Carrying value	13,692	11,579	1,093	26,364	188,811	215,175
As % of face value	37.49%	66.50%	70.33%	47.51%	99.43%	-
As % of total loans	6.36%	5.38%	0.51%	12.25%	87.75%5	-

Figure 4.4: Unicredit S.p.A. Non-Performing Loans at the end of 2015

Figure 4.5: comparison of level of write-down for NPLs held in portfolio on a prudent basis and in Unicredit S.p.A.

Category	Description	Likely recovery	Appropriate write-down	Write-down as above	Under-provision	Further write-down in €millions
Bad exposures	in default, little likelihood of recovery	10%	90%	62.51%	27.49%	10,040
Unlikely to pay	in default, some chance of a recovery	10-50% = 30% on average	70%	33.5%	36.5%	6,355
Non-performing & past due	it has to meet both of these tests, and there should be a meaningful recovery	50-90% = 70% on average	30%	29.67%	0.33%	€5
Further writedown on book value needed to meet likely recovery rates						€16,400

Figure 4.5: comparison of level of write-down for NPLs held in portfolio on a prudent basis and in Unicredit S.p.A.

Chapter 5 – the response to the Pandemic

Chapter introduction

The EU/Eurozone's emergency response to the Pandemic crisis came in several channels. The first was a doubling-down on its bond buying, up to then mounted through its APP programmes, and then a series of other measures. In total these were:

- The Pandemic Emergency Purchase Programme (PEPP)
- The relaxation of associated rating and creditworthiness criteria
- The extension of ECB Targeted Longer Term Refinancing Operations
- The EU Coronavirus Recovery Fund within the 2021-7 Multiannual Financial Framework
- European Guarantee Fund
- Expansion of TARGET2 Imbalances
- Legal moratoria on loan payments and on actions to recover defaulted loans

In the process several Rubicons were crossed.

The terms of the PEPP have meant that Eurosystem operations no longer have to be carried on a 'whole Eurozone' basis, by the global amounts transacted having to be broken down into allocations to each NCB in line with the NCB's Capital Key in the ECB.

The relaxation of criteria mean that Eurosystem operations no longer have to be carried out solely with Investment Grade securities, let alone ones that count within the accepted definition of 'central bank money'.

The EU Coronavirus Recovery Fund will involve borrowings being taken up by the EU and relayed as grants, not as back-to-back loans. This causes a certain future deficit in the EU cash budget which must either be filled with new taxes or levies, or increased member state cash contributions.

It also repositions the member states as the primary source of repayment for the portion of the funds relayed as grants, whereas before they were the secondary source, the primary source being the taker of the back-to-back loan. The positioning of member states as secondary backers has been repeatedly represented to investors in the EU's bonds – either directly in investor presentations or by its being included in reports on the EU by a public credit rating agency – as being a credit strength of those bonds.

If all of that was not enough, the TARGET2 balances have inexorably increased, and under the same pattern: Germany lends more, Spain and Italy borrow more.

5.1 The Pandemic Emergency Purchase Programme (PEPP)

The PEPP has been examined in our Bruges Group paper of April 2021.[103] It consists of more buying of bonds but with important differences compared to the APP programme, implying weaker controls and a higher degree of credit risk.

The PEPP was established through the EU legal instrument DECISION EU 2020/440 ECB of 24 March 2020.[104] The amount upon establishment was €750 billion. This was raised by €600 billion on 4 June 2020 to €1.35 trillion, and further increased by €500 billion on 10 December 2020 to a ceiling of €1,850 billion.

The PEPP balance as of 8 April 2022 was €1,695.7 billion, near to 92% of the ceiling.[105]

---

[103] https://www.brugesgroup.com/blog/the-ecb-s-pandemic-emergency-purchase-programme-the-undermining-of-the-eurozone-as-a-free-financial-market-the-epitome-of-the-failure-of-the-euro-project-and-a-coup-d-etat-by-the-european-central-bank accessed on 1 June 2022

[104] https://www.ecb.europa.eu/mopo/implement/pepp/html/index.en.html accessed on 31 March 2021

[105] https://www.ecb.europa.eu/mopo/implement/omo/html/index.en.html accessed on 17 April 2022

What the PEPP can buy

The PEPP may buy any bonds that are permissible for the four pre-existing APP programmes to buy, noting that non-financial institution commercial paper was added to the APP scope after the four programmes had been established such that the PEPP can buy this as well.

All bonds purchased must be on the ECB list of eligible collateral.[106]

The Purchase Limits for public sector securities in the portfolio that were built into the PSPP are absent in the PEPP. The PSPP limits are:
- The PSPP can own no more than 50% of any individual bond issue or of the total of bonds issued by a recognised supranational
- The PSPP can own no more than 33% of any individual bond issue or of the total of bonds issued by any other entity

The PEPP can buy entire issues and the entire outstandings of any issuer, subject only to the guideline explained below connected to ECB Capital Keys.

Bonds of a supranational issuer can be purchased by any Eurosystem member.

Bonds of a non-supranational issuer can only be purchased by the Eurosystem member – the NCB – of the member state where the issuer is domiciled: only the Bundesbank can buy German government bonds (Bundesanleihe) into the PEPP and only the Banca d'Italia can buy Italian government bonds (BTPs).

PEPP portfolio limits

This leads on to the limit of the make-up of the PEPP portfolio: it need only be guided by the Capital Key of each Eurozone NCB in the ECB, not to adhere to it.

The comparison of the terms of the PEPP with those of the PSPP is important. The terms of the PSPP were revised multiple times since its establishment but all those changes were consolidated into DECISION EU 2020/188 ECB of 3 February 2020. These include the limitations by International Securities Identification Number of what percentages of an issue and of an issuer's bonds the PSPP can hold which are absent in the PEPP.

The PEPP can buy entire issues.

The PSPP was the focus of the legal case brought in front of the German Constitutional Court (Bundesverfassungsgericht or BVG) and which gave rise to this court's verdict of May 2020. That verdict was based upon the assumption of the presence of certain conditions in the PSPP that are absent in the PEPP, to the extent that the PEPP has rendered some of those conditions meaningless.

The PEPP held, in April 2021, a greater proportion of public sector securities (93%) to its entire portfolio, than did the PSPP as a percentage of the four pre-existing APPs (82%).

How the PEPP dispensed with the comfort that the BVG read into the conditions of the PSPP

The Bruges Group paper on pp. 28-32 explains how the PEPP's conditions sweep away the comfort that the BVG read into the conditions of the PSPP.

Figure 5.1 is a summary.

---

[106] https://www.ecb.europa.eu/mopo/assets/html/index.en.html accessed on 1 June 2022

The PEPP can buy primary market securities of member states and can thus engage in the direct monetary financing of member states, and indeed buy up the entirety of their individual bond issues.

The PEPP activity does not have to be conducted across all member states equally: its portfolio make-up does not have to match ECB Capital Keys. This means that the PEPP is not supporting the euro currency as a unitary entity, but is supporting Eurozone member states individually.

The PEPP is linked tenuously to keeping inflation to 2% - the ECB's core mandate.

The ECB's freedom-of-action is further extended.

The BVG's assumption that bonds held in an ECB scheme must be of 'a minimum credit quality assessment that provides access to the bond markets' is challenged in a number of ways.

The Eurosystem have gone better than circumventing this test that appears six times: they have liquidated its meaning. When the BVG formulated its test of an issuer having a 'minimum credit quality' enabling it to 'access the bond markets', they cannot have conceived how the ECB would design a series of programmes whose upshot was to make the Eurosystem itself 'the bond market', enabling it in turn to determine the access criteria to the bond market and to set them at a lower level than 'Investment Grade'.

These actions disable both 'credit quality' and 'access to bond markets' as supposedly independent benchmarks applied by credit rating agencies and market forces: the Eurosystem alters the credit rating criteria as it wishes and the Eurosystem is the sole market force of significance in the Euro bond market.

Degree ownership and control of the Eurozone bond market exercised by the Eurosystem

As regards the Eurosystem defining 'access to bond markets', pp. 24-7 of the Bruges Group paper gave a working model, as of December 2020, of how much of the Euro bond market was owned or controlled by the Eurosystem.

There were some unknowns around the gross size of the TARGET2 balances, to what extent they were secured with collateral that is already part of 'General government gross debt', and whether the collateral was released at the end of the day for other purposes, or whether rather it remained where it is under the effective control of a Eurosystem member but became, for a very short period, unhypothecated.

Appendix 3 goes into further depth about the interpretational difficulties.

Notwithstanding those difficulties, we set out below the blocks of money that correlated to bonds owned or controlled as collateral by the Eurosystem, and drew out cumulative figures:
- What was owned: the APP + the PEPP
- Plus what was held as collateral
- Plus what was held as collateral if only the net-net balance in TARGET2 was regarded as a loan requiring to be supported by collateral
- Plus if the TARGET debtors balance was regarded as loans requiring to be supported by collateral as well
- But not including the gross balances in TARGET2 that were eliminated by the end-of-day netting, even though they either still required to be supported by collateral or if the collateral remained operationally in place overnight where it had been held intraday, albeit that it became unhypothecated[107]

At each level the market share owned or controlled by the Eurosystem increased, until it was nearly half, with figures in € millions.

---

[107] Intraday – during the business day; unhypothecated – not subject to a security interest in favour of another party

To recap, the figures are as at 31 December 2020, except for TARGET2 where the amounts are as per the end of October 2020:

Total nominal value of Eurosystem eligible collateral	€15,800,000
Collateral lodged in the Eurosystem	€2,600,000
TARGET2 net-net balance (end October)	€323,700
TARGET2 creditors - balance (end October)	€1,546,200
TARGET2 debtors - balance (end October)	€1,222,500
PEPP portfolio	€718,000
APP/CSP	€243,000
APP/PSPP	€2,309,000
APP/ABSPP	€29,000
APP/CBPP3	€286,000
Total pre-existing APP portfolio	€2,868,000
APP + PEPP	€3,586,000
APP + PEPP + Collateral	€6,186,000
APP + PEPP + Collateral + TARGET net-net balance	€6,509,700
APP + PEPP + Collateral + TARGET debtors balance	€7,732,200
Relationship of indicator to total value of Eurosystem eligible collateral:	
APP + PEPP	23%
APP + PEPP + Collateral	39%
APP + PEPP + Collateral + TARGET net-net balance	41%
APP + PEPP + Collateral + TARGET debtors balance	49%

Table 5.1: degree of ownership and control by the Eurosystem of the euro financial market at the end of 2020

At that stage the Eurosystem itself owned or controlled as much as 49% of the entire bond supply.

The PEPP was a major step-up in the Eurosystem's intervention and of its overall ownership and control of the financial market in Euro. This undermined the concept of the Euro financial market being a free market, when its administrator owns it and tilts market conditions so far in favour of itself, if one defines 'itself' as a pyramid of public sector bodies of which the Eurosystem members are a part, with the member states at the top, all with high debts and needing to keep the cost of debt service low. What better than to have the Eurosystem members rig the market in their favour by first managing to own and control half of it, and then fixing interest rates at a negative level?

5.2 The relaxation of associated rating and creditworthiness criteria

At the same time as setting up the PEPP, the Eurozone authorities greatly weakened the credit rating and creditworthiness standards for Eurosystem monetary and payment operations. This is explained in the Bruges Group PEPP paper pp. 34-39. The respective ECB press releases are quoted in full in that paper as Appendix 7: ECB Monetary Policy press release of 22 April 2020 pp. 59-60 and as Appendix 8 – ECB Monetary Policy press release of 22 April 2020 pp. 61-2, with the key dispensations highlighted in red.

The extract of pages 34-39 is Appendix 2. A summary is given below.

Eurosystem Credit Assessment Framework for Monetary Policy Operations

Pre-pandemic the Eurosystem Credit Assessment Framework for Monetary Policy Operations or ECAF, with five rungs or Credit Quality Steps (CQS), defined the eligibility for securities to be on the ECB list and therefore investable by the APP and the PEPP.

A CQS rung equates to given public credit ratings or approved equivalents, one of the equivalents being an IRB methodology.

A minimum rating of Credit Quality Step 3 ('CQS3') applied: securities had to be of Investment Grade to be bought by the APP or PEPP. That meant, for securities above 1 year:

Standard & Poor's	BBB-
Moody's	Baa3
Fitch	BBB-
DBRS	BBBL

The minimum short-term ratings for a security to meet CQS3 were:

Standard & Poor's	A-3
Moody's	P-3
Fitch	F-3
DBRS	R-3

Any security only has to have one rating for the purposes of the ECAF; if there are multiple ratings, the best one applies, including where one meets CQS3 and the others fall below.

Reduction in Eurosystem standards

The ECB relaxed the standards to permit CSQ4 and CSQ5 securities to continue to be held by the PEPP and other APPs where they had come down into that rung from CSQ3. The securities did not have to be sold if their ratings fell below Investment Grade. The long-term ratings in these categories are:

	CSQ4	CSQ5
Standard & Poor's	BB+	BB
Moody's	Ba1	Ba2
Fitch	BB+	BB
DBRS	BBH	BB

These long-term ratings class the security as Speculative Grade.

A delusion suffuses the PEPP on the issue of ratings downgrades that securities purchased when they met CQS3 do not have to be sold even if they fall to CQS5 (Ba2 using the Moody's scale), but they do have to be sold if they fall below CQS5 to B1 in the Moody's system, its equivalent in the three other systems, or worse. There will be no-one wanting to buy the securities under that eventuality.

PEPP stance as opposed to investment 'Best Practice'

The PEPP's stance on buying and then selling securities flies in the face of 'best practice' for investments.[108] This is to buy securities rated no lower than Baa1, and to sell any that fall into Baa2. The investor has then disposed of its holding before the security risks falling out of Investment Grade, Baa3 being the lowest rung of Investment Grade. This avoids an investor getting caught up in a firesale when a security ceases to meet the criteria of collective investment vehicles. These vehicles are obliged to sell, and all at the same time, which will drive prices down and precipitate the firesale. The prudent investor gets out early. The Eurosystem, knowing it cannot get out, simply re-writes the rules for itself so that it does not have to sell securities in portfolio when they fall out of Investment Grade. In fact the Eurosystem only has to sell them after the firesale has already taken place; at that point the securities will not meet the buying criteria of any investors, and the Eurosystem will be forced to hold the security until maturity, and hope that the issuer repays.

This reversal of normal logic is, in a way, a statement of the facts for a market actor who controls the market and controls the rules upon which the market operates: they cannot step out of their investments given that they are the only major buyer, and have, by their interventions, already caused all the securities in the market to be over-priced. When the Eurosystem wants to sell, there will not be willing buyers in the market at the price the Eurosystem wants to sell at.

---

[108] For example, the "Investment" module of the Cash Management course offered by Accountingcpd.net and written by the author

Dissolution of safeguards – Eurosystem becomes a commercial bank

The Eurosystem has dissolved the BVG-quoted safeguard that the 'issuer has a minimum credit quality assessment that provides access to the bond markets'.

These collateral-easing measures affect the PEPP and all the APPs. These measures were announced as temporary on 7 April 2020 but were extended until June 2022 on 10 December 2020.

Further weakenings were:
- increase of 20% in the Eurosystem loan size against all types of collateral, achieved by reducing the 'haircuts' specified in the ECB list of eligible collateral. Haircuts were reduced by around 20% - 1/5th of themselves;
- 'credit claims' (i.e. an instrument giving the Eurosystem a collateral interest in bank loans) were accepted onto the ECB list. These could come in the form of a debt security like a Collateralised Loan Obligation, in which case they were eligible for the PEPP and APP. If they did not come in the form of a debt security, they were not investable by the PEPP or APP but could still serve as eligible collateral;
- 'Credit claims' could include loans of lower credit quality, loans to types of debtors not accepted in the ECB's general framework, and foreign-currency loans. COVID-19 emergency loans, guaranteed by a public entity, were also eligible;
- the ECB eased the acceptance of banks' own IRB models as arbiters of creditworthiness and as an alternative to a public credit rating. IRB would play a particular role in attesting to the quality of 'credit claims';
- Republic of Greece bonds were returned to the ECB list: their inclusion in the PEPP on 24 March 2020 opened the gates for them to be included on the ECB list in April 2020.

The Eurosystem had in effect become a commercial bank, only one without its own credit assessment function. Credit assessment was and is outsourced to third-parties, including ones – banks – with a very high vested interest in attesting to their expertise in credit assessment, but with an inconsistent track record of success.

The further measures announced on 22 April 2020 had the intention of <u>temporarily</u> (our underlining) mitigating 'the effect on counterparties' collateral availability from rating downgrades arising from the economic impact of coronavirus, while continuing ensuring collateral adequacy'.

They did not ensure collateral adequacy: on the contrary, they compromised it.

Grandfathering of credit ratings at their March 2020 level

Whilst the haircut reductions applied to all types of asset, several measures only applied to marketable assets, and they crystallized the credit ratings – and thus the eligibility – of issuers and issues at their level on 24 March 2020, inoculating issuers and issues from downgrades by rating agencies. These measures – as well as their worst-case implications - are shown in Figure 5.2, as well as being in Appendix 2.

They amounted to extraordinary weakenings of the quality of assets owned and held as collateral within Eurosystem operations. Assets would be treated as central bank money and be exchanged for Eurosystem central bank money when they were clearly some way distant from being that.

IRB grades as interchangeable with public credit ratings, with both being de-based

Eurosystem policy has come to regard public credit ratings as interchangeable with internal ones generated by banks. Both have been debased. Internal ratings have been debased by the IRB methodologies used to ascertain them, as described earlier. Public credit ratings had already been debased in the Eurozone by two factors.

Firstly, the independence of the rating agencies had been compromised by EU Regulation, leading to Eurozone issuers – and particularly sovereign issuers - continuing to be rated at a level significantly higher than their economic fundamentals merit. This is evidenced by the worsening Debt-to-GDP ratio referenced above, which have not led to ratings downgrades. Indeed, Greece was upgraded by DBRS on 21 Mar 2022 to BB (high) and by S&P on 25 April 2022 to BB+.

Secondly the rating agencies seem to have not grasped – or have been compelled not to grasp – the intrinsic difference between Eurosystem central bank money (which has no single sovereign behind it which is the sole user of the currency), and central bank money in GBP or USD (where the single sovereign has control of the levers of monetary policy). The proof of this point lies in the fact that Eurosystem central bank money is not *de iure* fully fungible: issuers of it have different credit ratings. The Stability & Growth Pact and the Fiscal Stability Treaty are attempts to make Eurosystem central bank money *de facto* fully fungible by harmonizing the statistics of economic performance of its users, but that is not the same as *de iure* fungibility. Eurozone 'sovereign issuers' having inflated public credit ratings as a result, as do all supranational and public sector entities and banks connected to Eurozone sovereigns as part of the Eurozone monetary policy system.[109]

So, since Eurozone sovereigns, supranational and public sector entities were already systemically over-rated, it follows that the quality of the Eurosystem's assets and collateral was already lower than it appeared on paper.

Degree of over-rating of Eurozone parties by public credit rating agencies and implications

The key question is by how many notches. If one were to posit that Eurozone sovereign ratings were too high by one notch because of political influence and by a further two notches for the failure to appreciate the flaw in Eurozone central bank money, that would be three notches. The systematic under-reporting of the size of Eurozone public sector debt that is the subject of this paper should add another notch at least. We will revisit this point at the conclusion with reference to the anomaly identified earlier whereby there is no consistency between what one notch of credit rating correlates to as a percentage of Debt-to-GDP Ratio. If the shadow debts and contingent liabilities represent a high proportion of member states' GDP, then a downgrade of more than one notch for this aspect may be merited.

It might seem unfair on the likes of Germany and the Netherlands with AAA ratings to subject them to a 4-notch downgrade, but these are the member states upon whom reliance is being placed by investors for the debt service on the shadow debts: the balance sheets and contingent liabilities that the rating agencies consider when ascribing AAA ratings to these countries do not capture the full position.

In consequence many assets formally rated as Investment Grade are already intrinsically Speculative Grade and not necessarily at the top of it. Now that assets formally rated as sitting at the top end of Speculative Grade will remain eligible for Eurosystem operations, it follows that the real minimum credit quality for Eurosystem operations is at the middle or low end of the range of Speculative Grade.

For example, Republic of Italy's formal rating of Baa3 (Investment Grade/Moderate Credit Risk) reflects an intrinsic rating of Ba3 (Speculative Grade/Substantial Credit Risk). If Italy's formal rating is allowed to fall to Ba2 (Speculative Grade/Substantial Credit Risk), its intrinsic rating would by then be B2 (Speculative Grade/High Credit Risk).

Furthermore, where IRB methodologies of the institutions originating a covered bond or ABS are permitted as a proxy for a public credit rating, one has no quality assurance at all beyond that the methodology has been approved by a financial regulator. These are the same methodologies in wide use in Greece, Cyprus, Spain, Portugal and Italy, under which their user banks can discount their nominal book of business by 60-70% to attest their Risk-Adjusted Assets, against which they have a comfortable cushion of Common Equity Tier 1. And yet these are the same methodologies that gave rise to such a high proportion of Non-Performing Loans.

Summary of degradation of Eurosystem standards

As stated before, this list of measures represents an extraordinary weakening of the quality of assets owned and held as collateral within Eurosystem operations.

It is a comprehensive degradation of the asset quality in Eurosystem operations. Against this it cannot be claimed that the safeguard exists that the 'issuer has a minimum credit quality assessment that provides access to the bond markets'.

---

[109] 'Managing Euro Risk', p. 3, p.30, p.33

While none of the securities permissible can have Junk ratings as the rating agencies classify them, the portfolio will have increasing elements of Speculative Grade in it and even assets that have no formal public credit rating, but which are disgorged by a bank's IRB system. These assets can safely be assumed to equate to the lower end of Speculative Grade if they had public ratings, and will harbour individual assets, within a batch that ranks as Speculative Grade on average, that are Junk.

5.3 The extension of ECB Targeted Longer Term Refinancing Operations

The TLTRO balance at the end of 2021 was €2.2 trillion, compared to €616 billion at the end of 2019, an increase of €1.6 trillion. This came about largely through ECB Open Market Operations that were in the TLTRO Series 3:[110]

Month	TLTRO Op.	Amount	Maturity
March 2020	3.3	€115 billion	3 years
June 2020	3.4	€1,308 billion	3 years
September 2020	3.5	€174 billion	3 years
December 2020	3.6	€50 billion	3 years
March 2021	3.7	€331 billion	3 years
June 2021	3.8	€110 billion	3 years
September 2021	3.9	€98 billion	3 years
December 2021	3.10	€52 billion	3 years

Table 5.2: TLTRO Series 3 operations from March 2020

December 2021 should be the final operation and indeed there was none in March 2022. The total of these operations was €2.2 trillion, which is not a coincidence because the operations took over, as explained above, any maturities under TLTRO Series 2 falling during the same timespan, either directly upon their maturity, or by first refinancing them out of the Bridge LTRO and refinancing them again through the next-following TLTRO Series 3 operation.

It is worth noting that these operations are unsecured. The borrowing bank simply needs to send to its NCB its response to a questionnaire in which it lists the current outstanding balances under different loan types. The borrowing bank can then bid for TLTRO funds up to 55% of the cumulative outstanding balance.[111]

The interest rate applied 'is linked to the participating banks' lending patterns. The more loans participating banks issue to non-financial corporations and households (except loans to households for house purchases), the more attractive the interest rate on their TLTRO III borrowings becomes'. This means that, the more the bank borrows, the lower the cost of its TLTRO funds.

Borrowing rates on TLTRO Series 3 'can be as low as 50 basis points below the average interest rate on the deposit facility over the period from 24 June 2020 to 23 June 2022, and as low as the average interest rate on the deposit facility calculated over the life of the respective TLTRO Series 3 during the rest of the life of the same operation'. The ECB deposit facility rate is one of the three interest rates the ECB sets for monetary policy purposes.[112] As at 6 June 2022 the deposit rate was -½%.[113] The theoretical best interest rate (for the borrower) is -1%, if the deposit rate continues at its current level: this is based on the first half of the above statement.

TLTRO thus represents a very low cost of financing for banks, especially unsecured financing. For the Eurosystem it is an exercise in commercial banking – unsecured lending to other banks at term.

---

[110] https://www.ecb.europa.eu/mopo/implement/omo/html/index.en.html accessed on 6 June 2022

[111] https://www.ecb.europa.eu/mopo/implement/omo/tltro/html/index.en.html accessed on 6 June 2022

[112] https://www.ecb.europa.eu/ecb/educational/explainers/tell-me/html/what-is-the-deposit-facility-rate.en.html accessed on 6 June 2022

[113] https://www.ecb.europa.eu/stats/policy_and_exchange_rates/key_ecb_interest_rates/html/index.en.html accessed on 6 June 2022

5.4 The EU Coronavirus Recovery Fund within the 2021-7 Multiannual Financial Framework

The European Union reached an agreement on its next budget (the Multiannual Financial Framework or MFF) for the period 2021-27 at an 'ECOFIN' European Council summit meeting lasting from 17th to 21st July 2020.[114] It included the Coronavirus Recovery Fund, a €750 billion exercise to borrow-and-spend. The borrowings will be taken up by the European Union, and are therefore on the customary joint-and-several-liability basis: each member state is theoretically liable for the whole amount. The amount of the Coronavirus Recovery Fund represents a major expansion of the EU's loans and guarantees at the end of the 2014-20 MFF, the calculation of which is given later.

Size of the 2021-7 EU budget

For 2021-27, the EU has set an 'overall budget' of €1.82 trillion, of which €1.07 trillion is shown as the MFF and €750 billion is shown as 'Next Generation EU', or the Coronavirus Recovery Fund.[115] Council Decision 2020/2053 both raised the 'normal' budget percentages to 1.40% and 1.46% of EU GNI from 1.23% and 1.29% respectively, and allowed a 'temporary' expansion of both just for this MFF by 0.6% of EU GNI to 2.00% and 2.06% respectively.

The lower figure can be understood as all the money going into the EU budget and out again during the period (the payments appropriation), and the higher figure to include the actual or anticipated effect on future cash budgets of funds, facilities and guarantees that the EU can engage during the current budget period.

€1.82 trillion is 1.93% of EU 2020 GNI extrapolated over 7 years and equates to €260 billion per annum.

If €1.07 trillion of this is the MFF, it allows annual disbursements under the new Fund of the balance - €75 billion per annum. However, 1/7th of the Fund per annum is €107 billion. This amount should be spent annually in order to exhaust the fund by 2027, whereas the amounts in the budget for the Fund are lower: 0.6% of 2020 EU GNI is only €80 billion, and the budget allowance for the Fund is only €75 billion. Inflation should raise EU GNI, but the purchasing power of the money will decline, and the connection of the disbursement of the money to Coronavirus diminishes with time, making the connection of the expenditure to its cause the more tenuous.

If €1.07 trillion is the entire MFF, then it contains the 0.06% as the amount the EU can engage in funds, facilities and guarantees. €1.026 trillion is in that case the cash budget, and €44 billion is the allowance for funds, facilities and guarantees.

How the size of the Fund is expressed as a percentage of GNI

It is uncomfortable to read that the Coronavirus Recovery Fund will be accommodated under a special extra ceiling of 0.6% of GNI per annum under Council Decision 2020/2053, when the normal ceiling for such exercises is 0.06%. Are no other numbers possible? Was it hoped that readers would become confused by the different placing of the decimal point and overlook the size of the new fund compared to all previous funds? For the member states, this means they have a new contingent liability up to 0.6% of the 2021-27 GNI out to 2058, with a declining balance in the meanwhile, over and above the contingent liabilities built up through the usage of the 0.06% of GNI over many years in the past, during the current MFF and over future ones.

The Fund challenges assumptions about EU interventions

The large size of the fund challenges the accepted extent of EU interventions. It appears that the EU can borrow a very large amount as long as the repayments are spread over a long enough period and, if the processes and controls limiting the EU's expenditure threaten to be infringed, they can be altered to accommodate the new exercise, as has happened with Council Decision 2020/2053.

What has been agreed appears to some extent to have dissolved the basis for and controls on the EU budget and borrowings, and thereby undermined representations made by credit rating agencies to financial market investors.

---

[114] 'Special meeting of the European Council (17, 18, 19, 20 and 21 July 2020) – Conclusions' reference EUCO 10/20
[115] https://ec.europa.eu/info/live-work-travel-eu/health/coronavirus-response_en accessed on 10.8.20

Rating agencies seem unable to deliver a consistent explanation of the grounding for and amount of the member state contingent liability for the EU's debts:

- The Moody's Investor Service rating report of 2015, on p. 1, refers to 'the European Commission's right to call for additional resources of on average up to around 0.26% of EU Gross National Income (around €40 billion on average) each year during 2014-20 from its member states, on a joint and several basis'.
- The 2015 EU Investor Presentation quotes, on p. 7, Standard and Poor's stating that the 'EU has an additional contingent claim on Member States of about €30 billion annually over the 2014-2020 MFF period. This pledge is made for the express purpose of backing EU's financial obligations'.
- DBRS's rating report of 3 April 2020 p. 5 states that 'EU legislation obliges member states to provide additional contributions necessary to repay the debt and balance the budget, up to a ceiling of 1.20% of EU GNI. If needed, EU legislation allows member states to contribute independently of their share to the EU budget'.

We see 0.26% of GNI and 1.20% of EU GNI, and we have €30 billion and €40 billion. DBRS do not provide a reference for the 'EU legislation' and the other agencies do not prove either 'the European Commission's right to call' or the 'EU [ ] additional contingent claim'.

Difficulties in understanding the EU budgetary process

The figure of 0.26% might be the difference between the MFF ceiling set at 1.23% of EU GNI for 2014-20 and the 0.97% of EU GNI that the EU was said to be spending in cash. With average EU GNI of about €12.5 trillion per annum between 2014 and 2020, the cash budget would have sat at around €121 billion per annum and the MFF at €154 billion, leaving a supposed cushion for backing borrowings and guarantees of €33 billion per annum.[116] This is speculation, however, and the point needs to be officially and authoritatively clarified.

Where we have €8 billion per annum (0.06% of EU GNI) within the 2021-27 MFF, this can correlate to €56 billion of losses on operations approved during the MFF: there is no annual pro rata allocation. The whole amount could be committed on the final day of the MFF or even up to a year afterwards under the carryover provisions.

While the difference between our €8 billion per annum and rating agency statements of €30-40 billion per annum needs to be addressed, the new Fund is of a different order of magnitude. The subsequent five MFFs will have to cater for bond maturities of around €150 billion each.

Size of the new Fund, drawdown and source of repayment

The €750 billion of debt will be repayable over 31 years from 2027 to 2058, with maximum 7.5% of it falling due each year.[117] That maximum is €56.25 billion, which is within the €80.5 billion that is 0.6% of 2020 EU GNI. The average annual repayment is €24.19 billion. 52% of repayments to bond investors (€29 billion of the maximum or €12.58 billion of the average) will have no borrower repayments against them. The EU's annual cash budget for the 2014-20 MFF was around €135 billion so such debt payments would have shrunk the remaining cash budget by 9-21% if they had been due during the MFF in which they were agreed upon.

The debt drawdown during 2021-27 will result in a very low net interest burden on the EU cash budget in the short term, limited to the shortfall on interest receivable on the €390 billion being disbursed as grants, compared to the interest payable on the entire €750 billion.[118] Any shortfall is likely to be minimised by the negative rates set by the ECB; indeed, not receiving negative loan interest on the grants portion could actually result in additional Own Resource in 2021-27.

The new borrowings will have an impact on future MFFs, for which either the member state cash contributions will have to rise or new EU-level taxes will have to be imposed to cover the EU's debt service for that portion of the €750 billion that is to be relayed as grants, and of course for any credit losses on the portion that is to be relayed as loans.

---

[116] EU's 'GNI_data_collection_2019' with current foreign exchange rates applied to non-Euro currency figures, totalled and averaged to reach average EU GNI, with factors of 0.97% and 0.26% applied
[117] EUCO 10/20 p. 3; points A7 and A8
[118] EUCO 10/20 p. 3; point A6

The usage of the EU as the borrowing vehicle was hailed as a breakthrough – even though the EU had borrowings already – because it showed the member states acting in concert and creating debts that were backed by all EU taxpaying entities. Indeed that is the case, but this should not be at all to the taste of the citizenry of member states, because of the means arrogated to itself by the EU to make this come about. Nor should it be to the taste of financial market investors. In sum, the outcome of the ECOFIN summit was a major power grab by the EU apparatus, and one scarcely if at all within their legal powers. It ought to have been greeted both as a democratic outrage and a financial one, both for the suppliers of money – financial market investors and their helpmeets the credit rating agencies – and for receivers and re-payers, the EU's citizenry and businesses.

Firstly the framework and controls around the EU's budget, how much it can spend on its citizens' behalf and how much it can borrow, have been effectively dissolved. Up until this point the amount that the EU could borrow – and the amount it could extend in guarantees to other entities like the EIB Group to allow them to borrow – was assumed to be limited to 0.06% of EU GNI per annum, and to be relatively trivial. Now it appears to be possible, and may always have been possible, to establish a fund in an amount of 5.6% of EU GNI - over 90 times that amount. This brings into question what the 0.06% represented.

2021-7 could see new contingent liabilities created of 0.06% of GNI per annum under the normal limit and 0.796% of GNI under the Fund, which are cumulative with existing ones. It was therefore possible to create very large quantities of future liabilities with minor changes to the existing framework and controls, meaning that the framework and controls were substantially ineffective.

The accumulation of amounts incurred under this difference of 0.06% of GNI over all MFFs is (or was) known as the 'Reste à liquider', but the ECOFIN document[119] says this will rise to only €308 billion during the 2021-27 MFF, even though the EU will borrow €750 billion, and there were – according to our calculations – around €150 billion in loans and guarantees outstanding already at the time the new MFF was agreed, with another €24 billion in the pipeline for completion during the then-current MFF.[120] That would have raised the 'Reste à liquider' to €174 billion by the end of the 2014-2020 MFF. The ECOFIN document causes previous assumptions about the 'Reste à liquider' to themselves be liquidated. The Fund will not form part of the 'Reste à liquider', as the Fund does not form part of the MFF. It now appears possible that the EU can create an envelope for new borrowings that is not part of the MFF, when the MFF was previously be assumed to be one and the same as the budget, which was assumed to govern all that the EU could spend and all that it could commit to in such a way as to create a contingent liability for the member states.

Repayment will require new taxes or higher member state cash contributions

The next major issue is that the debts are only affordable out of new taxes imposed at the EU level, which will create a new burden on citizens and businesses in member states but which, because the EU categorizes them as its Own Resources and due to the EU directly, can be statistically masked from the member states' cash contributions. This diminishes the appearance of the cash contributions and misrepresents the total cost of EU membership. Facts4EU.Org revealed that the EU, in Christmas week of 2021, floated the concept of new taxes to bring in an amount of €380 billion between 2026 and 2030, of which €85 billion would flow to Brussels.[121] €247 billion of the new taxes are carbon-related, and €133 billion are new taxes on companies. As Facts4EU.Org points out, the need for new lines of Own Resources is connected to the Coronavirus Recovery Fund.

The EU represent that the extra debt service will not be problematical, on the basis that the EU will have its own money to pay the debt service, but by 'own money' they mean Own Resources, and by extension new taxes. The wording disguises that all of the EU's resources are either diverted from the resources of member states, or imposed and collected by member states when the member state might not have chosen to place that imposition on its businesses, citizens and economy.[122]

---

[119] EUCO 10/20 p. 12; point 7

[120] The €24 billion in the pipeline materialized as the European Guarantee Fund; we raised the issue above as to what the relationship is between this fund and the MFF, given that only a subset of member states have set up the EGF and directly guaranteed the EIB Group

[121] https://facts4eu.org/news/2021_dec_uk_escapes_eu_taxes accessed on 28 December 2021

[122] EUCO 10/20 page 64: "New Own Resources"

The impact of the Coronavirus Recovery Fund will be deflationary in the medium term, and will necessitate either (i) raised payments to the EU (under whatever budget heading and however well disguised) and an equal-and-opposite cut in the funds available for the day-to-day running of the member state or (ii) a cut in the funds available for the day-to-day running of the EU.

How the EU has justified the fund as legal

To legitimize this the EU has manipulated the meaning of Article 122 of the Treaty on the Functioning of the EU. Article 122 is to do with the giving of 'Union Financial Assistance' in the case of natural disasters. Article 122 allows that 'the [European] Council, on a proposal from the Commission, may grant, under certain conditions, Union financial assistance', and this is indeed the way in which matters were presented by the Commission to ECOFIN, which consists of Finance Ministers or heads of government of all Member States and is thus a valid meeting of the European Council.

However the triggering event for this 'Union financial assistance' should be where a 'Where a Member State is in difficulties or is seriously threatened with severe difficulties caused by natural disasters or exceptional occurrences beyond its control'. Article 122 should only be invoked in the case of 'natural disasters or exceptional occurrences beyond its control' affecting one member state at a time, not all of them at once. Article 122 must surely have been drafted to deal with situations such as if the Netherlands had a suffered a repeat of the 1953 floods.

Article 122 says nothing about the 'Union Financial Assistance' being spent on anything other than direct and immediate remedying of the disaster. The €750 billion need not be used to remedy the direct results of coronavirus, such as to replenish medical supplies: it can be used to remedy matters that may or may not have been caused by coronavirus, directly/indirectly, definitely/arguably and so on.

Article 122 says nothing about the affected member state having to wait years for relief. The €750 billion will be disbursed over a period of 7 years and, given the linkage to a GNI which needs to expand before €107 billion per annum can be released, the disbursement pattern will be back-loaded, further lessening the connection between the expenditure and its supposed motivation.

The grants, if not the loans, will be subject to each supplicant member state submitting its national coronavirus recovery plan to the EU apparatus for approval. Article 122 says nothing about this new obligation.

These are major conditions not grounded in Article 122, and their imposition represents a great expansion of competence by the EU apparatus. It is surprising that no commentators or politicians have argued that these conditions are beyond the EU's powers – 'ultra vires'.

Failing other available mechanisms, the Commission has overlooked the exact wording of Article 122 so as to shoehorn its proposal into this Article and thereby legitimize it, dissolving any protection the wording might have afforded to individual member states and their citizenry and businesses. The EU's actions are justified in a 68-page legal opinion from the EU's own legal service, under reference EDK-2020-AK-310708.[123] It is surely indicative that it required so many pages to argue that the EU's actions were consistent with its powers.

What this means for the TFEU and for investor assumptions about the EU's bonds

After this usage of Treaty and Council Decisions, the TFEU must now be construed as not limiting the EU apparatus directly, but as conferring delegated powers on it, through which, in an emergency declared as such by itself, the EU can circumvent any controls on it. Even the Council Decision on the system of the European Communities' own resources was easily replaced to meet the needs of the moment, to increase the centralized powers of the EU apparatus, and to diminish member state controls and protections. The manner of the establishment of the Coronavirus Recovery Fund undermines the representation made to investors that EU borrowings are based on Treaty.

---

[123] EU NGEU Legal Opinion EDK-2020-AK-310708

EU presentations to investors[124] and EU briefings to credit rating agencies[125] have repeatedly inferred that the EU's borrowings were governed directly by the TFEU and were part of the MFF framework.

The Coronavirus Recovery Fund challenges assumptions amongst the EU's creditors and amongst the credit rating agencies about the structure of the EU budget and the basis of the EU's claim on member state budgets if the EU's funds, loans and guarantees result in losses. The 2021-7 'overall budget' is much larger than what was thought to be the MFF and the ceiling, because the Coronavirus Recovery Fund comes on top of it. The manner of its establishment and legitimization appear to have dissolved accepted assumptions around the basis for and controls on the EU budget and borrowings, and the Fund undermines representations made by credit rating agencies to financial market investors.

5.5 European Guarantee Fund[126]

A 'European Guarantee Fund' or EGF was established in 2020.[127] Its ceiling was €24.4 billion and it 'was set up by the EIB Group with contributions from 22 EU Member States. By mobilizing extra finance from the private sector, we aim to generate up to €200 billion for the economy.

The EGF is explained in the EIB 2021 Annual Financial Report 'as designed to complement other actions undertaken at the EU level in response to the crisis triggered by the COVID-19 pandemic'.[128] Five member states do not participate in it. The template for the financing to be raised strongly resembles the InvestEU template.

The products offered by EIB Group sound identical to those it offers under InvestEU. The financings under EGF now appear to be complete: 'The approval and signature of guarantee products were finalised in December 2021, whereas the allocation period was extended until 30 June 2022 and 31 December 2022, depending on the applicable state aid framework, thanks to the approval of the state aid third notification package. Similar to guarantee products, the approval of equity and equity-type operations under the EGF ended in 2021, while signatures can continue until February 2022 for a limited number of transactions'.[129]

Transactions nearly up to the ceiling had been approved by the end of 2021: 'As of 31 December 2021, the EGF Contributors' Committee and EIB governing bodies have approved projects for a total of EUR 23.2 billion'. The remaining €1.2 billion may now have lapsed, as no more approvals could be made after the end of 2021, although this needs to be confirmed.

The EGF was established during the 2104-20 MFF and it has been used mainly during the 2021-7 MFF but its relationship to either is unclear, as it does not run through the legal person of the EU. It is more akin to the EFSF in its structure, while being akin to InvestEU in the operations it enables.

What business the EGF has done and of what type

The EGF webpage stated that as of 30 April 2022 €23.3 billion of the commitments that the EGF could make had been approved, and that the financing documents in respect of €19.1 billion of this figure had already been signed. It also states that it is expected that what had been approved would 'mobilize' €175.6 billion of investment. Once again we have a semantic difficulty: with a guarantee of €24.4 billion, EGF was meant to 'mobilize' €200 billion of financing. €23.3 billion of the €24.4 billion or 95.5% - has been approved, but that should 'mobilize' only €175.6 billion, which is 87.8% of the programme size. When examining InvestEU, we took the term 'mobilized' to refer to the amount of money raised (i) against the EIF's engagement and (ii) directly by the project. If €175.6 billion is based on the same calculation, it means that only €152.3 billion was raised directly by EGF projects over and another €23.3 billion raised on the back of the EGF engagement. If the two are cumulative, we come to a total raised of €198.9 billion, or 99.5% of the programme size.

[124] European Union Investor Presentations of December 2010 and July 2015
[125] Moody's Rating Report on the European Union 30 September 2015
[126] https://www.eib.org/en/products/egf/index.htm accessed on 29 May 2022
[127] https://www.eib.org/en/products/egf/index.htm accessed on 25 May 2022
[128] EIB 2021 Annual Financial Report p. 13
[129] EIB 2021 Annual Financial Report p. 14

The InvestEU calculations were anyway clouded by some transactions in the EIF annual report not being tagged with any programme name. In addition neither €23.3 billion nor €175.6 billion appear to be final figures.

It appeared reasonable to resolve this by stating a total amount 'mobilized' thanks to EGF and InvestEU together of €612 billion at the end of 2021, without being able to exactly determine the relative size of each programme, or of other programmes. Our assumptions made earlier appear reasonable:
- InvestEU accounted for €612 billion of this type of financing put on by the EIF by the end of 2020;
- EGF accounted for the €141 billion of EIF's expansion of this type of financing in 2021;
- EGF will have contributed a further €60 billion or so in 2022;
- InvestEU will now have restarted under the 2021-7 MFF guarantee.

What the EGF guarantees consist of

The EGF webpage states that 'Participating countries in the European Union provide guarantees proportional to their share in the EIB or other institutions. The EGF Contributors' Committee, made up from representatives of these countries, decides on the availability of guarantees. The guarantees will cover losses that may occur in the EGF operations of the EIB Group - including the EIB and its specialized SME-financing arm, the European Investment Fund'. The arrangement operates as InvestEU does, other than that the EIB/EIF do not have blanket recourse to all member states up to a ceiling of the amount of the EU guarantee, but that the guarantees are issued selectively by the 22 member states participating in the EGF.

The list of members of the EGF contributors' committee as of February 2022 shows which countries are not part of it. They are Estonia, Czech Republic, Hungary, Romania and Latvia.[130] It does not state explicitly that the guarantees are joint-and-several as they would be if issued through the legal person of the EU. Instead the inference of the statement that 'Participating countries in the European Union provide guarantees proportional to their share in the EIB or other institutions' is that the liability is several-but-not-joint: as with the unpaid portion of capital in the EIB, each country is only liable up to the amount against its name. It is not responsible for paying in the shares of other countries if those countries cannot pay. However it also means that each country is guaranteeing financings of other countries: a member state does not just stand guarantor for the financings taking place in its own member state. In addition it cannot be the case that one member state's guarantee is either conditional on the other member states paying their shares, or that a member state's pay-out under a particular guarantee call is calculated in accordance with its share in the EIB and other institutions. One member state might pay a larger share of a call if another could not, but it could not be asked to pay more than the ceiling of its guarantee.

The EGF webpage shows the guarantees issued so far, and the operations they enable follow the pattern of the InvestEU programme. The EGF-backed projects financed by EIB Group will have several-but-not-joint backing from 22 member states, whilst InvestEU will continue to expand based on joint-and-several backing from all 27 member states as before.

5.6 Expansion of TARGET2 imbalances

Previous work

We have tracked the issue of the TARGET2 imbalances since 2016 and have issued two major papers, firstly as an overview of the subject upon the request of a senior UK political figure.[131] That overview was based on the following papers:

- Guideline for TARGET2 2005
- Amending Guideline for TARGET2 2016
- Harmonized conditions for participation in TARGET2 (Banque de France version only)
- TARGET2 Information Guide v4.0 from 2010 for the Single Shared Platform

---

[130] egf-contributors-committee-composition-030222.pdf downloaded from the EGF webpages
[131] TARGET imbalances research august 2017 available through Research Papers on www.lyddonconsulting.com

- Target functional specification V2_1_070122 for the Single Shared Platform
- Target 2016 annual report
- ECB 2016 annual report
- ECB 2016 annual accounts (contained in the ECB annual report)
- Eurosystem balance sheet 2016 (also contained in the ECB annual report)
- CCBM information for counterparties - summary of legal instruments of January 2017
- CCBM procedures for Eurosystem counterparties January 2017

This left a number of open points, subsequent to which we visited the Deutsche Bundesbank in Frankfurt in December 2018 to obtain clarification. We obtained an explanation, but it did not fully clarify what all the account balances were at the end of the TARGET2 processing day, what they were at the finish of the end-of-day processes, and what accounting entries were put through in order to marry the two together.

We received three supplementary documents:
- 2012 TARGET Guideline ECB/2012/27
- Agreement of 3 August 2018 on the Multilateral Netting of End-of-Day Obligations in TARGET2
- Deutsche Bundesbank presentation on TARGET2 dated 27th November 2018

We have further collected the ECB annual reports in the meantime, the TARGET2 annual reports, and the ECB monthly reports on the TARGET2 balances.

Public debate on TARGET2 balances, current size, and legal and operational procedures

The subject of TARGET2 imbalances has been much discussed in the media, with two views expounded:
   a.   The balances are mere accounting entries and of no significance;
   b.   The balances represent disguised government-to-government loans and are a form of Eurozone bailout mechanism.

At the end of October 2020, as discussed above, the ECB had a net-net liability to the TARGET2 participants of €324 billion, and participating NCBs had debts to other participating NCBs which netted off at €1.2 trillion. At the end of October 2021 these figures had risen to €352 billion and €1.3 trillion respectively.[132]

The problem is that these are not the complete figures. There is an extra amount that disappears before the amounts in the ECB reports are ascertained. It could be another €1.5 trillion, or even more if the €1.5 trillion is itself the result of a prior zero-balancing of some of the accounts involved.[133]

The TARGET2 balances are derived from the balances on the 600 nostro and vostro accounts held at the ECB and the 24 TARGET2-participating NCBs. These accounts have their own balances at the end of the processing day, and these balances are then subjected to a procedure to net them during the TARGET2 end-of-day.

Appendix 4 contains our full analysis of the legal and operational situation after we had received the supplementary documents referred to above.

However, our own thinking has moved on from then. It does not now seem credible that any zero-balancing takes place on the balances on the 600 TARGET2 accounts as they stand at the end of the processing day. They finish one business day with a balance that is shown on their end-of-day statement (in the SWIFT MT950 format) as the ledger balance and the available balance. The same figures are the opening balances for the following business day.

The TARGET2 balances are a large and impenetrable subject, lacking transparency, but we can start with the ECB's accounting of the net balances, which is incorrect.

---

[132] http://www.lyddonconsulting.com/invisible-eurozone-liabilities-require-action-by-global-financial-regulators/ accessed on 7 June 2022

[133] Zero-balancing: a computer-programmed operation to make a balance on a slave account come to zero, and have its balance reappear on the master account. A genuine zero-balance operates on the balances as they are after all of the day's debits and credits across both the slave and maser accounts have been passed and confirmed. As such it is carried out within the bank's end-of-day processes, and normally towards to end of them

ECB wrongly treats the TARGET2-participating NCBs as a Single Counterparty

The ECB's monthly reports show its claim on or liability to NCB. This treatment is the one justified by the legal papers.

In its annual report, though, the ECB offsets the liabilities against the claims and only books the difference. This is incorrect given the legal documentation.

The ECB is granted no right under the legal documentation to net off the assets and liabilities that match in their amounts but not in their counterparties, so as to produce a single liability position on its own balance sheet. The assets and the liabilities are separate debts to and claims on individual NCBs, and the ECB possesses no offset agreement from the NCBs permitting the claims of some to be netted against the debts of others. The ECB should carry all the assets and liabilities on its balance sheet at least at the level at which they novated to it from the NCBs.

This would inflate the ECB's balance sheet by around €1.5 trillion.

Legal documentation mismatches operational steps

A good basis of banking is that any operational procedure should reflect the legal documentation that governs it. An accounting entry has to have a motivation, be that a payment order, a foreign exchange contract or a standing mandate. Without such a motivation, the bank's internal audit department should not allow the accounting entries to be passed.

The TARGET2 netting fails to meet this test. The legal documentation foresees four steps to bring about the result. However, in the way the Bundesbank explains it, there is only one operational step - a zero-balancing of NCBs' accounts with one another into an ECB account – to cover all of the legal construct of Article 6 of the TARGET Guideline and the phases in the Multilateral Netting agreement. Our current view is that there are no operational steps at all.

Even if the Bundesbank's version is correct, the operation fails to deliver the correct result. The legal procedure indicates that the balances need to end up in the 24 accounts in the books of the ECB that are owned by the NCBs. The legal technique used is novation and that calls for a physical movement of funds in order to prove the transfer of ownership. The zero-balancing should link the nostro accounts of each NCB at the 23 other NCBs to the same NCB's nostro at the ECB. That would be 576 zero-balancing linkages running in parallel, into 24 master accounts.

The operational procedure, according to the Bundesbank, indicates that the balances end up in the 24 accounts in the books of the NCBs that are owned by the ECB. If this is occurring, it transfers ownership, but between the wrong parties: it links the 23 vostro accounts opened at one NCB by the 23 others, to the vostro account of the ECB at the same NCB.

This mismatch between documentation and operations would be bring into question the validity and enforceability of the arrangement were it contracted between a bank and a multinational corporate.

TARGET2 documentation weaker than that need to achieve the same outcome in corporate banking

The documentational backing for the legal procedure is weak compared to what would be needed in the corporate banking world to achieve the same outcome. In particular the main agreement explicitly states that it only treats the end-of-day balances, not the intraday ones, whilst the other element – Article 6 in the TARGET Guideline – claims to constantly merge any two positions between two NCBs into just one position, and therefore to have force for 24 hours a day.

It is a weakness to have legal documentation split into two elements, and a worse weakness to have one element valid 24 hours a day, and another valid for end-of-day, and still worse when there is no definition of 'end-of-day' in the agreement that describes operationally what happens at end-of-day and then at the start of the next day.

The novation should be reversed at the start of the next day, so that each NCB gets its money back and can start to transact against its balance. The Multilateral Netting agreement makes no mention of this reversal, and the Bundesbank made no mention of the zero-balancing being reversed , as it should be if it happened in the first place, under what is known as a 'Cinderella Sweep'.

Short end-of-day and overnight

The TARGET2 day lasts for over 23 hours in 24 on the TARGET2 business days, although it is closed over weekends. The netting process purports to convert the balances to the way the ECB presents them for 50 minutes per business day at most, given that the zero-balancing must occur in the TARGET2 end-of-day between 18:15 and 18:45 CET, and be reversed using the 'Cinderella' function at around 19:05 CET when the books are opened for the following business day.

Given the number of other functions that need to be carried out during this short period and the partially-centralized architecture of TARGET2, it seems unlikely that any zero-balancing occurs at all.

Intraday position

One thing is certain: for the remaining 23+ hours of the business day, the NCBs have direct positions vis a vis one another, either without any netting if one believes that Article 6 fails to achieve it, or in the amount of their single, net bilateral obligation, whatever that is.

Notional or real netting

The key question remains: is real netting applied to the 600 accounts – meaning zero-balancing – or notional netting? Article 6 is notional – no accounting entries result from it. It is a legal measure that alters the complexion to be put on a pair of NCBs each having a balance in one another's books: they are to be considered as one and all the time, but with no operational impact.

The Multilateral Netting dictates no operational steps for its fulfilment, and there are no provisions for the obligatory reversal.

In sum one must conclude that the netting is completely notional. There is no zero-balancing in any direction, and no 'Cinderella Sweep'.

Amount of direct risk

The amount of direct risk being taken is not made clear by the ECB in its annual report or monthly reports, or in the TARGET2 annual report. It is bound to be higher than the amount by which the net positive balances in the ECB's monthly reports match the net negative balances, because the ECB's figures have already gone through more than one stage of netting.

The author's view, expressed above, is that the total amount is €1.5 trillion more than the amount by which the net positive balances in the ECB's monthly reports match the net negative balances. This latter figure is itself €1.8 trillion, which, if correct, means that the unnetted balances are €3.2 trillion.

Credit risk and collateral

The credit risk is either a direct, unsecured risk on the NCB by virtue of maintaining a credit balance on a nostro account with it, or a secured risk through granting an overdraft to the NCB on its vostro account.

The security may well be securities issued by a public sector entity in the same country as the NCB, which represents 100% correlated security: since the debt of the NCB is guaranteed by the government of its Member State, securities issued by that same Member State or its agencies carries the same credit risk.

This leads on to the key question of whether the credit risk should be regarded as gross or net, and net in which sense:

- Net of equal-and-opposite cash positions in other TARGET2 accounts?
- Net of collateral?

Our answer to those questions are, firstly, that the cash positions should be regarded as gross. The documentation underpinning the netting is weak, and it mismatches what happens operationally. If the documentation was tested in a court of law, it is highly likely that an NCB would be able to 'cherry-pick' the arrangement and successfully argue, for example, that it ought not to surrender deposits in its books into the netting when its own position would thereby be converted in an overdraft to the system as a whole.

Secondly the collateral in TARGET2 cannot be considered as genuine collateral: it is 100% correlated.

Member states should find out and take account of the gross end-of-day balances their NCB has in TARGET2, visible from the daily statements on the NCB's TARGET2 accounts at the level of the balance prior to any final operations to execute the netting, if indeed there are any: it remains a possibility that the entire netting is notional and does not include any operations at all.

Which is the better credit risk to have? NCB risk or ECB risk?

It is a further important question whether it is a better result, from the credit risk point of view, for the NCBs to have overnight risk on the ECB than on one another. They have intraday risk on one another, and converting that to ECB risk for at most an hour is not necessarily a superior outcome. The ECB is unrated and thinly capitalised, and can only pay back the TARGET2 Obligations if it receives payment on the TARGET2 Assets.

The only benefit, to major TARGET2 creditors like Germany, of the novation and netting is that the ECB loss-sharing mechanism would serve to reduce their share of any loss from the amount that is owed to them by the NCBs direct, to a portion of the loss determined through their ECB capital key.

The comfort derived from this may prove to be illusory as it is contingent upon other NCBs (and member states) being willing to accept a larger share of the loss than their direct exposure would indicate, and the loss share will naturally rise as the member state/NCB causing the loss will not be able to pay its share.

The situation is clouded further by the avenues open to member states and NCBs to 'cherry-pick' the arrangement in the ways that are open in the corporate banking world. Given that the underlying bank accounts are distributed around the NCBs and subject to their local laws and divergent applicable 'General banking conditions' issued by each NCB, the avenues available for 'cherry-picking' are wider than is the case in a corporate banking set-up, which is customarily established in a single location and subject to a single governing law.

The netting agreement makes no mention of its taking precedence over 'General banking conditions' applicable to the accounts within its scope, so it fails to address this conflict between different agreements: the conflict must be resolved in favour of the netting agreement for the netting agreement to be effective.

How matters would play out in practice if there were a major problem is a matter of conjecture. It cannot be held as certain that the incident would be handled in line with what is written in the agreements.

Indeed, given the questionable efficacy, the possibility of challenge and the likely need for swift remedial action, it is more likely that the TARGET2 imbalances will be formally converted into what they are latently: government-to-government loans from the solvent countries to a universe of ones requiring ongoing financing and in large amounts, concentrating on Italy, Spain, Portugal and Greece.

What are the TARGET2 balances in that case

There is no secret what the net balances and the net-net balance were at year-end 2021:
- The debts and claims of different Eurosystem members that matched one another were €1,457 billion;
- The overhang of claims over debts – which became a liability of the ECB – was €335 billion;
- The total volume of debts and claims shown openly by the ECB was €1,792 billion.

The amount netted away prior to that has been induced from the difference between the Eurosystem's business conducted in euro with 'Monetary Financial Institutions' in the Eurozone (i) shown in its Aggregate Balance Sheet, and (ii) shown in its Consolidated Balance Sheet.

The difference between the two is €1.5 trillion.

'Monetary Financial Institutions' includes central banks and commercial banks: both would figure in an Aggregate Balance Sheet but the business between central banks would be eliminated in a Eurosystem Consolidated Balance Sheet.

The Eurosystem consists of the ECB and the Eurozone central banks: business in between these entities is excluded upon consolidation. There are no other Eurosystem operations that this difference can relate to.

It can therefore be induced that it relates to the TARGET2 gross balances which are eliminated from view by the netting. They are €1.5 trillion. As a result the original TARGET2 balances, before the netting, are €3.3 trillion.

Full illumination could be brought in by an examination of the SWIFT MT950 Statement Messages that are produced on each of the 600 accounts in the TARGET2 structure. These could be produced for 31 December 2021 and for the next-following TARGET2 business day. The statement messages would show all the debits and credits across the accounts, and the day's end ledger balance and available balance.

The debts and credits would show any zero-balancing operations at the beginning and end of the day, and the balance would include the processing of related debits and credits.

Through seeing the entire TARGET2 activity for two successive business days, including the one on which the ECB issues its report, one would see what the original balances were, how these were arrived at operationally, and how the operations were or were not underpinned by the legal documentation.

5.7 Legal moratoria on loan payments and on actions to recover defaulted loans

A further line of official action in connection with the pandemic was to allow moratoria on loan payments and a stay on legal processes to recover loans where debt service has been missed. These actions were applied in particular where the borrower was an SME or a consumer. These were included, for example in Italy, with numerous other support measures.[134]

The impact of this line of action is to create a potential new set of Non-Performing Loans on bank balance sheets and/or to introduce qualifications against existing categories of both Performing and Non-Performing Loans.

For example, a loan that is 'Past due' but not yet 'Non-performing' as well (i.e. with debt service less than 90 days overdue) might, thanks to the moratorium, reach 90 days overdue. Does it then get classed as 'Past due and non-performing', or does it remain in 'Past due' with a note against that category for all the loans that have been affected by the moratorium and which should normally be moved to the next category down?

The line of action will for sure have inhibited banks from their enforcement actions on their portfolios of NPLs, and they will likewise have inhibited the analogous actions by the agents acting for Special Purpose Companies within NPL securitization structures.

---

[134] https://www.esrb.europa.eu/home/search/coronavirus/countries/html/esrb.covidpmc_Italy.en.html accessed on 9 June 2022

The point is that this official response to the pandemic does not directly cause new and higher shadow debts of member states, but it is likely to weaken the credit quality of bank loan portfolios and aggravate five problems described above:

1. A member state's potential loss, caused by its obligations under its Deposit Insurance Scheme, when the assets it acquires as a result of the resolution of a bank are worth less than the debt it took out in order to pay out depositors;
2. A member state's liability to pay out on its guarantee on the A tranche of an NPL securitization;
3. The Eurosystem's credit risk under TLTRO;
4. The Eurosystem's credit risk when it is accepting 'credit claims' as collateral;
5. The Eurosystem's credit risk when it is buying Collateralised Loan Obligations into its APP or PEPP.

Chapter summary

The Pandemic response by the European authorities was firstly to radically expand the Eurosystem balance sheet through the establishment of the Pandemic Emergency Purchase Programme and the expansion of TLTRO, together adding around €2.7 trillion. In addition the TARGET2 net balances have increased to €1.8 trillion, with the gross balances – observable in the difference between the Eurosystem Consolidated Balance Sheet and the Eurosystem Aggregated Balance Sheet – adding a further €1.5 trillion.

Possibly of even greater significance is the weakening of the Eurosystem criteria, moving decisively away from its operations being conducted in 'central bank money'. Operations can be conducted in assets that are below Investment Grade, and any linkage to independent benchmarks is disabled by the total size of Eurosystem interventions: the Eurosystem came to own or control nearly 50% of the market.

The Eurosystem began to operate as a commercial bank but without a credit assessment department. Instead it came to accept the work of third parties, expressed in the interchangeable reliance on public credit ratings and banks' IRB.

The EU, not to be left behind, makes its own budgetary mechanisms even harder to understand, manipulates the treaty establishing itself to justify an intervention, and conducts that intervention in a manner that contradicts representations made to investors in its bonds as to how borrowings are controlled and repaid. The upshot is an uncovered gap in the EU's future cashflow that will eventually be filled either with new taxes or higher member state cash contributions.

Lastly there were moratoria at member state level on banks collecting on loans: that can only have fed through to more NPLs, existing in NPLs declining in quality, and securitized NPLs failing to produce the income needed pay out all the bondholders in full and on time.

Figures:
- 5.1: how the PEPP's conditions sweep away the comfort that the BVG read into the conditions of the PSPP
- 5.2: ECB collateral-easing measures of 2020 and worst-case implications

Figure 5.1: how the PEPP's conditions sweep away the comfort that the BVG read into the conditions of the PSPP

PEPP condition	Which BVG point of comfort is undermined
There is no limitation on the PEPP's buying to the secondary market only: it can buy in the primary market as well	Assumption of the prohibition of direct monetary financing of member states, taken to mean the purchase of member state government bonds in the primary market
The tenuous linkage of the PEPP to price stability, that the Pandemic could cause inflation to fall well below 2%	That ECB programmes are governed by treaty and the ECB's mandate to keep inflation below 2% per annum
ECB Capital Keys need only act as a guideline for the make-up of the PEPP portfolio	'Purchases are carried out in the accordance with the ECB's capital key'
There are no Purchase Limits in the PEPP	'The purchase limit of 33% per International Securities Identification Number (ISIN) is observed'
ECB is granted an unfettered right to amend Decision 2020/440 if they feel that its text might hinder their actions	Assumption of democratic control over the ECB and the PEPP via treaty and the ECB's mandate
The PEPP can buy Republic of Greece bonds	'Issuer has a minimum credit quality assessment that provides access to the bond markets'
The PEPP can buy non-financial commercial paper with the lowest short-term public credit ratings	'Issuer has a minimum credit quality assessment that provides access to the bond markets'
Credit assessment can be based on banks' IRB methodologies as an alternative to public credit ratings	'Issuer has a minimum credit quality assessment that provides access to the bond markets'
Securities do not have to be sold when their public ratings fall below 'Investment Grade'	'Issuer has a minimum credit quality assessment that provides access to the bond markets'
Debt securities based on 'Credit claims' would now be eligible	'Issuer has a minimum credit quality assessment that provides access to the bond markets'
'Credit claims' can include loans with lower credit quality, loans to types of debtors not accepted in the ECB's general framework, and foreign-currency loans. COVID-19 emergency loans, guaranteed by a public entity, are also eligible	'Issuer has a minimum credit quality assessment that provides access to the bond markets'

Figure 5.1: how the PEPP's conditions sweep away the comfort that the BVG read into the conditions of the PSPP

Figure 5.2: ECB collateral-easing measures of 2020 and worst-case implications

Clause	Worst-case Implications
Marketable assets and issuers of these assets that met the minimum credit quality requirements for collateral eligibility on 7 April 2020 (BBB- for all assets, except asset-backed securities (ABSs)) will continue to be eligible in case of rating downgrades, as long as their rating remains at or above credit quality step 5 (CQS5, equivalent to a rating of BB) on the Eurosystem harmonised rating scale. This ensures that assets and issuers that were investment grade at the time the Governing Council adopted the package of collateral easing measures remain eligible even if their rating falls two notches below the current minimum credit quality requirement of the Eurosystem	• Issuers and issues are downgraded to below Investment Grade but this does not require them to be sold off as Eurosystem assets or replaced as collateral for Eurosystem-extended loans • A meaningful portion of Eurosystem-owned assets and of the collateral for Eurosystem-extended loans starts to rank as Speculative Grade • Eurosystem members have paid out central bank money – supposedly risk-free – in exchange for assets that become Speculative Grade (noting that Eurosystem central bank money is not fully-fungible and risk-free in the first place, as was explained earlier)
Future issuances from grandfathered issuers will also be eligible provided they fulfil all other collateral eligibility criteria	• New issues by issuers that have become Speculative Grade can nevertheless be purchased by the Eurosystem and accepted by it as new collateral • Eurosystem members pay out fresh central bank money – supposedly risk-free – in exchange for assets that are only of Speculative Grade • Speculative Grade assets progressively displace Investment Grade assets as Eurosystem-owned assets and as the collateral for Eurosystem-extended loans • This trend will be accelerated if the largest eligible issuers are also the ones with reduced credit ratings
Currently eligible covered bond programmes will also be grandfathered, under the same conditions	• The degradation, as described above, of the quality of the Eurosystem's assets and collateral • It is exacerbated in relation to covered bonds because of the opportunity for the usage of IRB methodologies to warrant the credit quality of the underlying assets instead of public ratings (albeit that the rating agencies and their opinions are already flawed as explained below) • Credit claims – if presented as a debt security – can become eligible for purchase on this basis, or just eligible as collateral if they are not
Currently eligible ABSs to which a rating threshold in the general framework of CQS2 applies (equivalent to a rating of A-) will be grandfathered as long as their rating remains at or above CQS4 (equivalent to a rating of BB+).	• The degradation, as described above, of the quality of the Eurosystem's assets and collateral • Exacerbated by usage of IRB methodologies, possibly even more so than for covered bonds • Credit claims – if presented as a debt security – can become eligible for purchase on this basis, or are just eligible as collateral if they are not
Assets that fall below the minimum credit quality requirements will be subject to haircuts based on their actual ratings	• Haircuts will increase as ratings fall, but in such a way as not to reflect the deterioration in credit quality, because Eurosystem haircuts were already low and have been further reduced on 7 April 2020

Figure 5.2: ECB collateral-easing measures of 2020 and worst-case implications

145

Chapter 6 – interim summary on how the 'shadow debts' began and have been added to

At this point we can make an interim summary of the implications of the material in the chapters so far.

What began as emergency measures to deal with the Global Financial Crisis and/or the Eurozone sovereign debt crisis have now become fully normalized into the business-as-usual practices of the EU and of Eurozone public financing. The responses to the Pandemic crossed a Rubicon not so much in terms of the nature of the interventions, but rather in terms of liquidating the meaning of any quantitative and qualitative controls on them.

The results can be summed up as:
- the direct monetary financing by the Eurosystem of member states, not just at government level but at several levels in the pyramid of public sector entities at the apex of which sits the member state government;
- a dramatic increase in volume;
- a degrading of credit quality both in terms of lower security margins, the acceptance of assets with public credit ratings below Investment Grade, and the acceptance of bank-internal methodologies for warranting that an asset is of Eurosystem-eligible quality as an alternative to the asset having a public credit rating;
- the general acceptance of the reliability of bank-internal methodologies for assessing the likelihood and amount of losses in banks' business, where the banks from whom the methodologies have been borrowed have not shown a consistent and excellent track record in risk management;
- an increasing ownership and control of financial assets by the Eurosystem itself, creating a single nexus of market power and diminishing the role of private markets;
- a concentration of market and credit risk into the Eurosystem, the EU, the EIB Group, the ESM and the EFSF, and through such a variety and disparity of mechanisms that it is extremely difficult to ascertain where risk ultimately lies.

Fragility in size and degree

These results have introduced a new layer of fragility into the EU and, in particular, the Eurozone, a layer that is expanding in both size and degree: in effect the EU/Eurozone financial market is becoming akin to an example of state-driven capitalism, in which resource allocation is decided by state bodies as opposed to its being decided by market forces. This points to a dwindling role for an independent private sector in the provision of capital, and a reduction in the checks and balances the private sector brings in terms of credit assessment and market discipline.

Instead the authorities are taking on commercial banking risk, most notably through the PEPP, the APP programmes other than the PSPP, the eligible collateral list, and TLTRO. However the authorities are doing this without making a credit assessment of that risk themselves. They are relying firstly on the four EU-regulated public credit rating agencies, whose independence must now be viewed as questionable. Secondly they are relying on the Internal Ratings-Based methodologies of banks, and normally of the ones who are selling the resultant assets to the Eurosystem or offering them as collateral. We have above set a major question mark against such methodologies, as their results have been to demonstrate that the banks have adequate capital even under the severe stress scenarios constructed for the Stress Tests, without the banks having strengthened their capital from profits, new share issuance, or corporate restructurings.

Lack of controls and limitations

Official interventions have no monetary ceiling, as has been shown by the ease with which the PEPP was created and then had its ceiling increased twice. The Coronavirus Recovery Fund, InvestEU and TLTRO are further examples where a substantial official intervention was mounted without all previous assumptions about controls and limitations being adhered to.

The ease with which controls and limitations can be circumvented demonstrates that there is no obvious point at which the activity has to stop. There always seems to be a reason to hand for the EU and Eurosystem to do more of what they wanted to do anyway, whether that be the Pandemic, Ukraine, or the supposed imperative of Net Zero.

Creation of shadow debts as the path of least resistance

The continued expansion of the shadow debt mechanisms is now the path of least resistance, when member state financing pots are becoming difficult to tap, in the light of a supposed determination to comply with the Stability & Growth Pact and to achieve compliance by 2030 with the Fiscal Stability Pact. Indeed the borrowing through shadow mechanisms can assist compliance as it can be expanded to directly create GDP growth, the denominator in the calculations for compliance. The numerator – 'General government gross debt' – can be kept steady or even reduced via the build-up of borrowings that do not qualify for inclusion in it.

This pathway of manipulation is aided by interest rates being kept low by the Eurosystem's own interventions: if a given amount per annum can be afforded for debt service, it can be expended to reduce the principal amount rather than on interest. In that way the current member state budgets can be protected, and the deflationary effect of future debt service can be kept manageable.

Implications for global financial markets

This might work for the member states but it should not be acceptable to global financial markets, as they are investing in or taking market or credit risk positions on EU and Eurozone counterparties without having a complete view of the on- and off-balance obligations of those counterparties, or else they are relying on public credit rating agencies approved by the EU whose view also appears to be incomplete.

The preceding chapters bear witness to the lack of transparency which inhibits financial markets from understanding the nature, size, and location of all the liabilities that track back to the pyramid of public sector entities.

Baseline information required from each member state to justify 'General government gross debt'

As a baseline, every EU member state should issue a list of all the entities whose debts are included in their 'General government gross debt', and what the debts of each entity were as at 31 December 2021, such that the total reconciles with the Eurostat figures.

The debts of each entity should be broken into categories of (i) debt represented by a bond; (ii) loan debts; (iii) finance lease debts; (iv) other debts, with the numbers totaling the same as the entity's entire debt.

'General government gross debt' as Eurostat reports it represents 'The indicator [ ] defined (in the Maastricht Treaty) as consolidated general government gross debt at nominal (face) value, outstanding at the year in the following categories of government liabilities (as defined in the ESA 2010: currency and deposits, debt securities and loans. The general government sector comprises the subsectors: central government, state government, local government and social security funds'.[135]

Central banks' debts are not included, as the BIS confirms in its definition of 'general government': 'Sectoral classification that refers collectively to the central government, state government, local government and social security funds. General government excludes the central bank and publicly owned corporations.'[136]

This is a point that requires explicit confirmation by the inclusion of the central banks in the above list, or by their exclusion.

The same applies to 'Recognised Agencies'. These are the government agencies listed in Appendix 5 whose bonds enjoy a special status as ECB-eligible collateral.[137] However, they do not explicitly fall within the above definitions of General government. The point needs to be confirmed by the inclusion of the 'Recognised agencies' in the above list, or by their exclusion.

---

[135] Ec.europa.eu > tables on EU policy > Euro indicators/PEEIs > National accounts > Public finance – excessive debt procedure statistics accessed on 21 June 2022
[136] https://www.bis.org/statistics/glossary.htm?selection=314&scope=Statistics&c=a&base=term accessed on 21 June 2022
[137] https://www.ecb.europa.eu/mopo/assets/standards/marketable/html/index.en.html#agencies accessed on 21 June 2022

One then expects a considerable list of regional, provincial and municipal government entities, but not of publicly-owned corporations or transport, power or water utilities. The debts of the latter should come under the debts of other public sector entities below.

That will at least baseline how the 'General government gross' debt is made up, and allow a reconciliation back to Eurostat's figures.

Transparency over public sector indebtedness outside 'General government gross debt'

There now follows an enumeration of the areas outside 'General government gross debt' that lack transparency and, as a best estimate, what data should be produced, going forward and on a consistent basis, in order to deliver transparency. There are ten areas and they are:

1. Member State contingent liabilities for the debts and guarantees of the EU both as a total and as the total divided by the member state's normal share of the EU budget
2. Member State contingent liabilities for the debts of the EFSF, ESM, EIB and EIF, both as the member state's subscribed-but-not-called capital, and as a share of these mechanisms' total liabilities and commitments divided by the member state's normal share of the EU budget
3. Debts of public sector entities that are not included in 'General government gross debt' as Eurostat reports it
4. Liabilities (contractual or financial) of public sector entities created by structures like InvestEU, with a focus on ESG financing schemes
5. Net debts in TARGET2 of Eurozone Member State central banks
6. Debts in TARGET2 of Eurozone Member State central banks that are eliminated by the netting
7. Member State contingent liability for replenishing the capital of the ECB if the ECB made **market** losses on its Asset Purchase Programmes
8. Member State contingent liability for replenishing the capital of the ECB if the ECB made **credit** losses on its programmes including MRO and LTRO
9. Member State contingent liability on bonds issued as part of Eurozone bank Non-Performing Loan securitizations, for example in Italy, Greece and Cyprus
10. Member State contingent liability on their Deposit Insurance Scheme where a bank has a 'carrying value' of Non-Performing Loans in excess of the bank's equity

Each one of these is the subject of a chapter that follows, and in each such chapter an attempt is made to quantify the amount debt outstanding in the area concerned or, if there is insufficient information in the public domain, to devise a plausible 'placeholder' amount. Should the liability be in the form of a Contingent Liability, that is quantified as well.

In each case either the debt or the contingent liability amount is allocated down to member state level. The book concludes with an aggregation of all the amounts.

Chapter 7 - quantification of liabilities: The European Union

This chapter quantifies, to the degree possible given information gaps, member states' liabilities for the debts and guarantees of the EU both as a total (because the debts are on a joint-and-several liability basis) and as the total divided by the member state's normal share of the EU budget.

The information gaps are listed.

The approach is then to go through each of the EU's programmes and derive the amount at risk.

At the end of the chapter the amounts-at-risk in each programme are totaled to reach a global amount-at-risk.

That figure is then apportioned to member states in line with their GNIs.

EU budgetary framework

In order to close the information gaps, the EU should be asked to state the following:
- What is the amount that the EU believes it can call up from member states if there is a shortfall in its budget:
  - As a formula and in respect of both 'Own resources ceiling to cover the annual appropriations for commitments' and 'Own resources ceiling to cover the annual appropriations for payments';
  - As an amount of money;
  - Both of the above for past 4 MFFs and the current one;
- What is the basis for the statements by rating agencies that the EU can call upon €30-40 billion per annum from member states in case its budget goes into deficit;
- What programmes were set up under that qualify for member state support in this way in each MFF period, their size, their dates and the legal instrument enabling them;
- What individual operations and their amounts and dates were carried out under each programme;
- What amount of the ceiling expired unused in each period;
- Which of the individual operations remain open from each period;
- What the ceiling is for the MFF 2021-7 both as a formula and an amount;
- What programmes are contemplated as using up a portion of the ceiling during the MFF 2021-7, their size, their dates and the legal instrument enabling them;
- What individual operations and their amounts and dates were carried out under each such programme so far;
- What programmes are contemplated as using up a portion of the Coronavirus Recovery Fund; their size, their dates and the legal instrument enabling them;
- What individual operations and their amounts and dates were carried out under each programme so far;
- A separate list of legal instruments with dates and reference numbers that supports each of the responses to the above.

European Financial Stabilisation Mechanism

The EFSM ceiling is €60 billion. Ireland currently owes €15.6 billion and Portugal €14.25 billion with maturities out to 2042. These amounts are contained within their respective GGGD. €30.15 billion remains nominally available. Other member states are responsible as guarantors for the whole amount.

The EU needs to issue:
- A statement of whether the €30.15 billion remains available or not;
- If it does, a further statement is required of the circumstances under which it could be drawn.

The amounts-at-risk here are:
- Debts: €0.0 billion
- Contingent liabilities: €60.0 billion

The Balance of Payments Facility[138]

The BoP ceiling appears to be €12 billion, although this is not stated explicitly on the respective EU webpage, and this amount appears to be undrawn.

The EU needs to:
- confirm that COUNCIL REGULATION (EC) No 332/2002 of 18 February 2002 remains the legal instrument governing the BoP;
- state whether any monies are still owing from Hungary, Latvia or Romania deriving from their usage of BoP;
- state what each borrower owes;
- state the current total amount owed;
- issue a run-off table for each borrower;
- issue a programme run-off-table.
- confirm that the difference between the current total amount at risk and €12 billion remains available.

The amounts-at-risk here are:
- Debts: €0.0 billion
- Contingent liabilities: €12.0 billion

Macro Financial Assistance (MFA)[139]

MFA is for support to non-EU countries that are undergoing a financial programme under the International Monetary Fund. The European Commission supplies an annual report on the 'implementation of macro-financial assistance to third countries' and the most recent one is for 2020 under reference COM(2021) 375. The preceding ones were COM(2020) 296 for 2019 and COM(2019) 324 for 2018.

There is a grants portion that comes out of the Payments Appropriation, and the ceilings for this were €27 million (2019), €20 million (2020) and €56.4 million (2021 provisional), of which €10.3 million (2019) and €15.3 million (2020) were used.

The loans are far larger, and neither on the EC webpages nor in the annual report does one find the full inventory of them. All we see in COM(2021) 375 is a list of disbursements in 2019 and 2020 and a plan for 2021, which we have supplemented for 2017 and 2018 from COM(2019) 324.

That is contained in Figure 7.1.

The total is €6 billion of new loans over the last five years, whilst COM(2016) 376 showed the addition of €1.36 billion in 2014 and €1.25 billion in 2015, whereas COM(2018) 511 showed only €10.0 million added in 2016.

The EU should show the full inventory of its MFA loans by maintaining a table:

Date of loan	Borrower	Amount	Current amount	Interest rate & payment frequency	Run-off profile	Final maturity

Table 7.1: ongoing data table to be maintained by the EU on Macro Financial Assistance

[138] https://ec.europa.eu/info/business-economy-euro/economic-and-fiscal-policy-coordination/financial-assistance-eu/funding-mechanisms-and-facilities/balance-payments-bop-assistance-facility_en accessed on 13 June 2022
[139] https://ec.europa.eu/info/business-economy-euro/economic-and-fiscal-policy-coordination/international-economic-relations/macro-financial-assistance-mfa-non-eu-partner-countries_en accessed on 13 June 2022

The EU should further include on its webpage concerning the MFA:
- the legal instrument that established the MFA and all subsequent legal instruments that amended it, prolonged it or whatever;
- the legal instruments or decisions by which it was agreed that the MFA would participate in each of the programmes under which it has made loans;
- the current MFA ceiling;
- the current balance of loans under each programme;
- the current cumulative balance of all loans.

The amounts-at-risk here are:
- Debts: €6.0 billion
- Contingent liabilities: €0.0 billion

Euratom[140]

This loan programme relates to nuclear power stations and it is stated that the 'total amount of lending for these activities is limited to €4 billion, of which €3.67 billion has already been allocated'. As of 31 December 2021, Euratom had '€349.5 million of loans outstanding stemming from projects in Romania (€49.5 million) and Ukraine (€300 million)'. Loan tranches 'have a maturity of 10 years and are due between 2027 and 2031'.

The EU needs to:
- confirm that only €330 million can still be drawn from this programme (€4 billion less €3.67 billion);
- confirm that amounts repaid are not redrawable;
- issue run-off tables for the loans to Romania and Ukraine;
- issue a programme run-off-table.

The amounts-at-risk here are:
- Debts: €3.7 billion
- Contingent liabilities: €0.0 billion

First-loss guarantees for EIB loans outside the EU

The two main guarantees in issue are:
- Decision 1080/2011 in respect of the 2007-13 MFF in an amount of €29.5 billion
- Decision 2018/412 in respect of the 2014-20 MFF in an amount of
- Total up to the end of the 2014-20 MFF: €61.7 billion

We have catered for a small amount remaining outstanding from guarantees issued prior to 2007, in respect of loans signed before that year that are now in the late stages of run-off.

Each EU Decision appears to have been the final raising of the amount for the respective MFF. In order to qualify for reimbursement from the EU in the case of a loan loss, the loan needs to have been signed during the respective MFF, rather than approved (the preceding stage) or disbursed (the subsequent stage).

As the loans are for projects, one should expect an availability period of up to 3 years between loan signature and the final disbursement, failing which the undisbursed amount would lapse. EIB's standard loan period is 15 years, with repayment in 30 equal semi-annual instalments beginning six months after full drawdown.

The EU/EIB should confirm this understanding by supplying extra information as laid out below. As it is one can only estimate what the current amount-at-risk is.

---

[140] https://ec.europa.eu/info/business-economy-euro/economic-and-fiscal-policy-coordination/international-economic-relations/euratom-loans_en accessed on 13 June 2022

The data supplied by the EIB on its loans outside the EU is as follows, in € billions:

	2010	2011	2012	2013	2014	2015	2016	2017	2018	2019	2020	2021
Page[141]	2	3	3	3	3	3	3	3	4	4	4	4
Approved	€10.4	€7.3	€8.2	€10.0	€7.5	€9.0	€9.7	€8.0	€10.3	€7.6	€13.0	€4.5
Signed	€8.8	€7.1	€7.4	€7.7	€7.9	€7.8	€7.9	€7.3	€7.8	€7.9	€9.3	€7.5
Disbursed	€6.4	€5.0	€6.6	€5.5	€4.8	€5.0	€6.8	€6.3	€5.7	€4.3	€6.1	€6.0

Table 7.2: EIB data on its loans outside the EU

It is noticeable that disbursements run at 60-70% of approvals: large amounts committed are not taken up. Nevertheless, if one assumes that €7.5 billion was signed in each year of the 2007-13 MFF of which only €6 billion will ever have been disbursed, and the disbursed loans have an average final maturity of 15 years from full drawdown and an average duration of 8½ years[142], the result is a loan book for that MFF of €42 billion. A portion of that would only have been fully drawn by the end of 2016. A reasonable estimate is that 70% is still drawn, which is €29.4 billion and just €0.1 billion less than the guarantee of €29.5 billion supporting it.

Similarly regarding the 2014-20 MFF, a loan book of €42 billion might well emanate from that MFF, but the loans signed towards the end of the MFF may not yet be fully drawn. We are now almost two years after the latest date for signature, so we would be confident that the loan book is now 90% drawn, which would lead to outstandings of €37.8 billion, well in excess of the guarantee of €32.2 billion supporting them.

There might also be some residual lending from before 2007. If there is, it would continue to be supported by the EU guarantee issued for the MFF in which the loan was signed. For convenience's sake we have posited that the outstanding is €0.1 billion. In that case the entirety of the amount of the two guarantees of €61.7 billion would be on risk because the outstandings – at €67.3 billion - exceed the guarantees, albeit that €0.1 billion of the underlying loans was booked before 2007.

A sanity check can be carried out by deriving the outstandings from the EIB's 2021 statement of its lending outside the EU as 11% of its current loans of €433 billion, and by assuming this means that 11% of €123 billion 'to be disbursed' amount relates to outside the EU. That would set the EIB's current loans outside the EU at €47.6 billion with €13.5 billion to be disbursed, totaling €61.1 billion, €0.6 billion less than the total derived from the other calculation. Under this scenario the EIB is also fully inoculated against credit risk on borrowers outside the EU.

The difference between the two calculations lies in the undisbursed amount: the figure of €13.5 billion for undisbursed, signed loans at the end of 2021 infers an even longer timelag between signature and first drawdown, and then an even longer period during which instalments of the loan are drawn.

Presumably the EU will now issue a further guarantee for activity in the 2021-7 MFF, and this is catered for in an amount of €35.0 billion. It is assumed that €3.0 billion of this has gone on-risk in 2021 thanks to loan agreements being signed and drawn.

The EU and EIB should issue and maintain five tables as set out in Figure 7.2.

Here then are the amounts guaranteed by the EU from this area in € billions:

Guarantee period	Ceiling	Drawn	Undrawn	Amount-at-risk
Guarantees from before 2007	n/a	€0.1	€0.0	€0.1
Guarantee I/EIB Loans outside EU 2007-13	€29.5	€29.4	€0.0	€29.4
Guarantee II/EIB Loans outside EU 2014-20	€32.2	€32.2	€0.0	€32.2
Guarantee III/EIB Loans outside EU 2021-7	€35.0	€3.0	€32.0	€35.0
Totals	€96.7	€64.7	€32.0	€96.7

Table 7.3: EU guarantees to EIB for its lending outside the EU

---

[141] Page in EIB Financial Report in which the data appears
[142] The loan being taken up one year before full drawdown, and being repayable in 15 semi-annual instalments commencing 6 months after full drawdown

The amounts-at-risk here are:

- Debts: €64.7 billion
- Contingent liabilities: €32.0 billion

First-loss guarantees to EIB Group regarding InvestEU

InvestEU, set up as EFSI, had an original ceiling of €315 billion at its establishment, which was raised to €500 billion by the end for the 2014-20 MFF. The picture becomes blurred because, from some point in 2020 onwards, the European Guarantee Fund (EGF) began to feature and then, for 2021, became the main scheme under which the EIF put on this type of funding.

It had been assumed that a supplementary EU guarantee would be needed, of about €10 billion, to accommodate the programme increase of €185 billion to €500 billion, assuming the same proportions as the initial programme, but possibly not if EGF served instead of it.

It is possible that 5 member states refused to countenance the EU guarantee being raised during the 2014-20 MFF, and wanted to limit the size of the EU guarantee for the 2021-7 MFF. Under that reading the other 22 member states went ahead with the EGF to keep the total of this type of financing rising on its established trajectory through 2020 and 2021, and saw the new InvestEU guarantee as able to maintain the trajectory until 2027.

EGF's 'beginning to feature' in 2020 does not mean that EGF transactions would necessarily be visible in the EIF's 2020 accounts. The EGF programme is supposed to have a size of €200 billion, and most of it is supposed to have been committed by the end of 2021.

That does not mean, though, that the EIF's guarantees and equity commitments under EGF qualified for inclusion in the EIF's accounts in the year they were agreed to. We do not know the exact trigger for a transaction to appear in the EIF's accounts: when it is committed, when it is signed, when the financing that it covers is drawn. We suspect that there is some delay which would impact all of the EIF's 2020, 2021 and 2022 accounts:

- Transactions agreed to in 2020 meet the trigger to be entered into EIF's accounts only in 2021;
- Most of EGF is visible in the 2021 accounts;
- A significant amount of EGF will only become visible in the EIF's 2022 accounts because it was committed in late 2021.

This is why we have posited that virtually no EGF financings fell within the €471 billion at the end of 2020 that the EIF had enabled through this type of scheme, that the €141 billion added in 2021 was all attributable to EGF, and that the EGF's balance of about €60 billion will have been added in 2022.

The EIB 2021 Annual Financial Report mentions only the initial InvestEU guarantee. InvestEU 'is a EUR 16 billion guarantee from the EU budget, complemented by an allocation of EUR 5 billion of EIB's own capital'.[143]

The EIB Group was permitted to put €5 billion of its own money at risk, over and above the EU's €16 billion guarantee. In fact it appears to have been the EIF who put EIB Group money at risk by engaging in the bottom slice/highest risk tranche, whilst the traditional EIB funding was not deemed to be putting money at risk.

Figure 7.3 contains the structure of InvestEU as originally proposed, with a €16 billion EU guarantee and €5 billion of risk taken by EIB Group on top enabling a total financing volume of €315 billion.

Now it appears that €471 billion of InvestEU financing has been done by the end of 2020, but without the EU guarantee being raised.

---

[143] EIB 2021 Annual Financial Report p. 169

The EU/EIB need to reveal:
- Under what legal instrument the InvestEU programme size was increased from €315 billion to €500 billion in the 2014-20 MFF;
- Whether the EU guarantee was increased so as to enable the programme size increase, what was the size of the new EU guarantee, and through what legal instrument it was created;
- What was the total of EU guarantees at the end of the 2014-20 MFF in respect of InvestEU;
- How much of EIB Group's own money it was allowed to put at risk at the end of the 2014-20 MFF in respect of InvestEU;
- Whether the EIB's 'traditional loans' are deemed by it to be EIB Group money put at risk.

The EIB's 'traditional loans' into InvestEU/EGF were estimated above at around €77 billion.

As regards the 2021-7 MFF, we have a new EU guarantee of €26.2 billion issued on 26 March 2021 via legal instrument 2021/523, and it is assumed that €5.0 billion of that was mobilized during 2021.

The EU/EIB need to reveal:
- The intended InvestEU programme size at the end of the 2021-7 MFF;
- How much of EIB Group's own money it is allowed to put at risk in respect of InvestEU during the end of the 2021-7 MFF.

Here then are the amounts of the EU's guarantees for InvestEU in € billions:

Guarantee period	Ceiling	Drawn	Undrawn	Amount-at-risk
Guarantee I/InvestEU	€16.0	€16.0	€0.0	€16.0
Guarantee II/InvestEU	€26.2	€5.0	€21.2	€26.2
Totals	€42.2	€21.0	€21.2	€42.2

Table 7.4: EU guarantees to EIB for InvestEU

The amounts-at-risk here are:
- Debts: €21.0 billion
- Contingent liabilities: €21.2 billion

European Guarantee Fund (EGF) in favour of EIB Group

The EGF is taken not to be an arrangement that runs through the EU legal entity, but to be a guarantee extended directly by member states to the EIB Group. This arrangement is similar to the EFSF. As a result the EGF is classified as an EU supranational and is treated in the following chapter.

Coronavirus Recovery Fund

There have been some operations of this fund prior to the end of 2021, but the main part is yet to be drawn. Our assumption is that 0.6% of EU 2020 GNI had been disbursed prior to the end of 2021, the time scope of this book. That would be €80.0 billion out of the programme ceiling of €750.0 billion.

This fact ensures that the member states' liability for the debts of the EU will continue to rise through the period 2021-7. This will mean, as regards the tables below, that the figure for what is drawn and what is an actual liability will rise, as the figure for a contingent liability falls. The contingent liability already exists as the fund has been fully authorized as part of the 2021-7 budget.

The EU should maintain a rolling inventory of tables showing the bonds issued for this fund, the amounts disbursed as grants, and the amounts disbursed as loans, as per Figure 7.4.

The amounts-at-risk here are:
- Debts: €80.0 billion
- Contingent liabilities: €670.0 billion

Other funds, facilities and guarantees not included above

The EU should be asked to state any other funds, facilities and guarantees not included in this section, and to disclose the details of them in line with the details requested of operations similar to them that are discussed here.

Collation of actual and contingent liability amounts created through the legal person of the EU

We have laid out in the table below the aggregate liabilities created for member states through the legal person of the EU in € billions:

Facility	Ceiling	Drawn – actual liability	(Re)drawable – contingent liability	Maximum possible loss
EFSM	€60.0	€0.0	€60.0	€60.0
Balance of Payments Facility	€12.0	€0.0	€12.0	€12.0
Macro Financial Assistance	€6.0	€6.0	€0.0	€6.0
Euratom	€4.0	€3.7	€0.0	€3.7
Guarantee/EIB loans before 2007	€0.1	€0.1	€0.0	€0.1
Guarantee I/EIB Loans outside EU 2007-13	€29.5	€29.4	€0.0	€29.4
Guarantee II/EIB Loans outside EU 2014-20	€32.2	€32.2	€0.0	€32.2
Guarantee III/EIB Loans outside EU 2021-7	€35.0	€3.0	€32.0	€35.0
Guarantee I/InvestEU	€16.0	€16.0	€0.0	€16.0
Guarantee II/InvestEU	€26.2	€5.0	€21.2	€26.2
Coronavirus Recovery Fund	€750.0	€80.0	€670.0	€750.0
	€970.9	€175.4	€795.2	€970.6

Table 7.5: aggregate liabilities created for member states through the legal person of the EU in € billions

The assumptions around these figures are contained in the following table:

Facility	Assumptions
EFSM	The difference between the ceiling and current balance is redrawable. The entire amount is a contingent liability for all member states, but the drawn amount is within the GGGD of Ireland and Portugal
Balance of Payments Facility	It is unused and fully redrawable
Macro Financial Assistance	Its ceiling is the current balance, which is new loans in the last five years
Euratom	It is now closed to new loans
Guarantee/EIB loans before 2007	A very small amount in run-off
Guarantee I/EIB Loans outside EU 2007-13	The loan balance supported by the guarantee is almost the same as the guarantee amount
Guarantee II/EIB Loans outside EU 2014-20	The loan balance supported by the guarantee is above the guarantee amount and may even increase as signed loans are drawn
Guarantee III/EIB Loans outside EU 2021-7	A new guarantee will be or has been issued, and at least as large as the one for 2014-20, but very few loans will have been signed and disbursed under it
Guarantee I/InvestEU	The guarantees and equity commitments made by the EIF and supported by the guarantee are substantially higher than the guarantee amount, and than the guarantee amount plus the permission to EIB Group to 'put its own funds at risk'
Guarantee II/InvestEU	It is too early for a substantial volume of new guarantees and equity commitments to have been issued such as to put the guarantee on-risk, especially since the exhaustion of the EGF programme appears to have been the priority in 2021
Coronavirus Recovery Fund	0.6% of EU 2020 GNI has been disbursed so far
General	The Coronavirus Recovery Fund, InvestEU and the EIB's loans outside the EU will be engaged aggressively and will reach their ceilings

Table 7.6: assumptions around aggregate liabilities created for member states through the legal person of the EU

Liability of each member state in € billions

Now we can break down the aggregate liability into the liability per member state, calculated in the same way as member state shares of the EU budget - i.e. through GNI shares – in € billion:

Country	GNI	Percentage share of EU budget	Share of actual liability	Share of contingent liability	Share of Maximum Possible Loss
Belgium	€416.2	3.10%	€ 5.4	€ 24.6	€ 30.1
Bulgaria	€111.6	0.83%	€ 1.5	€ 6.6	€ 8.1
Czech Rep	€287.9	2.14%	€ 3.8	€ 17.0	€ 20.8
Denmark	€244.4	1.82%	€ 3.2	€ 14.5	€ 17.7
Germany	€3,141.1	23.4%	€ 41.0	€ 186.0	€ 227.0
Estonia	€33.2	0.25%	€ 0.4	€ 2.0	€ 2.4
Ireland	€237.8	1.77%	€ 3.1	€ 14.1	€ 17.2
Greece	€198.8	1.48%	€ 2.6	€ 11.8	€ 14.4
Spain	€1,205.4	8.98%	€ 15.7	€ 71.4	€ 87.1
France	€2,180.1	16.24%	€ 28.5	€ 129.1	€ 157.6
Croatia	€79.5	0.59%	€ 1.0	€ 4.7	€ 5.7
Italy	€1,685.5	12.55%	€ 22.0	€ 99.8	€ 121.8
Cyprus	€22.3	0.17%	€ 0.3	€ 1.3	€ 1.6
Latvia	€40.0	0.30%	€ 0.5	€ 2.4	€ 2.9
Lithuania	€70.7	0.53%	€ 0.9	€ 4.2	€ 5.1
Luxembourg	€35.4	0.26%	€ 0.5	€ 2.1	€ 2.6
Hungary	€210.0	1.56%	€ 2.7	€ 12.4	€ 15.2
Malta	€13.6	0.10%	€ 0.2	€ 0.8	€ 1.0
Netherlands	€630.1	4.69%	€ 8.2	€ 37.3	€ 45.5
Austria	€332.7	2.48%	€ 4.3	€ 19.7	€ 24.0
Poland	€816.0	6.08%	€ 10.7	€ 48.3	€ 59.0
Portugal	€232.2	1.73%	€ 3.0	€ 13.8	€ 16.8
Romania	€407.2	3.03%	€ 5.3	€ 24.1	€ 29.4
Slovenia	€55.7	0.41%	€ 0.7	€ 3.3	€ 4.0
Slovakia	€113.4	0.84%	€ 1.5	€ 6.7	€ 8.2
Finland	€190.5	1.42%	€ 2.5	€ 11.3	€ 13.8
Sweden	€394.4	2.94%	€ 5.2	€ 23.4	€ 28.5
Totals	€13,428.30	99.68%	€ 174.8	€ 792.7	€ 967.5

Table 7.7: liability for member states created through the legal person of the EU according to GNI share

The discrepancy referred to in the Disclaimed has an effect here that is modestly material, because published GNI shares only add up to 99.68% when published GDP shares add up to 99.96%.

Since EU budgets are allocated according to GNI shares, there is a modest understatement of the debt and contingent liabilities that track onto the member states in this area.

This is not considered to be a serious issue in the light of the information gaps both in this area and others: no claim is made here that these figures are watertight. For that reason it remains legitimate that debt of €204.6 billion and contingent liabilities of €762.9 billion be carried through into the overall aggregation.

These numbers per member state would hold as long as all the others could pay, which is an unlikely event, given that the claim would emanate from financial difficulties in one of them.

The claim could escalate all the way up to a single member state paying the entire amount, or 'it all tracks back onto Germany'.

The balance between liability for an actual debt of the EU and a contingent liability will tilt dramatically towards responsibility for an actual debt once the Coronavirus Recovery Fund is drawn.

Figures:
- 7.1: Macro Financial Assistance - list of disbursements 2017-20 and a plan for 2021
- 7.2: tables that the EU and EIB should issue regarding the EU's guarantees of EIB loans outside the EU
- 7.3: original proposed structure of EFSI (InvestEU), showing €21 billion highest-risk slice taken by EIB Group
- 7.4: tables to be maintained by the EU on the Coronavirus Recovery Fund

Figure 7.1: Macro Financial Assistance - list of disbursements 2017-20 and a plan for 2021

In € millions	2017	2018	2019	2020	2021
Georgia	€13	€0	€0	€0	€0
Tunisia I	€100	€0	€0	€0	€0
Georgia II	€0	€15	€0	€20	€0
Moldova	€0	€0	€20	€20	€0
Ukraine III	€600	€0	€0	€0	€0
Ukraine IV	€0	€500	€0	€500	€0
Jordan II	€100	€0	€100	€0	€0
Jordan III	€0	€0	€0	€100	€400
Tunisia II	€200	€0	€300	€0	€0
Georgia - COVID	€0	€0	€0	€75	€75
Moldova – COVID	€0	€0	€0	€50	€50
Ukraine – COVID	€0	€0	€0	€600	€600
Jordan – COVID	€0	€0	€0	€150	€50
Tunisia – COVID	€0	€0	€0	€0	€600
Albania – COVID	€0	€0	€0	€0	€180
Bosnia and Herzegovina - COVID	€0	€0	€0	€0	€250
Kosovo - COVID	€0	€0	€0	€50	€50
Montenegro - COVID	€0	€0	€0	€30	€30
North Macedonia - COVID	€0	€0	€0	€80	€80
	€1,013	€515	€420	€1,675	€2,365

Figure 7.1: Macro Financial Assistance - list of disbursements 2017-20 and a plan for 2021

Figure 7.2: tables that the EU and EIB should issue regarding the EU's guarantees of EIB loans outside the EU

Table 1 – usage of guarantees for MFFs preceding 2007-13

Loan maturity	2021	2022	2023	20[ ]	20[ ]	Final
Amount under guarantee	€[ ] bn	€[ ] bn	€[ ] bn	€[ ] bn	€[ ] bn	€[ ] bn
Guarantee amount	€[ ] bn	€[ ] bn	€[ ] bn	€[ ] bn	€[ ] bn	€[ ] bn
Maximum loss under guarantee[144]	€[ ] bn	€[ ] bn	€[ ] bn	€[ ] bn	€[ ] bn	€[ ] bn

Table 2 – usage of guarantee for MFF 2007-13

Loan maturity	2021	2022	2023	20[ ]	20[ ]	Final
Amount under guarantee	€[ ] bn	€[ ] bn	€[ ] bn	€[ ] bn	€[ ] bn	€[ ] bn
Guarantee amount	€29.5 bn	€29.5 bn	€29.5 bn	€29.5 bn	€29.5 bn	€29.5 bn
Maximum loss under guarantee	€[ ] bn	€[ ] bn	€[ ] bn	€[ ] bn	€[ ] bn	€[ ] bn

---

[144] The maximum loss will be the lesser of the 'Amount under guarantee' and the 'Guarantee amount' as the loan portfolio runs off over time to be lower than the guarantee

Table 3 – usage of guarantee for MFF 2014-20

Loan maturity	2021	2022	2023	20[ ]	20[ ]	Final
Amount under guarantee	€[ ] bn	€[ ] bn	€[ ] bn	€[ ] bn	€[ ] bn	€[ ] bn
Guarantee amount	€32.2 bn	€32.2 bn	€32.2 bn	€32.2 bn	€32.2 bn	€32.2 bn
Maximum loss under guarantee	€[ ] bn	€[ ] bn	€[ ] bn	€[ ] bn	€[ ] bn	€[ ] bn

Table 4 – usage of guarantee for MFF 2021-7

Loan maturity	2023	2024	2025	20[ ]	20[ ]	Final
Amount under guarantee	€[ ] bn	€[ ] bn	€[ ] bn	€[ ] bn	€[ ] bn	€[ ] bn
Guarantee amount	€32.2 bn	€32.2 bn	€32.2 bn	€32.2 bn	€32.2 bn	€32.2 bn
Maximum loss under guarantee	€[ ] bn	€[ ] bn	€[ ] bn	€[ ] bn	€[ ] bn	€[ ] bn

Table 5 – aggregation of Tables 1-4

Loan maturity	2021	2022	2023	20[ ]	20[ ]	Final
Amounts under guarantee	€[ ] bn	€[ ] bn	€[ ] bn	€[ ] bn	€[ ] bn	€[ ] bn
Guarantee amounts	€[ ] bn	€[ ] bn	€[ ] bn	€[ ] bn	€[ ] bn	€[ ] bn
Maximum loss under guarantees	€[ ] bn	€[ ] bn	€[ ] bn	€[ ] bn	€[ ] bn	€[ ] bn

Figure 7.2: tables that the EU and EIB should issue regarding the EU's guarantees of EIB loans outside the EU

Figure 7.3: original proposed structure of EFSI (InvestEU), showing €21 billion highest-risk slice taken by EIB Group

LEVEL/MULTIPLIER	AMOUNT
EFSI-supported funding/bottom-slice	€21 billion
First-level Multiplier	190%
EIB 'traditional loans'/middle-slice	€40 billion
EFSI-supported funding and EIB funding combined	€61 billion
Second-level multiplier	416%
Private loans/top-slice	€254 billion
Total funding raised	€315 billion
Leverage of Total funding to EFSI funding	15 times
Leverage of Total funding to EFSI+EIB Loans funding	5.2 times

Figure 7.3: original proposed structure of EFSI (InvestEU), showing €21 billion highest-risk slice taken by EIB Group

Figure 7.4: tables to be maintained by the EU on the Coronavirus Recovery Fund

Table 1- bonds issued

Issue date	ISIN	Currency and amount	Final maturity	Coupon and interest payment dates	Capital repayments

Table 2 – amounts disbursed as grants

Date of grant	Recipient name	Grant's purpose and timeline	Amount	EU programme name	Authorizing legal instrument

Table 3 – amounts disbursed as loans

Date of loan	Borrower	Loan purpose	Original and current amount, interest rate, payment frequency	Run-off profile and final maturity	EU programme name	Authorizing legal instrument

Figure 7.4: tables to be maintained by the EU on the Coronavirus Recovery Fund

Chapter 8 – quantification of liabilities: EU supranationals

This chapter attempts to quantify member states' liabilities for the debts and commitments of the EFSF, ESM, EIB, and European Guarantee Fund (EGF).

The EIF is dealt with here even though the EU guarantees that support its InvestEU have been dealt with in the previous chapter, and Chapter 10 addresses the issue of what kind of borrowers the EIF is funding in InvestEU and EGF. The material on the EIF in this chapter deals with the supplementary information we should have about its guarantees and equity commitments in InvestEU, and this is similar data to that required of it in connection with the EGF.

8.1 European Financial Stability Facility

Notwithstanding the 'over-guarantee' built into the EFSF mechanism, the member states have a contingent liability for the €191 billion of debt securities of the EFSF in issue, noting that the EFSF is closed to further borrowings.

For completeness' sake we should also consider the liabilities both in the case that borrowing members can meet their guarantee liabilities and where they cannot.

Drawing on the table in the section on the EFSF above, we can show what the allocations would be in both cases, having already re-based the ECB Capital Keys to 100% by eliminating both the non-Eurozone shareholders and Latvia and Lithuania. These are shown in Figure 8.1.

The primary recourse is to the non- borrower member states who should record a contingent liability in the amount in the fourth column of Figure 8.1.

The amounts-at-risk here are:
- Debts: €0.0 billion
- Contingent liabilities: €190.9 billion

8.2 European Stability Mechanism

The member state contingent liability in respect of the ESM is in the first instance the member state's callable capital, and this is shown in Figure 8.2 at €624 billion. This is too high as a global amount because the ESM has a ceiling on its loans of €500 billion and because the ESM's debts are far smaller than that. They are currently €118 billion and, with the €81 billion of paid-in capital, make up the funding for its loans of €203 billion.

There is headroom for new operations of €214 billion. Member states could either be asked to inject this in cash, or to back new bonds.

The total capital call is up to €332 billion, the headroom of €214 billion and the current bonds outstanding of €118 billion.

Borrowers' debts to the ESM - the loans outstanding to Spain, Greece, Portugal, Ireland and Cyprus in an amount of €203 billion – are already part of their General government gross debt.

As in the case of the EFSF, investors are primarily looking to the non-borrowers for payment.

For the sake of completeness Figure 8.3 was compiled to calculate the share of the ESM's outstanding bonds as it might fall upon member states under their ESM keys:
1. If every member state were called upon to pay in their share of the €118 billion, even the ones whose default had caused the need for the capital call;
2. With the contributions of the borrower countries reversed out, and the ESM keys re-based to make 100%.

It is case (2) that reflects the investor view, so the amounts of actual and contingent liabilities that the member states should reflect would be as per Figure 8.4.

The amounts-at-risk here are:
- Debts: 0.0 billion
- Contingent liabilities: €332.1 billion

8.3 European Investment Bank

The EU member states all have a contingent liability to pay in the uncalled capital of the EIB and the size of those claims as at 31.12.21 in € billions is contained in Figure 8.5. They total €226.6 billion.

This is the base case figure, but a possible addition to that should be discussed of the difference of €191 billion between that figure and the €440 billion of debts that the EIB has to capital markets. These debts are arguably an obligation that the member states could not allow to go bad.

The uncalled capital should be regarded as the EIB's third loss cushion, as it benefits from guarantees from the EU and the EGF, upon which it can call first, before calling up more capital. The EIB's loan portfolio is €433 billion, with loans to be disbursed of €123 billion, and we can analyze the first two loss cushions.

The first cushion is the EU guarantee for EIB's loans outside the EU. These are 11% of its portfolio at €48 billion and it appears to have total guarantee coverage for this amount.

The second cushion is the EU guarantee for InvestEU and the EGF guarantee. 18% of the EIB's loan portfolio - estimated at €77 billion - is into InvestEU/EGF projects, and the coverage which EIB individually enjoys from the InvestEU/EGF guarantees is low and possibly zero. EIF's commitments appear to be higher than all of the guarantees plus the permission to 'put funds at risk'. EIF would consume the guarantees first because it is taking higher risk than the EIB. In addition, the EIB, as majority shareholder, would be the main contributor if the EIF lost the amount of EIB Group funds it is permitted to 'put at risk' in the context of InvestEU/EGF.

We estimate this loss as €4 billion to EIB as a 60% shareholder in the EIF, out of a loss of €7 billion. This figure is composed of the €5 billion of the initial InvestEU programme size of €315 billion which we know about explicitly, plus a placeholder of €2 billion for an amount of EIB Group funds put at risk by the EIF in EGF and in the increase in InvestEU beyond its initial ceiling.

That would make EIB individually exposed for around €81 billion on InvestEU/EGF: €77 billion of loans and this extra €4 billion at risk, and there is a high risk-of-loss.

The remaining 71% of the EIB's portfolio - €307 billion portfolio - is its loans into the EU outside the context of InvestEU/EGF. The EIB itself regards this as low-risk business, hence its CET1 Ratio.

If we were to press the point of the possibility of member states being compelled to pay back the €191 billion of bonds, we should at least offset the EU guarantee for lending outside the EU of €48 billion, reducing the €191 billion to €143 billion.

Then it would need to be considered how the member states could be called upon to contribute more than their subscribed-but-not-called capital, so as to make sure the EIB was still able to meet its bond payments. That could either be a further capital call in the same proportions as member states' existing capital in EIB, or in line with the GNI-based contributions to the EU. If existing capital was used as the reference point, the contributions to the €143 billion would be as per the third column in Figure 8.5.

These contributions would then be added to the member state's uncalled capital in the fourth column of Figure 8.5, to reach a total potential liability in the fifth column.

The result appears harsh. So much would need to go wrong within the EU's core business of loans to the EU public sector for the EIB to need more than its subscribed-but-not-called capital of €226 billion. This ability represents a very thick first-loss cushion, and we do not believe it is realistic to increase that amount by factoring in a possible member state liability for the EIB's debts to capital markets.

There are some information gaps, and these are set out below. Notwithstanding those, it would appear churlish to posit that member states could be called upon for more than their subscribed-but-not-called capital.

What is needed to round out the information on the EIB Group is the table set out in Figure 8.7 as of 31/12/21, which specifically exempts its InvestEU/EGF loans.

The fourth and seventh columns in Figure 8.7 will serve the reconciliation with 'General government gross debt', as the figures in these columns do or will fall within it. The fifth and eighth columns will serve the quantification of the size of the public sector debt of the EU outside of 'General government', by showing how large EIB's loan book is into that type of borrower.

The disclosure, below, of the EIB's loans in the context of InvestEU/EGF will serve the quantification of the size of debt for which no public sector entity is the direct borrower but for the debt service on which the investor or lender is placing reliance on the public sector.

It is not felt to be equitable to increase the member state liability beyond the uncalled capital, so the amounts-at-risk here are:
- Debts: €0.0 billion
- Contingent liabilities: €226.6 billion

8.4 European Investment Fund (EIF) and InvestEU

The EIF does not represent a direct risk to member states, and that is in itself a problem when it has been used to 'mobilize' a large amount of finance. The main issue is transparency.

What is required of the EIF is a complete list of equity commitments it has made and the guarantees it has issued under the InvestEU programme. The EIF issues some lists but they are not so as to enable the reader to judge either the possibility of a loss or the actual face amounts that the EIF has engaged. These tables will also capture the EIB's loans in the context of InvestEU.

It will not, though, capture the full volume of liabilities created through the InvestEU template (or the EGF one) that track back onto the public sector. These liabilities come in three layers:
1. the liabilities of the projects enabled by the EIF guarantees/equity commitments;
2. the EIB's loans into these templates;
3. further private financing taken on by the projects.

This section only deals with the first one, and it is important not to double-count it by recording the liability for the loan enabled by the EIF guarantees/equity commitments on top of the EIF guarantees/equity commitments themselves.

The second one - the EIB's loans that are part of its loan portfolio - and are funded by its debts: the previous section has recognized a potential member state liability in respect of the EIB's debts, over and above the member state liability for uncalled capital, even though it has not included a figure for it.

The third one is dealt with in the next-but-one chapter.

Turning just to the EIF guarantees/equity commitments, the EIF 2020 Annual Report has been chosen as the reference point because the list in the EIF 2021 Annual Report has a preponderance of deals connected with the EGF, and it is therefore difficult to track the progress of InvestEU separately.

The EIF 2020 Annual Report contains tables on five types of operation:
1. Equity – Private Equity (p. 66)
2. Equity - Venture Capital (pp. 67-8)
3. Equity - Private debt (p. 69)
4. Guarantees (pp. 70-4)
5. Inclusive Finance Signatures (p. 75)

'Venture Capital' and 'Private Debt' are listed before the double horizontal purple line that appears to delineate the end of the section of Equity, so the requested table on 'InvestEU equity commitments' should embrace all three, and contain an entry on every equity commitment currently on the EIF's books, other than those coming under the heading 'European Guarantee Fund'.

Likewise the tables of 'Guarantees' and 'Inclusive Finance Signatures' contain an entry on every piece of business under these headings currently on the EIF's books, other than those falling under the heading 'European Guarantee Fund'

Five tables are needed as set out in Figures 8.8 – 8.12. In each case the data required is contrasted with the data that the EIF makes available now. 'Inclusive Finance' is covered, although it may be small, because it is opaque what these operations are. Their total amount appears to be far smaller than Equity Commitments and Guarantees. The 'Deal Name' could infer either an equity commitment or a guarantee, but if they did, why are the operations assigned their own heading? One must assume a mixture of the two broad types so there should be one table for each type.

The information required by Figures 8.8 – 8.12 will serve the quantification of the size of debt for which no public sector entity is the direct borrower but for the debt service on which the investor or lender is placing reliance on the public sector. A further example of this phenomenon is the EGF below. The EIF needs to break out its InvestEU, its EGF and its 'any other business' into separate tables. It is possible that 'Inclusive Finance Signatures' sit outside InvestEU, although this is not made clear.

This does not mean that EIF is an EU supranational that itself creates an actual debt or a contingent liability for member states. Losses on the EIF's business would be fed through to the member states through the legal persons of the EU and EIB, as a result of calls on EU guarantees or as payments of capital calls made by the EIF on the EU or made by the EIB on member states, this last one being a feed-through of a call by the EIF or the EIB. The EIF's potential losses are of course only a fraction of the extra indebtedness of the EU public sector caused by its schemes, which is quantified in Chapter 10.

We can revert to the table in the earlier chapter about what liabilities the EIF has undertaken as both guarantees and equity commitments, and which enable projects to take on finance, and what the total amount of that finance is, including what the EIB has lent into the same projects:

Overall estimate total of EIF book – aggregate of estimated total of EIF guarantees and equity books											76,002
Estimated total book of finance enabled – aggregate of estimated books of finance enabled by EIF guarantees and equity books											611,964

Table 8.1: estimate of total EIF book of engagements and finance enabled by them

This €76 billion is meaningfully larger than the aggregate of the EU guarantee for InvestEU (€26.2 billion), the guarantees in its favour from the EGF (€24.4 billion), and the permission for it to put 'EIB Group's own funds at risk under InvestEU (€5 billion). These total €51.6 billion. The discrepancy of €24.4 billion could point to further schemes existing beyond InvestEU and EGF, or to the EIF having exceeded its brief.

Because any loss for member states would reach them either (i) via a call by EIB Group on the InvestEU guarantees; or (ii) via a demand from the EIB for a portion of the uncalled capital; or (iii) via direct call on an EGF guarantee, it has been considered unnecessary to state a separate amount-at-risk against EIF.

This is itself indicative of the overriding problem: a large amount of indebtedness has for sure been created, but it is neither visible in the accounts of the entity sitting at the fulcrum of the debt's creation, nor does the risk filter through to member states transparently via the Eurostat contingent liabilities table. The risk tracks through but via several tracks, like a river delta.

The amounts-at-risk are captured under other headings, so the specific amounts are:
- Debts: €0.0 billion
- Contingent liabilities: €0.0 billion

8.5 European Guarantee Fund (EGF) in favour of EIB Group

EGF, like InvestEU, suffers from a lack of transparency.

The EU/EIB need to confirm what is the relationship between the EGF and the MFF. As the EGF was established in the second half of 2020, it might sit within the 2014-20 MFF. Alternatively it might either sit right outside the MFFs for both 2014-20 and 2021-7, or be accommodated in some way under the 2021-7 MFF.

The timing of the roll-out of EGF infers that initial EGF transactions might only have registered in the EIF's annual report for 2021, not 2020, even if approval had been given for an allocation out of the EGF ceiling in 2020. This would point in the same direction as our calculation that up to €60 billion of EGF financing would be put on in 2022, even if approval for almost all of it had been given in 2021.

Approvals 'are expected to mobilise total investment of EUR 174.4 billion, with projects spread over all 22 participating Member States. Signatures stand at EUR 18.1 billion for the whole EIB Group (EIB EUR 10.1 billion and EIF EUR 8 billion) — which shows that EGF funding is effectively reaching businesses across the European Union.':

In € billions	Approved	Signed	Expected amount mobilized
EIB (loans)	€10.4	€10.1	€82.4
EIF (guarantees & equity commitments)	€12.8	€8.0	€92.0
Total	€23.2	€18.1	€174.4

Table 8.2: EGF project amounts

The EU/EIB need to confirm:
- Whether the EIB and EIF receive an EGF guarantee for every loan, guarantee or equity commitment they make under this programme, and in the exact principal amount of the loan, guarantee or equity commitment they make, or whether they have a permission to put EIB Group money at risk over and above the amounts guaranteed to the EIB Group by the EGF, as is the case within InvestEU;
- That the programme is now closed with €1.2 billion unused;
- Whether the 'Expected amount mobilized' includes the €23.2 billion EIB Group commitment and, if it does not, what the total amount of money is which is the addition of the €23.2 billion EIB Group commitment and all the finance from other sources obtained by the projects;
- What the final mobilized amount is and the total of all finance if different;
- An inventory of the projects financed on the back of the EGF as below.

The comparison with the data that the EIF does provide is taken from the EIF 2021 Annual Report, in which EGF-backed business is mixed into single tables per operation type with InvestEU. The EIF should in future provide separate tables per programme, as well as for each operation type within a programme. There is a slight difference in the overall figure from the €175.6 billion quoted elsewhere.

At least a total figure is stated for EGF, rather than needing to be extrapolated as we have had to do for InvestEU. It leaves open the reconciliation between InvestEU and EGF: how much of the totals of €471 billion at the end of 2020 and €612 billion at the end of 2021 are attributable to InvestEU, EGF or other, similar financing schemes?

Regarding EGF the EIF should produce five new tables; EGF-based 'Inclusive Finance Signatures' may include both equity commitments and guarantees. These are set out in Figures 8.13 to 8.17 and follow the pattern of the supplementary information needed on InvestEU.

The information as per Figures 8.13 to 8.17 will further serve the quantification of the size of debt for which no public sector entity is the direct borrower but for the debt service on which the investor or lender is placing reliance on the public sector.

The EGF webpage states that 'Participating countries in the European Union provide guarantees proportional to their share in the EIB or other institutions'. Estonia, Czech Republic, Hungary, Romania and Latvia do not take part.

Taking therefore the EIB as a model, and re-basing the shareholdings of the EGF participants to 100%, Figure 8.18 shows the contingent liability for the participating member states based on the size of the EGF at its closure of €23.2 billion.

Unlike InvestEU, losses from which track back to member states from the EIF via the EIB and the EU, losses from the EGF programme will reach participating member states directly from the EIF through their guarantees. EIB loans into EGF projects are dealt with in the section on EIB within this chapter. The third-party finance raised by the same projects is dealt with in a later chapter. The amounts-at-risk here are then simply the EGF guarantees:

- Debts: €0.0 billion
- Contingent liabilities: €23.2 billion

8.6 Collation of member state liabilities created through the legal persons of the EU/Eurozone supranationals

Below is a table showing all of the actual and contingent liabilities created for the member states through the legal persons of the EU and Eurozone supranationals, tracked back to the member state level in accordance with the methodology used in the respective section in this chapter, with the figures in € billions. There are rounding errors on the totals against EIB and EGF of €0.1 billion which are considered to be immaterial.

Table 8.3: collation of member states liabilities created through the EU/Eurozone supranationals in € billions

Country	EFSF/contingent liability	ESM/contingent liability	EIB/ contingent liability	EGF/ contingent liability	Total
Belgium	€ 7.50	€ 14.10	€ 11.80	€ 1.20	€ 34.60
Bulgaria	--	--	€ 0.50	€ 0.10	€ 0.60
Czech Rep	--	--	€ 2.00	--	€ 2.00
Denmark	--	--	€ 6.00	€ 0.60	€ 6.60
Germany	€ 54.50	€ 110.30	€ 42.50	€ 4.50	€ 211.80
Estonia	€ 0.60	€ 0.70	€ 0.20	--	€ 1.50
Ireland	--	--	€ 1.50	€ 0.20	€ 1.70
Greece	--	--	€ 3.20	€ 0.30	€ 3.50
Spain	€ 24.70	--	€ 25.50	€ 2.70	€ 52.90
France	€ 42.30	€ 82.80	€ 42.50	€ 4.50	€ 172.10
Croatia	--	--	€ 0.90	€ 0.10	€ 1.00
Italy	€ 35.20	€ 72.80	€ 42.50	€ 4.50	€ 155.00
Cyprus	--	--	€ 0.30	€ 0.00	€ 0.30
Latvia	--	€ 1.10	€ 0.20	--	€ 1.30
Lithuania	--	€ 1.70	€ 0.40	€ 0.00	€ 2.10
Luxembourg	€ 0.70	€ 1.00	€ 0.30	€ 0.00	€ 2.00
Hungary	--	--	€ 1.90	--	€ 1.90
Malta	€ 0.00	€ 0.40	€ 0.10	€ 0.00	€ 0.50
Netherlands	€ 12.10	€ 23.20	€ 11.80	€ 1.20	€ 48.30
Austria	€ 6.10	€ 11.30	€ 5.80	€ 0.60	€ 23.80
Poland	--	--	€ 10.40	€ 1.10	€ 11.50
Portugal	--	--	€ 2.10	€ 0.20	€ 2.30
Romania	--	--	€ 1.50	--	€ 1.50
Slovenia	€ 1.00	€ 1.90	€ 0.70	€ 0.10	€ 3.70
Slovakia	€ 2.40	€ 3.40	€ 0.70	€ 0.10	€ 6.60
Finland	€ 3.80	€ 7.30	€ 3.40	€ 0.40	€ 14.90
Sweden	--	--	€ 7.80	€ 0.80	€ 8.60
	€ 190.90	€ 332.00	€ 226.50	€ 23.20	€ 772.60

Table 8.3: collation of member states liabilities created through the EU/Eurozone supranationals in € billions

Figures:
- 8.1: member state liability under guarantee for the debts of the EFSF
- 8.2: callable capital in the ESM as at 31 December 2020 in € billions
- 8.3: member state liability for the outstanding debts of the ESM, using the same formula as the callable capital
- 8.4: most plausible member state liability position deriving from the ESM
- 8.5: member states contingent liability for uncalled capital of the EIB at 31.12.21 in € billions
- 8.6: total member state liability for EIB if all EIB debts had to be repaid
- 8.7: supplementary information required on EIB loan portfolio
- 8.8: Inventory of InvestEU equity commitments
- 8.9: Inventory of InvestEU guarantees
- 8.10: Inventory of InvestEU/Inclusive Finance equity commitments
- 8.11: Inventory of InvestEU/Inclusive Finance guarantees
- 8.12: Extract from inventories of equity commitments, guarantees and Inclusive Finance for projects with public sector involvement
- 8.13: Inventory of EGF-based equity commitments
- 8.14: Inventory of EGF-based guarantees
- 8.15: Inventory of EGF-based Inclusive Finance equity commitments
- 8.16: Inventory of EGF-based/Inclusive Finance guarantees
- 8.17: Extract from inventories of equity commitments and guarantees for EGF-based projects with public sector involvement
- 8.18: contingent liability for the participating member states in the EGF

Figure 8.1: member state liability under guarantee for the debts of the EFSF

Country	Re-based Capital Keys	Allocation of €191 billion	Capital Keys after removal of borrowers	Re-allocation of €191 billion
Belgium	3.6789%	€7.0 billion	3.9468%	€7.5 billion
Germany	26.6192%	€50.8 billion	28.5578%	€54.5 billion
Estonia	0.2845%	€0.5 billion	0.3052%	€0.6 billion
Ireland	1.7099%	€3.3 billion	--	--
Greece	2.4977%	€4.8 billion	--	--
Spain	12.0412%	€23.0 billion	12.9181%	€24.7 billion
France	20.6240%	€39.4 billion	22.1260%	€42.3 billion
Italy	17.1546%	€32.8 billion	18.4039%	€35.2 billion
Cyprus	0.2173%	€0.4 billion	--	--
Latvia	--	--	--	--
Lithuania	--	--	--	--
Luxembourg	0.3327%	€0.6 billion	0.3569%	€0.7 billion
Malta	0.1059%	€0.2 billion	0.1136%	€0.2 billion
Netherlands	5.9177%	€11.3 billion	6.3487%	€12.1 billion
Austria	2.9555%	€5.6 billion	3.1707%	€6.1 billion
Portugal	2.3634%	€4.5 billion	--	--
Slovenia	0.4862%	€0.9 billion	0.5216%	€1.0 billion
Slovakia	1.1564%	€2.2 billion	1.2406%	€2.4 billion
Finland	1.8548%	€3.5 billion	1.9899%	€3.8 billion
Total	100.00%	€191.0 billion	100.00%	€191.0 billion

Figure 8.1: member state liability under guarantee for the debts of the EFSF

Figure 8.2: callable capital in the ESM as at 31 December 2020 in € billions

Country	ESM Key	Shares	Subscribed	Paid-in	Callable
Belgium	3.4513%	243,244	€24.3 billion	€2.8 billion	€21.5 billion
Germany	26.9449%	1,899,071	€189.9 billion	€21.7 billion	€168.2 billion
Estonia	0.1847%	13,020	€1.3 billion	€0.1 billion	€1.2 billion
Ireland	1.5804%	111,383	€11.1 billion	€1.3 billion	€9.8 billion
Greece	2.7957%	197,044	€19.7 billion	€2.3 billion	€17.4 billion
Spain	11.8153%	832,743	€83.3 billion	€9.5 billion	€73.8 billion
France	20.2346%	1,426,131	€142.6 billion	€16.3 billion	€126.3 billion
Italy	17.7807%	1,253,184	€125.5 billion	€14.3 billion	€111.0 billion
Cyprus	0.1948%	13,729	€1.4 billion	€0.2 billion	€1.2 billion
Latvia	0.2746%	19,353	€1.9 billion	€0.2 billion	€1.7 billion
Lithuania	0.4063%	28,634	€2.9 billion	€0.3 billion	€2.6 billion
Luxembourg	0.2486%	17,519	€1.8 billion	€0.2 billion	€1.6 billion
Malta	0.0899%	6,338	€0.6 billion	€0.1 billion	€0.5 billion
Netherlands	5.6746%	399,945	€40.0 billion	€4.6 billion	€35.4 billion
Austria	2.7627%	194,718	€19.5 billion	€2.2 billion	€17.3 billion
Portugal	2.4906%	175,534	€17.6 billion	€2.0 billion	€15.6 billion
Slovenia	0.4678%	32,973	€3.3 billion	€0.4 billion	€2.9 billion
Slovakia	0.8184%	57,680	€5.8 billion	€0.7 billion	€5.1 billion
Finland	1.7841%	125,744	€12.6 billion	€1.4 billion	€11.2 billion
Total	100.0000%	7,047,987	€704.8 billion	€80.5 billion	€624.3 billion

Figure 8.2: callable capital in the ESM as at 31 December 2020 in € billions

Figure 8.3: member state liability for the outstanding debts of the ESM, using the same formula as the callable capital

Country	ESM Keys	All pay their share	Re-based ESM Keys	Borrowers do not pay
Belgium	3.4513%	€4.07 billion	4.2544%	€5.02 billion
Germany	26.9449%	€31.79 billion	33.2148%	€39.19 billion
Estonia	0.1847%	€0.22 billion	0.2277%	€0.27 billion
Ireland	1.5804%	€1.86 billion	--	--
Greece	2.7957%	€3.30 billion	--	--
Spain	11.8153%	€13.94 billion	--	--
France	20.2346%	€23.88 billion	24.9430%	€29.43 billion
Italy	17.7807%	€20.98 billion	21.9181%	€25.86 billion
Cyprus	0.1948%	€0.23 billion	--	--
Latvia	0.2746%	€0.32 billion	0.3385%	€0.40 billion
Lithuania	0.4063%	€0.48 billion	0.5008%	€0.59 billion
Luxembourg	0.2486%	€0.29 billion	0.3064%	€0.36 billion
Malta	0.0899%	€0.11 billion	0.1108%	€0.13 billion
Netherlands	5.6746%	€6.70 billion	6.9950%	€8.25 billion
Austria	2.7627%	€3.26 billion	3.4056%	€4.02 billion
Portugal	2.4906%	€2.94 billion	--	--
Slovenia	0.4678%	€0.55 billion	0.5767%	€0.68 billion
Slovakia	0.8184%	€0.97 billion	1.0088%	€1.19 billion
Finland	1.7841%	€2.11 billion	2.1992%	€2.60 billion
Total	100.0000%	€118.00 billion	100.0000%	€118.00 billion

Figure 8.3: member state liability for the outstanding debts of the ESM, using the same formula as the callable capital

Figure 8.4: most plausible member state liability position deriving from the ESM

Country	Non-borrowers' liability for ESM debts now	Non-borrowers' total callable capital	Non-borrowers' contingent liability for headroom	Total ESM contingent liability
Belgium	€5.02 billion	€21.5 billion	€9.1 billion	€14.1 billion
Germany	€39.19 billion	€168.2 billion	€71.1 billion	€110.3 billion
Estonia	€0.27 billion	€1.2 billion	€0.5 billion	€0.7 billion
Ireland	--	--	--	--
Greece	--	--	--	--
Spain	--	--	--	--
France	€29.43 billion	€126.3 billion	€53.4 billion	€82.8 billion
Italy	€25.86 billion	€111.0 billion	€46.9 billion	€72.8 billion
Cyprus	--	--	--	--
Latvia	€0.40 billion	€1.7 billion	€0.7 billion	€1.1 billion
Lithuania	€0.59 billion	€2.6 billion	€1.1 billion	€1.7 billion
Luxembourg	€0.36 billion	€1.6 billion	€0.7 billion	€1.0 billion
Malta	€0.13 billion	€0.5 billion	€0.2 billion	€0.4 billion
Netherlands	€8.25 billion	€35.4 billion	€15.0 billion	€23.2 billion
Austria	€4.02 billion	€17.3 billion	€7.3 billion	€11.3 billion
Portugal	--	--	--	--
Slovenia	€0.68 billion	€2.9 billion	€1.2 billion	€1.9 billion
Slovakia	€1.19 billion	€5.1 billion	€2.2 billion	€3.4 billion
Finland	€2.60 billion	€11.2 billion	€4.7 billion	€7.3 billion
Total	€118.00 billion	€506.5 billion	€214.0 billion	€332.0 billion

Figure 8.4: most plausible member state liability position deriving from the ESM

Figure 8.5: member states contingent liability for uncalled capital of the EIB at 31.12.21 in € billions

Nr	Country	Subscribed capital	Called capital	Uncalled capital
1	Germany	€46.7	€4.2	€42.5
2	France	€46.7	€4.2	€42.5
3	Italy	€46.7	€4.2	€42.5
4	Spain	€28.0	€2.5	€25.5
5	Netherlands	€12.9	€1.1	€11.8
6	Belgium	€12.9	€1.1	€11.8
7	Poland	€11.4	€1.0	€10.4
8	Sweden	€8.6	€0.8	€7.8
9	Denmark	€6.6	€0.6	€6.0
10	Austria	€6.4	€0.6	€5.8
11	Finland	€3.7	€0.3	€3.4
12	Greece	€3.5	€0.3	€3.2
13	Portugal	€2.3	€0.2	€2.1
14	Czech Republic	€2.2	€0.2	€2.0
15	Hungary	€2.1	€0.2	€1.9
16	Ireland	€1.6	€0.1	€1.5
17	Romania	€1.6	€0.1	€1.5
18	Croatia	€1.0	€0.1	€0.9
19	Slovakia	€0.8	€0.1	€0.7
20	Slovenia	€0.7	<€0.1	€0.7
21	Bulgaria	€0.5	<€0.1	€0.5
22	Lithuania	€0.4	<€0.1	€0.4
23	Luxembourg	€0.3	<€0.1	€0.3
24	Cyprus	€0.3	<€0.1	€0.3
25	Latvia	€0.2	<€0.1	€0.2
26	Estonia	€0.2	<€0.1	€0.2
27	Malta	€0.1	<€0.1	€0.1
	Total	€248.8	€22.2	€226.6

Figure 8.5: member states contingent liability for uncalled capital of the EIB at 31.12.21 in € billions

Figure 8.6: total member state liability for EIB if all EIB debts had to be repaid

Nr	Country	Percentage	Amount	Uncalled capital	Total liability
1	Germany	18.77%	€26.8	€42.5	€69.3
2	France	18.77%	€26.8	€42.5	€69.3
3	Italy	18.77%	€26.8	€42.5	€69.3
4	Spain	11.25%	€16.1	€25.5	€41.6
5	Netherlands	5.18%	€7.4	€11.8	€19.2
6	Belgium	5.18%	€7.4	€11.8	€19.2
7	Poland	4.58%	€6.6	€10.4	€17.0
8	Sweden	3.46%	€4.9	€7.8	€11.7
9	Denmark	2.65%	€3.8	€6.0	€9.8
10	Austria	2.57%	€3.7	€5.8	€9.5
11	Finland	1.49%	€2.1	€3.4	€5.5
12	Greece	1.41%	€2.0	€3.2	€5.2
13	Portugal	0.92%	€1.3	€2.1	€3.4
14	Czech Republic	0.88%	€1.3	€2.0	€3.3
15	Hungary	0.84%	€1.2	€1.9	€3.1
16	Ireland	0.64%	€0.9	€1.5	€2.4
17	Romania	0.64%	€0.9	€1.5	€2.4
18	Croatia	0.40%	€0.6	€0.9	€1.5
19	Slovakia	0.32%	€0.5	€0.7	€1.2
20	Slovenia	0.28%	€0.4	€0.7	€1.1
21	Bulgaria	0.20%	€0.3	€0.5	€0.8
22	Lithuania	0.16%	€0.2	€0.4	€0.6
23	Luxembourg	0.12%	€0.2	€0.3	€0.5
24	Cyprus	0.12%	€0.2	€0.3	€0.5
25	Latvia	0.08%	€0.1	€0.2	€0.3
26	Estonia	0.08%	€0.1	€0.2	€0.3
27	Malta	0.04%	€0.1	€0.1	€0.2
	Total	100.00%	€143.0	€226.6	€369.6

Figure 8.6: total member state liability for EIB if all EIB debts had to be repaid

Figure 8.7: supplementary information required on EIB loan portfolio

Nr	Country	Outstanding loans to all public sector entities	Outstanding loans to 'General government' entities	Outstanding loans to other public sector entities	Loans to be disbursed to all public sector entities	Loans to be disbursed to 'General government' entities	Loans to be disbursed to other public sector entities
1	Germany	€ billion	€ billion	€ billion	€ billion	€ billion	€ billion
2	France	€ billion	€ billion	€ billion	€ billion	€ billion	€ billion
3	Italy	€ billion	€ billion	€ billion	€ billion	€ billion	€ billion
4	Spain	€ billion	€ billion	€ billion	€ billion	€ billion	€ billion
5	Netherlands	€ billion	€ billion	€ billion	€ billion	€ billion	€ billion
6	Belgium	€ billion	€ billion	€ billion	€ billion	€ billion	€ billion
7	Poland	€ billion	€ billion	€ billion	€ billion	€ billion	€ billion
8	Sweden	€ billion	€ billion	€ billion	€ billion	€ billion	€ billion
9	Denmark	€ billion	€ billion	€ billion	€ billion	€ billion	€ billion
10	Austria	€ billion	€ billion	€ billion	€ billion	€ billion	€ billion
11	Finland	€ billion	€ billion	€ billion	€ billion	€ billion	€ billion
12	Greece	€ billion	€ billion	€ billion	€ billion	€ billion	€ billion
13	Portugal	€ billion	€ billion	€ billion	€ billion	€ billion	€ billion
14	Czech Republic	€ billion	€ billion	€ billion	€ billion	€ billion	€ billion
15	Hungary	€ billion	€ billion	€ billion	€ billion	€ billion	€ billion
16	Ireland	€ billion	€ billion	€ billion	€ billion	€ billion	€ billion
17	Romania	€ billion	€ billion	€ billion	€ billion	€ billion	€ billion
18	Croatia	€ billion	€ billion	€ billion	€ billion	€ billion	€ billion
19	Slovakia	€ billion	€ billion	€ billion	€ billion	€ billion	€ billion
20	Slovenia	€ billion	€ billion	€ billion	€ billion	€ billion	€ billion
21	Bulgaria	€ billion	€ billion	€ billion	€ billion	€ billion	€ billion
22	Lithuania	€ billion	€ billion	€ billion	€ billion	€ billion	€ billion
23	Luxembourg	€ billion	€ billion	€ billion	€ billion	€ billion	€ billion
24	Cyprus	€ billion	€ billion	€ billion	€ billion	€ billion	€ billion
25	Latvia	€ billion	€ billion	€ billion	€ billion	€ billion	€ billion
26	Estonia	€ billion	€ billion	€ billion	€ billion	€ billion	€ billion
27	Malta	€ billion	€ billion	€ billion	€ billion	€ billion	€ billion
	Total	€ billion	€ billion	€ billion	€ billion	€ billion	€ billion

Figure 8.7: supplementary information required on EIB loan portfolio

Figure 8.8: Inventory of InvestEU equity commitments

Project name, its capital, and sponsor	Project purpose and timeline	What equity asset EIF has committed to buy, who from, and at what price	Amount of EIF's commitment and how long it is open for	Nature and timing of EIF's exit route if it buys the equity asset	Amount of EIB loans into the same project and run-off profile	Amount of other loans into the same project and run-off profile

Figure 8.8 - Inventory of InvestEU equity commitments

This contrasts with the information given in the EIF 2020 Annual Report on equity commitments issued:

Breaking it down

Equity Signatures
as at December 2020

Deal Name	Resource	Team location	Commitment (EURm)	EFSI SMEW	EFSI SMEWII
Private Equity			128.9		
ABAC SUSTAINABLE VALUE II FCR	EFSI - SMEW, OWN FUNDS	Spain	40,0	Yes	No
Abenex VI	OWN FUNDS, RCR	France	20,0	Yes	No
Aksia Capital V	OWN FUNDS, RCR	Italy	30,0	No	No
Alcedo V	AMUF - GC, OWN FUNDS, RCR	Italy	60,0	No	No
Argos Wityu Mid-Market VIII	OWN FUNDS, RCR	France	60,0	No	No
ASEF SCSp	EFSI - SMEW, OWN FUNDS, NPI SM - HBOR	Croatia	25,0	Yes	No
Avallon MBO Fund III SCA SICAV-RAIF	AMUF - GC, EFSI - SMEW, OWN FUNDS	Poland	30,0	Yes	No
Axcel VI K/S 2	AMUF - GC	Denmark	20,0	Yes	No
Beyond Capital Partners Fund II GmbH & Co. KG	COSME-EFG, OWN FUNDS, RCR	Germany	30,0	Yes	No
BlackPeak Southeast Europe Growth Equity Fund SCSp	COSME-EFG, OWN FUNDS, JER-009 BULGARIA	Bulgaria	32,0	No	No
Blue Sea Capital Fund II SCSp	EFSI - SMEW, OWN FUNDS	Croatia	25,0	Yes	No
Bluegem III SCSp	OWN FUNDS, RCR	United Kingdom	30,0	No	No
CMF-Cipio Partners	German CMF	Luxembourg	10,3	No	No
Crest II FCR	OWN FUNDS, NPI SM - IFD (Portugal Growth), RCR	Portugal	20,0	No	No

It is not even clear whether the EIF's table is of all equity commitments on its books, or just the ones signed in 2020. The details given are sparse, and all of 'Resource', 'Team location', 'EFSI SMEW' and 'EFSI SMEWII' may be interesting to the EIF itself and possibly to the EIB, but they convey little idea of what the EIF has bought into.

172

Figure 8.9: Inventory of InvestEU guarantees

Project name, its capital, and sponsor	Project purpose and timeline	Who EIF has issued a guarantee to, and who has issued a counter-indemnity to EIF for it	Under what circumstances the guarantee can be called	Original and current amount of EIF's guarantee and its run-off profile	Amount of EIB loans into the same project and run-off profile	Amount of other loans into the same project and run-off profile

Figure 8.9: Inventory of InvestEU guarantees

This contrasts with the information given in the EIF 2020 Annual Report pp. 70-4 on guarantees issued:

Breaking it down

Guarantee Signatures
as at December 2020

Deal Name	Resource	Team location	Commitment (EURm)	EFSI SMEW	EFSI SMEWII
Austria Wirtschaftsservice (AWS) - CCS GF	CCS GF	Austria	3,5	Yes	No
Banco Comercial Portugues (BCP) - CCS GF	CCS GF	Portugal	25,2	Yes	No
Cassa Depositi e Prestiti (CDP) - CCS GF	CCS GF	Italy	8,4	Yes	No
CERSA - CCS GF (COVID)	CCS GF	Spain	27,9	Yes	No
Credito Emiliano – CCS GF	CCS GF	Italy	14,0	Yes	No
Finora Capital - CCS	CCS GF	Estonia	1,1	Yes	No
IFCIC - CCS GF - CG	CCS GF	France	1,8	Yes	No
IFCIC - CCS GF - DG (COVID)	CCS GF	France	15,8	Yes	No
Raiffeisenbank EAD – CCS GF	CCS GF	Bulgaria	1,8	Yes	No

The 'Deal name' is not the Account Party, and the details of 'Resource', 'Team location', 'EFSI SMEW' and 'EFSI SMEWII' are scarcely enlightening.

Figure 8.10: Inventory of InvestEU/Inclusive Finance equity commitments

Project name, its capital, and sponsor	Project purpose and timeline	What equity asset EIF has committed to buy, who from, and at what price	Amount of EIF's commitment and how long it is open for	Nature and timing of EIF's exit route if it buys the equity asset	Amount of EIB loans into the same project and run-off profile	Amount of other loans into the same project and run-off profile

Figure 8.10: Inventory of InvestEU/Inclusive Finance equity commitments

Figure 8.11: Inventory of InvestEU/Inclusive Finance guarantees

Project name, its capital, and sponsor	Project purpose and timeline	Who EIF has issued a guarantee to, and who has issued a counter-indemnity to EIF for it	Under what circumstances the guarantee can be called	Original and current amount of EIF's guarantee and its run-off profile	Amount of EIB loans into the same project and run-off profile	Amount of other loans into the same project and run-off profile

Figure 8.11: Inventory of InvestEU/Inclusive Finance guarantees

This contrasts with the single table of information given in the EIF 2020 Annual Report p. 75 on Inclusive Finance Signatures:

Breaking it down

Inclusive Finance Signatures
as at December 2020

Deal Name	Resource	Team location	Commitment (EURm)	EFSI SMEW	EFSI SMEWII
Agricover - EaSI Funded MF	EaSI - Funded	Romania	7.2	No	No
FAER - EaSI Funded MF	EaSI - Funded	Romania	2.1	No	No
Opportunity Bank Serbia (OBS) - EaSI Funded MF	EaSI - Funded	Serbia	10.0	No	No
Lithuanian Central Credit Union (LCCU) - EaSI CBI	EaSI CBI	Lithuania	2.0	No	No
Qredits - Easi CBI - MF	EaSI CBI	Netherlands	5.0	No	No
Vitas - Easi CBI - MF	EaSI CBI	Romania	1.9	No	No
Alpha Bank Greece - EaSI MF	EaSI GFI	Greece	3.6	Yes	No
Aros Kapital - EaSI MF	EaSI GFI	Sweden	1.5	Yes	No
Attica Bank - EaSI MF	EaSI GFI	Greece	1.2	Yes	No
Banca Intesa ad Beograd - EaSI MF	EaSI GFI	Serbia	2.4	No	No
Banco Comercial Portugues (BCP) - EaSI SE	EaSI GFI	Portugal	9.6	Yes	No

This information suffers from the same problems mentioned above.

Figure 8.12: Extract from inventories of equity commitments, guarantees and Inclusive Finance for projects with public sector involvement

Project name and sponsor	Equity commitment or guarantee	What public sector entity is involved	What is their role in the project, their liability towards it, the liability amount, timing and so on	What further public sector entities are involved and in what way

Figure 8.12: Extract from inventories of equity commitments, guarantees and Inclusive Finance for projects with public sector involvement

Figure 8.13: Inventory of EGF-based equity commitments

Project name, its capital, and sponsor	Project purpose and timeline	What equity asset EIF has committed to buy, who from, and at what price	Amount of EIF's commitment and how long it is open for	Nature and timing of EIF's exit route if it buys the equity asset	Amount of EIB loans into the same project and run-off profile	Amount of other loans into the same project and run-off profile

Figure 8.13: Inventory of EGF-based equity commitments

This contrasts with the data in the combined tables for InvestEU/EGF in the EIF 2021 Annual Report pp. 62-6:

2021
Transactions

Equity Signatures as at December 2021

Deal Name	Resource(s)	Team Location	EFSI/SMEW	EFSIIW	Commitment (€ m)
Infrastructure					
Everwood Renewables Fund V	Intra Climate Funds	Spain	No	No	50,0
Ginkgo Co-Investment A SCSp	Intra Climate Funds - Co-Investments	Switzerland	No	No	56,4
Ginkgo Fund III SCA SICAV-RAIF	Intra Climate Funds	Switzerland	No	No	50,0
Impax New Energy Investors IV SCSp	Intra Climate Funds	Luxembourg	No	No	50,0
Mirova Energy Transition V Fund	Intra Climate Funds	France	No	No	20,0
Pioneer Infrastructure Partners SCSp	Intra Climate Funds	United Kingdom	No	No	50,0
Infrastructure Total					276,4
Private Debt					
Acto Heritage	EGF Minimum & Target Fund size Facility	France	No	No	40,0
All Seas Capital I SCSp	EGF Minimum & Target Fund size Facility, EIF, RCR 20	United Kingdom	No	No	60,0
Armada Fund V	EGF Minimum & Target Fund size Facility	Sweden	No	Yes	50,0
Bootstrap Europe III SCSp	EGF Minimum & Target Fund size Facility	United Kingdom	No	No	40,0
BPM Mezzanine Fund II	Baltic Innovation Fund 2, COSME-EFG, EIF in COSME-EFG	Estonia	No	No	30,0
Brightr Capital Credit Fund III SCSp	BMWi-MDD 2, EGF Selective Loan Funds Facility, LfA CV-MDD 2, NRW-MDD 2, SAB-MDD 2	Germany	No	No	40,0
Croatian Mezzanine Debt Fund	EGF Minimum & Target Fund size Facility	Croatia	Yes	No	7,0
Enterprising Finance The Netherlands Unitranche Fund SCSp	EGF Selective Loan Funds Facility	Netherlands	No	No	40,0
Equita Private Debt Fund II	EGF Minimum & Target Fund size Facility	Italy	Yes	No	20,0
Fondo Impresa Italia II	EGF Selective Loan Funds Facility	Italy	No	No	50,0
IEF Private Debt Fonds II SCSp	BMWi-MDD 2, EGF Selective Loan Funds Facility, LfA CV-MDD 2, NRW-MDD 2, SAB-MDD 2	Germany	No	No	50,0

Figure 8.14: Inventory of EGF-based guarantees

Project name, its capital, and sponsor	Project purpose and timeline	Who EIF has issued a guarantee to, and who has issued a counter-indemnity to EIF for it	Under what circumstances the guarantee can be called	Original and current amount of EIF's guarantee and its run-off profile	Amount of EIB loans into the same project and run-off profile	Amount of other loans into the same project and run-off profile

Figure 8.14: Inventory of EGF-based guarantees

This contrasts with the data in the combined tables for InvestEU/EGF in the EIF 2021 Annual Report pp. 67-71:

Guarantee Signatures as at December 2021

Deal Name	Resource	Team Location	EPSF/SMEW	EFSF/IW	Commitment (Euro)
Capped					
AB SEB bankas EGF-CDG	EGF Capped Guarantees (unfunded)	Lithuania	No	No	5,6
Allianz Bank Bulgaria EGF-CDG	EGF Capped Guarantees (unfunded)	Bulgaria	No	No	2,9
Alpha bank EGF-CDG	EGF Capped Guarantees (unfunded)	Greece	No	No	46,2
Atum S&E GP	EPSI S&E Pilot	Latvia	Yes	No	3,5
AB9 EGF-CDG	EGF Capped Guarantees (unfunded)	Poland	No	No	9,9
Attica Bank EGF-CDG	EGF Capped Guarantees (unfunded)	Greece	No	No	12,5
Banca Transilvania S&E GP	EPSI S&E Pilot	Romania	Yes	No	4,5
Banco BPI EGF-CDG	EGF Capped Guarantees (unfunded)	Portugal	No	No	15,2
Banco Comercial Portugues (BCP) EGF-CDG	EGF Capped Guarantees (unfunded)	Portugal	No	No	172,0
Banco Santander Totta EGF-CDG	EGF Capped Guarantees (unfunded)	Portugal	No	No	87
Banque Populaire Occitane FOSTER Midi Pyrenees ERDF	ESIF MP ERDF (G&S)	France	No	No	7,6
BCR Social Finance IFN SA S&E GP	EPSI S&E Pilot	Romania	Yes	No	2,5
BGK EGF-CCG	EGF Capped Guarantees (unfunded)	Poland	No	No	76,2
Brain Capital S&E GP	EPSI S&E Pilot	Germany	Yes	No	5,6
Caisse d'Epargne FOSTER Midi Pyrenees ERDF de	ESIF MP ERDF (G&S)	France	No	No	7,8
Caixa Geral de Depósitos EGF-CDG	EGF Capped Guarantees (unfunded)	Portugal	No	No	150,2
Caixa Geral de Depósitos S&E GP	EPSI S&E Pilot	Portugal	Yes	No	3,0
Cassa Depositi e Prestiti EGF-CCG	EGF Capped Guarantees (unfunded)	Italy	No	No	1.050,0
CERSA EGF-CCG	EGF Capped Guarantees (unfunded)	Spain	No	No	191,1
CHANCEN eG S&E GP	EPSI S&E Pilot	Germany	Yes	No	5,0

176

Figure 8.15: Inventory of EGF-based Inclusive Finance equity commitments

Project name, its capital, and sponsor	Project purpose and timeline	What equity asset EIF has committed to buy, who from, and at what price	Amount of EIF's commitment and how long it is open for	Nature and timing of EIF's exit route if it buys the equity asset	Amount of EIB loans into the same project and run-off profile	Amount of other loans into the same project and run-off profile

Figure 8.15: Inventory of EGF-based Inclusive Finance equity commitments

Figure 8.16: Inventory of EGF-based/Inclusive Finance guarantees

Project name, its capital, and sponsor	Project purpose and timeline	Who EIF has issued a guarantee to, and who has issued a counter-indemnity to EIF for it	Under what circumstances the guarantee can be called	Original and current amount of EIF's guarantee and its run-off profile	Amount of EIB loans into the same project and run-off profile	Amount of other loans into the same project and run-off profile

Figure 8.16: Inventory of EGF-based/Inclusive Finance guarantees

This contrasts with the data in the single table on Inclusive Finance Signatures for InvestEU/EGF in the EIF 2021 Annual Report p. 72:

Inclusive Finance Signatures as at December 2021

Deal Name	Resource(s)	Team Location	EFSI/SMBW	EFNBW	Commitment (€.m)
Capacity Building Investments					
Fed Invest EaSI-CBI-MF	EaSI-CBI	Albania	No	No	2.0
Hefenos-EaSI-CBI-MF/SE	EaSI-CBI	Belgium	No	No	5.0
Microcredito di Impresa-EasiCBI-MF	EaSI-CBI	Italy	No	No	1.5
Capacity Building Investments Total					8.5
Capped					
Adie-EGF-C2IG	EGF Capped Guarantees (unfunded)	France	No	No	17.6
Almi Företagspartner AB-EGF-CDG	EGF Capped Guarantees (unfunded)	Sweden	No	No	11.5
Arus Kapital 2-EaSI-MF	EaSI-GFI-MF	Sweden	No	No	4.0
Banca Popolare Etica-EGF-CDG	EGF Capped Guarantees (unfunded)	Italy	No	No	6.0
BOBI Leasing EAD-EGF-CDG	EGF Capped Guarantees (unfunded)	Bulgaria	No	No	2.2
Caisse des dépôts et consignations-EaSI-MF Guarantee	EaSI-GFI-MF	France	No	No	4.9
Colonya Caixa d'Estalvis de Pollença-EaSI 2-SE	EaSI-GFI-SE	Spain	No	No	0.3
COOPERATIVE BANK OF KARDITSA-EGF-CDG	EGF Capped Guarantees (unfunded)	Greece	No	No	2.0
Erste & Steiermärkische Bank 2-EaSI-MF	EaSI-GFI-MF	Croatia	No	No	0.5

177

Figure 8.17: Extract from inventories of equity commitments and guarantees for EGF-based projects with public sector involvement

Project name and sponsor	Equity commitment or guarantee	What public sector entity is involved	What is their role in the project, their liability towards it, the liability amount, timing and so on	What further public sector entities are involved and in what way

Figure 8.17: Extract from inventories of equity commitments and guarantees for EGF-based projects with public sector involvement

Figure 8.18: contingent liability for the participating member states in the EGF

Country	EIB shareholding	Re-based to 100%	Share of contingent liability of €23.2 billion
Belgium	5.18%	5.33%	€1.24 billion
Bulgaria	0.20%	0.21%	€0.05 billion
Czech Rep	0.00%	0.00%	--
Denmark	2.65%	2.73%	€0.63 billion
Germany	18.77%	19.29%	€4.48 billion
Estonia	0.00%	0.00%	--
Ireland	0.64%	0.66%	€0.15 billion
Greece	1.41%	1.45%	€0.34 billion
Spain	11.25%	11.57%	€2.68 billion
France	18.77%	19.29%	€4.48 billion
Croatia	0.40%	0.41%	€0.10 billion
Italy	18.77%	19.29%	€4.48 billion
Cyprus	0.12%	0.12%	€0.03 billion
Latvia	0.00%	0.00%	--
Lithuania	0.16%	0.17%	€0.04 billion
Luxembourg	0.12%	0.12%	€0.03 billion
Hungary	0.00%	0.00%	--
Malta	0.04%	0.04%	€0.01 billion
Netherlands	5.18%	5.33%	€1.24 billion
Austria	2.57%	2.64%	€0.61 billion
Poland	4.58%	4.71%	€1.09 billion
Portugal	0.92%	0.95%	€0.22 billion
Romania	0.00%	0.00%	--
Slovenia	0.28%	0.29%	€0.07 billion
Slovakia	0.32%	0.33%	€0.08 billion
Finland	1.49%	1.53%	€0.35 billion
Sweden	3.46%	3.55%	€0.82 billion
	97.31%	100.00%	€23.2 billion

Figure 8.18: contingent liability for the participating member states in the EGF

Chapter 9 - quantification of liabilities: other public sector entities

This will be a particularly difficult area to get complete figures on. It comprises all of the public sector entities whose debts are not included in 'General government gross debt'.

That will include the central bank and any 'Recognised agencies', unless, under the exercise undertaken pursuant to Chapter 7, they have been confirmed as qualifying as 'General government'.

As an anchor figure we have the EIB's loans into the EU outside of the context of InvestEU and EGF. We have calculated above that these stood at €307 billion at the end of 2021, and we have surmised that the majority of this figure has been lent to public sector entities outside General government. This was 71% of EIB's total loan portfolio.

If it can be proven that the EIB is one of the main sources of finance of public sector entities outside General government, then the indebtedness of this sector may not be a major concern. This would be the case if, for example, the 71% of EIB's total loan book turned out to be 50% of the sector's indebtedness, meaning the indebtedness was around €600 billion. If, on the other hand, the EIB turned out not to be main source of the indebtedness of the sector and its €307 billion of loans into it was only 10% of the whole, we have a different picture entirely.

Difficulties in setting the scope and a taxonomy

Other public sector entities may come in a number of legal forms, all being non-natural legal persons: partnerships, trusts, country-specific forms such as a German 'open trading company' (Offene Handelsgesellschaft or OHG). Partnerships could have limited or unlimited liability; they could be a German 'Kommanditgesellschaft' whose style ends in '& Co KG' indicating an unlimited liability on behalf of the members ('Kommanditisten'), and the same but ending 'auf Aktien' which indicating a liability limited by shares ('Aktien'). Many will be constituted as private or public limited liability companies: these being a GmbH or AG in Germany, or a B.V. or N.V. in Belgium and the Netherlands, equivalent to Ltd. and plc in the UK.

Any of these entities would qualify as an 'other public sector entity' if it is owned, managed or controlled by one or more entities either within General government or which themselves are 'other public sector entities'.

It would be difficult to devise a fool-proof definition for 'other public sector entities'. The definition cannot be one that captures only the entities whose figures are consolidated into those of others. On the contrary it needs to be resistant to where an entity is held at arm's-length from its owners/controllers, such that there is no consolidation, and both the entity and its owners/controllers can indebt themselves based on what is actually a single base of capital.

It specifically needs to capture minority interests, particularly where a controlling interest is spread around minority holdings by several public sector entities who would tend to act 'in concert' with one another, such as if ownership was spread at 20% each into a national government, a development agency, a regional government, a municipal government and a public power utility.

The definition needs also to 'look through' intermediate arrangements such as a legal entity form which is an open partnership and which has no substance of its own, but enables entities behind it to exercise control, use the recourse to themselves as a way of enabling the entity to have an activity, without the backers having to invest their own money in cash. The EFSF and ESM are perfect examples of 'look-through' entities.

Borrowing a taxonomy from Anti-Money Laundering legislation

The most appropriate approach to formulating a workable and comprehensive definition would appear to be to borrow from another area of finance, where the aim is to identify what is behind a business proposition that is presented to bank, namely in the legislation for combatting Money Laundering and the Financing of Terrorism, known as AML/CFT.

The relevant aspect is to identify Ultimate Beneficial Ownership, for which the requisite definition comes from the Financial Action Taskforce Guidance: Transparency and Beneficial Ownership of 9 March 2015 p. 8.[145] The relevant wording is:

'Beneficial owner refers to the **natural person(s)** who ultimately[50] owns or controls a customer[51] and/or the natural person on whose behalf a transaction is being conducted. It **also includes those persons who exercise ultimate effective control** over a legal person or arrangement.

[50] Reference to "ultimately owns or controls" and "ultimate effective control" refer to situations in which the ownership/control is exercised through a chain of ownership or by means of control other then direct control
[51] This definition should also apply to beneficial owner or beneficiary under a life or other investment linked insurance policy.'

FATF's Ultimate Beneficial Ownership test identifies a natural legal person. In the case-in-hand it will be a non-natural legal person. The basic FATF threshold for ultimate ownership/control is set at 25%, unless indicators of higher risk are present such as to require Enhanced Due Diligence. In that case the Ultimate Beneficial Ownership threshold falls to 10%.

The risk in the case-in-hand is high that ownership and control structures have been designed so as to keep debt out of sight and to frustrate the kind of comprehensive stock-taking of public debt that is the subject of this book. The threshold for the purposes of this exercise should be set at the lower of the two FATF levels, namely at 10%.

There is in the case-in-hand no need to prove that the ownership or control is 'beneficial': it simply needs to exist. In other words it is 'effective' control, which can come about in a number of forms, such as a golden share of no monetary value, rights embedded in applicable law or in an entity's constitution. Control can be 'effective' without the controlling entity or entities making any monetary investment.

Requirement for member state lists

Each member state should be asked to issue a comprehensive list of such entities in their member state, where an entity is ultimately owned or controlled to a percentage of 10% or more by either one or more entities that fall within their list of 'General government' entities pursuant to Chapter 7, or which are themselves 'other public sector entities' and are included on the list produced pursuant to this chapter. There may be some circularity in the creation of the list and it is to be expected that certain entities will appear to be owned or controlled by one another.

The debts of each entity on the list should be broken into categories of (i) debt represented by an ECB-eligible bond; (ii) debt represented by an ECB-ineligible bond; (iii) loan debts; (iv) finance lease debts; (v) other debts, with the numbers totaling the same as the entity's entire debt.

Portugal: an example of the challenges involved

To give an illustration of the challenges involved, we have taken the example of Portugal, and used the EIB's list of projects and the ECB list of eligible collateral as the pointers to what 'other public sector entities' may exist there.

The result has been to underline the opacity of this area.

Portugal emerged from a long period of Fascist dictatorship until a brief one of Marxism in the early 1970s, to become the democracy it is today. It is in some ways an advertisement for EU membership and has been a major beneficiary of development funds, that is until its financial bailout in 2010. In true EU style it emerged from bailout, but without repaying all the bailout funds.

---

[145] http://www.fatf-gafi.org/documents/documents/transparency-and-beneficial-ownership.html accessed on 14 June 2022

The Republic of Portugal sits at the top of the pyramid. Then there is the central bank: the Banco de Portugal. There are two 'Recognised agencies':

- Infraestruturas de Portugal S.A. (IP)
- PARPÚBLICA - Participações Públicas S.A. (SGPS)

A search of the EIB's 'All projects' database on 'Portugal' returned, on 22 June 2022, 500 projects financed in Portugal in the EIB's history. The details on earlier projects are somewhat sparse, not even giving the name of the borrower in all cases, but here are some examples from the early years:

Project	Signed	Amount	Sector
Centr Electr de Sines III	10/12/1985	€30 million	Energy
Electricite Acores	28/6/1984	€15 million	Energy
Route Lisbonne/Algarve	17/12/1981	€31 million	Transport
Forestier Celbi	16/6/1981	€11 million	Agriculture, forestry, fisheries
Aeroport de Madeira	2/8/1979	€11 million	Transport
Qimigal I	14/12/1978	€8 million	Industry
Quai d'Alcantara	13/10/1977	€8 million	Transport
Odivelas-Vigia	18/01/1977	€12 million	Water/sewerage
Setubal II	22/05/1979	€20 million	Energy

Table 9.1: EIB Portuguese projects from the 1970s and 1980s

It is taken as read that there was a sponsoring 'other public sector entity' for each of these projects and we can make a tentative picture their profiles:

Project	Sponsor profile
Centr Electr de Sines III	Publicly-owned power utility company
Electricite Acores	Publicly-owned power utility company
Route Lisbonne/Algarve	Publicly-owned toll motorway company
Forestier Celbi	Publicly-owned area forestry management company
Aeroport de Madeira	Publicly-owned airport management company
Qimigal I	Publicly-owned chemical plant management company
Quai d'Alcantara	Publicly-owned docks management company
Odivelas-Vigia	Publicly-owned water and sewerage utility company
Setubal II	Publicly-owned power utility company

Table 9.2: profiles of project sponsors of EIB Portuguese projects from the 1970s and 1980s

In fact the Sines Area project was an extensive development of an area centered around the Port of Sines, and in 1983 Lloyds Bank International made a proposal to the sponsoring entity – Gabinete de Area de Sines – for a Dutch export credit loan structured very similarly to the one described in the section on sovereign risk. This was in support of a tender by the same Dutch company – Royal Dutch Harbourworks N.V. – to dredge the channels into the port area and the port basin. 85% of the financing would have been insured towards the bank by the Dutch Credit Insurance Company (Nederlandsche Credietverzekering N.V.), whose insurance policies were reinsured by the Dutch Ministry of Finance. The Dutch authorities were willing to take this risk on behalf of Royal Dutch Harbourworks N.V. because the liabilities of Gabinete de Area de Sines were to be guaranteed by the Republic of Portugal acting through a regional development agency. In that way one 'other public sector entity' - Nederlandsche Credietverzekering N.V. – was willing to take risk on another - Gabinete de Area de Sines. The debt, however, was to be lent by Lloyds Bank International, and borrowed outside the scope of 'General government gross debt'.

If we go forward to the first year of the existence of the euro and record the first 9 loans signed in 1999 by the EIB into Portugal:

Project	Signed	Amount	Sector
Soporcel Paper II	3/5/1999	€100 million	Industry
SETAS II	19/5/1999	€45 million	Energy
LIPOR Thermal Waste Disposal	17/6/1999	€86 million	Solid waste
Chaves Motorway (PPP)	8/7/1999	€450 million	Transport
Optimus Mobile Telephony	12/7/1999	€249 million	Telecom
Urban Rehabilitation Lisbon	14/7/1999	€5 million	Urban development
Portgas	19/7/1999	€58 million	Energy
JAE Estradas VII-XI	26/7/1999	€643 million	Transport
SCUT (DBFO) Beira Interior	24/9/1999	€358 million	Transport

Table 9.3: the first nine of EIB's loans into Portugal in 1999

And to 2009, shortly before Portugal's fall into bailout:

Project	Signed	Amount	Sector
Baixo Alentejo Motorway	30/1/2009	€225 million	Transport
EDP Repowering	4/2/2009	€145 million	Energy
GALP Refinacao – Projecto de Conversao	3/3/2009	€500 million	Industry
BPI Loans for SMEs I	18/5/2009	€175 million	Credit lines
Modernizacao Parque Escolar	22/5/2009	€300 million	Education
Hospital de Braga PPP	3/6/2009	€65 million	Health
ANA Airport Extension	23/7/2009	€72 million	Transport
REN – Sistema Nacional de Gas Natural	28/7/2009	€150 million	Energy
Banco Popular Portugal Loan for SMEs I	2/9/2009	€50 million	Credit lines

Table 9.4: the first nine of EIB's loans into Portugal in 2009

We have motorways, hospitals, airports, gas supply, waste disposal – all being within the normal spheres of activity of public sector entities outside General government.

We do not have the exact borrowefr's name but we can be sure that a good number of the loans were made directly to a public sector entity. This certainty diminishes with the onset of structured finance techniques like InvestEU, and this reducing certainty is reflected in a growing difficulty in identifying who the EIB's loans have been made to and for what purpose.

Usage of structured finance templates

The usage of these structured finance techniques is not limited to InvestEU and, latterly, EGF. At least two other schemes are mentioned where the description of the financing structure is similar: 'Private Finance for Energy Efficiency' or 'PF4EE' and 'Efficient Private Housing Programme'. These will be discussed further in the next chapter. 'PF4EE' and 'Efficient Private Housing Programme' differ from InvestEU and EGF in that there is no involvement of the EIF.

Where the loan purpose is not given as 'Credit lines', the projects – right through to 2021 - do appear to fall into the category of being in the public interest. This would have, in the early part of the time period, indicated that the direct borrower would be a public sector entity.

Where InvestEU, EGF, PF4EE loans and Efficient Private Housing Programme are in play, the financial structures used place all or part of the credit risk with public sector entities but do not normally have a public sector entity as the direct borrower. This type of structure would fall within the scope of the following chapter.

Full list of EIB loans into Portugal 2105-2022

Figures 9.1 through 9.8 contain the full lists of EIB projects regarding Portugal, with full years for 2015-2021 and up to June 2022 at the time of writing: only two loans had been signed. Appendix 6 contains a click-through for each loan to the page on the EIB website that contains the fullest information about the project: in some cases this is quite sparse. The Appendix also indicates where these webpages state a connection to InvestEU or EGF. InvestEU was to begin with termed 'the Juncker Plan', then 'the Investment Fund for Europe', then the 'European Fund for Strategic Investments' or 'EFSI', before settling into 'InvestEU', albeit that the lists of projects in the EIF Annual Reports still use the tag 'EFSI'.

The indication that an EIB loan was made into an InvestEU or EGF project is taken as definitive. The following chapter contains a list from the annual reports of the EIF of all the EIF's projects that involve Portugal. The intention was to reconcile the EIB's loans into Portugal outside schemes like InvestEU and EGF, and inside them as EIB 'traditional' loans, and to reconcile the latter back to where the EIF inserts its 'guarantees', 'equity commitments', and 'Inclusive Finance signatures' in Portuguese projects. The outcome would, it was hoped, be to indicate how many of the EIB's loans are being made into structured financings, but this has not been successful.

We were, however, able to total all the EIB projects from 2009 to 2021, and to break them down into loans to banks – called 'Credit Lines' – and those for all other purposes – 'Non-banks' in Figure 9.10.

Loans to banks have increasingly come to dislodge loans to non-banks: the balances of both are now about equal (€12.7 trillion against €13.0 trillion).

These are loans to banks for them to on-lend to SMEs and Midcaps – occasionally via Asset-Backed Securities – and they became predominant in the period 2013-2016.

As time goes on it becomes less and less obvious who the end-user of the borrowed funds is and on exactly what the money is being spent. There are even instances of 'n/a' against the amount.[146]

Loan signings are increasingly bunched into December, inferring the existence of a quota to be met and which, if unmet, expires unused.

Loans within InvestEU/EGF and outside

Several of the 2021 loans are connected to the EGF; several others before 2021 were, and from 2022 on will be, connected to InvestEU, referred to also as 'EFSI'. These are broken out in Figure 9.10, also for the period 2015-21.

The portion of loans related to InvestEU and EGF is below 20%, and a significant proportion of what is linked to these programmes is in the form of 'Credit lines' to banks for on-lending.

Total EIB loan exposure into Portugal and discrepancy

EIB appears to have committed €26 billion into Portugal over the 13-year period 2009-21, or €2 billion per annum. 50% of this may have been going directly to public sector borrowers; the rest went through banks but could then have gone to public sector borrowers or projects.

The normal profile of a loan is along the lines of (i) a period of 3½ years from signature through full drawdown to the commencement of the semi-annual instalments; plus (ii) repayment in 30 equal semi-annual instalments spread over 15 years; (iii) an average duration of a loan of 11 years (iv) final maturity up to 19 years from signature. Using this pattern and the average of new lending per annum, the total EIB portfolio of loans into Portugal should now be €2 billion x 11 = €22 billion. Indeed, this figure should be higher if there were amounts against the 3 cases where 'n/a' is given.

---

[146] In all but 3 cases where 'n/a' is stated in the main listing there is an amount within the 'Summary Sheet'

EIB states its loans into Portugal at the end of 2021 as being 2.6% of its loan portfolio, its loan portfolio being sized at €433 billion on p. 4.[147] €433 billion x 2.6% is €11.3 billion, so there is a significant discrepancy between that figure and our extrapolated one of €22 billion.

Possible reasons for the discrepancy

This discrepancy could be attributable, for example, to:
1. Portugal, in 21 cases, not being the sole destination of funds, meaning that Portugal's share may have been well below the amount given in EIB's 'All projects' listing;[148]
2. Funds disbursed being significantly lower than the ceilings to which the EIB has committed. This factor has already been noted in the general failure of the EIB balance sheet to expand since the first Eurozone debt crisis, and the pattern whereby disbursed amounts fall well below signature amounts;
3. The loan term being far shorter than an 11 years' average life;
4. Banks not being able to find SME and Midcap borrowers on whom they are willing to take the credit risk when relaying EIB funds for 15 years. It has always been the principle for EIB loans to banks that EIB has credit risk on the bank, and the bank takes the credit risk on the end-user of the funds.

One can only speculate as to which of these four possible reasons, or others, may be at play in Portugal, and in what combination. The first one applies to 13% of the loans, and where the loan is shared with Spain, it is likely that Spain received six times as much money as Portugal based on their respective GDPs. Nevertheless, in 87% of cases Portugal was the sole destination.

The second one appears to be endemic to all of EIB's lending. An impression is given of large lending ceilings being agreed, with elaborate signing ceremonies and attendant public relations actions, in order to meet quotas, but then the funds disbursed fall well below the ceilings, particularly when they were facilities for banks under which the banks would then look out for specific projects to fund.

The third one does not ring true. EIB does not offer a wide range of loan types. Several currencies are available, but the loan product offered is homogenous: the long maturity of EIB loans and their fixed rate of interest are the EIB's unique selling points. They are providing loan capital, and stepping in for sources of finance that are not available to the end-user of the money. InvestEU was specifically justified as an exercise in which the EIB Group acts as a 'missing private investor': the private lender who will not offer loan capital for longer maturities and on a junior level of seniority. Even EIB's 'traditional' loans act as a 'missing private investor': banks able and willing to lend for a long maturity and at a fixed rate of interest.

It is the fourth one that rings most true in this case: SMEs and Midcaps are not going to indebt themselves for 15 years just because their banks have an available loan product, not unless they themselves have a reason to borrow and invest.

Evaluating whether EIB's Portugal loan book is a guide to its 'other public sector debt'

If €11.3 billion really is EIB's total book of loans into Portugal, and 50% has gone to bank borrowers, we only have €5.65 billion of EIB money that may have gone into the Portuguese public sector, and that will be split down into direct loans to 'other public sector borrowers' and loans into structures where the ultimate credit risk may lie with the public sector but the direct borrower is a private entity. Those structures will fall both under the EGF and InvestEU programmes, and possibly under other programmes of a similar nature like PF4EE.

At any rate, €5.65 billion of EIB money that may have gone into the Portuguese public sector represents only 2.0% of Portugal's 2021 'General government gross debt' of €269.2 billion and 2.7% of its 2021 GDP of €211.3 billion.

It is viewed as unlikely that this figure of €5.65 billion provides firm evidence of the size of the direct or indirect debts of Portugal's 'other public sector entities'. Nor is it viewed as plausible that the list of EIB's projects provides a reliable listing of Portugal's 'other public sector entities'.

---

[147] EIB 2021 Annual Financial Report p. 13
[148] 4 programmes are labelled 'Multicountry', 15 quote Spain as co-destination, with 1 quoting Finland and one quoting France

Another angle through which to look at this is via the Portuguese entities that appear on the ECB's list of eligible collateral. The list contains the following Portuguese issuers aside from banks, the Republic and the 'Recognised agencies'. One ISIN is quoted for each issuer, even where there are multiple issues against the name of the issuer. Here is our assessment as to which category each issuer should be assigned to:

ISIN	Issuer	Category	Activity
PTSAOBOM0009	Região Autónoma dos Açores	General government	Azores administration
XS0365137990	SAGRES S.d.T.d.C. S.A.	Other public sector entity	Algarve development corporation
PTNOSFOM0000	NOS, SGPS, S.A.	Not public sector	Cable and Satellite TV
PTEIEAOE0000	EDIA - EMPRESA DE DESENVOLVIMENTO E INFRA-ESTRUTURAS DO ALQUEVA S.A.	Other public sector entity	Public infrastructure company
PTLSNHOM0001	Ares Lusitani - STC, S.A.	Not public sector	Securitization of non-performing loans
PTRAMYOM0005	REGIÃO AUTONOMA DA MADEIRA	General government	Madeira administration
PTMTLBOM0007	Metropolitano de Lisboa EPE	Other public sector entity	Lisbon metro railway company
PTTCPEOE0002	SOCIEDADE DE TRANSPORTES COLECTIVOS DO PORTO S.A.	Other public sector entity	Porto public transport company
PTTGUIOM0007	Tagus - Sociedade de Titularização de Créditos, SA	Not public sector	Securitization of credit card debts
PTGMMBOM0001	Gamma - Sociedade de Titularização de Créditos, SA	Not public sector	Securitization of credit card debts
PTRELDOM0007	REN - Redes Energeticas Nacionais, SGPS, S.A.	Other public sector entity	National power distribution company
PTBSSJOM0014	BRISA-Concessao Rodoviaria, SA	Other public sector entity	Toll road company
PTRAMDOM0018	Vice-Presidência do Governo Regional da Região Autónoma da Madeira	General government	Madeira administration
PTEDPNOM0015	EDP - Energias de Portugal SA	Other public sector entity	National power generation company

Table 9.5: Portuguese issuers on ECB eligible collateral list beyond the Republic and 'Recognised agencies'

This evidence is also inconclusive. Once again one has to speculate as to why there appear to be relatively few 'other public sector entities' that have issued bonds which are on the ECB list. This could either indicate that:
1. there are no such entities; or
2. that there are and they have issued no bonds; or
3. that there are, they have issued bonds and they are ineligible for inclusion.

The last possibility might appear to contradict the impact of the ECB's admission criteria: the ECB actively encourages issuers, in its Marketable Securities' page referenced above, to apply for their securities to be included in the list. The demands in the 'General Framework' are not demanding, and they have been relaxed further by the 'Temporary Framework', which was discussed earlier in relation to the Pandemic Emergency Purchase Programme. The ECB permits eligible securities to be traded and listed on a quite extensive list of unregulated markets, as opposed to stipulating that they trade on regulated markets, in which liquidity can be supervised. To repeat an assumption made earlier in relation to the estimate of what proportion of all bonds in euro are on the ECB list, it was taken to be 95%+. Put another way, it was taken that there was no hidden bond market of any size. We now need to place a condition against this assertion – there is no hidden market in tradeable bonds of any size. Bonds may exist, but for some reason not be tradeable or traded.

Evaluating ECB lists against EIB borrower lists, and what is missing

The EIB information infers the existence of a large number of borrowing Portuguese public sector entities, albeit that they are not named in the EIB information. We can discount the idea that no such entities exist.

If there are numerous borrowing entities, they might well be eligible to have their bonds listed by the ECB if they wanted to and if they had issued bonds that met the ECB's conditions. This is not the same as saying that these entities had issued no bonds at all.

This leaves another possibility: Portuguese 'other public sector entities' raise their borrowings privately – i.e. not through public capital markets - and the EIB is one source, although specialized in major projects, not working capital or general-purpose finance. Raising borrowings privately can include a number of borrowing techniques. A bilateral contract between two parties to lend and borrow money does not have to be done in the form of a loan contract. It can be done as a private placement or as an issue of a security which is then not traded. If such securities exist and they are not traded, there will be no market in them, they will not be listed on an exchange and they will fail the ECB eligibility criteria on that point alone. If the investor is not a Eurozone financial institution, they may have no access to credit from the ECB/Eurosystem anyway and would not have any requirement for a security they own to be on the ECB list. The wording of the second possibility should be adapted: Portuguese 'other public sector entities' raise their borrowings primarily through private finance contracts, whether these result in loans, private placements or securities.

Testing the hypothesis through the example of EDP - Energias de Portugal, S.A.

To test this hypothesis the 2021 annual report and accounts of EDP - Energias de Portugal, S.A. was examined.[149] This company was chosen because it appears both in the EIB and ECB lists, and because it has been an 'other public sector entity' in the past, though it has been privatized now. Its annual report, on p. 99, shows there was a shareholders' agreement from 2007 involving Parpublica, the Portuguese 'Recognised agency', through which shareholdings in companies were held. The statement attests that Parpublica no longer has a shareholding but that the shareholders' agreement still appears to be in place.

EDP - Energias de Portugal, S.A. is also the exact type of organisation that could be an 'other public sector entity': a power utility and critical national infrastructure of a member state. Indeed, even if the Republic of Portugal no longer owns shares in it, the Republic will continue to exercise significant influence over it, and this may even add up to 'effective' control. Such control can exist in a variety of ways such that as to meet tests of ultimate effective ownership, or even ultimate beneficial ownership: it is not unknown in the world of trusts and partnerships that a party with no financial stake nevertheless is in control and is therefore the entity's beneficiary. EDP remains a critical national Portuguese infrastructure: if EDP went bankrupt, it has to be regarded as a strong possibility that the Republic would step in to re-nationalize its Portuguese business and thereby become responsible for its debts. Indeed a situation has arisen in France, where nationalization has been threatened by President Macron on EDF (Electricite de France) in a way that bears out this point: critical national infrastructures, even if privatized, operate at the grace and favour of the government of the country for which they perform a critical service.[150]

EDP's debts

The EDP balance sheet on p. 268 shows €15.2 billion of long-term debt and €.5 billion of short-term debt. Note 34 on pp. 370-1 breaks the debt out by instrument and by who the direct borrower is. Short-term debt consists for €0.2 billion of bank loans, €0.2 billion of accrued interest, and €1.1 billion of bonds (the short-term portion of long-term debt). Of the loans and bonds of €1.3 billion, €0.3 billion has been borrowed by operating subsidiaries and €1.0 billion by the group's Finance B.V. in the Netherlands.

---

[149] RC EDP_ENG_Unofficial Version – Unaudited downloaded from www.edp.com/en/investors/investor-information on 23 June 2022

[150] https://journalstar.com/news/national/govt-and-politics/french-government-plans-to-nationalize-electricity-giant-edf/article_3115351d-c186-5129-a285-5746bdcbb19b.html accessed on 6 July 2022

Long-term debt €1.0 billion of bank loans (all to operating subsidiaries), and securities as follows:

Borrower	Commercial paper	Bonds	Hybrid bonds	Total
EDP S.A.	€0.2 billion	€0.7 billion	€3.7 billion	€4.6 billion
EDP Finance B.V.	€0.2 billion	€7.1 billion	€0.0 billion	€7.3 billion
EDP Brasil Group.	€0.1 billion	€1.1 billion	€0.0 billion	€1.2 billion
EDP Espana Group	€0.0 billion	€1.1 billion	€0.0 billion	€1.1 billion
	€0.5 billion	€10.0 billion	€3.7 billion	€15.2 billion

Table 9.6: EDP debt securities in issue

It is the hybrid bonds of EDP S.A. (five issues) that are on the ECB eligible list. The issue details are given on p. 372. Similarly EDP Finance's long-term debt is in the form of Medium-Term Notes, which are listed on p. 372. They include notes in USD (US$1.85 billion) and GBP (£325 million).

There is no mention of the EIB in EDP's annual report. There is no mention of the 'EDP Repowering' project for which €145 million were signed by the EIB on 4/2/2009, even though a balance would still exist were the loan conditions to have been standard and the borrower to have been within the perimeter of EDP Group's consolidation.

These subsidiaries should not have their own external debts other than the ones that are recorded in the group annual report. Where the report states 'EDP Brasil Group' the direct borrower could be any one of the Brazilian companies listed, but the total external debts cannot exceed what is stated against 'EDP Brasil Group'. The presumption is that the debt financing raised by EDP Finance B.V. is distributed around the group as intercompany loans that are excluded from the accounts upon consolidation, and that these loans needed to be carefully routed for tax purposes, so that unrecoverable withholding tax is not deducted from interest, so that the interest is tax-deductible for the borrower and so on. Using a B.V. in the Netherlands as the lender is favourable in this regard, due to the Netherlands' wide network of beneficial Double Taxation treaties, although the barriers to doing any cross-border lending into Brazil remain considerable, and using domestic financing sources may be the only feasible option for EDP Brasil Group.

'Effective' and 'beneficial' ownership within the EDP Group

The EDP annual report contains a lengthy list of companies that fall within the perimeter of consolidation, on pp. 436-49. The companies within the generation, supply and distribution sectors are 100% owned, with a few exceptions (Brazil, Spain). Lower shareholdings are very common in the renewables sector, with many instances of the shareholdings of the 74.98% and 63.73%. The interesting point is that there are several instances where the shareholding is below 50% but the company still falls within the perimeter of consolidation: in that case there must be indicators of control present whereby EDP is the ultimate effective or beneficial owner.

EDP as an archetype as a major power utility

The example of EDP is used because its profile – a major power utility – would be one of a typical 'other public sector entity'. It has debt, but not all of it is used to finance the Portuguese operations. It has had EIB debt in the past but does not record any EIB debt on its balance sheet. It makes use of bank financing in modest amounts compared to its main financing needs. It has a series of bonds on the ECB list of eligible collateral, but it has over twice as much as that issued in the form of Medium-Term Notes that are not ECB-eligible. It is possible that all or part of these Notes are owned by banks, although the aim of having such a programme is to diversify away from bank sources of finance, so as to achieve longer maturities and fixed rates of interest.

Perhaps all that we can conclude here is firstly that the EIB project data does not give a useful list of who its borrowers are, which could then have been extrapolated into a base list of 'other public sector entities'.

We can also conclude that the ECB list of eligible collateral does not give up a useful list of borrowers that are public sector but not 'General government'.

Conclusions on sources of funding used by EDP

The sources of finance used by EDP also place a question mark against another contention: that entities whose bonds are not on the ECB list use bank finance, not bonds. EDP has bonds issued that are both ECB-eligible and ECB-ineligible, and it has bank finance as well. In fact, EDP has twice as much ECB-ineligible debt in issue through its Medium-Term Notes than it has ECB-eligible debt in issue.

The conclusion from this is simply that entities like EDP can access substantial amounts of debt privately, from banks and other types of lender and investor, where the debt is documented as a loan, as a private placement, as a bond, as a note, with some such instruments being in the same form as ones that are traded, even if these ones are not. An instrument being listed on a stock exchange is no guarantee of its being traded: certain investors have it in their investment rules that they must only buy instruments that are listed, possibly on the assumption by the committee or person who wrote that rule that the terms 'listed', 'tradeable' and 'traded' are synonyms. A listed instrument is tradeable, but unless there is a panel of banks appointed to act as market-makers in the secondary market, it will not be 'readily tradeable on a two-way price in standard lot sizes in unstressed market conditions during normal business hours', a working definition of 'liquid'. It may be possible to find a buyer for the instrument by negotiation, and possibly by appointing an intermediary to do that for a finder's fee. But the instrument will not be 'liquid', even if it is legally tradeable. The Luxembourg stock exchange is the archetype for an exchange that acts as a 'flag of convenience' for instruments where the investor insists on its being listed but where there is no intention that it be either liquid or traded in the secondary market: the instrument will meet the investor's rules in name only. The instrument is legally tradeable – and without obtaining the borrower's permission.

Private placements are not legally tradeable, but can be sold by private arrangement with the borrower's permission. That process can be time-consuming and expensive.

A loan agreement may have clauses built into it that allow substitution of the lender in whole or in part, together with clauses governing the extent to which the borrower needs to give their permission. Loans can generally only be made by banks, and a lending bank might wish to alter the lending office, which it ought to be able to do without the borrower's permission as long as the change did not encumber the borrower with paying withholding tax on the interest. The transfer of ownership can be effected in a number of ways: a sub-participation in the loan where the original lender remains the lender of record, as an assignment, or as a novation where the original lender steps completely out of the contract.

The conclusion is that there is a sizeable block of debt taken on privately by 'other public sector entities', using a range of borrowing instruments. Little of this debt is included in the ECB list of eligible collateral. The EIB is one source of this private debt, but far from a leading one.

Limitation to further private enquiry and need for further information

It does not therefore seem productive to make further attempts to extrapolate the debts of 'other public sector entities' using ECB or EIB data as the point-of-entry. The requirement is as set out in the early part of this chapter: member states need to produce their own lists of 'other public sector entities' using the guidelines based on FATF Ultimate Beneficial Ownership at the 10% level or above, and to state the debts of each such entity.

The debts of each entity on the list should be broken into categories as per the table in Figure 9.11, and then collated by each member state as per the table in Figure 9.12.

'Placeholder' amount for the debts of 'other public sector entities'

For the purposes of this book we can only hazard a global 'placeholder' amount for the direct debts of public sector entities which fall outside the scope of General government.

An argument could be made to offset the EIB's €307 billion of lending into the EU that is not part of InvestEU/EGF from any such 'placeholder' amount, on the basis that the EIB has lent this amount to 'other public sector entities'.[151]

---

[151] with the balances of its EU loan portfolio - €77 billion - lent through financing templates like InvestEU/EGF

We do not see an offset as merited at this stage, when the amount against which the offset would be made is so nebulous, and because EIB appears to be far from a major provider of funds to this sector.

The 'placeholder' amount is €2 trillion, which was 13.8% of EU 2021 GDP of €14.5 trillion, and 15.7% of the EU's GGGD of €12.7 trillion.

EDP has €12 billion of debt with a profile of an 'other public sector entity' in a country that represents 1.73% of EU GNI. That would infer a debt amount of €693 billion in EDP's peer group of power companies across the EU, where EDP is only active in electricity generation sector of the energy market.

€2 trillion would be just less than three times the debt inferred to be owed by EDP's peer group of electric power companies across the EU. Several other industry sectors with public sector suppliers would then need to be factored in: the gas and nuclear sectors of the energy market, transportation, water, waste disposal, health and housing sectors as well.

€2 trillion seems entirely plausible in that context, and it will be allocated to member states as debt that tracks onto them, in line with their GNI key, as follows:

Country	GNI Key	Share of debt of €2 trillion
Belgium	3.10%	€62.0 billion
Bulgaria	0.83%	€16.6 billion
Czech Rep	2.14%	€42.9 billion
Denmark	1.82%	€36.4 billion
Germany	23.39%	€467.8 billion
Estonia	0.25%	€4.9 billion
Ireland	1.77%	€35.4 billion
Greece	1.48%	€29.6 billion
Spain	8.98%	€179.5 billion
France	16.24%	€324.7 billion
Croatia	0.59%	€11.8 billion
Italy	12.55%	€251.0 billion
Cyprus	0.17%	€3.3 billion
Latvia	0.30%	€6.0 billion
Lithuania	0.53%	€10.5 billion
Luxembourg	0.26%	€5.3 billion
Hungary	1.56%	€31.3 billion
Malta	0.10%	€2.0 billion
Netherlands	4.69%	€93.8 billion
Austria	2.48%	€49.6 billion
Poland	6.08%	€121.5 billion
Portugal	1.73%	€34.6 billion
Romania	3.03%	€60.6 billion
Slovenia	0.41%	€8.3 billion
Slovakia	0.84%	€16.9 billion
Finland	1.42%	€28.4 billion
Sweden	2.94%	€58.7 billion
	99.68%	€1,993.7 billion

Table 9.7: placeholder for debts of other public sector entities

That the amounts do not add up to €2 trillion is attributable to the issue discussed in the Disclaimer.

Figures
- 9.1: full list of 14 EIB projects for 2015 in Portugal
- 9.2: full list of 15 projects for 2016 in Portugal
- 9.3: full list of 14 projects for 2017 in Portugal
- 9.4: full list of 19 projects for 2018 in Portugal
- 9.5: full list of projects for 2019 in Portugal
- 9.6: full list of 16 projects for 2020 in Portugal
- 9.7: full list of 14 projects for 2021 in Portugal
- 9.8: projects in Portugal signed in 2022 up to June 22
- 9.9: EIB loans into Portugal to banks, non-banks and totals
- 9.10: breakout of EIB loans into Portugal connected to InvestEU/EGF
- 9.11: template for the statement of the debts of 'other public sector entities'
- 9.12: template for summary from each member state of the debts of 'other public sector entities'

Figure 9.1: full list of 14 EIB projects for 2015 in Portugal

Project	Signed	Amount	Sector	EFSI/EGF
Montepio Loan for SMEs Midcaps & Other Priorities 3	15/4/2015	€200 million	Credit lines	N
EIB-IADB Joint Facility for SMEs & Midcaps PT	15/4/2015	€30 million	Credit lines	N
BES Loan for Midcaps and Other Priorities III	16/4/2015	€300 million	Credit Lines	N
Credito Agricola for SMEs and Other Priorities I	16/4/2015	€50 million	Credit Lines	N
Banco Popular SMEs and Midcaps V	28/5/2015	€500 million	Credit lines	N
IHRU III – Rental Housing Rehabilitation	28/5/2015	€25 million	Urban development	N
SAPEC Agro RDI	10/7/2015	€25 million	Industry	N
Deutsche Bank KMU & Midcap Loan V	29/7/2015	€250 million	Credit lines	N
PF4EE Collateral Agreements	5/8/2015	€55 million	Credit lines	N
BIAL Inovacao RDI II	21/9/2015	€60 million	Industry	N
BPI Loan for Agriculture SMEs & Midcaps	25/11/2015	€50 million	Credit lines	N
BCP Loan for SMEs and Other Priorities 3	25/11/2015	€500 million	Credit lines	N
REN – Electricity System Upgrade III	25/11/2015	€170 million	Energy	N
BST Loan for SMEs Midcaps & Other Priorities IV	27/11/2015	€500 million	Credit lines	N

Figure 9.1: full list of 14 EIB projects for 2015 in Portugal

Figure 9.2: full list of 15 projects for 2016 in Portugal

Project	Signed	Amount	Sector	EFSI/EGF
Bankinter Loan for SMEs & Midcaps IV	3/3/2016	€350 million	Credit lines	N
Portucel Cacia Mill Optimisation	22/3/2016	€25 million	Industry	N
Growth Equity Fund Midcaps	22/4/2016	€40 million	Credit lines	EFSI
Portugal Employment & Startups Programme	16/6/2016	€300 million	Credit lines	N
Wave Energy Device (FDP)	6/7/2016	€10 million	Energy	N
EU Funds Co-Financing 2014-2020 (PT)	1/8/2016	€250 million	Various	N
Midcap programme Loan Spain	23/9/2016	€248 million	Credit lines	N
BST Employment & Startups Programme	26/9/2016	€70 million	Credit lines	EFSI
BPI Employment & Startups Programme	26/9/2016	€70 million	Credit lines	EFSI
BCP Employment & Startups Programme	26/9/2016	€70 million	Credit lines	EFSI
CGD Employment & Startups Programme	26/9/2016	€70 million	Credit lines	EFSI
Montepio Employment & Startups Programme	24/10/2016	€20 million	Credit lines	EFSI
Lisbon Urban Regeneration Climate Housing FL	8/11/2016	€160 million	Urban regeneration; Water & sewage	N
BPI Loan for SMEs and Other Priorities 5	20/12/2016	€400 million	Credit lines	N
BPI Energy Efficiency FL PF4EE	20/12/2016	€50 million	Energy; Industry	N

Figure 9.2: full list of 15 projects for 2016 in Portugal

Figure 9.3: full list of 14 projects for 2017 in Portugal

Project	Signed	Amount	Sector	EFSI/EGF
BCP Loan for SMEs and Other Priorities 4	26/6/2017	€50 million	Credit lines	N
CGD Loan for SMEs and Other Priorities III	26/6/2017	€300 million	Credit lines	N
Parenteral Solutions Industrial project Portugal	30/6/2017	€20 million	Industry	N
Natural Gas Distribution Portugal 2016-2019	6/7/2017	€29 million	Energy	EFSI
NOVA SBE Campus	26/7/2017	€16 million	Education	EFSI
Usine du Futur & Innovation	28/7/2017	€40 million	Industry	EFSI
Suma Capital Energy Efficiency	2/8/2017	€20 million	Solid Waste; Energy	EFSI
IFRRU 2014-2020	9/8/2017	€300 million	Urban development	N
Portugal Water Supply & Sanitation	12/9/2017	€420 million	Water; Sewerage	EFSI
Efficient Private Housing Programme PT	16/10/2017	€70 million	Credit lines	N
SCIENCE4YOU (EGFF)	6/11/2017	€10 million	Industry	EFSI
BPI Innovfin Mid-Cap Guarantee	21/12/2017	€150 million	Credit lines	N
Loan 4 SMEs & Midcaps Forest Fire Support	29/12/2017	€75 million	Credit lines	N
CGD Efficient Private Housing Programme	29/12/2017	€30 million	Credit lines	N

Figure 9.3: full list of 14 projects for 2017 in Portugal

Figure 9.4: full list of 19 projects for 2018 in Portugal

Project	Signed	Amount	Sector	EFSI/EGF
IFD Loan for SMEs and Other Priorities	2/1/2018	€250 million	Credit lines	N
Plysa Forest Fire Extinction Fleet	19/1/2018	€20 million	Transport	N
Portugal Irrigation Plan	21/2/2018	€200 million	Water; Sewerage	N
Innovative Diagnostics Tools (MGF)	14/3/2018	€17 million	Industry	N
Midcap Programme Loan Spain & Portugal 2	5/3/2018	€400 million	Credit lines	EFSI
BCP Efficient Private Housing Programme PT	13/4/2018	€25 million	Credit lines	N
Novobanco Efficient Private Housing Programme PT	13/4/2018	€15 million	Credit lines	N
Portuguese Ports Private Investment Plan 2017-19	17/5/2018	€40 million	Transport	N
Figueira Mill Optimisation	6/7/2018	€40 million	Industry	N
Tamega Iberdrola Hydropower & Storage Portugal	23/7/2018	€650 million	Industry	N
CIE Automotive RDI & Convergence	24/7/2018	€120 million	Industry	EFSI
Lisbon Climate Adaptation Drainage System	18/9/2018	€65 million	Water; Sewerage	N
BPI Loan for SMEs and Other Priorities 6	19/9/2018	€250 million	Credit lines	N
Credito Agricola Loan for SMEs and Other Priorities 2	28/9/2018	€100 million	Credit lines	N
Windfloat Innovfin FDP	18/10/2018	€60 million	Energy	N
Bial Pharmceutical RDI	14/11/2018	€n/a million	Industry	Unknown
Advanced Automotive Fabrics Project Portugal	12/12/2018	€25 million	Credit lines	EFSI
IFD Restart & Modernise Programme	14/12/2018	€100 million	Credit lines	N
Energy & Environmental Sustainability Project	21/12/2018	€55 million	Various	N

Figure 9.4: full list of 19 projects for 2018 in Portugal

Figure 9.5: full list of projects for 2019 in Portugal

Only 8 projects were signed, noting that no amount has been disclosed for three of them.

Project	Signed	Amount	Sector	EFSI/EGF
Fresh Vegetable Food Portugal	16/7/2019	€35 million	Industry	N
BPI Loan for SMEs & Midcaps	22/7/2019	€n/a million	Credit lines	Unknown
Madeira New Central Hospital	15/10/2019	€n/a million	Health	N
Wind Farms PT 1	27/11/2019	€47 million	Energy	N
Novo Banco Loan for SMEs & Midcaps	17/12/2019	€225 million	Credit lines	N
Portugal Solid Waste Investment Plan	19/12/2019	€75 million	Solid waste	N
BCP Innovative Midcap Linked Risk Sharing	20/12/2019	€100 million	Credit lines	N
Montepio Loan for SMEs Midcaps & Other Priorities 4	30/12/2019	€300 million	Credit lines	N

Figure 9.5: full list of projects for 2019 in Portugal

Figure 9.6: full list of 16 projects for 2020 in Portugal

Project	Signed	Amount	Sector	EFSI/EGF
UCI Green Energy Mortgages MBIL SFSB	12/5/2020	€100 million	Urban development	N
Iberia Covid-19 Healthcare Programme Loan	25/5/2020	€750 million	Health	N
EV Charging Stations Iberia Programme Loan	11/6/2020	€200 million	Transport	N
SCF Portugal Covid-19 Loan for SMEs and Midcaps	22/7/2020	€434 million	Credit lines	N
SCF Portugal Covid-19 ABS for SMEs and Midcaps	22/7/2020	€55 million	Credit lines	N
Figueira Environmental Enhancement	31/7/2020	€28 million	Industry	N
Elderly Care Investment in Portugal	7/8/2020	€200 million	Health	N
Bizay (EGFF)	30/10/2020	€20 million	Services	EFSI
IFD Covid-19 Loan for SMEs and Midcaps	2/11/2020	€340 million	Credit lines	N
Portugal Irrigation Plan – Reguengos Subproject	4/11/2020	€30 million	Water, sewerage	N
Madeira Electricity Network Optimization	15/12/2020	€65 million	Energy	N
Global Shares (EGFF)	18/12/2020	€n/a million	Services	EFSI
Montepio Covid-19 Loans for SMEs and Midcaps	18/12/2020	€158 million	Credit lines	N
Montepio ABS Covid-19 Loans for SMEs and Midcaps	18/12/2020	€71 million	Credit lines	N
Portugal Water Distribution Optimization North	22/12/2020	€28 million	Water, sewerage	N
Icicle Wind Farm	23/12/2020	€65 million	Energy	EFSI

Figure 9.6: full list of 16 projects for 2020 in Portugal

Figure 9.7: the full list of 14 projects for 2021 in Portugal

Project	Signed	Amount	Sector	EFSI/EGF
Sugal Agro Sustainable Investment Programme	25/3/2021	€40 million	Industry	N
UCI Building Renovation MBIL	6/5/2021	€50 million	Urban development	N
CGD EGF Midcaps Risk Sharing	31/5/2021	€113 million	Credit lines	EGF
Midcap Programme Loan Spain & Portugal 3	17/6/2021	€250 million	Credit lines	N
AFR-IX Medusa Submarine Cable System	2/8/2021	€163 million	Telecom	N
Galp EV Sustainable Charging Network	21/10/2021	€42 million	Transport	N
Alco Solar PV Green Energy Loan	21/10/2021	€40 million	Energy	N
NAV Portugal ATM Upgrade	10/12/2021	€100 million	Transport	N
Energy Efficient Refurbishments Spain & Portugal	16/12/2021	€45 million	Services	N
Unitranche Bridge Financings	17/12/2021	€100 million	Energy	N
BCP EGF Midcaps Risk Sharing	22/12/2021	€200 million	Credit lines	EGF
NB EGF Midcaps Risk Sharing	23/12/2021	€100 million	Credit lines	EGF
Montepio EGF Midcaps Risk Sharing	23/12/2021	€116 million	Credit lines	EGF
Medway Cargo Rolling Stock	23/12/2021	€45 million	Transport	N

Figure 9.7: the full list of 14 projects for 2021 in Portugal

Figure 9.8: projects in Portugal signed in 2022 up to June 22

Project	Signed	Amount	Sector
Innovation Programme Loan for Spain & Portugal	15/6/2022	€n/a million	Credit Lines
Iberdrola Solar PV Green Loan Portugal	13/5/2022	€n/a million	Energy

Figure 9.8: projects in Portugal signed in 2022 up to June 22

Figure 9.9: EIB loans into Portugal to banks, non-banks and totals

Year	Deals	No amount	Credit lines	Non-banks	Totals
2009	16	0	€575 million	€2,467 million	€3,042 million
2010	13	0	€300 million	€4,003 million	€4,303 million
2011	8	0	€493 million	€770 million	€1,263 million
2012	4	0	€300 million	€230 million	€530 million
2013	9	0	€1,292 million	€160 million	€1,452 million
2014	9	0	€1,322 million	€119 million	€1,441 million
2015	14	0	€2,435 million	€280 million	€2,715 million
2016	15	0	€1,638 million	€495 million	€2,133 million
2017	14	0	€675 million	€855 million	€1,530 million
2018	18	1	€1,165 million	€1,202 million	€2,367 million
2019	8	1	€625 million	€381 million	€1,006 million
2020	16	1	€1,058 million	€1,426 million	€2,484 million
2021	14	0	€779 million	€625 million	€1,404 million
Totals	158	3	€12,657 million	€13,013 million	€25,670 million

Figure 9.9: EIB loans into Portugal to banks, non-banks and totals

Figure 9.10: breakout of EIB loans into Portugal connected to InvestEU/EGF

Year	# of EFSI/EGF loans	Amount of EFSI/EGF loans	EIB total loans	EIB non-EFSI/EGF loans
2015	0	€0 million	€2,715 million	€2,715 million
2016	6	€340 million	€2,133 million	€1,793 million
2017	6	€535 million	€1,530 million	€995 million
2018	3	€545 million	€2,367 million	€1,822 million
2019	0	€0 million	€1,006 million	€1,006 million
2020	2	€85 million	€2,484 million	€2,399 million
2021	4	€529 million	€1,404 million	€875 million
Total	21	€2,034 million	€13,639 million	€11,605 million

Figure 9.10: breakout of EIB loans into Portugal connected to InvestEU/EGF

Figure 9.11: template for the statement of the debts of 'other public sector entities'

[Name of 'other public sector entity']	Debt represented by an ECB-eligible bond[152]	Debt represented by an ECB-ineligible bond[153]	Loan debts	Finance lease debts	Other debts	Totals
Short-term[154]	€ million	€ million	€ million	€ million	€ million	€ million
Long-term	€ million	€ million	€ million	€ million	€ million	€ million
Totals	€ million	€ million	€ million	€ million	€ million	€ million

Figure 9.11: template for the statement of the debts of 'other public sector entities'

Figure 9.12: template for summary from each member state of the debts of 'other public sector entities'

[Member state name]: debt of 'other public sector entities'	Debt represented by an ECB-eligible bond	Debt represented by an ECB-ineligible bond	Loan debts	Finance lease debts	Other debts	Totals
Short-term	€ million	€ million	€ million	€ million	€ million	€ million
Long-term	€ million	€ million	€ million	€ million	€ million	€ million
Totals	€ million	€ million	€ million	€ million	€ million	€ million

Figure 9.12: template for summary from each member state of the debts of 'other public sector entities'

[152] Including commercial paper
[153] Including commercial paper
[154] Including the current portion of long-term debt

Chapter 10 - quantification of liabilities: public liabilities under financial templates like InvestEU

The objective of this chapter is to draw up an approach for the capture of the amounts of debt taken on within structures like InvestEU, EGF, PF4EE and Efficient Private Housing Programme where the ultimate credit risk falls on public sector entities, whether within General government or not.

InvestEU, EGF and other EU templates apply the principles of PFI

InvestEU and EGF are clear applications of the principles behind the UK's PFI to the EU. The EIB Group has further programmes like PF4EE. The objective under this chapter will be to design a methodology to uncover the full amount of debts taken on by projects where the debt service is made thanks to the rentals or other payments coming from a 'General government' entity or an 'other public sector entity' in an EU member state.

Under 'other payments' these could be payments for the project's offtake, such as for a renewables energy project, and this may not be a straightforward supply agreement, but a jigsaw of subsidies and agreements to buy.

We can examine two EIB projects for 'Credit Lines' not related to InvestEU or EGF which show characteristics of this type of structured financing:

| PF4EE Collateral Agreements | 5/8/2015 | €55 million | https://www.eib.org/en/projects/all/20150420 |
| BCP Efficient Private Housing Programme PT | 13/4/2018 | €25 million | https://www.eib.org/en/projects/all/20170844 |

Table 10.1: PF4EE and Efficient Private Housing

PF4EE Collateral Agreements

The EIB's amount of €55 million is part of a total project cost of approximately €1 billion, with 8 member states explicitly quoted under 'Location', but then 'EU countries' quoted as well.

The financing is described as a 'group of collateral agreements supported by the Private Finance for Energy Efficiency (PF4EE) instrument', which is taken to mean that the instrument is the legal authorization for the scheme to exist, and that EIB inserts the highest-risk tranche into the financing package. This interpretation is borne out by the assertion that the 'PF4EE instrument aims to stimulate the supply of private debt financing to complement national energy efficiency support schemes and, through this leverage, to support the priorities set by Member States in their national energy efficiency action plans for the period 2014-2020.'

In other words the financing structure is similar to InvestEU and EGF, with the public creditor – EIB Group – supporting the tranche at the bottom of the priority list, in order to offer a loss cushion to creditors whose claims rank higher in priority.

The fact that the project is 'in the public interest' is borne out by the references to the 'national energy efficiency action plans' of member states. It is left unclear whether the direct borrowers under the financings are public sector entities, but the double negatives in the following suggest they are not, but that they rank as the 'final beneficiaries': 'The specific project pipelines proposed by the financial intermediaries will be assessed by the EIB; if the final beneficiaries are private companies not operating in the utilities sector and not having the status of a contracting entity, the projects will be considered as not being subject to EU rules on public procurement.'

The expected base case is that the 'final beneficiaries' will either be public companies or, if they are private companies, they will be operating in the utilities sector and will have 'the status of a contracting entity'. In either of those eventualities the project will be 'considered as [ ] being subject to EU rules on public procurement'. These are public projects, even if the borrower of funds is a private entity. The objective of the projects is energy efficiency, which meets EU policy priorities.

The key detail is missing from the information supplied by the EIB: what is the source of repayment of the loans? We are left to infer that it is a power distribution company – which may itself have the status of an 'other public sector entity' or which, like EDP, is a critical national infrastructure and sits under the effective control of a member state.

BCP Efficient Private Housing Programme PT

The EIB will fund the Portuguese bank BCP, who will make loans under this 'dedicated EIB facility to support energy and water efficiency investments in private residential households in Portugal'. The project's supposed scope is that it 'will help the financing of small/medium projects carried out by small sized enterprises and private individuals'.

As regards 'Environmental Aspects' and 'Procurement', 'final beneficiaries will be requested to comply with applicable national and EU legislation, as appropriate'.

'Small/medium projects' do not sound like the kind of work that a private person would carry out on their own home for energy and water efficiency. They sound more like the kind of projects that a building contractor – either an SME or sole trader – would undertake on a housing development or renovation, possibly for a local authority or housing cooperative.

There is an EU policy priority at play here, but it is even less clear than in the case PF4EE who the borrower of the funds is, and what is the source of repayment of the loans. If this were a project in France, the borrowers could be any one of the many 'Recognised agencies' that are public housing enterprises, specializing in HLMs ('Habitation à Louer Modéré' – low-rent accommodation).

The conclusion here is that the structured financing template is in play but that EIB does not supply enough information about the individual financings for one to know whether the credit risk falls ultimately on the public sector in all cases, in some of them or in none.

Other financing templates
We can also examine two specific EIB projects of which, again, neither is tagged as related to InvestEU or EGF. This is a concerning point in itself. The extent of the usage of the structured financing template may be far larger even than the total mobilized amounts under InvestEU and EGF, involve programmes like PF4EE and Efficient Private Housing Programme, other programmes not identified by name in this book, and ad-hoc examples of the template outside any recognized programme. EIB Group has no monopoly on these financing structures.

The two EIB projects are:

Unitranche Bridge Financings	17/12/2021	€100 million	https://www.eib.org/en/press/all/2022-075-eib-to-provide-eur100-million-to-co-finance-solar-photovoltaic-and-wind-energy-projects-on-the-iberian-peninsula
Medway Cargo Rolling Stock	23/12/2021	€45 million	https://www.eib.org/en/projects/all/20200410

Table 10.2: example EIB projects using structured finance templates that are not InvestEU, EGF, PF4EE or EPHP

Unitranche Bridge Financings

It is apt in this case to quote the EIB's own project description:

'The European Investment Bank (EIB) has signed an agreement under which it will grant unitranche loans for solar photovoltaic and onshore wind projects in Spain and Portugal from 2021 to 2024. These projects will not need power purchase agreements (PPAs) to receive unitranche loans, which combine two tranches of financing (senior and junior) in a single loan.

The EIB will act as the lead lender to a Ben Oldman-managed investment fund, which will in turn lend the funds as bridging loans to final beneficiaries as senior debt, normally via special purpose vehicles (SPVs) set up to implement the projects. Ben Oldman is an alternative investment manager and will handle the origination of the loans.

The project is expected to generate about 430 MW of new renewable energy, equivalent to the annual energy use of more than 200 000 households. It will therefore contribute to the national renewable energy targets set out in the national energy and climate plans of Spain and Portugal.'

The key points are:
- the project serves the EU's policy priority of renewable energy;
- the financing will be inserted into separate, project-specific special purpose vehicles, which, in the case of Italian bank securitizations of non-performing loans, we termed an SPC or 'special-purpose company';
- the equity tranche of each financing is being contributed by an investment fund;
- the junior debt financing is being contributed in the form of bonds of which the investment fund will take a portion;
- the senior debt financing is being contributed by the EIB: in this case the EIB is not taking the highest risk;
- to qualify for financing, a project does not have to have a Power Purchase Agreement (PPA) in place.

This last point is a vital one: the Unitranche arrangement is depicted as an exception to a rule. The rule is that the project already has a guaranteed buyer for its offtake, in the form of a PPA. That PPA would then either be with an 'other public sector entity' or a private company which, like EDP, is a critical national infrastructure and sits under the effective control of a member state.

This transaction conforms to the structured financing template, and the ultimate credit risk is on the public sector even if, in this case, the EIB is not taking the highest-risk tranche of debt.

Medway Cargo Rolling Stock

This project's purpose is the 'acquisition of 16 electric locomotives and 113 intermodal wagons to provide new rail cargo services in Spain and Portugal'.

The strategic statements about the project are:
1. It 'contributes to expanding rail freight transport services, thus enabling a more efficient supply chain in Portugal and Spain and reducing transport costs for import and export goods. The project is therefore expected to increase the competitiveness and regional development of the region and contribute to sustainable growth and employment in Iberia. Additionally, the project is to be considered under the Climate Action (CA) objectives of the Bank, as it fosters a modal shift from road to rail and supports investments in electric rail transport, a zero direct emissions transport technology'; and
2. 'The rolling stock will provide services predominantly in less developed or transition regions and thereby support the strengthening of the EU's economic, social and territorial cohesion. The project supports the deployment of the European Rail Traffic Management System, which creates network-wide benefits that are higher than those experienced by each operator individually'.

Once again EU policy priorities are in play. The 'Promoter/Financial Intermediary' is Medlog S.A., a Swiss logistics company (company number 922654), chemin Rieu, 12-14, Genève, 1208. It is part of the MSC Group.[155] This does not mean that Medlog S.A. is the borrower: again the identity of the borrower is not disclosed but we can infer that it is a special-purpose company established to operate this new fleet of rolling stock.

The key commercial issue is in the statement that the 'rolling stock will provide services predominantly in less developed or transition regions'. The aim of the project is to create economic development, not to service existing demand or to capitalize upon an opportunity created by visible or anticipated economic growth. Entrepreneurs either create demand for goods and services, or anticipate there being a demand for goods and services. They take a risk with their own money, and either make a profit, or lose their money.

This is not what is happening in this case: Medlog will not be taking meaningful entrepreneurial risk. The impetus for the project is coming from public authorities, to improve transportation links in the hope that this will lay the groundwork for economic development in areas that are lagging behind. The project does not stand up on its own as a commercial proposition for an entrepreneur.

---

[155] https://www.msc.com/en/about-us/msc-group accessed on 29 June 2022

The respective public authorities do not want to, or are precluded from acting to, furnish the train operator that will service these transportation links themselves, so a commercial scheme and a financial scheme behind it are devised to induce a private-sector company to act in loco.

The relevant question is how Medlog was induced to step up to play this role. The availability of long-term, fixed rate loans from the EIB will have been part of the package of public support. The remainder of the package of public support is undisclosed, but it might include a reduced tariff for the usage of the rail network, and/or a fallback guarantee for the volume of space that is rented on the wagons and the price paid by actual businesses.

The special-purpose company will probably be owned by Medlog but it will be thinly capitalized: the majority of the financing will be debt, €45 million from the EIB and €48 million from other sources. The EIB webpages do not state whether the EIB debts ranks senior, equal ('pari passu') or junior to the other debt, but we can infer that it is junior.

The papers that would be of the greatest interest would be (i) the board paper put to the board of directors of Medlog S.A. to convince them to approve their investment in and their running of the project; and (ii) the credit application put to the Credit Committee of the supplier(s) of the other €48 million of debt financing.

These papers would indicate the risk/return for Medlog, as well of the levels of credit support from public authorities, in whatever shape they were to be furnished. Without this information we cannot draw firm conclusions other than to extrapolate from experience:
- The deal will have looked very attractive for Medlog: a small cash investment in exchange for a guaranteed minimum level of return and the possibility of a very high return if the project did actually result in economic growth, and ample possibilities within the commercial structure to take revenues along the way, thereby reducing their need for returns on their shares;
- The deal will have looked eminently bankable to the supplier(s) of the other €48 million of debt financing: effective or actual security over the rolling stock, a loan-to-value on these assets of just over 50%, a commercial structure with several levels of public subsidy built in, and a direct borrower that can easily afford the debt service in view of these levels of public subsidy.

The debt supplier, putting the deal through its Internal Ratings-Based methodology, would be able to assign a very favorable Facility Weighting based on the loan-to-value and on the parties committed to pay the levels of public subsidy.

It might not be possible to substitute a guarantor as the party upon whom the Customer Weighting was performed, in place of the special-purpose company, because the subsidy might be coming in pieces from several different public entities, but it would be possible to enhance the Facility Weighting based both on the subsidies committed by public entities and the Customer Weightings of those entities.

It is perfectly possible that one of the subsidizing parties in Portugal is Infraestruturas de Portugal S.A., a 'Recognised agency', and similarly in Spain that Instituto de Finanzas de Cantabria might feature, Cantabria being a remote region.

This transaction is a good example of a usage of the financing template but outside InvestEU and EGF. The transaction would not be commercially viable for Medlog to undertake without levels of public subsidy. The driving force is the fulfilment of EU policy priorities. The debts of the special-purpose company will not be serviceable without public support, so the debts should be counted as ones which ultimately track back onto Spain and Portugal.

Amount of structured finance facilitated by the EIB, using Portugal as the example

In order to ascertain the amount of financing under such structures that the EIB Group has facilitated into Portugal, we have extracted into Figure 10.1 all the Portugal signatures in EIF annual reports, since 2015 when InvestEU was established, up to and including 2021 when the EGF programme concluded.

The list is not broken down into every different type of EIF operation but is left at the level of 'Guarantee', 'Equity commitment', or 'Inclusive Finance'. It is sequential in time in order inter alia to facilitate the comparison with the EIB's list of all projects in Portugal, it being the supposition that the EIB made 'traditional' loans into the same projects into which the EIF had made an engagement in whatever form.

The total amount of the financings was €7 billion.

It has not proven possible to tie up this list with the full list of EIB projects for the same period because of:
- differences existing in the project name as given by EIB and EIF, even though they are part of the same group;
- there being no clear statement in the EIB list of whether the amount they state is inclusive or exclusive of the EIF's commitment;
- the wording inferring in certain cases that the EIB is receiving a guarantee from the EIF, which is implausible as they are part of the same group.

EIB Group should instead be asked to produce for each member state a reconciliation of the lists in the EIF annual reports and the EIB lists of 'All projects' via this table for EIB loans that are part of InvestEU and EGF financings, which will draw on tables requested earlier:

Year	Project names used by EIB and EIF	EIF operation type	EIF operation amount	EIB loan amount	Should EIF be netted off against EIB amount?	InvestEU or EGF
			€ million	€ million		
			€ million	€ million		
			€ million	€ million		

Table 10.3: reconciliation table between EIB and EIF lists of projects by member state

This is not the same as the total debt for the member state involved that derives from this form of financing template. There first needs to be a stock-take of all the programmes of this type beyond InvestEU and EGF. From the EIB information we know only of the existence of PF4EE and the Efficient Private Housing Programme. There could be further programmes, and also ad-hoc implementations of the template with and without EIB involvement.

Once all the programmes have been identified, a stock-take is required of all the individual transactions, and of the total mobilized amount against each one, identifying where the InvestEU or EGF commitment is additional to that amount, or whether it rather enables the raising of part of that amount.

That at least would tell us whether a far larger amount had been raised than the total mobilized amounts under InvestEU and EGF, which we have estimated at over €612 billion at the end of 2021.

Obtaining a balanced view of the amount of financing in play

It is not certain that a public sector entity is being relied upon for the debt service in all cases, albeit that this conclusion is signposted by the very low Risk-Weighted Asset figures the EIB (and by inference the EIF) calculate on their exposures. Particularly the EIF, through InvestEU and EGF, reports very low values-at-risk for its engagements, strongly inferring public sector involvement.

We could also use the case of Portugal, which has signed €7 billion of such financings since 2015 and which accounts for 1.73% of EU GNI. Dividing €7 billion by 1.73% delivers a whole-EU figure of €405 billion, far less than the EIF claims to have mobilized.

The figure of €612 billion for the total amount 'mobilized' through the EIF up to the end of 2022 is an extrapolation. It includes an estimated €77.7 billion lent by the EIB into the same projects. In addition to this, the member states can be made responsible for €16.0 billion via the InvestEU guarantee extended through the EU and for €23.2 billion via their direct EGF guarantees: €39.2 billion already accounted for as contingent liabilities elsewhere.

With the EIB's loans into InvestEU/EGF projects, that would add up to €116.9 billion of potential offsets to the figure of €612 billion.

On the other hand, our extrapolation of €612 billion for the total book of financing enabled by EIF's commitment may turn out not to be complete. We also know that another amount of EGF financing of about €60 billion will have been added in 2022.

Furthermore, we know that a new InvestEU guarantee of €26.2 billion has been issued for the 2021-7 MFF and that it would enable €1 trillion of new financing to be 'mobilized' if the same multiples are applied to it as have been to the €16.0 billion guarantee under the 2014-20 MFF.

There are more templates in use by EIB Group than just InvestEU and EGF, and there are templates which do not involve EIB Group at all. We do not claim €612 billion to be more than an indicator for the size of one area of this financing market at the end of 2021.

It is not possible to make a more accurate assessment of the total size of this financing market, under all templates, via information that is currently public and, even if more information was in the public domain, the onus should fall on the public sector to publish the total extent of their liabilities, not for an independent analyst to try and guess at them.

For the purposes of this book we can only hazard a 'placeholder' amount for these off-balance sheet debts that track back, via whatever pathway, to public sector entities which fall inside or outside the scope of General government.

The following arguments seem to us the salient ones in discerning a realistic 'placeholder' amount:
i.   it is not certain that all finance transacted under the InvestEU and EGF schemes tracks back onto the public sector;
ii.   on the other hand there are more EIB Group-backed schemes than InvestEU and EGF: neither the Medway Cargo nor the Unitranche transactions were connected to InvestEU or EGF;
iii.   EIB Group has no monopoly on the usage of the financing templates: they can be employed without any involvement of EIB or EIB Group schemes;
iv.   The new EU guarantee of €26.2 billion issued for the 2021-7 MFF will enable a sharp increase in InvestEU financings, possibly as much as another €1 trillion;
v.   That would take the total volume of funding under InvestEU alone to €1.6 trillion;
vi.   A 'placeholder' is what it says and is not warranted as being watertight.

Our 'placeholder' amount €1.25 trillion, or just over double the amount that appears to have been mobilized through the InvestEU and EGF schemes based on the EIF up to the end of 2021.

€1.25 trillion was 8.6% of EU 2021 GDP of €14.5 trillion, and was 9.8% of the EU's GGGD of €12.7 trillion.

This global 'placeholder' amount will be allocated to member states as debt that tracks onto them, in line with their GNI key, as follows:

Country	GNI Key	Share of debt of €1.25 trillion
Belgium	3.10%	€38.7 billion
Bulgaria	0.83%	€10.4 billion
Czech Rep	2.14%	€26.8 billion
Denmark	1.82%	€22.8 billion
Germany	23.39%	€292.4 billion
Estonia	0.25%	€3.1 billion
Ireland	1.77%	€22.1 billion
Greece	1.48%	€18.5 billion
Spain	8.98%	€112.2 billion
France	16.24%	€202.9 billion
Croatia	0.59%	€7.4 billion

Allocation of 'placeholder' amount for usage of structured finance templates (cont'd):

Country	GNI Key	Share of debt of €1.25 trillion
Italy	12.55%	€156.9 billion
Cyprus	0.17%	€2.1 billion
Latvia	0.30%	€3.7 billion
Lithuania	0.53%	€6.6 billion
Luxembourg	0.26%	€3.3 billion
Hungary	1.56%	€19.5 billion
Malta	0.10%	€1.3 billion
Netherlands	4.69%	€58.7 billion
Austria	2.48%	€31.0 billion
Poland	6.08%	€76.0 billion
Portugal	1.73%	€21.6 billion
Romania	3.03%	€37.9 billion
Slovenia	0.41%	€5.2 billion
Slovakia	0.84%	€10.6 billion
Finland	1.42%	€17.7 billion
Sweden	2.94%	€36.7 billion
	99.68%	€1,246.0 billion

Table 10.4: allocation of 'placeholder' amount for usage of structured finance templates

Figures
- 10.1: all EIF deals in Portugal 2015-21

Figure 10.1: all EIF deals in Portugal 2015-21

Year	Project	Amount	EIF operation type	EFSI	EGF
2015	Pelican SME N2 - Montepio - OR 2015	€200 million	Guarantee	N	N
2015	BANIF - IFSMEG 2015	€10 million	Guarantee	Y	N
2015	Novo Banco_IFSMEG_2015	€100 million	Guarantee	Y	N
2015	BCP Millenium IFSMEG 2015	€100 million	Guarantee	Y	N
2016	Montepio	€10 million	Guarantee	Y	N
2016	Novo Banco 2	€20 million	Guarantee	Y	N
2016	Lusitano SME No.3	€260 million	Guarantee	N	N
2016	Millennium bcp (MF)	€1.5 million	Guarantee	N	N
2016	Millennium bcp III	€5 million	Guarantee	N	N
2017	Co-investment with Oxy Capital Mezzanine Fund	€5.1 million	Equity commitment	N	N
2017	Novo Banco 2 – IFSMEG	€130 million	Guarantee	N	N
2017	Banco BPI 2 – IFSMEG	€100 million	Guarantee	N	N
2017	Millennium BCP 2 - IFSMEG	€50 million	Guarantee	Y	N
2017	Novo Banco 3 - IFSMEG	€75 million	Guarantee	Y	N
2018	Oxy Capital II	€40 million	Equity commitment	Y	N
2018	Co-investment with HCapital - ESID - Icebel	€1.8 million	Equity commitment	Y	N
2018	Mustard Seed Maze Social Entrepreneuship Fund I. FES	€17.5 million	Equity commitment	Y	N
2018	Caixa Geral de Depositos - CCS GF	€.4 million	Guarantee	Y	N
2018	Banco Comercial Portugues (BCP) - COSME LGF EFSI	€40 million	Guarantee	Y	N
2018	Banco Comercial Portugues 2 (BCP) - IFSMEG	€80 million	Guarantee	Y	N
2018	Caixa Geral de Depósitos - IFSMEG	€100 million	Guarantee	Y	N
2019	Faber Tech II, FCR	€15 million	Equity commitment	Y	N
2019	FCR Armilar Venture Partners Tech Transfer Fund	€30 million	Equity commitment	Y	N
2019	Caixa Geral de Depósitos - COSME LGF (digit)	€15 million	Guarantee	Y	N
2019	Banco Comercial Portugues 2 (BCP) - IFSMEG	€100 million	Guarantee	Y	N
2019	Caixa Geral de Depósitos - IFSMEG	€50 million	Guarantee	Y	N
2020	Crest II FCR	€20 million	Equity commitment	N	N
2020	HCapital II FCR	€25 million	Equity commitment	N	N
2020	Vallis Sustainable Investments II	€7.5 million	Equity commitment	Y	N
2020	Banco Comercial Portugues (BCP) - CCS GF	€25.2 million	Guarantee	Y	N
2020	Caixa Geral de Depósitos (CGD) - COSME LGF (digit- COVID)	€27.6 million	Guarantee	Y	N
2020	Montepio SME Synthetic 2020 - OR/SLA Fronted (COVID)	€387.8 million	Guarantee	Y	N
2020	Banco BPI - Agri Portugal	€10 million	Guarantee	N	N
2020	Banco Santander Totta - Agri Portugal	€7.3 million	Guarantee	N	N
2020	Caixa Central de Credito Agricola Mutuo - Agri Portugal	€11.9 million	Guarantee	N	N
2020	Caixa Geral de Depósitos - Agri Portugal	€10 million	Guarantee	N	N
2020	Banco BPI 2 - IFSMEG (COVID)	€85 million	Guarantee	Y	N
2020	Banco Comercial Portugues 2 (BCP) - IFSMEG (COVID)	€130 million	Guarantee	Y	N
2020	Caixa Geral de Depósitos (CGD) - IFSMEG (COVID)	€85 million	Guarantee	Y	N
2020	Santander Consumer Portugal 2020 - OR/SLA (COVID)	€97.6 million	Guarantee	Y	N
2020	Banco Comercial Portugues (BCP) - EaSI SE	€9.6 million	Inclusive Finance	Y	N
2020	Montepio EaSI SE	€12 million	Inclusive Finance	Y	N
2021	Vallis Sustainable Investments II	€11 million	Equity commitment	Y	Y
2021	Blue Pioneers Fund	€21 million	Equity commitment	N	Y

Figure 10.1 (cont'd): all EIF deals in Portugal 2015-21

Year	Project	Amount	EIF operation type	EFSI	EGF
2021	Banco BPI - EGF - CDG	€15.2 million	Guarantee	N	Y
2021	Banco Comercial Portugues (BCP) - EGF - CDG	€132 million	Guarantee	N	Y
2021	Banco Santander Totta - EGF - CDG	€8.7 million	Guarantee	N	Y
2021	Caixa Geral de Depósitos - EGF - CDG	€130.2 million	Guarantee	N	Y
2021	Caixa Geral de Depositos – S&E GP	€3 million	Guarantee	Y	N
2021	Fundacao Jose Neves (FJN) – S&E GP	€1 million	Guarantee	Y	N
2021	Novo Banco SA - EGF - CDG	€27.3 million	Guarantee	N	Y
2021	Banco BPI - EGF - UDG	€560 million	Guarantee	N	Y
2021	Banco Comercial Portugues (BCP) - EGF – UDG	€1,068.9 million	Guarantee	N	Y
2021	Banco Santander Totta - EGF – UDG	€560 million	Guarantee	N	Y
2021	BBVA - Sucursal em Portugal – EGF – UDG	€21 million	Guarantee	N	Y
2021	Caixa Geral de Depósitos - EGF - UDG	€805 million	Guarantee	N	Y
2021	Caixa Geral de Depósitos (CGD) - IFSMEG (COVID)	€15.9 million	Guarantee	Y	N
2021	Montepio - EGF – UDG	€700 million	Guarantee	N	Y
2021	Novo Banco SA - EGF – UDG	€367.5 million	Guarantee	N	Y
	Total	€6,959.1 million			

Figure 10.1: all EIF deals in Portugal 2015-21

Chapter 11 - quantification of liabilities: net debts in TARGET2

This category is considerably easier to quantify than the previous two. It is the net debts in TARGET2 of Eurozone Member State national central banks (NCBs). If one believes in the efficacy of the first two stages of the netting of the TARGET2 balances, they cause each NCB to have either a single claim on or debt to the ECB.

Central banks' debts are not part of 'General government gross debt', even if they are reinsured by the central bank with its paymaster – the exchequer or treasury of the country for whom it acts as central bank.

The TARGET2 net debts represent debts of Eurozone member states, even if they are not accounted for as such, and the amounts in the ECB December 2021 TARGET2 Report should be added to the respective member state's 'General government gross debt':

Borrower NCBs	€ billions
Belgium	85.7
Greece	104.2
Spain	512.8
Italy	590.0
Latvia	5.3
Netherlands	22.5
Austria	57.4
Portugal	79.3
	1,457.2

Table 11.1: TARGET2 net debts

The ECB should also have the entire claims of NCBs on it on its balance sheet, and not just the difference between the claims and the debts. This would add €1,457.2 billion to the ECB's balance sheet footing, because at present the ECB only carries the difference between NCBs' claims and NCBs' debts of €334.6 billion:

The NCB claims on the ECB as at 31 December 2021 were:

Depositor NCBs	€ billions
Germany	1,260.7
Estonia	0.6
Ireland	84.8
France	25.8
Cyprus	12.6
Lithuania	14.9
Luxembourg	326.6
Malta	7.3
Slovenia	9.2
Slovakia	23.9
Finland	25.3
Non-Eurozone	5.8
	1,791.8

Table 11.2: TARGET2 net claims

Chapter 12 - quantification of liabilities: gross debts in TARGET2

The above figures only go part of the way to incorporating all of the debts in TARGET2 of Eurozone Member State central banks. They do not include the portion of the original balances that are supposedly eliminated by the netting.

In the earlier chapter we contrasted the Eurosystem 'aggregate' balance sheet with the 'consolidated' one and extrapolated the following as at 31 December 2021:

In € billions	Amount
Loans between Euro-area 'Monetary Financial Institutions'	€5,527
Less loans to credit institutions - MRO/TLTRO	(€2,202)
Produces loans between Eurosystem members	€3,325
TARGET2 creditor NCBs	€1,792
TARGET2 debtor NCBs	€1,457
ECB balance (creditor NCBs less debtor NCBs)	€335
Original balances eliminated by netting (3,325 – 1,792)	€1,533

Table 12.1: original TARGET2 balances eliminated by the netting

There is an amount of €1.5 trillion of debts of one Eurosystem member to another that are eliminated in the netting, a netting which in our view would not hold water in a court of law. The debts should not be netted off.

We have assumed that every NCB has claims on and debts to other NCBs that (i) match up per NCB; (ii) add up to €1.5 trillion in toto, and that the debts of each NCB accord to their Capital Key in the ECB.

Based on that, here are the extra debts in TARGET2 that are debts of central banks, and which should therefore be tracked back onto each member state:

Country	ECB Capital Key	Keys re-based to 100%	NCB's extra debt
Belgium	2.9630%	3.6432%	€54.65 billion
Germany	21.4394%	26.3615%	€395.42 billion
Estonia	10.2291%	0.2817%	€4.23 billion
Ireland	1.3772%	1.6934%	€25.40 billion
Greece	2.0117%	2.4735%	€37.10 billion
Spain	9.6981%	11.9246%	€178.87 billion
France	16.6108%	20.4243%	€306.36 billion
Italy	13.8165%	16.9885%	€254.83 billion
Cyprus	0.1750%	0.2152%	€3.23 billion
Latvia	0.3169%	0.3897%	€5.85 billion
Lithuania	0.4707%	0.5788%	€8.68 billion
Luxembourg	0.2679%	0.3294%	€4.94 billion
Malta	0.0853%	0.1049%	€1.57 billion
Netherlands	4.7662%	5.8604%	€87.91 billion
Austria	2.3804%	2.9269%	€43.90 billion
Portugal	1.9035%	2.3405%	€35.11 billion
Slovenia	0.3916%	0.4815%	€7.22 billion
Slovakia	0.9314%	1.1452%	€17.18 billion
Finland	1.4939%	1.8369%	€27.55 billion
Total	81.3286%	100.0000%	€1,500.00 billion

Table 12.2: allocation of original TARGET2 balances down to the NCBs

The assumptions upon which this table is built have no validity other than that it would be considered questionable to base the calculation on different ones.

Transparency is needed - by revealing what the actual balances were on the 600 TARGET2 accounts held by the ECB and NCBs on the same business day as the ECB issues its monthly report.

This would only reveal the end-of-day situation.

The netting does not even govern the balances other than for the brief period of about an hour when TARGET2 is only closed. On an intraday basis the balances could be even larger.

Chapter 13 - quantification of liabilities: market losses on ECB programmes

This area is the potential loss for Eurozone Member State NCBs – and therefore for their governments – deriving from the need to replenish the capital of the ECB if the ECB made market losses on its programmes.

This is a contingent liability.

The assumption is that the replenishment would be up to the ECB's present level, such that the loss would be allocated in full to the Eurozone NCBs in line with the ECB Capital Keys, re-based to 100% so that no claim was made on non-Eurozone NCBs.

Programmes that entail market risk

This is principally about the APP and the PEPP, about Outright Monetary Transactions if they ever materialize, and about the new Transmission Protection Mechanism, should it be mobilized. Bonds are bought into these programmes by NCBs at the behest of the ECB. Bonds are bought in both primary and secondary markets, and if interest rates go up while bonds are in portfolio, their re-sale value drops, such that a secondary-market investor experiences the higher yield-to-maturity equating to the annual interest coupon that would be attached to a new bond issue in the primary market and which is set in line with currently prevailing interest rates.

Eurosystem-owned bonds are subject to credit risk and market risk. Credit risk is dealt with in the next chapter, and within its scope is the issue of collateral, where the Eurosystem has accepted collateral from a borrower, which the Eurosystem executes upon and sells when the borrower defaults. The risk that the collateral may be worth less than the loan is a market risk only in the sense that the haircut may have been inadequate: the haircut is set and should be monitored so as to be adequate to the risk that the collateral might decline in value between when the borrower defaults and when the bank sells the collateral.

What the Eurosystem's market risk is

The more substantive risk for the Eurosystem, when it buys long-term fixed rate bonds, is market risk. It materializes when interest rates increase. If interest rates increase by 1% from 2% to 3% in the 10-year maturity and the Eurosystem is holding bonds in that maturity, its bonds will fall by approximately 10% in value, such that a buyer of the bond in the secondary market will enjoy a 3% yield-to-maturity on the bond, even if they only receive a 2% per annum coupon. The remaining 1% in yield-to-maturity derives from their paying only 90% of face value for the bond instead of 100%: this discount of 10% of face value will be accounted for by an institutional investor as a 1% per annum income, to add to the 2% per annum coupon, making an annual effective income of 3% per annum.

The Eurosystem had purchased €4.9 trillion into APP and the PEPP as of April 2022. The holdings of bonds are in accordance with the ECB Capital Keys for the APP, and guided by the ECB Capital Keys for the PEPP. The overall make-up is therefore strongly weighted towards Germany, France, Italy and Spain.

ECB loss-sharing mechanism

The loss-sharing mechanism means that all NCBs can be asked to pay in their proportion of the loss, however high the loss is: the amount of the loss that the NCBs collectively can be asked to pay is unlimited, but the proportion of the loss that can be allocated to each NCB is limited.

The loss-sharing mechanism works as follows. The NCB in the country of the issuer of the bond is the place where the loss crystallizes, as only that NCB is permitted to buy the bonds of issuers in its country. That NCB sells a bond for a lower price than it originally paid, and realizes a loss. Having booked the loss, it invokes the loss-sharing through the ECB. The ECB first credits the entire loss back to the loss-crystallizing NCB, then calculates the loss allocations to each NCB in accordance with its Capital Key, and finally debits the capital account of each NCB with its loss allocation. If the loss is large enough – i.e. €109 billion or more – it will expunge the ECB's entire capital and reserves.

Assessing a reasonable figure for the loss and difficulties in the case of the Eurosystem

The Maximum Possible Loss on the APP and PEPP is €4.9 trillion: a total loss. The challenge is to devise a methodology to quantify a reasonable contingent liability, especially since the Eurosystem has the option of holding bonds until maturity. The loss-sharing is only triggered if a loss in cash is made, by the respective NCB selling it for less than it paid for it. The Eurosystem produces no mark-to-market valuations of its portfolio and need hold no capital, as a commercial bank would do, in order to take account of market risk.

A commercial bank would run what is called a Monte Carlo simulation on the bonds, to indicate the degree to which interest rates could rise such as to push down the market value of the bonds during their remaining life. The key components in such a simulation are what actual interest rates have been over the past 20 or 30 years, and their volatility. Since for the last 10 years the ECB has kept interest rates either falling or static and low, the Eurosystem's running a simulation on its portfolio using the standard components is likely to produce a benevolent view of the risks it is running. During that period the Eurosystem has been the major buyer of bonds and has backstopped prices in the secondary market, keeping them high and keeping yields correspondingly low.

As long as the Eurosystem is capable of sustaining that posture, and in whatever quantity is required, it should not have to sell its portfolio and realise any market losses. In fact, with no other buyer in the market of the same scale, the Eurosystem's attempting to liquidate its portfolio would for sure cause the very risk to materialize that it has been trying to eschew: bond price falls, increasing yields, and higher coupons for member states when they come to issue new bonds, worsening their deficits and General government gross debt.

Why a quantification is needed

Stating that the Eurosystem's intention is to avoid this market risk materializing is not the same, though, as contending that the risk of a market loss does not exist. The issue is the capability of the Eurosystem to maintain the current market structure and what happens if it is unable to. A quantification of a potential market loss is needed for three reasons:
1. per se; and
2. to act as a proxy for the increased risk to member states that would be caused by extra measures and programmes that the Eurosystem might have to undertake, in fact would probably find itself obliged to undertake, if a large Eurozone member state could not fund itself on acceptable terms in the open market;[156] and
3. to reflect the risk to member states if the Eurosystem was unable to sustain the current market structure.

The ECB has found itself in the position of having to frame a new programme – the Transmission Protection Mechanism – to anticipate the case of another member state having to access support. The Eurosystem's support mechanisms lack firepower: the ESM's firepower would be reduced by the member state having to swap positions from Guarantor to Debtor, the EFSF is closed and the EFSM has only €30 billion of headroom. The Transmission Protection Mechanism would buy up member state bonds in the primary market, as well as the secondary market, and increase the Eurosystem portfolio, only in such a way that the portfolio mix becomes heavily tilted towards the member state that was unable to fund itself in the open market.

Where the portfolio make-up is either in accordance with or guided by the ECB Capital Keys, an NCB can argue that it has risk on itself if it is investing primarily in public sector securities of its own member state, albeit that this is not how the loss reallocation system works: every NCB will be presented with its percentage share of every loss.

Where the portfolio make-up moves considerably away from any relationship with ECB Capital Keys, the member states are taking market risk on one another, and the above argument ceases to have validity.

---

[156] This is the stated reason why the Transmission Protection Mechanism has been established in July 2022

Quantum of risk is magnified by the ECB's low interest rate policy

The quantum of risk is aggravated by the very low levels of absolute interest rates over the last 10 years.

Bonds have been bought into Eurosystem programmes that are of long term (15-30 years) with scarcely an annual coupon at all in some cases (0.10-0.15%).

The effect of a 1%, 2% and 3% rise in absolute interest rates on the secondary market price of such a bond is dramatic and quite easy to calculate in broad numbers:

Price fall in % of face value	15 years	20 years	25 years	30 years
If yield rises by 1%	15%	20%	25%	30%
If yield rises by 2%	30%	40%	50%	60%
If yield rises by 3%	45%	60%	75%	90%

Table 13.1: impact of rises in interest rates on the price of fixed-coupon bonds of various maturities

The price changes more dramatically for a given rise in interest rates when the underlying bond carries a very low coupon as opposed to one carrying a higher coupon.

Here is an example of a fictitious bond issued in 2106 with a 12-year maturity and an annual coupon of 1%, showing its value after 2 years at lower yields to maturity of 0% and -0.5%, and then after 5 years when yields had risen to 2% and 3%. The profits and losses are measured against the original price paid in 2016:

Original:	12 year	Remaining:	7 year		
The investor paid 1,000,000; the sale proceeds are the top number in the remaining four columns					
Yields:	1.00%	0.00%	-0.50%	2.00%	3.00%
21/06/16	-1,000,000				
21/06/17	10,000				
21/06/18	10,000	1,100,000	1,154,209		
21/06/19	10,000	10,000	10,000		
21/06/20	10,000	10,000	10,000		
22/06/21	10,000	10,000	10,000	935,280	875,394
22/06/22	10,000	10,000	10,000	10,000	10,000
22/06/23	10,000	10,000	10,000	10,000	10,000
22/06/24	10,000	10,000	10,000	10,000	10,000
22/06/25	10,000	10,000	10,000	10,000	10,000
22/06/26	10,000	10,000	10,000	10,000	10,000
22/06/27	10,000	10,000	10,000	10,000	10,000
22/06/28	1,010,000	1,010,000	1,010,000	1,010,000	1,010,000
Profit		100,000	154,209		
Loss				-64,720	-124,606

Table 13.2: example profits and losses on a low fixed-coupon bond under falls and rises in interest rates

A 2% increase in yield from 1% to 3% causes a loss of 124,606, or 12.5% of nominal value.

Another fictitious bond, with the same timings, carried a coupon of 6%, and its yield fell to 4% and 5% after 2 years, but rose to 7%, 8% and 9% after 5 years:

Original:	12 year	Remaining:	7 year			
The investor paid 1,000,000; the sale proceeds are the top number in the remaining five columns						
	6.00%	4.00%	5.00%	7.00%	8.00%	9.00%
21/06/16	-1,000,000					
21/06/17	60,000					
21/06/18	60,000	1,162,218	1,077,217			
21/06/19	60,000	60,000	60,000			
21/06/20	60,000	60,000	60,000			
22/06/21	60,000	60,000	60,000	946,107	895,873	849,011
22/06/22	60,000	60,000	60,000	60,000	60,000	60,000
22/06/23	60,000	60,000	60,000	60,000	60,000	60,000
22/06/24	60,000	60,000	60,000	60,000	60,000	60,000
22/06/25	60,000	60,000	60,000	60,000	60,000	60,000
22/06/26	60,000	60,000	60,000	60,000	60,000	60,000
22/06/27	60,000	60,000	60,000	60,000	60,000	60,000
22/06/28	1,060,000	1,060,000	1,060,000	1,060,000	1,060,000	1,060,000
Profit		162,218	77,217			
Loss				-53,893	-104,127	-150,989

Table 13.3: example profits and losses on a high fixed-coupon bond under falls and rises in interest rates

The same increase in yield of 2% - but from 6% to 8% - causes only a 10.4% fall in price.

This shows how market risk causes a greater loss when the coupon on an existing bond in portfolio is low.

The ECB's own bond buying and ultra-low interest rate policy have magnified the Eurosystem's market risk.

Proposed scenario from which to extrapolate the ECB's market risk amount

However, so as not to appear to be over-dramatizing the situation, we should consider a scenario where bond yields rise by 2% and then the Eurosystem successfully mobilises the Transmission Protection Mechanism to stop the yields rising further.

The Eurosystem would probably find itself obliged to add €1.0 trillion of bonds to its portfolio in order to achieve this, raising its holdings through its programmes to €5.9 trillion, and with an average life for the Eurosystem's holdings of 7 years. The market risk is thereby limited to a 2% rise in yield-to-maturity on €5.9 trillion nominal for 7 years.

The potential loss – and consequent need for the capitalization of the ECB – would then be 14% of €5.9 trillion, or €826 billion.

If this loss was passed to the ECB and then re-allocated to the Eurozone NCBs in line with their ECB Capital Keys, the loss for each NCB would be as follows in € billions:

Country	ECB Capital Key	Keys re-based to 100%	Loss share
Belgium	2.9630	3.6432	€30.1
Germany	21.4394	26.3615	€217.7
Estonia	10.2291	0.2817	€2.3
Ireland	1.3772	1.6934	€14.0
Greece	2.0117	2.4735	€20.4
Spain	9.6981	11.9246	€98.5
France	16.6108	20.4243	€168.7
Italy	13.8165	16.9885	€140.3
Cyprus	0.1750	0.2152	€1.8
Latvia	0.3169	0.3897	€3.2
Lithuania	0.4707	0.5788	€4.8
Luxembourg	0.2679	0.3294	€2.7
Malta	0.0853	0.1049	€0.9
Netherlands	4.7662	5.8604	€48.4
Austria	2.3804	2.9269	€24.2
Portugal	1.9035	2.3405	€19.3
Slovenia	0.3916	0.4815	€4.0
Slovakia	0.9314	1.1452	€9.5
Finland	1.4939	1.8369	€15.2
Total	81.3286	100.0000	€826.0

Table 13.4: allocation of ECB market risk down to member state level

Once again, though, one has to confront the issue of circularity: if the bond market had collapsed such as to precipitate these losses, it would most likely be due to the payment difficulties of a large member state and probably the one that the Eurosystem had accommodated by mobilizing the Transmission Protection Mechanism. In that case it is hardly credible that the member state's NCB would be able to come good on the call for extra capital.

Chapter 14 - quantification of liabilities: credit losses on ECB programmes

This area is the potential loss for Eurozone Member State NCBs – and therefore for their governments – deriving from the need to replenish the capital of the ECB if the ECB made credit losses on its programmes.

This is a contingent liability.

The assumption is that the replenishment would be up to the ECB's present level, such that the loss would be allocated in full to the Eurozone NCBs in line with the ECB Capital Keys, re-based to 100% so that no claim is made on non-Eurozone NCBs.

Where the ECB is taking credit risk

The ECB is running a major credit risk on its Longer-Term Refinancing Operations, because these are unsecured.

It is also taking a credit risk where it has bought securities into its APP and PEPP.

Finally it is taking a credit risk where it is lending against eligible collateral, both on the borrower and on the collateral.

What is credit risk

Credit risk is the assessment of the likelihood of a failure of a counterparty to furnish debt service of capital and interest, and its anchor point is the face value of the loan made to that counterparty. Internal Ratings-Based methodologies routinely shrink that value by 70-80% in order to ascertain the respective Risk-Weighted Asset and, in the EU and Eurozone, public sector entities of all types have their loans disproportionately shrunk because of the wrongful attribution of a 0% risk-weighting to the sovereign and the resultant benevolent trickle-down of that into the risk-weightings assigned to other public sector counterparties.

0% is a clearly incorrect risk-weighting for Eurozone member states like Spain (rated A), Italy (rated BBB) and Portugal (rated BBB).

In order not over-dramatize the situation, though, let us construe the matter like this. The Eurosystem is undertaking the extension of credit within a series of central banks – the ECB and the NCBs – which do not run Internal Ratings-Based methodologies, and do not have to subject themselves to capital or liquidity adequacy metrics. In fact they are very thinly capitalized.

They can be thinly capitalized themselves because their risks are re-insured with their finance ministries in the case of the NCBs and, in the case of the ECB, its risks are effectively re-insured with the NCBs whose risks are in turn reinsured with their finance ministries.

The risks all track back to the finance ministries but the accounting does not reflect this.

Acceptance that the ECB's credit risk is 20% of the face value of its exposure

If one accepts that an average risk-weighting of 20% is correct for the credit risks the Eurosystem is running, or a shrinkage from face value to 80%, then it is simple to calculate the contingent liability that each member state is running.

It is based on the asset side of the Eurosystem consolidated balance sheet, as this captures all the business with parties that are not members of the Eurosystem. In effect this is the securities portfolio of €4.9 trillion and TLTRO of €2.2 trillion, or €7.1 trillion overall.

The Eurosystem's remaining €1.5 trillion of assets include €559 billion of gold and gold receivables, €500 billion of deposits and investments in other currencies, and €441 billion of miscellaneous assets. Regardless of what resides within these assets, it is felt to be more transparent and comprehensible to take €7.1 trillion as the nominal value of the Eurosystem's risk-bearing assets.

If we agree to apply a Credit Conversion Factor of 20% in accordance with a putative IRB methodology, then the amount at risk is 20% of €7.1 trillion, or €1.42 trillion.

Assessing the reliability of this figure

There is a counter-argument to this figure, and then a counter to the counter.

Firstly it could be deemed harsh to assign a further amount-at-risk against the securities portfolio when it has already had €826 billion assigned against it for market risk. If weight were given to this argument then the risk-weighting for credit risk might be reduced to below 20%.

On the other hand the risk-weighting at 20% both accepts some measure of the direct effect of the incorrect ubiquitous 0% risk-weighting of claims on Eurozone member states, and further accepts that assets are routinely risk-weighted at far below their face values, in order for them then to be reduced even further by the respective commercial bank's CET1 threshold.

The Eurosystem is uncapitalized

Due note needs to be taken that the Eurosystem is conducting similar business to commercial banks, but on a capital base of near to zero.[157] It has only €0.1 trillion of capital and reserves against total assets of €8.6 trillion, and a Leverage Ratio of 86-to-1 when commercial banks are limited to 20-to-1, if one takes account only of elements in the ECB's capital and reserves that a commercial bank could count as Tier 1 capital.

The ECB has a further €0.6 trillion of revaluation reserves, which a commercial could at best count as Tier 2 capital. If that amount is counted in and the total capital of the ECB is reckoned at €0.7 trillion, its Leverage Ratio is 12-to-1.

This calculation would not hold for a commercial bank, though, as the lion's share of its total capital must consist of Tier 1 capital elements. Applying that guideline, only some €0.025 trillion of the ECB's revaluation reserves could be counted within its total capital (an amount of ¼ of its Tier 1 capital of €0.1 trillion). The ECB's total qualifying capital would then be €0.125 trillion and its Leverage Ratio would only be slightly improved at 68-to-1.

The member states should absorb the risk, because the ECB cannot, and the risk has increased

The ECB is a creature of member state exchequers for the engagement of banking business without the maintenance within the ECB of a meaningful loss buffer. The acid test is whether it is possible and likely that the ECB might make credit risk losses on its business of €1.42 trillion, given that it has increasingly begun to engage in commercial banking business, relies for credit risk assessment on public credit rating agencies and commercial banks' IRB methodologies, has started making loans on an unsecured basis, reduced its 'haircuts' as a response to the Pandemic from levels that were already low, and has compromised the quality of the collateral it takes both thanks to the weak eligibility criteria for bonds to be admitted to its eligible collateral list, and thanks to the temporary relaxations which were introduced in the wake of the Pandemic and which have now been extended several times.

Others might argue that, even if losses on that scale were possible, the ECB should be permitted to do what commercial banks do: only hold capital in a fraction of about 10% of their Risk-Weighted Assets. The counter to that would be that central banking is supposed to be conducted on a risk-free basis in which all assets qualify as 'central bank money'.

---

[157] Eurosystem consolidated balance sheet at 31 December 2021 pp. 1-2

The ECB trades in assets that are not definitionally 'central bank money', and others that meet a definition of being euro 'central bank money' without taking heed of the qualification that a currency needs full sovereign backing to be regarded as 'central bank money' and the euro does not have that. The ECB has diverged from traditional central banking to a marked degree, and should not be permitted to benefit from methodologies that it has devised for commercial banks it supervises and which have served to mask risk.

Inoculation against the pitfalls of IRB and the 'resolution' regime

It would surely not be right to repeat the inadequacies of the Risk-Weighted Assets methodology, as currently applied in EU and Eurozone commercial banks, and allow that to act as a reason for underestimating the losses that could fall on member states through the activities of the central banks. When a commercial bank goes into resolution, its shareholders and suppliers of capital-like financing may lose all their money, but they cannot be called upon to contribute extra funds.

The ECB has no suppliers of capital-like financing into it, only its shareholders. It does not hold regulatory capital buffers. It only has its shareholders as sources of new money to prevent it going under. This line-of-recourse exists instead of the ECB having adequate capital. There is no limit on what the ECB's shareholders can be called upon to contribute, although each member state would only have to contribute its percentage of a call for new capital and the call has to be approved through the respective internal processes of the ECB.

In substance, though, the member states are at risk for the ECB's losses, and the ECB is running very substantial credit risk.

Allocation of 20% of the ECB's risk-bearing assets to member states

For these reasons it is correct to project a total possible loss of 20% of the ECB's risk-bearing assets, or of €1.42 trillion. The loss would be allocated to Eurozone NCBs as follows in € billions:

Country	ECB Capital Key	Keys re-based to 100%	Loss share
Belgium	2.9630	3.6432	€51.7
Germany	21.4394	26.3615	€374.3
Estonia	10.2291	0.2817	€4.0
Ireland	1.3772	1.6934	€24.0
Greece	2.0117	2.4735	€35.1
Spain	9.6981	11.9246	€169.3
France	16.6108	20.4243	€290.0
Italy	13.8165	16.9885	€241.2
Cyprus	0.1750	0.2152	€3.1
Latvia	0.3169	0.3897	€5.5
Lithuania	0.4707	0.5788	€8.2
Luxembourg	0.2679	0.3294	€4.7
Malta	0.0853	0.1049	€1.5
Netherlands	4.7662	5.8604	€83.2
Austria	2.3804	2.9269	€41.6
Portugal	1.9035	2.3405	€33.2
Slovenia	0.3916	0.4815	€6.8
Slovakia	0.9314	1.1452	€16.3
Finland	1.4939	1.8369	€26.1
Total	81.3286	100.0000	€1,420.0

Table 14.1: allocation of ECB credit risk down to member state level

Chapter 15 - quantification of liabilities: Non-Performing Loan securitization

A member state contingent liability arises on bonds issued as part of Eurozone bank Non-Performing Loan securitizations where a member state government adds its guarantee to a tranche of bonds issued by a special-purpose securitization company.

Scope Ratings have collated a large amount of data and analysis on such securitization deals and in Italy in particular, although they have also been carried out in Greece and Cyprus.[158]

The guaranteed portion is typically 85% of the funding raised by the special-purpose securitization company.

Information requirement

Each member state should be required to complete a simple table of its contingent liability as guarantor under structures for the securitization of its banks' Non-performing Loans:

Originating bank	Name/number of transaction	Value of bonds guaranteed by government	ISIN of these bonds	Eurosystem-eligible	Final maturity date
				Y/N	

Table 15.1: information table to be completed by member states for their guarantees of NPL securitizations

No basis to insert even a 'placeholder' amount

The data for the contingent liabilities of member states under this heading should come from the member states. We therefore have no basis on which to estimate a 'placeholder'.

---

[158] https://scoperatings.com/#!research/list

Chapter 16 - quantification of liabilities: Bank Deposit Insurance Schemes

This aspect is the member state contingent liability on their equivalent of the UK Financial Service Compensation Scheme where a bank has a 'carrying value' of Non-Performing Loans in excess of the bank's equity.

The Deposit Insurance Scheme creates a contingent liability for member states, but not a risk exposure if resolved banks have a surplus of assets over the amount of depositor claims that the member state has had to pay out.

However, the large number of defaulted loans – NPLs – on banks' balance sheets represent a potential shortfall for a member state, if it has to borrow to pay depositors out but finds that the assets of the resolved bank do not yield sufficient for it to repay its borrowings.

That eventuality would cause the member state to increase its borrowings permanently, and the risk of that occurring should be tracked.

Methodology for assessing when an event could happen and its severity if it did

The key to this is identifying firstly the banks most likely to go into resolution and then:
- how much the member state would have to borrow to pay out the depositors
- how much of the borrowing would either be repaid to the member state through the liquidation of the bank's assets, or could be netted off against the borrowing because the bank has first claim on a portfolio of good assets
- what the ultimate shortfall might be for the member state because a portion of the bank's assets, attested to on its balance sheet, is bad and does not exist

Given the known problems in banks' over-statement of their equity positions thanks to their IRB methodologies, and the routine understatement of 'Risk-Weighted Assets' or RWAs, it is the nominal value of banks' business that must be concentrated upon here. In order to deal with the problem in hand, it is the balance-sheet equity that needs to be considered, and the balance-sheet value of liabilities and assets, not ones that have been risk-adjusted.

Information required from member states about their banking systems

It is vital therefore to know, for each bank in each member state, what its eligible and ineligible liabilities are, its equity and its 'carrying value' of NPLs. Only then can one know what latent loss exists for the member state if the bank has to be resolved, and which would be permanently added to the member state's debt.

These figures are captured in the table below. Operationally, under a resolution of a bank, the member state will have to borrow amount 'B' straight away to make the compensation payments.

It will enjoy priority over the proceeds of the liquidation of the assets, from which it would be able to repay the borrowings from the liquidation – but not if the assets yield far less than the Balance sheet footing 'A'.

The member state will start to lose if the assets yield an amount inferior to the Balance sheet footing 'A' less Equity 'E' and less Ineligible liabilities 'C'. The thicker these cushions of Equity and of Ineligible liabilities are, the less likely it is that the member state will end up with a loss. The loss, as stated above, would crystallise as a permanent addition to borrowing.

Against this, the higher the 'carrying value' of NPLs, the more likely it is that the assets will leave a shortfall, and especially if they are higher than the Equity and Ineligible liabilities combined.

The information required is an inventory by member states of all their Credit Institutions, a simple table to be issued by the financial regulator of every member state on a quarterly basis:

Bank Name	Balance sheet footing 'A' = B + C + E	Total of eligible liabilities = B	Total of ineligible liabilities = C	'Carrying value' of NPLs = D	Balance sheet equity = E	Shortfall vs equity only = F	Equity + ineligible liabilities 'G' = C + E	Shortfall vs equity + ineligible liabilities = H
						@insert figure where D > E; @insert 0 where E > D		@insert figure where D > G; @insert 0 where G > D
[Bank]								
[Bank]								
Totals								

Table 16.1: information required from member states about their banking systems

The values are all nominal ones, rather than risk-adjusted ones.

The totals will show:
  A. Total assets of the eligible institutions per country
  B. Total of eligible liabilities per country – the amount the member state would have to borrow initially to compensate depositors
  C. Total of ineligible liabilities per country – the extra loss cushion in the member state's favour which is converted into equity-like instruments in the recovered bank
  D. 'Carrying value' of NPLs in that country's banking system
  E. Equity in that country's banking system - the primary loss cushion in the member state's favour which is expunged from the resolved bank
  F. Shortfall of Equity compared to NPLs in that country's banking system
  G. Total loss cushion in the member state's favour in that country's banking system
  H. Shortfall of the total loss cushion in that country's banking system

The figure 'H' is the extra member state liability latent in the NPLs of the banks in its banking system.

No basis to insert even a 'placeholder' amount

We have no figure for H and therefore no basis on which to estimate a 'placeholder'.

Chapter 17 – aggregation of the amounts involved

Now we come to the task of aggregating the amounts involved, such as to show the debts that are eliminated from 'General government gross debt' but which track back onto borrowers within its scope, the debts which track back onto borrowers in the public sector but who fall outside the scope of General government, and the contingent liabilities of both. The figures in the tables in this chapter have been copied over from the respective chapter quantifying the size of the liability under each heading.

There is a significant information gap. Nevertheless, with stated provisos, it is possible to quantify the overall shadow liabilities and track them back onto each EU member state individually.

Not even a 'placeholder' for two areas

Out of the ten headings discussed above, we have no basis upon which to estimate a 'placeholder' amount:
- Member state guarantees on bonds issued in connection with the securitization of banks' Non-performing loans (Chapter 15);
- Potential for a permanent addition to General government gross debt in the case of a bank resolution where the volume of Non-performing loans exceeds the bank's capital and its volume of deposits that are ineligible for compensation under the member state Deposit Insurance Scheme (Chapter 16).

Type of liability and quality of numbers

This leaves eight headings where the numbers are more visible. 'Placeholder' amounts have been used against two headings for the reasons explained in the respective chapter. There are separate tables for debts and contingent liabilities. The eight headings deliver twelve columns in tables 17.1 and 17.2 because the EU legal entity appears in both tables, and because each EU supranational entity is given its own column in Table 17.2:

Heading	Chapter	Debt or Contingent Liability	Solid or Placeholder Amount	Table	Column Name in Table
Debts on account of the EU legal entity	7	Debt	Solid	17.1	EU
Contingent liabilities on account of the EU legal entity	7	Contingent Liability	Solid	17.2	EU
EU/Eurozone supranationals	8	Contingent Liability	Solid	17.2	EFSF
EU/Eurozone supranationals	8	Contingent Liability	Solid	17.2	ESM
EU/Eurozone supranationals	8	Contingent Liability	Solid	17.2	EIB
EU/Eurozone supranationals	8	Contingent Liability	Solid	17.2	EGF
Direct debts of public sector entities outside the scope of General government	9	Debt	Placeholder	17.1	Other public sector entities
Debts of private sector entities under schemes like PF4EE and InvestEU where the debt service depends on public sector entities inside or outside the scope of General government	10	Debt	Placeholder	17.1	Structures like InvestEU
Net debts in TARGET2	11	Debt	Solid	17.1	TARGET2 net debts
Gross debts in TARGET2	12	Debt	Solid	17.1	TARGET2 gross debts
ECB market losses	13	Contingent Liability	Solid	17.2	ECB market losses
ECB credit losses	14	Contingent Liability	Solid	17.2	ECB credit losses

Consolidated table of shadow debts, excluded from GGGD

We can thus present a consolidated table for all the shadow debts that track back onto member states and which appear in each case in a table at the end of the respective chapter.

These debts are excluded from the General government gross debt of the member state, but there are debts outstanding, and they are the responsibility of member states. The figures are in € billions:

Country	EU	Other public sector entities	Structures like InvestEU	TARGET2 net debts	TARGET2 gross debts	Total
Belgium	€ 5.4	€ 62.0	€ 38.7	€ 85.7	€ 54.7	€ 246.5
Bulgaria	€ 1.5	€ 16.6	€ 10.4	--	--	€ 28.5
Czech Rep	€ 3.8	€ 42.9	€ 26.8	--	--	€ 73.5
Denmark	€ 3.2	€ 36.4	€ 22.8	--	--	€ 62.4
Germany	€ 41.0	€ 467.8	€ 292.4	--	€ 395.4	€ 1,196.6
Estonia	€ 0.4	€ 4.9	€ 3.1	--	€ 4.2	€ 12.6
Ireland	€ 3.1	€ 35.4	€ 22.1	--	€ 25.4	€ 86.0
Greece	€ 2.6	€ 29.6	€ 18.5	€ 104.2	€ 37.1	€ 192.0
Spain	€ 15.7	€ 179.5	€ 112.2	€ 512.8	€ 178.9	€ 999.1
France	€ 28.5	€ 324.7	€ 202.9	--	€ 306.4	€ 862.5
Croatia	€ 1.0	€ 11.8	€ 7.4	--	--	€ 20.2
Italy	€ 22.0	€ 251.0	€ 156.9	€ 590.0	€ 254.8	€ 1,274.7
Cyprus	€ 0.3	€ 3.3	€ 2.1	--	€ 3.2	€ 8.9
Latvia	€ 0.5	€ 6.0	€ 3.7	€ 5.3	€ 5.9	€ 21.4
Lithuania	€ 0.9	€ 10.5	€ 6.6	--	€ 8.7	€ 26.7
Luxembourg	€ 0.5	€ 5.3	€ 3.3	--	€ 4.9	€ 14.0
Hungary	€ 2.7	€ 31.3	€ 19.5	--	--	€ 53.5
Malta	€ 0.2	€ 2.0	€ 1.3	--	€ 1.6	€ 5.1
Netherlands	€ 8.2	€ 93.8	€ 58.7	€ 22.5	€ 87.9	€ 271.1
Austria	€ 4.3	€ 49.6	€ 31.0	€ 57.4	€ 43.9	€ 186.2
Poland	€ 10.7	€ 121.5	€ 76.0	--	--	€ 208.2
Portugal	€ 3.0	€ 34.6	€ 21.6	€ 79.3	€ 35.1	€ 173.6
Romania	€ 5.3	€ 60.6	€ 37.9	--	--	€ 103.8
Slovenia	€ 0.7	€ 8.3	€ 5.2	--	€ 7.2	€ 21.4
Slovakia	€ 1.5	€ 16.9	€ 10.6	--	€ 17.2	€ 46.2
Finland	€ 2.5	€ 28.4	€ 17.7	--	€ 27.6	€ 76.2
Sweden	€ 5.2	€ 58.7	€ 36.7	--	--	€ 100.6
	€ 174.8	€ 1,993.4	€ 1,246.1	€ 1,457.2	€ 1,500.1	€ 6,371.6

Table 17.1: shadow debts that track back onto member states

Consolidated table of shadow contingent liabilities

We can also present a consolidated table for all the shadow contingent liabilities of member states, all being towards EU/Eurozone supranationals. These figures appear in each case in a table at the end of the respective chapter. The figures are in € billions:

Country	EU	EFSF	ESM	EIB	EGF	ECB market losses	ECB credit losses	Total
Belgium	€ 24.6	€ 7.5	€ 14.1	€ 11.8	€ 1.2	€ 30.1	€ 51.7	€ 141.1
Bulgaria	€ 6.6	--	--	€ 0.5	€ 0.1	--	--	€ 7.2
Czech Rep	€ 17.0	--	--	€ 2.0	--	--	--	€ 19.0
Denmark	€ 14.5	--	--	€ 6.0	€ 0.6	--	--	€ 21.1
Germany	€ 186.0	€ 54.5	€ 110.3	€ 42.5	€ 4.5	€ 217.7	€ 374.3	€ 989.8
Estonia	€ 2.0	€ 0.6	€ 0.7	€ 0.2	--	€ 2.3	€ 4.0	€ 9.8
Ireland	€ 14.1	--	--	€ 1.5	€ 0.2	€ 14.0	€ 24.0	€ 53.7
Greece	€ 11.8	--	--	€ 3.2	€ 0.3	€ 20.4	€ 35.1	€ 70.8
Spain	€ 71.4	€ 24.7	--	€ 25.5	€ 2.7	€ 98.5	€ 169.3	€ 392.1
France	€ 129.1	€ 42.3	€ 82.8	€ 42.5	€ 4.5	€ 168.7	€ 290.0	€ 759.9
Croatia	€ 4.7	--	--	€ 0.9	€ 0.1	--	--	€ 5.7
Italy	€ 99.8	€ 35.2	€ 72.8	€ 42.5	€ 4.5	€ 140.3	€ 241.2	€ 636.3
Cyprus	€ 1.3	--	--	€ 0.3	€ 0.0	€ 1.8	€ 3.1	€ 6.6
Latvia	€ 2.4	--	€ 1.1	€ 0.2	--	€ 3.2	€ 5.5	€ 12.4
Lithuania	€ 4.2	--	€ 1.7	€ 0.4	€ 0.0	€ 4.8	€ 8.2	€ 19.3
Luxembourg	€ 2.1	€ 0.7	€ 1.0	€ 0.3	€ 0.0	€ 2.7	€ 4.7	€ 11.5
Hungary	€ 12.4	--	--	€ 1.9	--	--	--	€ 14.3
Malta	€ 0.8	€ 0.0	€ 0.4	€ 0.1	€ 0.0	€ 0.9	€ 1.5	€ 3.7
Netherlands	€ 37.3	€ 12.1	€ 23.2	€ 11.8	€ 1.2	€ 48.4	€ 83.2	€ 217.3
Austria	€ 19.7	€ 6.1	€ 11.3	€ 5.8	€ 0.6	€ 24.2	€ 41.6	€ 109.3
Poland	€ 48.3	--	--	€ 10.4	€ 1.1	--	--	€ 59.8
Portugal	€ 13.8	--	--	€ 2.1	€ 0.2	€ 19.3	€ 33.2	€ 68.6
Romania	€ 24.1	--	--	€ 1.5	--	--	--	€ 25.6
Slovenia	€ 3.3	€ 1.0	€ 1.9	€ 0.7	€ 0.1	€ 4.0	€ 6.8	€ 17.8
Slovakia	€ 6.7	€ 2.4	€ 3.4	€ 0.7	€ 0.1	€ 9.5	€ 16.3	€ 39.1
Finland	€ 11.3	€ 3.8	€ 7.3	€ 3.4	€ 0.4	€ 15.2	€ 26.1	€ 67.4
Sweden	€ 23.4	--	--	€ 7.8	€ 0.8	--	--	€ 32.0
Totals	€ 792.7	€ 190.9	€ 332.0	€ 226.5	€ 23.2	€ 826.0	€ 1,419.8	€ 3,811.1

Table 17.2: shadow contingent liabilities of member states

Being contingent liabilities, these would not appear in General government gross debt even if the EU/Eurozone supranational was counted within the scope of GGGD, which they are not.

So as to characterize them briefly in order to distinguish them from the shadow debts:
- EU – the main item is the undrawn portion of the Coronavirus Recovery Fund
- EFSF – the guarantees for the EFSF's debts
- ESM – the subscribed-but-not-called capital not in its entirety, but in the amount of the ESM's outstanding debts, and of the headroom which the ESM has to launch new assistance programmes, although the respective chapter highlights how this headroom may prove illusory if a large member state wanted to borrow
- EIB – the subscribed-but-not-called capital
- EGF – the guarantees issued in favour of EIB Group
- ECB – potential for 'market losses' that would have to be made up by member states through their NCB
- ECB - potential for 'credit losses' that would have to be made up by member states through their NCB

Combined incremental member state liabilities deriving from shadow debt and contingent liabilities

Then we can consolidate the above tables to show the increments to both General government gross debt (GGGD) and the Debt-to-GDP Ratio caused first by the addition of (i) the debts that track back onto the member state; and then by the further addition of (ii) the contingent liabilities ('CLs') that would track back onto the member state if they were realized into a call for cash:

	GDP	GGGD	GGGD/ GDP	Extra debts	Revised GGGD	Revised GGGD/ GDP	Extra CLs	Revised GGGD + Extra CLs	Revised GGGD + Extra CLs/GDP
Belgium	€ 507.1	€ 548.7	108.2%	€ 246.5	€ 795.2	156.8%	€ 141.1	€ 936.3	184.6%
Bulgaria	€ 67.7	€ 17.0	25.1%	€ 28.5	€ 45.5	67.1%	€ 7.2	€ 52.6	77.7%
Czech Rep	€ 246.3	€ 103.2	41.9%	€ 73.5	€ 176.7	71.7%	€ 19.0	€ 195.7	79.5%
Denmark	€ 336.2	€ 123.4	36.7%	€ 62.4	€ 185.8	55.3%	€ 21.1	€ 206.9	61.5%
Germany	€ 3,572.6	€ 2,475.8	69.3%	€ 1,196.6	€ 3,672.4	102.8%	€ 989.8	€ 4,662.2	130.5%
Estonia	€ 30.4	€ 5.5	18.1%	€ 12.6	€ 18.1	59.7%	€ 9.8	€ 27.9	91.8%
Ireland	€ 421.2	€ 235.9	56.0%	€ 86.0	€ 321.9	76.4%	€ 53.7	€ 375.6	89.2%
Greece	€ 182.8	€ 353.4	193.3%	€ 192.0	€ 545.4	298.4%	€ 70.8	€ 616.2	337.1%
Spain	€ 1,205.4	€ 1,427.2	118.4%	€ 999.1	€ 2,426.3	201.3%	€ 392.1	€ 2,818.4	233.8%
France	€ 2,491.7	€ 2,813.1	112.9%	€ 862.5	€ 3,675.6	147.5%	€ 759.9	€ 4,435.5	178.0%
Croatia	€ 57.3	€ 45.7	79.8%	€ 20.2	€ 65.9	115.1%	€ 5.7	€ 71.6	125.0%
Italy	€ 1,775.8	€ 2,677.9	150.8%	€ 1,274.7	€ 3,952.6	222.6%	€ 636.3	€ 4,588.9	258.4%
Cyprus	€ 23.5	€ 24.3	103.6%	€ 8.9	€ 33.2	141.2%	€ 6.6	€ 39.7	169.1%
Latvia	€ 33.0	€ 14.8	44.8%	€ 21.4	€ 36.2	109.8%	€ 12.4	€ 48.6	147.2%
Lithuania	€ 55.5	€ 24.6	44.3%	€ 26.7	€ 51.3	92.5%	€ 19.3	€ 70.6	127.3%
Luxembourg	€ 73.3	€ 17.9	24.4%	€ 14.0	€ 31.9	43.5%	€ 11.5	€ 43.4	59.2%
Hungary	€ 149.6	€ 114.9	76.8%	€ 53.5	€ 168.4	112.6%	€ 14.3	€ 182.8	122.2%
Malta	€ 14.6	€ 8.3	57.0%	€ 5.1	€ 13.4	91.6%	€ 3.7	€ 17.1	117.1%
Netherlands	€ 860.1	€ 448.1	52.1%	€ 271.1	€ 719.2	83.6%	€ 217.3	€ 936.5	108.9%
Austria	€ 403.5	€ 334.1	82.8%	€ 186.2	€ 520.3	129.0%	€ 109.3	€ 629.7	156.0%
Poland	€ 570.3	€ 306.8	53.8%	€ 208.2	€ 515.0	90.3%	€ 59.8	€ 574.8	100.8%
Portugal	€ 211.3	€ 269.2	127.4%	€ 173.6	€ 442.8	209.6%	€ 68.6	€ 511.4	242.0%
Romania	€ 239.1	€ 116.7	48.8%	€ 103.8	€ 220.5	92.2%	€ 25.6	€ 246.1	102.9%
Slovenia	€ 52.0	€ 38.9	74.7%	€ 21.4	€ 60.3	116.0%	€ 17.8	€ 78.1	150.2%
Slovakia	€ 97.1	€ 61.3	63.1%	€ 46.2	€ 107.5	110.7%	€ 39.1	€ 146.6	151.0%
Finland	€ 252.9	€ 166.4	65.8%	€ 76.2	€ 242.6	95.9%	€ 67.4	€ 310.0	122.6%
Sweden	€ 524.8	€ 192.6	36.7%	€ 100.6	€ 293.2	55.9%	€ 32.0	€ 325.1	62.0%
Totals	€ 14,455.1	€ 12,965.7	89.7%	€ 6,371.6	€ 19,337.3	133.8%	€ 3,811.1	€ 23,148.4	160.1%

Table 17.3: combined incremental member state liabilities deriving from shadow debt and contingent liabilities

Implications of the above figures
The above figures imply that Eurostat's Debt-to-GDP Ratio for the EU of 90% understates the situation by 44% if one takes account of the actual debts, and by 70% if one factors in the contingent liabilities as well.

It is important to face the fact that over half of the Coronavirus Recovery Fund is being distributed as grants not loans, and that this makes member states primarily responsible for repaying that portion, whether they bring the money forth as extra taxes and levies, as extra annual member state cash contributions, or, de post facto, as extra calls on them by the EU.

Up to now member states were only the secondary source of debt service for the EU's debts because there was always a borrower as the primary source. That has changed with the Coronavirus Recovery Fund and these debts are a primary responsibility of member states, even if the accounting does not reflect this.

Impact of 'placeholders' measured against two areas where no figures are included at all

Admittedly the consolidated figures include the 'placeholders' listed above, which could be overstated but which we have justified via a frame of reference that makes them plausible. On the other hand figures for two areas are completely missing and, if they were included, the totals would be even higher.

An effort has been made not to enter a debt twice as in cases like the ESM holding government bonds of the Republic of Greece, although this cannot be a complete exercise given the inadequacies of publicly available information. Where the figures can be challenged the onus should surely be on the respective public authorities in the EU and Eurozone to provide complete figures and fully reconciled ones.

Impact of joint-and-several liability overlooked

We have been at pains not to over-dramatize the situation, as would be possible by putting the entirety of the debts and contingent liabilities arising through the EU against each member state, on the basis that the liability is on a joint-and-several basis. Not doing that, however, risks submerging the fact that contributions from member states might rise in a crisis situation above their normal percentage share.

The above figures are calculated on the assumption that every member state will be able to pay their share in a crisis, when the crisis could have been caused by the inability of a member state to meet its obligations as they fell due. That member state's contributions would have to be backed out and the contributions of the other member states raised, if the entire required amount was to be brought forth.

Impact for Eurozone and non-Eurozone member states

The situation of the Eurozone member states is considerably worse than that of the non-Eurozone ones: the latter do not participate in the EFSF, the ESM, the APP/PEPP or TARGET2.

Of course Germany as the biggest EU economy and an even bigger one as a proportion of the Eurozone fares worst of all. If 'it all tracks back onto Germany' as financial markets view the Coronavirus Recovery Fund, then financial markets are expecting Germany to be good for the entirety of the extra debts of €6.7 trillion and the contingent liabilities of €3.7 trillion on top of its own existing debt of €2.5 trillion, which is already 69% of its GDP of €3.6 trillion. In other words Germany seems to be regarded as good for extra claims of €10.4 trillion, plus existing ones of €2.5 trillion, meaning a total burden of €12.9 trillion bearing on an economy of €3.6 trillion: that would equate to a Debt-to-GDP Ratio of 358%.

Ballooning of shadow debt and possibility of challenge

The ballooning of debt separate from General government gross debt is extreme. This is in effect the meaning of the phrase 'fully mobilize the EIB', that creative schemes can be devised to place the risk on the public exchequer without the accounting showing it.

There may be some challenge to the way we have treated the borrowings of Ireland, Portugal, Greece, Cyprus and Spain from the EFSM, EFSF and ESM. All those member states have debts to these mechanisms which already form part of the General government gross debt, and yet they have amounts marked against them in respect of these mechanisms, over and above the debts they have to the mechanisms. We have explained in the respective sections that a member state has no legal offset between its debts to such a mechanism and its liabilities to support it. We have made an allowance that borrowers from the EFSF and ESM are not expected to be able to come good on their liabilities as guarantor towards these mechanisms, but this does not mean that they are not legally liable. In eliminating the borrower member states from the contingent liabilities in respect of the EFSF and ESM we have understated their legal liability.

In addition these member states have the liability when other borrowers fail: Ireland would be liable to pay in case Portugal or one of the others failed. Borrower member states do share a liability for the failure of other borrower member states. The potentially missing offset is one to recognize that a member state would not be able to pay out on its contingent liability if it had failed to pay its debt to the same mechanism. However, we do not view it as our role to invent a methodology for reversing the circularity that is built into the architecture of these mechanisms. The total of debts and contingent liabilities from all sources are both plausible individually and in aggregate. The onus should now be on public authorities to make such disclosures as to disprove the figures, if they are able to and if they disagree with the methodologies used in this book and with the conclusions.

Chapter summary

It must have been a deliberate policy to build up shadow debts in areas that fall outside the scope of GGGD, and to manufacture debt- and risk-creating mechanisms that depend upon member state guarantees.

The former is at one step removed from inclusion in GGGD, the latter at two steps removed.

However, in both cases the risk tracks back onto the member states and any assessment of their creditworthiness – by public credit rating agencies, by financial market counterparties, or by the Eurosystem itself – should take account of the much higher total liabilities than are included in GGGD.

The main finding is that Eurostat's Debt-to-GDP Ratio for the EU of 90% understates the situation by 44% if one takes account of the actual debts, and by 70% if one factors in the contingent liabilities as well.

This ought to cost an average member a reduction of four or five notches on its public credit rating, in addition to the reductions for the structural issues in the euro revealed in 'Managing Euro Risk' and the influence that the European authorities exercise over the public credit rating agencies.

In effect the average EU member state is over-rated by six or seven notches.

Chapter 18 – response required from the European and global authorities

Chapter introduction

A response to the degree of hidden indebtedness and disguised liabilities is required from the European authorities, and also from authorities around the world.

What that response is will require some debate, and will follow a process whereby the figures and conclusions of this book are themselves debated.

According to the above calculations, the EU as a whole has a Debt-to-GDP Ratio of 134% when all the actual debts are tracked back to member states, primarily based on their share of EU GNI. When contingent liabilities are added, these and the actual debt combined are over 160% of GDP.

Furthermore the Coronavirus Recovery Fund will cause another €310 billion to move from the contingent liabilities category to the actual debt category by 2027, as the fund becomes drawn. €80 billion out of an eventual €390 billion has been recorded so far into the category where the EU has issued a bond but there is no loan to a member state behind it. The other €360 billion of the fund will be distributed as loans and will stay as a contingent liability of member states.

There is also the possibility that the ECB's Transmission Protection Mechanism will add a significant amount to the volume of the Asset Purchase Programmes, increasing both member states' market risk on ECB operations as well as credit risk.

Quality of Eurozone member state government risk and 'trickle-up' and 'trickle-down'

'Managing Euro Risk' proved that the quality of Eurozone member state government risk was lower than it appeared to be, because of the flaws in the structure of the euro, and that the risk did not merit a 0% risk-weighting under the Basel regime for bank capital adequacy. The book also proved the existence of the trickle-up' and 'trickle down' effects. The trickle-up is where EU and Eurozone supranationals obtain undeservedly low risk-weightings on the back of the support for them of a government that has obtained an unmerited 0% risk-weighting. The trickle-down is where public sector entities and structures like InvestEU in the same member state as the government obtain undeservedly low risk-weightings because the government has obtained an unmerited 0% risk-weighting.

Now this book shows that the debt and contingent liabilities are more numerous, on top of being of lower quality.

Taken together, the two indicators point to the EU and Eurozone as being a significant risk to global financial stability. That demands a response, both from the European authorities, from governments of other countries, and from international bodies dealing with global financial stability.

Information gaps

We have laid out the ten headings under which hidden indebtedness and disguised liabilities have arisen, but there are many information gaps.

The EU authorities should be required to furnish more detailed reporting so as to accurately capture EU public sector liabilities and compare them with EU Member State 'General government GNI gross debt'. The currently available information in some areas is wholly inadequate, such as the nature of the contracts entered into by the EIF under InvestEU and EGF, and the source of debt service for the transactions in which they have become involved.

The TARGET2 information is extremely lacking, given the amounts involved, and only the disclosure of the account statements on all 600 TARGET2-participating accounts for a series of business days that include the ECB reporting date will suffice in order to validate how the ECB works back from the figures in its reports to the original balances, and how that is underpinned – or not – by the legal documentation.

Data around two areas is entirely missing, namely the member state guarantees on banks' securitizations of Non-performing Loans, and member states' exposure to Non-performing Loans through their bank Deposit Insurance Schemes.

Future trajectory of the Stability & Growth Pact and the Fiscal Stability Pact

Over and above this, the EU and Eurozone authorities should be asked to explain how the Stability & Growth Pact and the Fiscal Stability Pact now feature in their calculations, and in particular the limitation of annual public deficits to 3% of GDP and the undertaking in the Fiscal Stability Pact that each signatory Member State should bring its Debt-to-GDP Ratio to 60% by 2030, and still further if there are significant age-related social costs weighing on the Member State's budget up to 2050.

The Debt-to-GDP Ratio has been enshrined as a key indicator of fiscal performance, and thereby as a key token both that the euro is a unitary currency and that its 'central bank money' is fully fungible and risk-free. Currently a monetary adjustment is needed if an investor wants to sell a seasoned Italian government bond with a coupon of 1% and buy a German government bond of the same face amount, coupon and maturity date: the investor must pay a balancing amount because the yields-to-maturity on the two bonds will not be the same, and neither will their prices. The German bond has a lower yield and a higher price, because of the respective credit ratings. These two forms of euro 'central bank money' are not fully fungible with one another. The Fiscal Stability Pact was meant to make the credit risk on them the same by 2030, thereby cementing the status of the euro as a unitary currency.

Advanced Internal Ratings-Based methodologies

This book only deals with the EU and Eurozone commercial banking system to the extent of discussing the volume of Non-performing Loans that it harbours, and the inadequacy of the methodologies for assessing banks' loss buffers, meaning Advanced Internal Ratings-Based methodologies, or AIRB. Global action is needed on AIRB and this is outlined below.

Initial response from non-EU countries

Non-EU countries would be well advised to firstly benchmark the nature and scale of their own financial 'support' measures against those being undertaken in the EU/Eurozone, so as to ensure that their own 'support' measures either conform to the spirit and letter of justifiable 'support' or are run down if they do not.

Support, or stimulus, ought to accelerate the business cycle as opposed to what has happened in the EU and Eurozone. There the 'support' has created a business cycle of its own. There may be some connection between how the money is being spent and long-term economic growth but it is far from obvious. Projects are undertaken and goods and services purchased to execute it, but without creating new capacity in the case of renewables or resulting in better, cheaper or more goods and services for sale. There is a degree of tax-and-spend that has manufactured GDP growth: this has had the byproduct of improving member states' Debt-to-GDP Ratios by boosting GDP thanks to the spending of the proceeds of debt, without impacting the Debt – because debts are taken on outside the scope of General government gross debt.

Displacement of private sector activity in the EU/Eurozone

Whilst the EU authorities may argue the case for the 'missing investor' and why it is vital that they step in with public sector money or support to make a certain project occur, the reality has been of a public sector being involved in an ever greater proportion of a member state's economic activity, and a displacement of private sector activity.

This is exemplified in the financial market, where the Eurosystem owns or controls as collateral at least 47% of all tradeable bonds denominated in euro. A spread of values exists because of issues discussed in this paper and in Appendix 3, notably the full extent of TARGET2 debts, how they come about, what collateral is placed by one NCB with another intraday, and whether it remains operationally tied up with that NCB even if the debt is reduced thanks to incoming payments prior to the end of the day's processing or is further reduced or even eliminated by the end-of-day netting.

Figure 18.1 repeats the layout of the chart given earlier as of the end of 2020 but it is updated to the end of Q1 2022, still with one or two date anomalies:
- 'Total nominal value of Eurosystem eligible collateral' and 'Collateral lodged in the Eurosystem' are as per end of Q1 2022;[159]
- APP and PEPP as of 8 April 2022;
- TARGET2 as of the end of March 2022.

In summary, Figure 18.1 points to the following, cumulative degree of ownership and control of tradeable bonds in euro by the Eurosystem:

APP + PEPP	30%
APP + PEPP + Collateral	47%
APP + PEPP + Collateral + TARGET net-net balance (ECB)	48%
APP + PEPP + Collateral + TARGET debtors balance	55%

Table 18.1: conclusions of Figure 18.1 on Eurosystem ownership and control of tradeable bonds denominated in euro

An ownership level of 47-55% is huge, and it may be worse still if there are intraday debts in TARGET2 requiring collateral. The figures are as at end-of-day, not during it. Our interpretation is that the ECB figure for collateral €2.8 trillion means 'hypothecated' collateral and does not include eligible collateral lodged within the Eurosystem that becomes unhypothecated overnight, for example because of the TARGET2 netting, but where it is needed as collateral during the day and where it is operationally impossible to move the collateral elsewhere given the time it becomes unhypothecated, which is during the TARGET2 end-of-day.

47-55% means that around half of the bonds on the ECB list of eligible collateral are tied up in the Eurosystem. That represents a displacement of private sector activity and a financial market that is dominated by a single market actor.

For completeness' sake Figure 18.2 breaks down two of the figures in Figure 18.1 into categories:
1. Elements in ECB eligible collateral list, which totals €16.6 trillion
2. Elements in collateral lodged in Eurosystem, which totals €2.8 trillion

Need for global financial markets to re-calibrate their risk assessments of dealings with EU/Eurozone actors

In the face of the dominance of a single market actor in the Eurozone, as well as the larger volume of public sector obligations discussed in this book and the lower quality of those obligations discussed in 'Managing Euro Risk', it behoves the financial regulators of other major economies and the international oversight bodies (such as the Bank for International Settlements and the Financial Stability Board) to ensure the correct risk calibration of dealings by the market actors under their purview with EU/Eurozone counterparties.

This calibration needs to be set to the scale of the EU/Eurozone public sector obligations which exist but which are excluded from 'General government gross debt', to their lower quality than is inferred by a 0% risk-weighting for dealings with a government, and to the significant information gaps that this book has revealed.

The re-calibration should come about in the form of:
1. Less benevolent risk-weightings assigned in IRB methodologies for any and all risk-bearing business undertaken;
2. Larger haircuts when collateral is taken, or when tradeable instruments are relied upon as part of compliance with ordinances such as Liquidity Coverage Ratio and Net Stable Funding Ratio;
3. Larger haircuts where tradeable instruments are accepted by Central Counterparties (CCPs) outside the EU.

---

[159] https://www.ecb.europa.eu/paym/coll/charts/html/index.en.html for the date as of end of Q1 2022

Central Counterparties (CCP), Brexit and legal certainty

There has been much public discussion about one of the impacts of Brexit, namely that the principal place in which Euro derivatives contracts clear and settle is London, which is now outside the EU. Since the Global Financial Crisis many types of derivative contract that have been entered into bilaterally by market actors ('over the counter' as it is known) must be novated to a CCP and margined, between trade date and maturity date. The margin will vary during the contract's life dependent upon whether the contract comes 'into the money' or goes 'out of the money'. The original, single contract becomes spilt into two contracts: separate ones between the CCP and the two trading parties. This is exactly the way in which the TARGET2 balances are split from being bilateral between one NCB and another, to being two separate balances between an NCB and the ECB.

The CCP is by definition a systemically-critical Financial Market Infrastructure and must be financially resilient. It becomes this thanks to the legal enforceability of its contracts with its members (the market actors), the width of the loss cushion it takes as margin, and the quality of the assets it accepts as margin. Margin can be in the form of cash or eligible collateral.

Legal enforceability means the validity of the transfer of the rights and obligations under the original trade between the two market actors, the right to accept margin against the risk emanating from a trade, the right to view all of a market actor's trades as one, the right to accept margin against the mark-to-market value of a market actor's portfolio of trades, the right to liquidate a market actor's trades, and the right to apply the margin to the liquidated value of the trades.

This relies on the concepts of netting that are integral to the TARGET2 netting, except that they apply in this case to discreet financial instruments, and all of the instruments are subject to a single applicable law – the law of the location of the CCP. Above all there can be no cherry-picking – a liquidator of a market actor cannot be able to come to the CCP with a list of trades that were 'in the money' at the point of liquidation and a list of those that were 'out of the money', and demand that the CCP pay over the liquidated value of the 'in the money' trades and accept a place in the queue of ordinary unsecured creditors to receive a portion of the liquidated value of the 'out of the money' trades in due course, and hand over assets held as collateral.

The avoidance of the risk of cherry-picking is integral to a CCP's status as a systemically-critical Financial Market Infrastructure, and of course, for the reasons that are discussed above regarding the TARGET2 netting, this would not be a given if clearing and settlement of derivatives was moved back into the EU.

Central Counterparties (CCP) accepting EU/Eurozone assets as collateral and Brexit

Aside from legal certainty, a CCP must be demanding about the quality and liquidity of assets accepted as margin.

There is a risk now, for the CCPs handling this business, deriving from the larger volume of public sector liabilities than are recorded in plain view and from their lower quality as demonstrated in 'Managing Euro Risk', that margins being taken are too thin, if the assets being offered as collateral are EU/Eurozone public sector securities.

CCPs outside the EU need to raise the haircuts straight away in order to re-calibrate for the risk they are taking. Adhering to the ECB list of eligible collateral and at the haircuts stated in it exposes the CCPs to considerable risk.

Of course this is exactly why the EU wishes to re-onshore this business, so that it can specify the assets and haircuts as per the ECB list: the EU authorities cannot have a different list or different haircuts for CCPs compared to the remainder of their operations. This would mean, were the business to be re-onshored, that global market actors would be dealing with a systemically-critical Financial Market Infrastructure which did not meet the highest standards of financial resilience.

It would be meeting a standard even below the benevolent pre-existing ECB collateral framework, thanks to the temporary relaxation agreed for the Pandemic and still in operation. That should not be acceptable and the UK ought not to be standing alone in resisting this. In fact, at present, the UK is digesting considerable Eurozone risk by allowing trades to be cleared and settled through its CCPs on terms that do not take account of the volume and quality of EU/Eurozone public sector securities.

Global issues, needing to be addressed on a global basis

There are three issues that need to be addressed on a global basis. The author having in the past been a critic of global bodies, it may appear inconsistent that this call be made, but it is made with the proviso that any new bodies act separately from the ones whose machinations have given rise to the issues in the first place.

It may admittedly prove difficult to form new bodies without involving the global bodies who must bear a partial responsibility for the current predicament. It must be steadfastly avoided that the new bodies come under the influence of the EU and Eurozone authorities given that the problems the bodies will be tasked to address are EU and Eurozone-created problems.

Global review of Internal Ratings-Based methodologies

The first task is to undertake a global review of Internal Ratings-Based methodologies for assessing Risk-Weighted Assets, covering both on-balance sheet assets and off-balance sheet contracts. The current approach has been formulated between the BIS, EU-level and national banking regulators, banking trade bodies, individual banks, major accounting firms, and major consultancy firms.

Were one to task a new body to review the current situation, it might be difficult to find any representatives who were both expert and who were not already bought into the current approach. An outcome that all is soundly based will not be acceptable.

Review of the four public credit rating agencies regulated in the EU

The second task is to review the four public credit rating agencies regulated in the EU and whether their ratings methodologies take adequate account of the factors set out in the book, and then to ensure that their methodology is being applied impartially, consistently and to absolute standards both inside the EU and outside it.

It should not be acceptable to countries outside the EU that the work of these companies, so important for all countries that issue debt, be specially regulated inside the EU for its work on EU borrowers. There cannot remain any suspicion that EU borrowers obtain special treatment because of commercial pressure on the agencies by the EU, or of an implicit threat of the loss of regulated status if the agency comes up with findings not to the taste of the EU authorities.

The status of being one of the four agencies whose ratings are accepted for the purposes of the EU's collateral quality framework is lucrative as it creates a closed market for borrowers who want to have their liabilities included on the list. Removal from the list would have severe financial consequences for the agency. This creates an avenue for the EU authorities to put pressure on the agencies to maintain or improve the ratings of EU public sector borrowers, which in turn legitimizes lower haircuts, higher borrowing, lower borrowing costs, all of which are on the agenda of the EU authorities.

By way of example, the UK had a AAA-rating until the Brexit referendum. Standard and Poor's immediately imposed a two-notch down grade to AA because of Brexit, and the UK's rating has remained there ever since.

Italy has had the same rating of BBB since October 2017.

Spain had a BBB+ rating in 2017 and this was improved to A- in 2018 and A in 2019.

Portugal was rated BBB- in 2017 and this was raised to BBB in 2019.

France has had an unchanged AA-rating since 2013 and Belgium a AA- rating since 2011.

The Trajectory of the Debt-to-GDP Ratio of these countries since 2017 has been as follows:

Country	2017	2018	2019	2020	2021
UK[160]	85.2%	84.5%	83.8%	102.4%	102.8%
Italy	134.2%	134.4%	134.1%	155.3%	150.8%
Spain	101.9%	100.5%	98.3%	120.0%	118.4%
Portugal	126.1%	121.5%	116.6%	135.2%	127.4%
France	98.1%	97.8%	97.4%	114.6%	112.9%
Belgium	102.0%	99.8%	97.7%	112.8%	108.2%

Table 18.2: trajectory of Debt-to-GDP Ratio of the UK and five Eurozone member states

France and Belgium should not have the same rating as the UK, even if they had their own sovereign currency, which they do not. There was no rationale for Spain's and Portugal's ratings to be raised. Italy's deterioration should have cost it at least one downgrade to BBB-, the lowest rung in Investment Grade, and arguably another down to BB+.

S&P's double downgrade of the UK's rating, directly after the Brexit referendum, smacks of a re-echoing of 'Project Fear', and the reasons S&P gave for their downgrade were as follows:[161]

- 'In the nationwide referendum on the U.K.'s membership of the European Union (EU), the majority of the electorate voted to leave the EU. In our opinion, this outcome is a seminal event, and will lead to a less predictable, stable, and effective policy framework in the U.K. We have reassessed our view of the U.K.'s institutional assessment and now no longer consider it a strength in our assessment of the rating.
- The downgrade also reflects the risks of a marked deterioration of external financing conditions in light of the U.K.'s extremely elevated level of gross external financing requirements.
- The vote for "remain" in Scotland and Northern Ireland also creates wider constitutional issues for the country as a whole.
- Consequently, we are lowering our long-term sovereign credit ratings on the U.K. by two notches to 'AA' from 'AAA'.
- The negative outlook reflects the risk to economic prospects, fiscal and external performance, and the role of sterling as a reserve currency, as well as risks to the constitutional and economic integrity of the U.K. if there is another referendum on Scottish independence.'

The downgrade was based on speculation: a 'negative outlook', the 'creation of wider constitutional issues', the 'risks of a marked deterioration' and so on, but not on anything that had actually happened. Events in the meantime, and in particular the UK's capacity to meet its debt service obligations, have not borne out the degree of negativity justifying such a major downgrade of two notches. S&P ought to have partially reversed its downgrade by raising the UK's rating to AA+.

S&P might counter that the Pandemic has caused a rise in the UK's Debt-to-GDP Ratio so as to preclude such a change, but S&P have not adjusted the ratings of the five captioned countries in the Eurozone for this reason, so they must see the Pandemic as 'credit neutral'. S&P has not reacted either to the deterioration in the financial status of EU member states, nor to the addition of the debt to be issued for the Coronavirus Recovery Fund. The former factor weakens the creditworthiness both of the member states and of the EU supranationals whose ratings rely on the support of the member state. The latter both adds a considerable block of new debt to one of the EU supranationals, and also increases the debt that tracks back onto the member states. This is inequitable when measured against the treatment of a country like the UK which harbours no supranationals for whose debts it is responsible.

There is a clear basis for doubt as to whether S&P's treatment of the UK has been even-handed compared to its treatment of these Eurozone countries. This is not acceptable and needs to be addressed.

160

https://www.ons.gov.uk/economy/governmentpublicsectorandtaxes/publicspending/bulletins/ukgovernmentdebtanddeficitfor
eurostatmaast/december2021 accessed on 13 July 2022

[161] https://disclosure.spglobal.com/ratings/en/regulatory/article/-/view/type/HTML/id/1664261 accessed on 13 July 2022

New taxonomy for EU/Eurozone measures

The third task is to decide whether the nature and degree of actions by the EU/Eurozone necessitate a new taxonomy to differentiate them from optically similar operations carried out by a sovereign country with its own currency. A certain number of basic issues need to be dealt with. The scope of 'General government gross debt' needs to be reviewed. A working definition for an 'other public sector entity' is required as it is assumed that not all public sector entities will fall within the new definition of 'General government gross debt'. A working definition is required for the type of private sector enterprise which is a special purpose company whose debt service depends on the public sector. The EU and Eurozone authorities need to undertake to maintain and publish all of the tables contained in this book with the intention of delivering transparency, and comfort that there is only one version of the truth about the levels of debt and contingent liability.

The task does not end there, however. The flaw in the Euro as a currency, proved out in 'Managing Euro Risk', means that the Eurozone member states should not be maintaining the same level of real and contingent liabilities as countries with their own sovereign currencies, but lower ones.

The currencies of non-Eurozone EU member states sit on a range of proximities to the Euro: currencies within the Exchange Rate Mechanism sit within tight proximity, others like Sweden's less so. These member states should not be maintaining the same level of real and contingent liabilities as countries with their own sovereign currencies albeit that theirs can sit somewhat higher than those of Eurozone member states.

In some way a methodology needs to be created for limiting and unravelling the circularity of arrangements in the EU and Eurozone, such as the ESM where all Eurozone member states on the face of it are guarantors and potential borrowers, but where this is cannot happen in practice: a different view is inherent in the mechanism's structure, and the true situation is opaque.

Specific action on TARGET2: it must settle at end-of-day

TARGET2 needs to be made to settle at the end of the business day. It is an oxymoron to have a Real-time Gross Settlement system where the business of commercial bank participants settles at once and on a gross basis, but where the business between the Eurosystem members does not settle at all. A genuine zero-balancing needs to be installed during the TARGET2 end-of-day process so that every one of the NCB nostros and vostros with one another shows a zero balance overnight, as well as the ECB's vostros with each NCB, and that the balances of each NCB at every other NCB are physically concentrated onto the nostro account held by each NCB at the ECB, and then onto a Reserve Account overnight. Every movement so executed in the end-of-day process on D needs to be reversed as a 'Cinderella' sweep during the start-of-day process on D+1. Then the ECB's monthly reports would reflect the operational situation and the actual book balances, although the ECB's Annual Report would still need to be altered to show each of the ECB's balances vis a vis an NCB either as an asset or a liability and in full.

Transmission Protection Mechanism

In July 2022 the ECB established the Transmission Protection Mechanism (TPM) as a way of avoiding what it described as the fragmentation of its own monetary policy actions. The TPM was originally referred to as a Fragmentation Tool.

We had a critique published of the language with which the TPM was announced, along with a rise in interest rates.[162] The issues with the TPM go deeper.

The TPM's motivator is the risk that yields on the bonds of different member states had diverged, with those of Italy rising sharply while those of Germany rose moderately. The ECB argued that it would be unable to transmit its monetary policy actions evenly throughout the Eurozone if bond yields were so divergent. Therefore there needed to be a way of bringing down the yield differentials in order to allow the ECB's monetary policy actions to take effect. It is not the aim here to attack this logic chain but simply to point out what the TPM is and its central logic flaw.

---

[162] https://en.irefeurope.org/publications/online-articles/article/european-central-banks-gaslighting-defies-eu-energy-shortage/ accessed on 26 September 2022

The TPM as creator of new member state contingent liabilities through the ECB

The TPM is a permission to the ECB to mandate the Banca d'Italia, for example, to buy unlimited quantities of Italian government bonds (BTPs). The Eurosystem would allow the Banca d'Italia to generate the cash to do this via the Banca d'Italia pledging the BTPs to other NCBs through the Correspondent Central Banking Model. The Banca d'Italia would then be able to overdraw its RTGS accounts in TARGET2 against the BTPs.

The TPM would make no reference to ECB Capital Keys. Where the PEPP was only 'guided by' ECB Capital Keys, the TPM need make no reference to them at all.

In consequence the overall portfolio of the Eurosystem would become tilted, and could no longer be regarded as member states lending to themselves. Instead the member states would be allowing the ECB, to whom losses track back, to be taking increased market and credit risk in their name, when neither the ECB nor the NCBs are adequately capitalized. The ECB and the NCBs are creatures through whom the member states undertake financial operations not by investing capital but by opening up a line of recourse to themselves.

The TPM, if it were mobilized, would thus cause a significant increase in the contingent liabilities of member states through the ECB in the two categories identified in this book:
- Market losses on ECB programmes
- Credit losses on ECB programmes

TPM logic flaw

The central logic flaw in the TPM is that, in order for it to conform to the ECB's contention that it is a monetary policy operation within the ECB's mandate, its mobilization to support a particular member state must not be caused by 'objective' financial difficulties for that member state. In other words, investors must be selling off the member state's bonds for a reason unconnected with the member state's financial condition. Numerous supposed 'objective' tests are quoted for proving an absence of financial difficulties, but this is a smokescreen: investors buy, hold and sell bonds due to financial considerations. The supposed 'objective' tests will have to be malleable if the TPM is ever to be mobilized, and no doubt this will prove possible given the ECB's track record, at least to the ECB's own satisfaction.

Whether it will satisfy the European Parliament, national politicians, governors of the NCBs called upon to fund the TPM's mobilization, the press, voters and financial markets is another question entirely. The logic flaws in the TPM's conception and in the criteria for its mobilization are of an order of magnitude sufficient to cause a keen focus where the ECB would prefer that matters were left to the professionals i.e. themselves.

Chapter summary

The conclusions of the book require serious action if the global financial system is to continue to be rules-based.

There will no doubt need to be a period of debate and consideration before the conclusions are accepted, but then the EU/Eurozone authorities will need to implement the measures to deliver transparency in the many areas where there are currently information gaps. A new taxonomy may need to be devised to distinguish Eurozone operations, in a currency with no sovereign borrower behind it, from optically analogous operations by countries like the US, UK and Japan that have sovereign powers over their currencies.

The EU/Eurozone authorities will need to give guidance as to the future of both the Stability & Growth Pact and the Fiscal Stability Pact.

On a global level the application of Basel III Internal Ratings-Based methodologies needs to be reviewed, alongside the operations and fairness of the public credit rating agencies.

Finally, TARGET2 needs to settle at the end of every TARGET2 business day. If there are loans and deposits within it at the end of the payment processing day, the end-of-day closing processes need to transfer those balances out of the TARGET2 payment system and into, at least, a TARGET2 loan and deposit system in which they are transparent and for their full amount: RTGS accounts must be brough to a zero balance overnight.

Figures:
- 18.1: Eurosystem degree of ownership or control of tradeable bonds denominated in euro at end of Q1 2022
- 18.2: elements in ECB collateral list and in actual collateral lodged with the Eurosystem at end of Q1 2022, in € billions

Figure 18.1: Eurosystem degree of ownership or control of tradeable bonds denominated in euro at end of Q1 2022

Total nominal value of Eurosystem eligible collateral	€16,563,000
Collateral lodged in the Eurosystem	€2,811,000
TARGET2 net-net balance (ECB)	€317,600
TARGET2 creditors balance	€1,774,500
TARGET2 debtors balance	€1,456,900
PEPP portfolio	€1,698,000
APP/closed programmes	€4,100
APP/CSP	€332,800
APP/PSPP	€2,535,800
APP/ABSPP	€27,200
APP/CBPP3	€296,800
Total pre-existing APP portfolio	€3,196,700
APP + PEPP	€4,894,700
APP + PEPP + Collateral	€7,705,700
APP + PEPP + Collateral + TARGET net-net balance (ECB)	€8,023,800
APP + PEPP + Collateral + TARGET debtors balance	€9,162,600

Relationship of indicator to total value of Eurosystem eligible collateral:	
APP + PEPP	30%
APP + PEPP + Collateral	47%
APP + PEPP + Collateral + TARGET net-net balance (ECB)	48%
APP + PEPP + Collateral + TARGET debtors balance	55%

Figure 18.1: Eurosystem degree of ownership or control of tradeable bonds denominated in euro at end of Q1 2022

Figure 18.2: elements in ECB collateral list and in actual collateral lodged with the Eurosystem at end of Q1 2022, in € billions

Elements in ECB eligible collateral list	Amount
Other marketable assets	€1,203 billion
Asset-backed securities	€578 billion
Corporate bonds	€1,851 billion
Covered bank bonds	€1,664 billion
Unsecured bank bonds	€1,626 billion
Regional government securities	€602 billion
Central government securities	€9,039 billion
	€16,563 billion
Elements in collateral lodged in Eurosystem	Amount
Credit claims	€918 billion
Other marketable assets	€56 billion
Asset-backed securities	€413 billion
Corporate bonds	€75 billion
Covered bank bonds	€711 billion
Unsecured bank bonds	€136 billion
Regional government securities	€84 billion
Central government securities	€418 billion
	€2,811 billion

Figure 18.2: elements in ECB collateral list and in actual collateral lodged with the Eurosystem at end of Q1 2022, in € billions

Chapter 19 - Summary and Conclusions

The EU and Eurozone member states are over-indebted. The statistics in the Eurostat database are adverse enough on their own without adding the shadow debts and shadow contingent liabilities.

These additional liabilities have been created within the level of EU supranational entities – like the EU itself and the EIB – and at the two levels below: in 'other public sector entities' and in private entities who have borrowed heavily and whose debt service derives from the public sector.

The EU/Eurozone is not on a trajectory to be compliant with the Fiscal Stability Pact by 2030. Not only are those accounting for the majority of GDP heading in the opposite direction-of-travel, but the distance to travel is far larger than is appreciated, given the scale of the shadow debts and shadow contingent liabilities.

These are also the areas of liability that are growing the most strongly.

It is ironic that the EU and Eurozone have made such extensive usage of financial templates that were associated by their politicians with 'Anglo-Saxon capitalism'. Michel Barnier was often accused of being against such arrangements, although the words on record are from politicians like Nicholas Sarkozy.[163]

When President Macron met with German Chancellor Scholz and proposed the invention of new financial solutions for the EU, it is exactly these types of arrangement that are contemplated.[164]

The current situation ought to be unacceptable to other countries in the global financial system, namely that a significant bloc of participants do not abide by the system's rules. The implication of the shadow debts and shadow contingent liabilities is that EU/Eurozone member states are far less able to meet their liabilities as they fall due than they appear to be, given Eurostat statistics, their public credit ratings, and the capital that other actors in the system allocate behind their dealings with these counterparties.

This is a threat to global financial stability, of which other system members and the public credit rating agencies appear to be oblivious. That should not be allowed to continue, but it would be unrealistic to imagine that this problem can be solved overnight: it has become entrenched within the day-to-day operations of the EU generally and the Eurozone in particular.

The process of debate, agreement on remedial actions and implementation of such actions is a multi-year project and one must hope that, in the meantime, no usage of the Transmission Protection Mechanism is required. In fact it is strongly in the interests of the EU/Eurozone authorities to put their house in order and bring the euro onto an even keel, if it is to survive in the long term. A mobilization of the TPM, far from being a necessary action to enable monetary policy, could prove to be a fatal overreach.

---

[163] https://berlinpolicyjournal.com/close-up-michel-barnier/ accessed on 14 October 2022
[164] https://www.politico.eu/article/macron-urge-scholz-invent-new-financial-solutions-for-eu/ accessed on 14 October 2022

Appendix 1 – the sanitization of Unicredit Group 2016-7

In mid-2016 the CEO of Unicredit, Jean-Pierre Mustier, made it known that radical action was needed to repair the bank's balance sheet and particularly that of the Italian bank, which was at the same time the group parent and holder of shares in Hypovereinsbank and Creditanstalt-Bankverein, which in turn owned the shares in the other banks in the Central and Eastern European network.

A five-point plan was unveiled:
1. Unicredit S.p.A, the group parent and Italian bank, would become the direct owner of the shares in the banks in the Central and Eastern European network;
2. A major rights issue would be undertaken to increase the capital of Unicredit S.p.A.;
3. The carrying value of NPLs on the books of Unicredit S.p.A. would be substantially written down under 'Project Porto';
4. A substantial block of NPLs on the books of Unicredit S.p.A. would be sold off into a 'market-based securitization' under the 'Project Fino';
5. A provision of €4.1 billion, over and above those needed for 'Port' and 'Fino', would be made to improve the quality of the assets, a euphemism for bringing their book value down so it was nearer to their true value.

These actions were carried through by March 2017 with a number of provisos as pointed out in our paper of the time entitled 'The recapitalisation of Unicredit S.p.A.: an examination of (i) the accounting of its 13-for-5 rights issue (ii) its level of provisioning for Bad and Doubtful Debts and (iii) the accounting of its investments in its banking subsidiaries and sub-subsidiaries'.[165]

The provisos were principally these:
1. The bank made provisions in the final quarter of 2016, both to write down the 'Porto' portfolio (€4.5 billion), the 'Fino' portfolio (€3.6 billion), and further assets (€4.1 billion), and these all but eliminated Reserves at the end of 2016;
2. The rights issue raised €13.0 billion – scarcely more than the 2016 provisions. It replenished Share Capital in just over the amount the bank had written off from Reserves;
3. The Italian bank had loans itself of 543% of its capital, of which 25% were accounted as NPLs, even after 'Porto' and 'Fino';
4. The de-layering of the banks in the Central and Eastern European network had not been completed;
5. Prior to it Unicredit was using its capital three times: in the Italian bank, in Hypovereinsbank and Creditanstalt-Bankverein, and in the banks in the Central and Eastern European network;
6. After it, it would only be using it twice;
7. It did this by failing to directly deduct back from the parent's capital on a 1-for-1 basis the capital the parent owned in subsidiary bank, in a flagrant breach of BIS rules;
8. Had it done so properly, the parent would have been well short of meeting a normal CET1 Ratio, let alone one increased due to the bank's status as a GSIFI.

Unicredit's 'Balance-sheet equity'

The bank's 'Balance-sheet equity' before the rights issue was €50.7 billion, consisting of €36.7 billion of Capital and €14.0 billion of Reserves.

The rights issue – which was paid in by 3 March 2017 - increased Unicredit's shares-in-issue by a factor of 260%, it being a 13-for-5 issue of rights, with a maximum of 1,606,876,817 new shares issued, for an aggregate amount of up to €16,068,768.17 in share capital (€0.01 per share) and up to €12,983,564,681.36 in share premium (€8.08 per share). The proceeds were therefore €13.0 billion, and ought to have raised the bank's 'Balance-sheet equity' from €50.7 billion to €63.7 billion (without accounting for the 2016 profit).

Tracking the bank's capital through the process was rendered the more difficult by its carrying out a Reverse Stock Split on 24 February 2017, whereby 6,177,818,177 Ordinary shares-in-issue had become 617,781,817. This paved the way for 13-for-5 rights issue.

---

[165] Available through Research Papers on www.lyddonconsulting.com

The rights issue was recorded anomalously in a series of communications from the bank, from which we extrapolated the following position for the bank's equity as it should have appeared on its balance sheet after its completion on 3 March 2017:

Ordinary Share Value	€22,246,586.34
Savings Share Value	€2,367,586.02
Total Share Value	€24,614,172.36
Share Premium	€49,682,912,714.11
'Balance-sheet capital'	€49,707,526,886.47
Reserves	€14,036,000,000.00
'Balance-sheet equity'	€63,743,526,886.47

However, 'Balance-sheet equity' was not €50.7 billion on 3 March 2017 and thus never rose to €63.7 billion, because prior to the rights issue being completed it had fallen to €38.5 billion. Reserves had been depleted by €12.2 billion to only €1.8 billion thanks to the provisions. Share capital rose to €49.7 billion after the pay-in of the rights on 3 March 2017, by which time the Reserves were €1.8 billion, meaning 'Balance sheet equity' was €51.5 billion, only €0.8 billion higher than before the rights issue, again without accounting for the 2016 profit.

Unicredit's 'Balance-sheet equity' and market capitalization

All the way through the process there was a major discrepancy between Unicredit's market capitalization and its Balance sheet equity. The Unicredit S.p.A share price on 24 February was €12.16, on the day of completion of the Reverse Stock Split: 617,781,817 shares at €12.16 each made for a bank's market capitalization on that day of €7.5 billion.

This was a discount of 85% to its pre-rights issue 'Balance-sheet equity' of €50.7 billion. The market was thereby expressing an opinion that there was an overvaluation of UniCredit's assets of €43.2 billion compared to its 'Balance-sheet equity' of €50.7 billion (which investors may have assumed still included the Reserves of €14.0 billion).

2,224,658,634 Ordinary shares were in circulation once the rights issue had been made, and once it had been paid in. If the market price after the issue were to have settled at the rights price of €8.09, Unicredit's market capitalization would have risen to €18.0 billion (an increase of €10.5 billion). That contrasted with a 'Balance-sheet equity' of €51.5 billion, a difference of €33.5 billion, closing up the discrepancy between market capitalization and 'Balance-sheet equity' by €9.7 billion but still representing an opinion of the share market that now only €33.5 billion of Unicredit's assets did not exist, and/or that liabilities were understated and/or that any operating profits made over the coming five years would not be attributable-to-shareholders.

Capital raised was immediately written off – or had already been

The rights were nevertheless taken up by investors and they must have failed to fully understand the meaning of the reference on p. 2 of the Prospectus to 'one-off negative impacts on the net financial result of Q4 2016 of €12.2 billion due to the increase in the degree of cover on the portfolio of loans subject to sale under the scope of the "Fino Project" and the impaired loans of the "Porto Project"'.[166]

This statement inferred that the entire €12.2 billion related to 'Porto' and 'Fino', whereas other statements say that €4.1 billion was for other purposes.

Page of 1 of the same document refers to these two projects as being part of the Unicredit Strategic Plan for 'the improvement of the quality of the assets', which all sounds positive.

It is only on the following page that there is clarity that this 'improvement' meant recognizing that they were overvalued and buying their 'improvement' with nearly the entire proceeds of the rights issue.

---

[166] Registration Document filed at CONSOB on 30 January 2017

We know that Unicredit made a net profit of €1.1 billion in the nine months to 30 September 2016, and it is reasonable to extrapolate that into a profit of €400 million on ordinary activities in Q4 2016, and one of €150 million for January 2017.

Therefore we can posit that the Porto-Fino-other projects had impacted Reserves as follows up to the 'Registration date' for the rights issue of 31 January 2017 as follows, this time including the accounting for the 2016 profit and an estimated profit for January 2017:

Reserves as at 30/9/16 excl Minority Interests	€14,036 million
Profits for Q1-3 2016	€1,100 million
Profit on ordinary activities for Q4 2016 (estimated)	€400 million
Reserves at 31/12/16 without Porto-Fino adjustments	€15,536 million
Porto-Fino-other adjustments in Q4 2016	(€12,200 million)
Reserves as at 31/12/16 with Porto-Fino-other adjustments	€3,336 million
Profit for January 2017 (estimated)	€150 million
Reserves as at 31/1/17 with Porto-Fino-other adjustments	€3,486 million
Reserves as at 31/1/17 without Porto-Fino-other adjustments	€15,686 million

At the time the Prospectus for the rights issue was issued, then, almost the entire amount had already been spent by Unicredit in the form of further loan loss write-downs, to decrease the value of loans that were being sold off into securitization vehicles and to increase the Loan Loss Provisions against loans retained.

The Porto-Fino-other adjustments reduced reserves from €14.0 billion down to €1.8 billion, and then the 2016 profit plus the January 2017 profit raised them up again to €3.5 billion, and this would have altered the financial position after the pay-in of the rights as follows:

	Claimed position 2/3/17	Actual position 2/3/17	Rights issue	Claimed position after rights pay-in	Actual position after rights pay-in
Share Capital	€20,846,893,436.94	€8,545,404.19	€16,068,768.17	€20,862,962,205.11	€24,614,172.36
Share Premium	€15,861,000,000.00	€36,699,348,032.75	€12,983,564,681.36	€28,844,564,681.36	€49,682,912,714.11
Balance-sheet capital	€36,707,893,436.94	€36,707,893,436.94	€12,999,633,449.53	€49,707,526,886.47	€49,707,526,886.47
Reserves	€14,036,000,000.00	€3,486,000,000.00	€0	€14,036,000,000.00	€3,486,000,000.00
Balance-sheet equity	€50,743,893,436.94	€38,543,893,436.94	€12,999,633,449.53	€63,743,526,886.47	€51,543,526,886.47

Unicredit's bad loans

Unicredit S.p.A.'s loan loss figures were quite confusing in the detail as they referred at length to adjustments made thanks to policy notes from the European and Italian banking supervisors.

Nonetheless the chart on p. 30 of the 2015 Unconsolidated Annual Report of Unicredit S.p.A. was enlightening:

As at 31/12/15 in €millions	Bad Exposures	Unlikely to pay	Non-performing &past due	Total Non-performing	Performing loans	Total loans
Gross exposure	36,523	17,411	1,554	55,488	189,898	245,386
As % of total loans	14.88%	7.1%	0.63%	22.61%	77.39%	-
Writedowns	22,831	5,832	461	29,124	1,087	30,211
As % of face value	62.51%	33.5%	29.67%	52.49%	0.57%	-
Carrying value	13,692	11,579	1,093	26,364	188,811	215,175
As % of total loans	6.36%	5.38%	0.51%	12.25%	87.75%5	-

In terms of gradation of seriousness, the author's experience would indicate the following as prudent levels of write-down for NPLs held in portfolio, and these are compared with Unicredit's levels of write-down:

Category	Description	Likely recovery	Appropriate write-down	Write-down as above	Under-provision	Further write-down in €millions
Bad exposures	in default, little likelihood of recovery	10%	90%	62.51%	27.49%	10,040
Unlikely to pay	in default, some chance of a recovery	10-50% = 30% on average	70%	33.5%	36.5%	6,355
Non-performing & past due	it has to meet both of these tests, and there should be a meaningful recovery	50-90% = 70% on average	30%	29.67%	0.33%	€5
Further writedown on book value needed to meet likely recovery rates						€16,400

By these measures of the gravity of the situation, the loans were under-provisioned in the 2015 Annual Report by €16,400 million or €16.4 billion. These figures would be improved by €12.2 billion through the extra 'coverage' afforded by the 'Porto' and 'Fino' projects and if the other provisions were also made for this purpose, leaving an under-provisioning of €4.2 billion. If the other provisions were not for reducing the 'carrying value' of NPLs, then the under-provisioning rises to €8.3 billion.

Conclusion

The investors in the rights issue were barely informed correctly about how their money would be used, or already had been used.

Unicredit S.p.A. was badly under-capitalized for two reasons.

Firstly, it owned the shares in Hypovereinsbank and Creditanstalt-Bankverein without deducting this investment in the CET1 of other banks from its own CET1. Unicredit S.p.A. leveraged up this CET1, as did both Hypovereinsbank and Creditanstalt-Bankverein. These banks owned the CET1 of numerous other banks in their networks in central and eastern Europe, without deducting this investment in the CET1 of other banks from its own CET1. The same small amount of CET1 in Unicredit S.p.A. was thus leveraged by three levels of banks.

Secondly, the CET1 that these levels of banks were all leveraging up did not really exist. Unicredit S.p.A. had bad loans well in excess of its CET1, and multiple times its CET1 after investments in subsidiary banks had been deducted back.

Full paper available at:

https://www.brugesgroup.com/blog/the-ecb-s-pandemic-emergency-purchase-programme-the-undermining-of-the-eurozone-as-a-free-financial-market-the-epitome-of-the-failure-of-the-euro-project-and-a-coup-d-etat-by-the-european-central-bank

The standing eligibility criteria, prior to the pandemic, as regards credit quality for securities to be on the ECB list and therefore investable by the APP and the PEPP are defined in the Eurosystem Credit Assessment Framework for Monetary Policy Operations or ECAF. There are five rungs in it, each called a Credit Quality Step or CQS, and a rung equates to given public credit ratings or approved equivalents, one of the equivalents being an IRB methodology.

A minimum rating of Credit Quality Step 3 ('CQS3') applies: securities must be of Investment Grade to be bought by the APP or PEPP, but no longer to be held by them.

Any security only has to have one rating for the purposes of the ECAF; if there are multiple ratings, the best one applies, including where one meets CQS3 and the others fall below.

For securities above one year's maturity the minimum to be classed as Investment Grade and to meet CQS3 is:

Standard & Poor's	BBB-
Moody's	Baa3
Fitch	BBB-
DBRS	BBBL

The minimum short-term ratings for a security to meet CQS3 are:

Standard & Poor's	A-3
Moody's	P-3
Fitch	F-3
DBRS	R-3

In the Moody's system, as a guideline, P-3 (or Prime-3) is regarded as a short-term rating equivalent to a long-term one of Baa2 or Baa3, the lowest rung in Investment Grade.

The lack of any lower ratings for short-term securities is a problem because the ECB has relaxed the standards to permit CSQ4 and CSQ5 securities to continue to be held by the PEPP and other APPs where they have come down into that rung from CSQ3. The long-term ratings in these categories are:

	CSQ4	CSQ5
Standard & Poor's	BB+	BB
Moody's	Ba1	Ba2
Fitch	BB+	BB
DBRS	BBH	BB

These long-term ratings class the security as Speculative Grade, but there are no public rating levels for short-term securities that are Speculative Grade. At best we have the Moody's rating that is NP, meaning Not Prime, which can equate to any long-term rating from Ba1 at the top of Speculative Grade down to C at the bottom end of Junk Grade (meaning 'In default with little chance of recovery'). NP does not appear in the Eurosystem Credit Assessment Framework and nor do equivalents from any of the other three approved rating agencies. In effect the PEPP, if it has bought short-term securities that fall from P-3 to NP under Moody's, or fall from A-3, F-3 or R-3 into the void, will have no option but to hold them until maturity.

A delusion suffuses the PEPP on the issue of ratings downgrades. It is that securities purchased when they met CQS3 do not have to be sold even if they fall to CQS5 (Ba2 using the Moody's scale), but they do have to be sold if they fall below CQS5 to B1 in the Moody's system, its equivalent in the three other approved systems, or worse. This condition overlooks the fact that there will be no-one out there wanting to buy the securities under that eventuality.

The PEPP's stance on buying and then selling securities flies in the face of 'best practice' for investments.[167] This is to buy securities rated no lower than Baa1, and to sell any that fall into Baa2. The investor has then disposed of its holding before the security comes close to falling out of Investment Grade, Baa3 being the lowest rung of Investment Grade. This avoids an investor getting caught up in a firesale when a security, falling out of Investment Grade, ceases to meet the criteria of collective investment vehicles. These vehicles are obliged to sell, and all at the same time, which will drive prices down and precipitate the firesale. The prudent investor gets out early. The Eurosystem, knowing it cannot get out, simply re-writes the rules for itself so that it does not have to sell securities in portfolio when they fall out of Investment Grade. In fact the Eurosystem only has to sell them after the firesale has already taken place; at that point the securities will not meet the buying criteria of any investors, and the Eurosystem will be forced to hold the security until maturity, and hope that the issuer repays.

This reversal of normal logic is, in a way, a statement of the facts for a market actor who controls the market and controls the rules upon which the market operates: they cannot step out of their investments given that they are the only major buyer, and have, by their interventions, already caused all the securities in the market to be over-priced. When the Eurosystem wants to sell, there will not be willing buyers in the market at the price the Eurosystem wants to sell at.

The Eurosystem has dissolved the BVG-quoted safeguard that the 'issuer has a minimum credit quality assessment that provides access to the bond markets'.

The press release of ECB Monetary Policy Decisions taken at its meeting on 10 December 2020 includes the following statement:

'Fourth, the Governing Council decided to extend to June 2022 the duration of the set of collateral easing measures adopted by the Governing Council on 7 and 22 April 2020. The extension of these measures will continue to ensure that banks can make full use of the Eurosystem's liquidity operations, most notably the recalibrated TLTROs. The Governing Council will reassess the collateral easing measures before June 2022, ensuring that Eurosystem counterparties' participation in TLTRO III operations is not adversely affected.'

These collateral-easing measures affect the PEPP and all the APPs. These measures were announced as temporary on 7 April 2020 but were extended until June 2022 on 10 December 2020.

The first major weakening was the increase in the Eurosystem loan size against all types of collateral, achieved by reducing the 'haircuts' specified in the ECB list of eligible collateral. Haircuts were reduced by around 20% - 1/5th of themselves - across all marketable asset classes, and non-marketable assets: the methodology through which the latter was achieved was expanded upon but the outcome was the same – the Eurosystem reduced its margin of security by 1/5th across the board and thereby took on more credit and market risk.

The second major weakening was the degree to which 'credit claims' (i.e. an instrument giving the Eurosystem rights over bank loans) were accepted onto the ECB list. These could come in the form of a debt security like a Collateralised Loan Obligation, in which case they were eligible for the PEPP and APP. If they did not come in the form of a debt security, they were not investable by the PEPP or APP but could still serve as eligible collateral.

Whichever type of instrument it was, it was highly likely to have been created by the same bank that originated the loans. The loans would have been an asset of that bank upon disbursement and could now be sold on to the PEPP (and indeed the ABSPP and the CBPP3 as well, but probably not the CSPP as the direct counterparty is not a corporate) or placed with the Eurosystem as collateral.

'Credit claims' could now include loans of lower credit quality, loans to types of debtors not accepted in the ECB's general framework, and foreign-currency loans. COVID-19 emergency loans, guaranteed by a public entity, were also eligible.

---

[167] For example, the "Investment" module of the Cash Management course offered by Accountingcpd.net and written by the author

The ECB also eased the acceptance of banks' own IRB models as arbiters of creditworthiness and as an alternative to a public credit rating. IRB would play a particular role in attesting to the quality of 'credit claims'. IRB was acceptable as long as the methodology had been 'approved by supervisors': this generally means that it had been installed and audited by one of the Big Four accountancy firms, normally the same one that audited the bank's accounts. This endorsement is usually enough to secure the approval of the bank's supervisor. Loan-level reporting requirements on 'credit claims' were also eased. The minimum size threshold for domestic 'credit claims' was abolished.

The Eurosystem had in effect become a commercial bank, only one without its own credit assessment function. Credit assessment was and is outsourced to third-parties, including ones – banks – with a very high vested interest in attesting to their expertise in credit assessment, but with an inconsistent track record of success.

Republic of Greece bonds were returned to the ECB list: their inclusion in the PEPP on 24 March 2020 opened the gates for them to be included on the ECB list in April 2020.

The further measures announced on 22 April 2020 had the intention of <u>temporarily</u> (our underlining) mitigating 'the effect on counterparties' collateral availability from rating downgrades arising from the economic impact of coronavirus, while continuing ensuring collateral adequacy'.

They do not ensure collateral adequacy: on the contrary, they compromise it.

Whilst the haircut reductions applied to all types of asset, the following measures only applied to marketable assets, and they crystallized the credit ratings – and thus the eligibility – of issuers and issues at their level on 24 March 2020, inoculating issuers and issues from downgrades by rating agencies:

Clause	Worst-case Implications
Marketable assets and issuers of these assets that met the minimum credit quality requirements for collateral eligibility on 7 April 2020 (BBB- for all assets, except asset-backed securities (ABSs)) will continue to be eligible in case of rating downgrades, as long as their rating remains at or above credit quality step 5 (CQS5, equivalent to a rating of BB) on the Eurosystem harmonised rating scale. This ensures that assets and issuers that were investment grade at the time the Governing Council adopted the package of collateral easing measures remain eligible even if their rating falls two notches below the current minimum credit quality requirement of the Eurosystem	• Issuers and issues are downgraded to below Investment Grade but this does not require them to be sold off as Eurosystem assets or replaced as collateral for Eurosystem-extended loans • A meaningful portion of Eurosystem-owned assets and of the collateral for Eurosystem-extended loans starts to rank as Speculative Grade • Eurosystem members have paid out central bank money – supposedly risk-free – in exchange for assets that become Speculative Grade (noting that Eurosystem central bank money is not fully-fungible and risk-free in the first place, as was explained earlier)
Future issuances from grandfathered issuers will also be eligible provided they fulfil all other collateral eligibility criteria	• New issues by issuers that have become Speculative Grade can nevertheless be purchased by the Eurosystem and accepted by it as new collateral • Eurosystem members pay out fresh central bank money – supposedly risk-free – in exchange for assets that are only of Speculative Grade • Speculative Grade assets progressively displace Investment Grade assets as Eurosystem-owned assets and as the collateral for Eurosystem-extended loans • This trend will be accelerated if the largest eligible issuers are also the ones with reduced credit ratings

Clause	Worst-case Implications
Currently eligible covered bond programmes will also be grandfathered, under the same conditions	<ul><li>The degradation, as described above, of the quality of the Eurosystem's assets and collateral</li><li>It is exacerbated in relation to covered bonds because of the opportunity for the usage of IRB methodologies to warrant the credit quality of the underlying assets instead of public ratings (albeit that the rating agencies and their opinions are already flawed as explained below)</li><li>Credit claims – if presented as a debt security – can become eligible for purchase on this basis, or just eligible as collateral if they are not</li></ul>
Currently eligible ABSs to which a rating threshold in the general framework of CQS2 applies (equivalent to a rating of A-) will be grandfathered as long as their rating remains at or above CQS4 (equivalent to a rating of BB+).	<ul><li>The degradation, as described above, of the quality of the Eurosystem's assets and collateral</li><li>Exacerbated by usage of IRB methodologies, possibly even more so than for covered bonds</li><li>Credit claims – if presented as a debt security – can become eligible for purchase on this basis, or are just eligible as collateral if they are not</li></ul>
Assets that fall below the minimum credit quality requirements will be subject to haircuts based on their actual ratings	<ul><li>Haircuts will increase as ratings fall, but in such a way as not to reflect the deterioration in credit quality, because Eurosystem haircuts were already low and have been further reduced on 7 April 2020</li></ul>

These are extraordinary weakenings of the quality of assets owned and held as collateral within Eurosystem operations.

Assets will be treated as central bank money and be exchanged for Eurosystem central bank money when they are clearly some way distant from being that.

Appendix 3 – Degree ownership and control of the Eurozone bond market exercised by the Eurosystem

Methodology

A model was created to show the total ownership and control of the Eurozone bond market being exercised by the Eurosystem, with some allowable mismatch of dates such as that the TARGET2 figures were as of the last business day in October 2020.

The total market size was taken to be the entire nominal value of the securities on the ECB list of eligible collateral. The ECB gave a figure for this of €15.8 trillion, even if the individual issue sizes were not on its list. The ECB list of eligible collateral includes issues in Euro by non-EU supranationals, issues by EU supranationals not in Euro, and issues by non-EU supranationals which are not in Euro: the two last categories had to be backed out of the ECB list as we were looking for the total size of the bond market in Euro, issued by Euro area residents and non-residents.

On the other hand any ineligible bonds issued in Euro by Euro-area residents and non-residents should have been added, had the figures been available. Our opinion was that the total of ineligible issues was not large because (i) ineligible issues would have been of much smaller individual size than those of recognized agencies and local/regional government entities, which in turn were only 3-4% of the volume of issuance by sovereigns;[168] (ii) the criteria for admission to the eligible list were so low that an overwhelming majority of bonds-in-issue were eligible.

Under this reasoning the ECB figure for the total nominal value of Eurosystem eligible collateral could be taken as a reasonable token for the total market size.

Collateral

The ECB gave a figure for the collateral – i.e. for the subset of the eligible collateral – that was then lodged in the Eurosystem as €2.6 trillion, but without a breakdown as to exactly which Eurosystem operations were secured by it. It could not be TLTRO because TLTRO is unsecured.

It is more likely to be the collateral lodged by commercial banks with their respective 'home' NCB to allow them to go into overdraft on their RTGS Accounts in TARGET2 intraday, and possibly to remain in overdraft overnight within the modules that TARGET2 makes available for NCBs to lend to their sponsored banks: the Home Accounts Module (HAM), which sits on the TARGET2 Single Shared Platform, or the Proprietary Home Account facility (PHA), which NCBs maintain themselves within their own IT environment instead of – and not as well as – using HAM to perform the same function.

The loans, whichever module of TARGET2 they are supported on, would count as either a 'marginal lending facility' or a 'standing facility'.

A 'marginal lending facility' is defined by the ECB as 'a standing facility of the Eurosystem which counterparties may use to receive overnight credit from a national central bank at a pre-specified interest rate against eligible assets'.[169]

By contrast a 'standing facility' is defined by the ECB as 'a central bank credit facility available to counterparties at their own initiative. The Eurosystem offers two overnight standing facilities: the marginal lending facility and the deposit facility'.

A 'deposit facility' is defined by the ECB as 'a standing facility of the Eurosystem which counterparties may use to make overnight deposits at a national central bank. Such deposits are remunerated at a pre-specified interest rate'.

---

[168] the relative size of different categories of issue is corroborated by the relative size of the PSPP compared to the CSPP, ABSPP and CBPP3

[169] https://www.ecb.europa.eu/services/glossary/html/glossm.en.html#227 accessed on 6 June 2022

The TARGET2 debts between the NCBs

The 'Breakdown of Eurosystem aggregated balance sheet: December 2021' showed loans by the Eurosystem to Euro-area 'Monetary Financial Institutions' of €5.5 trillion at the time when the TLTRO balance was €2.2 trillion. The definition 'Monetary Financial Institutions' embraces credit institutions as well as members of the Eurosystem.

Both the 'Disaggregated financial statement of the Eurosystem - Assets – December 2021' and the 'Consolidated balance sheet of the Eurosystem as at 31 December 2021' are consistent with the TLTRO figures: they both have a posting 5 of 'Lending to euro area credit institutions related to monetary policy operations denominated in euro' and the balance is €2.2 trillion, marked against Longer-term refinancing operations.

There is therefore an amount of €3.3 trillion of Eurosystem loans to 'Monetary Financial Institutions' that are either:

1. Made between 'Monetary Financial Institutions' that are not credit institutions but are still euro area residents: this can only be between Eurosystem members themselves;
2. Loans by Eurosystem members to euro area credit institutions that are related to payment operations denominated in euro, rather than monetary policy operations.

The second explanation would fit with the interpretation that this is to do with loans by NCBs to commercial banks across modules of TARGET2, but why should they then be off-balance sheet in the posting 5 of the 'Disaggregated financial statement of the Eurosystem - Assets – December 2021' and the 'Consolidated balance sheet of the Eurosystem as at 31 December 2021'? In addition, if there are €3.3 trillion of loans, why is there only €2.6 trillion of collateral? The collateral, even with the narrow Eurosystem haircuts, should be €3.4 trillion at least to secure €3.3 trillion of loans.

The first explanation is more plausible, that the €3.3 trillion is loans between Eurosystem members that appear in the Eurosystem's aggregated balance sheet but neither on its disaggregated nor consolidated one. If this is the case, then the only Eurosystem programme that this can relate to is TARGET2 and the balances between the NCBs participating in it. The implications of this, if it is the case, are explored further below.

Security for TARGET2 debts that are visible in ECB reports

For the purposes of this section it is assumed that the amounts that need to be secured in TARGET2 are:

1. Where the ECB is a borrower – the net-net balance that the ECB shows as due from itself in its monthly reports, and which appears under its name within 'Intra-Eurosystem Liabilities - Claims related to TARGET2 and correspondent accounts (net)' in the 'Disaggregated financial statement of the Eurosystem – Liabilities'; and
2. Where NCBs are borrowers from one another – all the situations where a negative number is shown against an NCB in the ECB's monthly reports, and in the 'Intra-Eurosystem Liabilities - Claims related to TARGET2 and correspondent accounts (net)' in 'Disaggregated financial statement of the Eurosystem – Liabilities'.

These figures are respectively named in the table below as follows:

1. TARGET2 net-net balance; and
2. TARGET2 debtors – balance.

This is an assumption, though. The €1.8 trillion total of these two figures does sit within the €2.6 trillion of eligible collateral that the Eurosystem claims was lodged with it, albeit that they secure unidentified operations and could be lodged with it for the contingency that a bank might need to borrow.

Some or all of the collateral would be unhypothecated if there was no loan which it was securing. The unhypothecated portion remains lodged with the Eurosystem, and controlled by it because its owner is not accessing it and using it for other purposes: it is not in free circulation.

The degree of collateralization of the TARGET2 balances depends upon which account has the liability on it. It does not follow that every liability must be collateralized.

There are 600 nostro and vostro accounts in TARGET2.

A debt from one NCB to another created by a deposit of the creditor with the debtor requires no collateral.

Collateral is needed only when an account a debtor in a creditor's books goes over drawn.

In that case the borrowing NCB must post collateral from the ECB list in favour of the lending NCB, either directly or through the Correspondent Central Banking Model.

If the borrowing NCB pledges collateral that is already within its member state's General government gross debt, there is no addition to the General government gross debt or to the member state's aggregate public sector debt.

If the borrowing NCB pledges collateral that is not within General government gross debt but is within the other types of public sector security: the borrowing does not add to the member state's aggregate public sector debt.

However this is not the case if the borrowing NCB pledges private sector collateral from the ECB list: the borrowing NCB has increased its member state's 'other public sector debt' and its aggregate public sector debt.

There is also the possibility that the borrowing NCB could pledge collateral that is from a different member state, and either of its General government, 'other public sector entity', or not public sector.

There is also the potential for correlation risk: the collateral so pledged consists of public sector securities of issuers in the same member state as the borrowing NCB. The collateral in that case carries the same credit risk as the borrower: the NCB sits towards the top of the pyramid of public sector entities in its member state, whilst the collateral will have been issued by entities at various levels within the same pyramid.

This logically the principle situation in hand where, for example, the Banca d'Italia pledges BTPs[170] to the Bundesbank, and the rarer situation is where the Banca d'Italia pledges Italian asset-backed securities to the Bundesbank, or even German asset-backed securities.[171]

The greater the offset within the TARGET2 balances of a borrower NCB pledging collateral that is public sector securities of its own member state, the greater is the degree of correlation risk. Were the Republic of Italy to pledge BTPs, the correlation risk is 100%: the collateral represents the exact same credit risk as the loan, so the loan must be regarded as uncollateralized.

All one can say about stating that the €1.8 trillion of TARGET2 balances in the ECB reports is that:
- Some may be uncollateralized;
- A portion will be collateralized with bonds issued by General government or 'other public sector' entities and contain correlation risk;
- A portion will be collateralized with bonds that are not subject to correlation risk;
- There could be another €1.5 trillion of debts on top, subject to the same uncertainty.

Once again the onus should be on public authorities to disclose what amounts each NCB has deposited and borrowed and, where it has borrowed, what type of collateral it has offered.

---

[170] BTPs are bonds issued by the Republic of Italy
[171] "Managing Euro Risk", Reynolds et al, pp. 37-9 and pp. 102-4

TARGET2 intraday balances

There is a further twist to this which is that the balances at the end of the processing day may have been lower than intraday, and a higher intraday balance needed to be collateralized. This would raise the possibility that even more eligible collateral needed to be tied up to enable TARGET2 to function intraday than either the original, gross balances at end-of-day and certainly than the netted balances in the ECB's reports. The amount of collateral would escalate if:

1. intraday balances arose that were higher than the original balances at the end of processing day; and/or
2. the original balances at the end of processing day were much higher than the netted version reported by the ECB; and/or
3. the balances were largely formed by overdrafts requiring collateral rather than deposits which did not.

If one or more of these eventualities are arising, and notwithstanding that the cash positions are netted after the end of the processing day, TARGET2 will be tying up a very large amount of eligible collateral. It is highly unlikely that the collateral is released operationally for the brief period of less than an hour for which the netted cash figures are valid before they are reversed so as to begin the following business day.[172] The collateral remains tied up, even if for that brief period it is not hypothecated.

Unfortunately, like the original gross size of the balances, the amount of collateral tied up by TARGET2 is opaque.

---

[172] http://www.lyddonconsulting.com/wp-content/uploads/2020/11/TARGET2-Imbalances-accounting-and-risk-January-2019.pdf

Appendix 4 – examination of the legal and accounting aspects of the TARGET2 netting

Introduction

The TARGET2 netting, occurring at the end of each TARGET2 business day, purports to transfer original balances in between NCBs and between NCBs and the ECB, into a single balance owed by one NCB to the ECB or vice versa. There is one position per NCB and its counterpart is in all cases the ECB. The position could be a positive balance for the NCB (liability of the ECB) or a negative balance for the NCB (asset of the ECB).

The positions are what the ECB states in its month-end report. The net balance derived from adding up all the positive balances (from the NCBs' point of view) and deducting all the negative balances, is the net liability that the ECB records on its annual balance sheet.

The key questions about that procedure are:
- Is it a legal procedure?
- Is it both a legal and an operational procedure?
- If there is an operational procedure, what accounting entries are passed during it?
- Does the operational procedure exactly match the legal procedure?

Any operational procedure should reflect the legal documentation that governs it. That is basic banking. An accounting entry has to have a motivation, be that a payment order, a foreign exchange contract or a standing mandate. Without such a motivation, the bank's internal audit department should not allow the accounting entries to be passed.

The TARGET2 netting fails to meet this test. The legal documentation foresees four steps to bring about the result. However, in the way the Bundesbank explains it, there is only one operational step. This mismatch between documentation and operations would be bring into question the validity and enforceability of the arrangement were it contracted between a bank and a multinational corporate.

ECB wrongly treats the TARGET2-participating NCBs as a Single Counterparty

This raises the issue of whether the documentation achieves the accounting result that the ECB presents, and on one point it definitely does not.

The ECB is granted no right under the legal documentation to net off the €1.3 trillion of assets and liabilities that match in their amounts but not in their counterparties, so as to produce a single liability position on its own balance sheet of €352 billion. The assets and the liabilities are separate debts to and claims on individual NCBs, and the ECB possesses no offset agreement from the NCBs permitting their claims to be netted against their debts. The ECB should carry all the assets and liabilities on its balance sheet at least at the level at which they novated to it from the NCBs.

The NCBs' debts, which appear in the ECB annual report and its monthly TARGET2 reports, form part of 'General government gross debt'. It is uncertain how much if any of the TARGET2 balances are included in 'General government gross debt' and that in itself is an issue that needs to be resolved.

Balances eliminated from ECB reports

The next problem is whether there is yet another layer of assets and liabilities, which do not appear in the ECB's annual report or monthly TARGET2 reports. The original balances on the 600 nostro and vostro accounts at the end of the processing day are not in the public domain. The balances on those accounts are netted before appearing in ECB reports so the gross amounts can only be larger than ones that the ECB shows.

In another sense this is all immaterial since what the ECB is doing is window-dressing. Its reports are produced for only one day per month. They are only for 'overnight' on that day, and 'overnight' lasts under an hour. TARGET2 processing concludes at 18:00 CET, and there are then the End-of-Day Processes from 18:00 until 18:45. The system is closed for 15 minutes, whereupon the Start-of-Day Processes for the following day begin and last until 19:30.

The timing of the single operational step (a 'zero-balancing') that is carried out on the 600 accounts is not in the public domain, but, in commercial banks, zero-balancing is carried out towards the close of the End-of-Day Processes e.g. in TARGTE2's case around 18:30. The TARGET2 zero-balancing is reversed, according to the Bundesbank, to reinstate the balances on the 600 accounts for the next day to be exactly what they were at the end of the previous day. This is known as a 'Cinderella Sweep', and can be expected to be done around 19:05 on the 'Last In, First Out' principle: the zero-balancing is done late in the End-of-Day Processes and is reversed early in the Start-of-Day Processes.

What the ECB reports is valid for at most one hour, and more likely 35 minutes, on just one day per month. We are left to guess what the netted figure would be at the end of other days, or during any business day, and we have no inkling of what the original balances are at any time or on any day.

TARGET2 logical structure and what documentation sits behind the netting

The TARGET2 structure is that twenty-four NCBs of EU Member States participate in it: that is all the nineteen Eurozone NCBs plus the NCBs of Bulgaria, Croatia, Denmark, Poland and Romania. All 24 NCBs and the ECB have signed a single netting agreement to determine how the balances are dealt with at the end of the business day. It is the 'Agreement of 3 August 2018 on the Multilateral Netting of End-of-Day Obligations in TARGET2', and we shall refer to it as the 'netting agreement'.

It confirms, in the way it sets out the end-of-day process in its Article 2.1 and refers to bilateral net obligations between NCBs, that there are bilateral gross obligations between the NCBs, and it states that these are first netted into one single bilateral net obligation between each pair of NCBs. The legal basis for this initial step of the netting is not accomplished by the agreement, but by paragraphs 1 and 2 of Article 6 of the 2012 TARGET Guideline ECB/2012/27.

In using this wording the netting agreement confirms that the basic, operational construction is that the 24 participating NCBs have mutual nostros and vostros - which amount to 552 accounts - and that each NCB has a nostro and a vostro account with the ECB as well - another 48 accounts - making 600 current accounts within the scope of TARGET2 in all.

Bilateral gross obligations arise on these accounts during the business day as part of the processing of TARGET2 payments, or, put in plain English, some of the accounts are in credit and some in overdraft. These bilateral gross positions still exist as balances on accounts as TARGET2 finishes its daily operational processing at 18:00 CET and goes into its end-of day processes. Following the 'successful technical completion of the end-of-day reconciliation procedures effected by the SSP-providing NCBs', the netting process starts (Netting agreement Article 2.1). This phrase confirms that the netting occurs towards the end of the TARGET2 end-of-day processes.

The first stage of the netting – which is governed by paragraphs 1 and 2 of Article 6 of the 2012 TARGET Guideline ECB/2012/27 and not by the netting agreement – claims to merge the two separate balances on the nostro and vostro accounts held between a pair of NCBs – so for example between the Central Bank of Ireland and the Banca d'Italia - into a single bilateral net position.

If, by way of example, the Central Bank of Ireland's vostro account in its books for Banca d'Italia showed a debit balance of €31.6 billion, and its nostro in Banca d'Italia's books showed a debit balance of €11.6 billion, the bilateral net balance would be a liability of the Banca d'Italia to the Central Bank of Ireland of €20.0 billion.

Then Article 2.1.a and 2.1.b of the netting agreement split this single, bilateral balance between each pair of NCBs into two figures that are 'novated' to the ECB. The result of this stage of the netting process – to continue with the above example – would be the creation of a liability of the ECB to the Central Bank of Ireland of €20.0 billion, and of a claim for the ECB on Banca d'Italia of €20.0 billion.

After the completion of that stage, each NCB has 23 separate claims on or liabilities to the ECB deriving from the 'novation' of its bilateral net positions with other NCBs, and it has its two direct positions with the ECB as well: the balances on its nostro and vostro with the ECB. This is the force of Article 2.1 of the netting agreement: each NCB ends up with 25 separate positions with the ECB.

The ECB, under Article 2.2, then totals its 25 separate positions with each NCB, and derives the figures that it releases in its monthly reports and which it puts in its own year-end balance sheet:

- One net liability to or claim on each NCB;
- One total position of ECB towards all NCBs combined (which has always been a liability in the past years, though not at the start of TARGET);
- This total only goes onto the ECB's balance sheet and it is its single largest liability.

ECB treatment and reports

The ECB's accounting treatment is an example of On-Balance Sheet Netting as envisaged under Basel 2.[173] The relevant BCBS publication confirms that the 'novation' technique used within TARGET2 is a valid technique. The ECB issues its monthly report, usually one month in arrears, of its claim on or liability to each NCB, and of its own net claim.[174]

The net claim as of year-end is what the ECB puts on its own balance sheet, along with a note of the total of all claims on and liabilities to the NCBs[175]. As at 31/12/21 these amounts were, as per Note 12.2:

In € millions	2020	2021
Due to euro area NCBs in respect of TARGET2	1,622,395	1,791,771
Due from euro area NCBs in respect of TARGET2	(1,285,567)	(1,457,153)
Matched TARGET2 imbalance	1,285,567	1,457,153
Net deposit as a result of TARGET imbalance	336,828	334,618

Up until June 2018 the ECB only issued quarterly averages of the TARGET2 balances, making it difficult to reconcile their statistics with their published balance sheet.

However, since June 2018 the ECB has published the statistics monthly, and the month upon which we have based this analysis is December 2021, when the ECB-to-NCB balances were as follows, with some rounding differences:

Borrower NCBs	€ billions	Depositor NCBs	€ billions
Belgium	85.7	Germany	1,260.7
Greece	104.2	Estonia	0.6
Spain	512.8	Ireland	84.8
Italy	590.0	France	25.8
Latvia	5.3	Cyprus	12.6
Netherlands	22.5	Lithuania	14.9
Austria	57.4	Luxembourg	326.6
Portugal	79.3	Malta	7.3
		Slovenia	9.2
		Slovakia	23.9
		Finland	25.3
		Non-Eurozone	5.8
	1,457.2		1,791.8

Matching Balance	1,457.2
Mismatch	334.6
Imbalance shown as "ECB"	334.6

---

[173] https://www.bis.org/publ/bcbs37.pdf
[174] http://sdw.ecb.europa.eu/reports.do?node=1000004859
[175] https://www.ecb.europa.eu/press/pr/date/2018/html/ecb.pr180222.en.html

By showing only €334.6 billion on its own balance sheet, the ECB treats its several relationships with the 24 NCBs as if they were with a Single Counterparty.

The Eurosystem plays no role in the TARGET2 construction. The Eurosystem is simply a term used to refer collectively to the ECB and the Eurozone NCBs (but not the Non-Eurozone ones).

As such the wording on page A37 of the ECB 2021 Annual Accounts is incorrect when it expresses the legal position of the TARGET2 balances as follows: 'These positions in the books of the ECB represent the net claim or liability of each NCB against the rest of the European System of Central Banks (ESCB)'.

The version on page A6 is the correct one from the point of view of who the parties are: 'Intra-Eurosystem balances of euro area NCBs vis-à-vis the ECB arising from TARGET2 are presented together on the Balance Sheet of the ECB as a single net asset or liability position'.

This version describes the parties correctly, but the accounts do not correctly reflect the ECB's legal position towards the parties. The netting agreement does not confer on the ECB the right to present its balances towards the separate NCBs as if they were towards a Single Counterparty.

The ECB's accounting, as stated, presents the TARGET2 balances as if they were, and this is incorrect.

It needs to be recognized that the NCBs, and the ECB itself, are separate legal entities, with no common parentage or cross-shareholding, they each have their own statutes, and they are each established under a given applicable law, with various corporate laws from their country of incorporation applying to them.

What commercial banks would need to do to achieve the ECB's accounting treatment

The ECB's accounting is a treatment which, in the corporate banking world of International Cash Management, is customarily only achieved between a Pooling Bank (e.g. Deutsche, Citibank, the specialist Bank Mendes Gans in Amsterdam) and the subsidiaries of a multinational company if several conditions are all met.

These conditions are cumulative:
- The participating subsidiaries all belong to the same ultimate parent company; **and**

- There is a system of accounts for the multinational's subsidiaries established with just one banking location of the Pooling Bank (e.g. London, Amsterdam, Frankfurt); **and**

- Accounts held in the country of incorporation of the subsidiaries (or indeed anywhere else) are zero-balanced cross-border into accounts of the same subsidiaries at the pooling location and in the same currency:

  ➤ These transactions are sometimes referred to as 'left pocket, right pocket' because the two accounts at either end of the zero-balancing belong to the same account-owner, are in the same currency and do not alter the General Ledger line in which the account-owner places the balance – 'Cash in banks' if the balance is in credit, or 'Overdrafts' if it is in debit;

  ➤ The zero-balancing will include the sweeping in of credit balances on the in-country accounts to the Pooling Bank accounts;

  ➤ It will also include the opposite: topping transactions to make payments out of the Pooling Bank and eliminate overdrafts on in-country accounts;

  ➤ Each such arrangement will have a Zero-Balancing Agreement to govern it, an example being an IBOS DZero Cash Agreement, and it will be signed between the Pooling Bank, the in-country Account Servicing Institution for each subsidiary, and the subsidiary itself as slave account owner and master account owner;

➢ If, for some reason, the master account owner is not the subsidiary, then the master account owner will sign the Zero-Balancing Agreement as well; **and**

➢ Both credit and debit balances thus escape the coverage of the General Banking Conditions of the Account Servicing Institution to each subsidiary, whether that be a branch or subsidiary of the Pooling Bank, its local strategic partner, or an unrelated third-party bank; **and**

- The subsidiaries all sign into a single pooling agreement with the Pooling Bank, relating to the treatment solely of the accounts within the scope of the pool at the Pooling Bank; **and**

- In it they submit to the applicable law of and the exclusive jurisdiction of the country of the pooling location; **and**

- The subsidiaries collectively agree in it that the balances on accounts in the pool – whoever nominally owns them – represent a single funds position towards the Pooling Bank.

This last condition is the crux, and the legal techniques for the subsidiaries to collectively agree that the balances on accounts in the pool represent this single funds position and to establish the subsidiaries as a Single Counterparty towards the Pooling Bank fall into two broad categories.

Firstly they are ones allowing the Pooling Bank to seize credit balances in the pool and apply them against overdrafts:
➢ Pledge: the subsidiaries, within the text of the pooling agreement, pledge their credit balances in the pool to the bank as security for the overdrafts in the pool of other subsidiaries[176]

➢ Close-Out: the subsidiaries grant a right in the pooling agreement to the Pooling Bank to zero-balance the system of accounts in its books at its discretion[177]

Secondly they are techniques whereby the subsidiaries make themselves liable for one another's debts:
➢ Cross-guarantee: the subsidiaries issue separate Letters of Guarantee without a maximum amount to the Pooling Bank, guaranteeing the overdrafts of other subsidiaries[178]

➢ Declaration of Joint and Several Liability: the pooling agreement contains a Declaration of Joint and Several Liability under which all subsidiaries make themselves liable for the overdrafts of all other subsidiaries at the Pooling Bank

No such technique is embedded in the TARGET2 netting agreement: the NCBs have separate relationships with the ECB. The ECB's accounting treatment is, as stated, invalid: the ECB should carry each of their Debtor positions towards an NCB as an asset, and each of their Creditor positions towards an NCB as a liability.

Indeed there is a further important point that we will return to later: all the techniques used in the corporate world are in force and effect 24x7, for every moment that the accounts they apply to exist. No distinction is made between the position overnight and during the business day.

In TARGET2, however, the netting and novation explicitly kick in after the end of the TARGET2 processing day, such that they are not in force and effect during TARGET2 processing hours.

Effect of correct accounting treatment of what is in the public domain

As at 31/12/21, the ECB should not have carried just a Creditor position in respect of TARGET2 of €334.6 billion, but an additional to the Creditor position of €1,457.2 billion and a Debtor position of €1,791.2 billion.

---

[176] Used by Bank Mendes Gans as per their specimen pooling agreement
[177] Used by BankBoston in the Optimizer Cash Pooling Schedule
[178] Used by US and UK banks, and the technique recognized by the US and UK banking regulators for On-Balance Sheet Netting of current account balances

This would have added €1,457.2 billion to their Balance Sheet Footing and made their key figures change as follows:

€ billions	Before adjustment	Adjustment	After adjustment
Assets	€680.1	€1,457.2	€2,137.3
Liabilities	€631.2	€1,457.2	€2,088.4
Capital & Reserves (Tier 1 Capital)	€8.4	€0	€8.4
Provisions & Revaluation Accounts (Tier 2 Capital)	€40.5	€0	€40.5
Total loss cushion (Total Capital)	€48.9	€0	€48.9
Capital & Reserves/Assets	1.2%	--	0.04%
Total loss cushion/Assets	7.2%	--	2.3%

NCBs' credit risk in having their balances novated to the ECB

A school of thought has emerged whereby the original bilateral balances between NCBs are unimportant because they are all novated to the ECB. This contention rests first on the acceptance that all balances are validly netted and novated to the ECB, and second on the assumption that the ECB's creditworthiness is superior to that of the NCBs.

We shall explore below the efficacy of the legal means by which the netting and novation are enacted, but from the point of view of credit risk, it matters very much who is responsible for the balances that creditor NCBs hold with the ECB.

The ECB's accounting – by eliminating the matching balance from its assets and liabilities – infers that the ECB is not responsible for the claims of creditor NCBs in their entirety. This cannot be the case if original bilateral claims have been novated to the ECB. The essence of novation of a claim is that the new debtor becomes solely and fully responsible for the claim that the claimant had on the original debtor.

Article 2.2 of the netting agreement releases the NCBs from their claims on one another, and replaces them with claims on or obligations to the ECB.

The claims on the original parties were a mix of:
   a) Unsecured claims on an NCB when a creditor NCB had a credit balance on its nostro at a debtor NCB;
   b) Secured claims when a debtor NCB went overdrawn on its vostro at a creditor NCB.

The nature of the security lodged in case (b) against an overdraft is not in the public domain, but because of the historical 'A' and 'B' lists of collateral that existed when TARGET was established, we can be confident that an NCB mainly lodges public sector securities of its own country i.e. the Austrian NCB lodges securities issued by the Republic of Austria or by other Austrian government entities, as they have a ready supply of them.

Since the NCB's debts are normally the responsibility of its government anyway – and in the case of the Austrian NCB that would be the Republic of Austria – we can say with reasonable certainty that it does not matter whether an NCB pledges security for its TARGET2 debts or not, because any security it does pledge carries 100% correlation with lending to the same NCB without security.

While the NCBs do not have a public credit rating, their government does. The credit risk being taken by any NCB in TARGET2 by either allowing another NCB to go overdrawn on its vostro account – with or without collateral – or by running a credit balance in that other NCB, is the credit risk on the government of the respective member state. This is a claim in 'central bank money', albeit that it is in euro, standing behind which there is not one single sovereign entity.

There are three types of 'central bank money'. In central banking theory all three types are assumed to carry the same credit risk – the risk of the government of the country in question:
   • Note and coin;
   • A credit balance on an account held at an NCB;
   • A security issued by the government which stands behind the NCB.

NCBs have government-to-government credit risk when they have bilateral balances in TARGET2.

The question is whether that is a preferable position to be in compared to having a single net claim on the ECB, when the ECB is:
- Unrated by any of the public credit rating agencies;
- Not explicitly backed by a single national government;
- Thinly capitalised;
- With a loss cushion that is composed for 83% of 'Provisions & Revaluation Accounts' which may have already been earmarked for other purposes and which may turn out not to be available to cushion credit losses in TARGET2.

The ECB's capital consists mainly of Tier 2 capital as it would apply to a commercial bank under Basel 3. Its share capital and Profit&Loss Reserves would count both as Tier 1 capital and as Common Equity Tier 1, but these are the lesser parts of the ECB's capital.

The phrase 'out of the frying pan into the fire' would be appropriate here. The credit risk of the ECB is different from the credit risk of an NCB (which is tantamount to the credit risk of the NCB's government), but it is not necessarily preferable. Indeed, since so many of the ECB's assets are the novated claims on NCBs, it could be argued that the credit risk of the ECB is no more than a blended version of the direct credit risks on the NCBs. The ECB's methodology for dealing with a credit loss it incurred is the clearest token of the ECB's blending role.

How a loss by the ECB on TARGET2 would be dealt with

TARGET2 counts as a 'payment operation' of the ECB that falls within the scope of its profit-and-loss allocation methodology.

This means that a credit loss incurred in the operation of TARGET2 is either incurred directly by the ECB, or is allocated to the ECB in full by whichever NCB incurred it.

In either case the ECB then allocates the loss out to the Eurozone shareholders through their capital accounts. This is the reason why Non-Eurozone NCBs cannot be Debtors in TARGET2 and be the cause of a loss, as they are not part of the loss-absorbing arrangement.

If, for example, a loss of €20 billion was incurred by the Luxembourg NCB in its dealings with the Portuguese NCB, the loss would be deducted from ECB capital accounts of the Eurozone NCBs, according to their Capital Keys. Because Non-Eurozone countries do hold capital in the ECB, the Eurozone NCBs' capital keys do not total 100% of the ECB's capital, but have to be re-based in order to determine their share of the loss in question.

ECB Capital Keys are determined by combining each Member State's share of the EU on two measures:
1. 50% x Member State Gross National Income/EU Gross National Income;
2. 50% x Member State Population/EU Population.

The first problem is that a €20 billion loss would exceed the ECB's Capital & Reserves and require a full replenishment of shareholdings and in cash.

The second problem is that the Portuguese NCB, having been the source of the loss, would be unlikely to be able to come up with its contribution of the replenishment multiplied by its Capital Key. Indeed the background to the problem would be likely to rest with the Republic of Portugal, the NCB's owner, and not with the NCB itself.

This is uncharted territory, but past experience would indicate that the matter would be resolved by one or more of the following means:
- a. The shareholdings are re-based again and without including the Portuguese NCBs, so that every other NCB pays more; or
- b. One or more of the NCBs lends the Portuguese NCB the money with which to make its contribution; or
- c. A separate bail-out is arranged through the entirety of the Eurozone Member States and this includes a loan to the Portuguese NCB with which to pay its contribution to the ECB.

In other words, a loss of that magnitude would not be worked through the agreed methodology.

Instead it would be met, one way or the other, by the same group of Member States whose NCBs are the original lenders to the NCB in question, and the only variables are the percentages of the loss allocated to each NCB and the financial means through which the loss is crystallized (i.e. as a direct loan, as a syndicated bail-out loan, but not by being written off as a loss).

It is a moot point whether an NCB is better off lending directly and bilaterally to another NCB, or by having its claims novated to the ECB. This is not a simple question to answer.

It should be of some comfort to Germany, Finland, and Luxembourg that their very large net claims on the ECB (which may be backed by even larger gross bilateral claims on NCBs) should be diminished through the loss-sharing methodology.

The result would be a share of any loss in line with the normal range of their support for other EU mechanisms, such as the EU Budget, the European Investment Bank, the European Financial Stability Facility and the European Stability Mechanism. Of course it is one thing to have the right to see one's claims diminished through the ECB's mechanism, and another to get the remaining Member States to step up to the plate to take these claims on. Germany and Luxembourg should be particularly concerned in this regard.

It remains a moot point whether the creditor NCBs might be better served by retaining their direct claims on the debtor NCBs, rather than having them intermediated by the ECB.

It can hardly be pretended that the ECB adds a layer of Credit Enhancement to the claims of creditor NCBs, when a claim on a debtor NCB is directly backed by a national government whereas a claim on the ECB is not.

The ECB is not well-capitalised and does not have such a spread of other assets as to be able to repay creditor NCBs in case debtor NCBs fail. The ECB is totally dependent upon the debtor NCBs in TARGET2 repaying in order for the ECB in turn to meet the claims of the creditor NCBs.

Gross claims and debts at the end of the processing day

We now turn to the size of the gross claims and debts at the end of the processing day, before any of the netting has kicked in. The size of the gross bilateral claims on the mutually-held current accounts, before the application of Article 6 of the 2012 TARGET Guideline ECB/2012/27 and the netting agreement, can only be guessed at or extrapolated from other data.

By the nature of netting – and especially a netting that is in multiple stages – the amounts will be larger than the ECB discloses, and in this case they will be unlimited: under Eurosystem rules the Eurozone NCBs must supply each other with credit only limited by the amount of eligible collateral that can be pledged. In commercial banks' pooling arrangement there is usually a ceiling on the amount by which any participating entity can overdraw its account but no such ceiling exists in TARGET2.

Since the government of the NCB is a ready source of collateral in the form of issuance of its government bonds, there is no effective limit on how much collateral can be brought forth and how much credit in TARGET2 taken, other than the overall limits on government deficits that are part of the Stability & Growth Pact.[179]

Validity of the legal procedures of the netting – Article 6 of the TARGET Guideline

We can examine the validity of the netting of NCBs' nostro and vostro balances with one another as per paragraphs 1 and 2 of Article 6 of the 2012 TARGET Guideline ECB/2012/27.

Any pair of NCBs maintain mutual current accounts. A cross-border TARGET payment originates in the high-value payment system of the originating NCB, who credits the account of the destination NCB in its books and sends a payment order to that destination NCB.

---

[179] https://ec.europa.eu/info/business-economy-euro/economic-and-fiscal-policy-coordination/eu-economic-governance-monitoring-prevention-correction/stability-and-growth-pact_en

The destination NCB debits the account of the originating NCB in its books and pays out to the beneficiary's bank in its respective high-value payment system.

This is how the TARGET imbalances arise, and if there were just one payment, the destination NCB would find its account at the originating NCB to be in credit, and the account of the originating NCB in its own books to be in debit.

This situation is an 'Intra-Eurosystem obligation' in the meaning of Article 6, and Article 6 states that any such obligation 'shall automatically be aggregated and form part of a single obligation in relation to each Eurosystem CB'.

Article 6 runs to four short paragraphs totaling 183 words. This seems quite thin for achieving its objective: re-construing the balances on two separate bank accounts held in different NCBs as one single balance.

This is the extent of the documentation for the first step of the netting, whereby each pair of current accounts held by two NCBs with one another are netted into a single obligation of one NCB to the other. The wording infers that this happens continuously during the business day, because there is explicit reference in the second half of Article 6.2 to 'an agreement between the Eurosystem CBs' – which we take to mean the netting agreement.

Article 6.2 states that this agreement applies to the balances 'at the end of the business day'. In making that statement Article 6.2 both points out that the agreement does not apply during the business day and distinguishes that agreement with itself: by inference Article 6.2 does apply during the business day and indeed all the time.

This continuous netting between the accounts that NCBs have with one another has no operational result: the balances on the accounts fluctuate with the processing of payments over them during the business day, and there is no zero-balancing of the pairs of accounts at the end of the business day.

Using again our example where the Central Bank of Ireland's vostro account in its books for Banca d'Italia showed a debit balance of €31.6 billion, and their nostro in Banca d'Italia's books showed a debit balance of €11.6 billion, there is no payment between these two accounts of €11.6 billion such that the nostro in Banca d'Italia's books is brought to zero, and the vostro in the Central Bank of Ireland's books is brought to €20.0 billion debit:

- By a discreet payment using a SWIFT MT200 or MT202 sent either over the SWIFT network or across the TARGET2 Single Shared Platform ('SSP'), the technical platform run by the Bundesbank, Banca d'Italia and Banque de France, on which TARGET2 runs and on which all the accounts are housed;
- By an automated zero-balancing function such as is possible within the SSP.

Zero-balancing can be performed on the SSP, but is not used to this end.

As a result and both intraday and at the end of the processing day, these accounts have balances on them, which are construed thanks to Article 6 as a single bilateral net obligation, and which are referred to in para 1(a) of the netting agreement as 'each original net obligation'. By using these words it is acknowledged that original gross obligations exist between the NCBs, as credit and debit balances on their mutually-held accounts.

The wording of Article 6 confirms that these are real claims and obligations, and on real accounts.

Article 6 and 'cherry-picking'

In the corporate world Article 6 would not be sufficient to achieve the effect of continuously netting balances on accounts that are held with different banks. The acid test would be whether the liquidator of one of the banks would be able, under the governing law and Terms&Conditions ('Ts&Cs') applying to the accounts, to unpick (sometimes referred to as 'cherry-pick') the arrangement.

A typical example of 'cherry-picking' would be where the liquidator would try to seize credit balances and put them into the general pool of funds available to meet creditor claims, and he/she would construe debit balances as claims on the pool by ordinary, unsecured creditors.

In other words the liquidator would attempt to strike down any claim by a creditor to have a priority claim over a credit balance.

In our example it would clearly be in the interests of the liquidator of the Central Bank of Ireland (for the benefit of other creditors) to lay claim to the entire asset – the loan of €31.6 billion to Banca d'Italia – and make the Banca d'Italia service it in line with its terms, whilst recording the loan made by Banca d'Italia to the Central Bank of Ireland of €11.6 billion as an ordinary creditor claim.

The liquidator would then try to realize the asset in its entirety, pay the proceeds into the general pool, and then propose to pay the Banca d'Italia a liquidation premium (or 'pence in the pound') in accordance with the proceeds of all the assets, first meeting the priority claims, and then using what is left over to divide between the ordinary, unsecured creditors.

Banca d'Italia's position would be that Article 6 conferred on it a priority status, and that it had the right to set-off its loan to the Central Bank of Ireland in its books against the Central Bank of Ireland's loan to Banca d'Italia.

This would set Irish bankruptcy law against Article 6, an issue that would have been addressed in the corporate banking world through legal advice before the arrangement had been put in place.

Place of establishment of the pooling accounts to defend against 'cherry-picking'

In the construction of TARGET2 one NCB acts as Account Servicing Institution ('ASI') for the other, and vice versa. Whilst all the accounts reside technically on the SSP, TARGET2 is decentralized from a logical and therefore also from a legal point of view. The nostro account of the Bundesbank with the Bank of Greece resides in the Bank of Greece's books, it is domiciled in Greece, and is subject to the Bank of Greece's Terms and Conditions.

In the corporate banking world it is customary to move all balances into a Pooling Bank, in one location and subject to a single set of Ts&Cs, with one governing law. The Pooling agreement involves the Pooling Bank having the right of set-off between credit and debit balances, and frustrating any attempt by a liquidator of one of the participating companies to cherry-pick credit balances in the pool while there are debit balances outstanding.

Establishing the agreement, the powers of each participating company to sign it, the absence of local legal powers to 'cherry-pick it' and so on, is a major undertaking, and the efficacy of the outcome needs to be confirmed with positive legal opinions 'from every relevant jurisdiction' and which are regularly refreshed. An objective of Pooling in the corporate world is normally to establish that the location of the Pooling is the only relevant jurisdiction, because all the accounts in the Pool are held there. This is not the case in TARGET2 because the accounts are distributed around 24 countries.

For both this reason, and because this stage of the netting has no operational consequence, it is hard to believe that Article 6 is watertight in causing the continuous netting of the mutually-held accounts, and that NCBs can be completely confident that their risk towards one another is one position, as opposed to two separate positions, which will each be treated independently if one of the NCBs goes into liquidation.

Validity of the legal procedures of the netting – alteration of NCBs' bilateral balances into claims on or debts to the ECB

The next step is to examine the validity of the novation of NCBs' single, netted bilateral balance with one another into two claims: one of an NCB on the ECB, and an equal one of the ECB on an NCB, under the netting agreement.

Where we state above that the first stage of the netting has no operational consequence, it is because the accounts held bilaterally by the NCBs are all zero-balanced directly into accounts of the ECB as part of the netting and novation at the end of the business day.

As explained by the Bundesbank, this zero-balancing causes the balances of all the vostro accounts held by 23 NCBs in the books of the 24th to be zero-balanced into the vostro of the ECB at the 24th NCB. After that has been done, 576 of the 600 original balances are now combined onto the 24 vostros of the ECB at NCBs, and the remaining 24 balances sit on the 24 vostros of NCBs at the ECB.

That may put the balances into the ECB but it does not follow the legal construct exactly. If it did, the balances on the nostro and vostro held between each pair of NCBs would firstly be combined into a single figure per relationship, via either a funds transfer using SWIFT MT202, or by a zero-balancing across the SSP. This would result in balances existing on 276 – half – of the 552 nostros and vostros held between NCBs. That would achieve the objective of Article 6.

Then, for each of those balances, there would need to be bookkeeping entries that released the claims between the NCBs on these accounts and caused them to reappear as claims on or debts to the ECB, on the vostro that each NCB held at the ECB. The ECB should also zero-balance its 24 vostros at the NCBs and pass equal-and-opposite entries to the NCBs' vostros in the ECB's books. The results would be:
1. To have split the NCB-NCB positions into series of NCB-ECB and ECB-NCB positions;
2. To have made those appear on the accounts that the NCBs hold with the ECB, putting 24 debit or credit entries over each one;
3. Automatically to have combined the sum of those entries with whatever balance was already on the respective NCB's vostro at the ECB; and
4. To have combined the balances on each NCB's vostro at the ECB with the balance on the ECB's vostro in that NCB's books, so as to crystallize a single position of each NCB vis a vis the ECB at the end of each day.

This is the chain of entries which would cause the legal and operational procedures to be identical, but the operational procedure is subject to a shortcut.

Operational steps (if they even occur) shortcut the legal steps

What actually happens is there is just one operational step for four legal steps:
1. The netting of bilateral gross balances pursuant to Article 6;
2. The novation of bilateral net balances to the ECB, pursuant to the netting agreement;
3. The splitting of bilateral net balances into individual ECB-to-NCB balances, pursuant to the netting agreement;
4. The aggregation by the ECB of all ECB-to-NCB balances into a single claim or obligation, pursuant to the netting agreement.

This is not a good principle to work on; it is better that there be an operational consequence to manifest the taking of each legal step. Otherwise a court-of-law has greater leeway, when looking first at what happened operationally, to 'look through' the legal arrangement that a party contends sat behind it, and impose their own, different legal construction.

In a situation where an NCB had an original claim on the Bundesbank, for example an overdraft balance on the Bundesbank's account at that NCB, and this had been novated to the ECB, the member state government owning that NCB might see it as being in their interests to try to have the netting agreement struck down in their own courts, so that their NCB could maintain its claim on the Bundesbank, rather than the NCB having a claim on the less-creditworthy ECB.

The inducement to do this would be all the larger if the Bundesbank owed that NCB an amount greater than that same NCB's netted claim on the ECB.

One cannot predict what the circumstances might be in which the TARGET2 balances become problematical, who would owe how much to whom at the time, what legal rights the creditor might then lay claim to, and how they might proceed so as to press their claim.

What one can say is that the mismatch between the operational manifestation of the netting and its supposed legal meaning opens up an area of risk that is impossible to quantify without extensive and costly due diligence – which is what commercial banks are obliged to undertake in order to participate in International Cash Management.

Using the 'novation' technique for pooling bank account balances

One can go further and state that the usage of the technique of novation for the netting of balances on current accounts is an oddity, as compared with its common usage in the world of derivatives. In that business it has become obligatory for a contract between two financial institutions to be split in two and settled though a Central Counterparty, or 'CCP'.

Article 2.1.a of the netting agreement splits the single, bilateral cash balance between NCBs into two figures that are 'novated' to the ECB. The ECB becomes the Central Counterparty for the bilateral balance.

This is the legal construct used for the clearing and settlement of derivatives: if Goldman Sachs and Credit Suisse enter into a derivatives contract over-the-counter, their bilateral contract is split into two separate contracts with the Central Counterparty for the purposes of reducing the risk between contract and settlement.

While this may be a workable technique to use when there is a known quantity – a discreet contract – and two counterparties to it, it is less plausible to use the technique in connection with balances on bank accounts where the accounts themselves still exist and where the balances are returned to the accounts the following day.

Conflict of applicable law

The issue of applicable law is relevant here too. A single derivatives contract will have a single agreed applicable law. The bank accounts underlying the TARGET2 netting have the applicable law of the ASI they are held with. By extension the balances on those accounts are subject to the same applicable law as the accounts themselves.

If it were accepted that the zero-balancing - that occurs but which is not mentioned in the netting agreement – moved the balances onto accounts held at the ECB and within the purview of the netting agreement, then the balances would become subject to German law, as the netting agreement Article 4 specifies: the governing law is the local law of the seat of the ECB from time to time.

The problem is once again the mismatch between the operational situation and the legal one: NCBs zero-balance the accounts they run for other NCBs into the account they run for the ECB in their own books, and not into the account they hold at the ECB in its books.

The account that Banca d'Italia runs for the ECB is subject to Italian law, and this is the master account under the zero-balancing in which the Banca d'Italia clears the 23 accounts of the other NCBs in its books to the ECB's account.

If it cleared them to its nostro at the ECB – in the ECB's books – then the amount would be sitting on an account subject to the same applicable law as the netting agreement.

While we have Article 6 and the netting agreement as governing documents for the arrangement, there is no zero-balancing agreement. In the corporate world there would have to be a separate zero-balancing agreement for every set of relationships under which zero-balancing was being carried out.

The TARGET2 zero-balancing is undertaken in the context of the netting agreement, but is not mentioned specifically in it. This is another area where the TARGET2 arrangement could be challenged.

Validity of the legal procedures of the netting – determination of a single position between each NCB and the ECB

As regards the legal validity of the merging by the ECB of its 24 novated claims or liabilities vis a vis each NCB, with the balances on its nostro and vostro with the same NCB, to reach a single claim on or liability to each NCB, under the netting agreement, this is somewhat simpler.

Since the NCBs and the ECBs are all parties to the netting agreement (and not just the NCBs as Article 6.2 states), the merging of the separate positions of each NCB with the ECB into one ECB-to-NCB position is less problematical, assuming the preceding stages have been successfully completed.

Our view is that this step is not vulnerable in itself: the legal vulnerabilities are in the two preceding stages, in the fact that the netting agreement is only in force overnight, and in the operational manifestation not mirroring the legal one.

Validity of the legal procedures of the netting – limitation of validity of the netting agreement to end-of-day

Finally we have the significance of the limitation of the netting agreement to balances at the close of the business day. While Article 6 infers that the bilateral gross balances between NCBs are continuously netted during the business day, there is no operational manifestation of that, and the efficacy of Article 6 is questionable for that reason.

This means it is possible that the NCBs are exposed to one another separately for the credit balances and debit balances they run with one another intraday. What is certain is that the netting agreement only functions for the 'overnight' period, and not intraday. If one believes in the efficacy of Article 6, the NCBs' intraday exposure to one another is limited to the 'single obligation' they have with one another. This is the obligation that is novated to the ECB pursuant to the netting agreement which, as stated, only impacts the situation overnight.

As explained in our initial paper of 2017, 'overnight' in TARGET2 for this purpose is at most 90 minutes out of 24 hours, and could be as short as 20 minutes. Under that perspective the entire netting and novation can be regarded as a window-dressing for a short period in order to obfuscate the risks being run intraday.

While TARGET2 supposedly is open on D from 07:00 until 18:00, in fact the start-of-day procedures for D begin at 19:00 the previous evening on D-1, with a window for initial Liquidity Provision from 19:00 to 19:30 on D-1.

There are then two Nighttime Settlement Procedures, from 19:30 on D-1 until 07:00 on D, when the normal day's business begins. The normal day finishes at 18:00, and there are then the End-of-Day Processes from 18:00 until 18:45.

The TARGET Information Guide lays out the End-of-Day Processes as follows (pages 61 – 62):
'Between 18:00 and 18:15, the following events will take place:
- transfer back of liquidity from sub-accounts to main accounts (emergency procedure);
- rejection of pending payments at 18:00 (immediately after the running of algorithm 3);
- automatic emergency procedure if a group of accounts manager was not able to balance the accounts in time and there is one uncovered overdraft on one account belonging to a group of accounts
- automatic transfer of liquidity to the PHA (optional);
- use of the standing facilities until 18:15 (18:30 on the last day of the minimum reserve period);
- transfer of liquidity to the SF accounts, booking of overnight credit to SF accounts, automatic transfer of overnight credit from the SF to the RTGS account in case of use of intraday credit at the end of the day (optional);
- automatic transfer of liquidity to the HAM account (optional);
- levelling out of group of accounts (emergency procedure);
- sending of balance information to the RM module; and
- sending of account statements MT940/950 (optional).

After 18:30 the internal central bank accounting takes place.'

Internal central bank accounting lasts until 18:45, TARGET2's final closure point.

The many 'events' are a testimony to the complexity of TARGET2, with its decentralized logical structure and several modules such as PM (Payments Module), PHA (Proprietary Home Account), SF (Standing Facilities), HAM (Home Accounts Module), and RM module (Relationship Management Module).

There is no specific 'event' listed that is verbatim what is stated in Article 2.1 of the netting agreement about when the netting and novation take place ('following the successful technical completion of the end-of-day reconciliation procedures effected by the SSP-providing NCBs').

When Zero-Balancing normally occurs and when it is reversed

In commercial banks Zero-Balancing is applied after the reconciliation of the customer accounting system, when the end-of-day customer account balances are known.

This could be coincident with the later 'events' in the list, meaning that the zero-balancing would be then occurring around 18:15. It could, however, fall under the heading of 'internal central bank accounting' occurring between 18:30 and 18:45, after the balances of credit institutions in the different TARGET2 modules had been finalized.

In the extreme case the zero-balancing would be happening at 18:45 CET; in the other case just before 18:15 CET. The system is only fully closed for 15 minutes.

As regards the start-of-day processes, the window at start-of-day for Liquidity Provision basically reverses the operations undertaken at end-of-day (page 56-57 of the TARGET Information Guide):
'Between 19:00 and 19:30 liquidity is provided for the day-time settlement and night-time settlement if applicable. The following liquidity movements can take place:
- from the SF to the PM;
- from the SF to the HAM;
- from the HAM to the PM; or
- from the PHA to the PM (optional).
These 30 minutes could also be used to update credit lines or to settle repos before opening.'

The zero-balancing into the ECB's vostros undertaken at the end of the previous day is reversed at the start of the following day.

It is in the nature of such systems that the last zero-balancing undertaken on D is the first one reversed on D+1, as frequently there is more than one zero-balancing cycle, and they need to be reversed in order: Last In, First Out, in a reverse cascade.

Since the 'liquidity movements' listed above in shorthand ('SF to HAM' and so on) may each affect the NCBs' positions with one another, it is logical to conclude that the zero-balancing we are discussing was the very last one executed on D and the very first one to be reversed on D+1.

This means the reversal is happening at 19:05 CET at the latest.

How the TARGET2 netting would be considered in the Cash Management world

Considering the nature of the End-of-Day and Start-of-Day processes from a Cash Management perspective, the end-of-day zero-balancing operations put through at either 18:15 or 18:45 are reversed as the first transactions of the following day. This would be known in the Cash Management world as a Cinderella Zero-Balancing System.

The initial set of transactions is a classic zero-balancing: a set of fully automated and computer-programmed operations to reduce/increase the balances on a slave accounts to zero and to credit that reduction or debit that increase in full to a master account as the final transaction on D.

The 'Cinderella' function is the reversal of all the zero-balancing transactions in full as the opening actions of D+1. Any lending or borrowing relationships that exist during the business day are reconfigured for the purposes of end-of-day accounting, and instantly reconfigured back to what they were afterwards.

We concluded that the initial set of transactions are reversed at 19:05. It could be that the initial transactions are undertaken as late as 18:45: that would not alter the point at which they are reversed.

The 'overnight' situation as crystallized by the netting agreement lasts for a maximum of 50 minutes and a minimum of 20 minutes.

For the remainder of the day the NCBs have at best the single net bilateral obligation at risk between one another, and at worst the unconnected balances on their vostro and nostro accounts, whatever they are.

Conclusions on the validity of the legal procedures of the netting

The ECB monthly reports give no hint as to the size of the gross, bilateral, intraday balances.

Intraday there is no physical manifestation of netting, and the balances on these accounts represent claims and liabilities from one NCB to another, and between an NCB and the ECB. We need to remind ourselves that these are real claims and liabilities, as the netting agreement confirms: they are not 'accounting balances', or 'mirror'/'reference'/'shadow'   accounts.

The intraday exposures could be within any possible range. They do not seem to be monitored and there are no limits on them. Between the pairs of NCBs the balances may be netted if one believes in the efficacy of Article 6.

But there is no intraday equivalent of the netting and novation applied overnight by the netting agreement.

This is because of the Article of Faith, inherent to the TARGET2 system, that central bank money in euro is homogenous and it does not matter which NCB it is held in.

If one takes the contrary view, credit balances of one NCB with another are a credit risk on the second NCB and with no further collateral beyond the second NCB's good name. Debit balances appear to be secured, but on government bonds of the respective borrowing NCB's owner, which is not real collateral at all, as the credit risk on the collateral is 100% correlated with the credit risk on the borrower.

The credit risk would only be measured if NCBs undertook a Credit Analysis on one another, and would only be limited if NCBs imposed a credit limit (expressed as a money limit and not as a percentage of eligible collateral pledged) both on their Credit balances held on nostro accounts with other NCBs, and on the Overdraft balances on the vostro accounts that other NCBs held with them.

The quantum of credit risk being taken is unreported and therefore not publicly known. It is at least the aggregate of an NCB's single net claims on other NCBs, without an offset for its single net obligations to others.

But it could be as much as the aggregate of all of an NCB's credit balances held with other NCBs and overdraft balances incurred by other NCBs in its own books, without any offset, depending on whether one believes in the efficacy of Article 6.

This quantum can only be larger than the netted figures that the ECB reports, and even those figures are at end-of-day over month-end. What the figures are at end-of-day during the month, and intraday, can only be guessed at.

How the single figure shown by the ECB for one NCB can mask larger positions behind

The end-of-day position of the Central Bank of Ireland as at 31/12/21, to continue with our example, could have been composed of the following claims and liabilities after the application of Article 6 but before the transference onto the ECB:

Claims in € billion

NCB	Country	Amount
EestiPank	Estonia	2.7
Bank of Greece	Greece	7.8
Banque de France	France	23.1
Banca d'Italia	Italy	20.0
Central Bank of Cyprus	Cyprus	3.9
Latvijas Banka	Latvia	2.4
Lietuvosbankas	Lithuania	1.3
Banquecentrale du Luxembourg	Luxembourg	18.1
Central Bank of Malta	Malta	6.2
Den Nederlandsche Bank	Netherlands	8.3
Banco de Portugal	Portugal	18.2
Banka Slovenije	Slovenia	2.2
Národnábanka Slovenska	Slovakia	1.7
Total claims		115.9

Liabilities in € billion

NCB	Country	Amount
Nationale Bank van België	Belgium	6.2
Deutsche Bundesbank	Germany	5.4
Banco de España	Spain	2.8
Oesterreichische Nationalbank	Austria	1.7
Suomen Pankki	Finland	3.3
Българсканароднабанка	Bulgaria	0.2
Danmarks Nationalbank	Denmark	3.1
Hravatska norodna banka	Croatia	2.8
Narodowy Bank Polski	Poland	3.2
Banca Naţională a României	Romania	0.7
ECB	--	1.7
Total liabilities		31.1

This would then have been followed by the netting and transference to the ECB:

Netting in € billion

NCB	Amount
Total claims	115.9
Total liabilities	31.1
Net position – a claim	84.8

€84.8 billion was indeed the net claim of the Central Bank of Ireland as at 31/12/21, as shown in the ECB's reports – but we can see here that it will be composed of higher 'gross' claims, offset by a certain amount of liabilities.

Even the figures shown here have already been netted once, as we saw with the example of the Central Bank of Ireland's relationship with Banca d'Italia. The €20.0 billion net claim is derived in our example from a gross claim of €31.6 billion offset against a liability of €11.6 billion.

The ECB's figures show none of:
- Bilateral gross positions between NCBs at end-of-day;
- Bilateral net positions between NCBs at end-of-day;
- NCB positions with the ECB at end-of-day, either gross or net.

In addition, the netting is only the overnight treatment.

Credit   *risk*   *considerations*

There is a credit risk on the intraday balances, and a lack of controls, based on the delusion that the quantum of risk does not matter.

TARGET2 rests on an Article of Faith that it transmits central bank money only, and central bank money is free of credit risk. If one believes this, it does not matter which TARGET2 participant one holds one's money with, and it is safe to hold an unlimited amount. If one believes in the Article, there is no need for credit limits on other participants, no need for a Credit Analysis, and no need for extra due diligence or possibly for any due diligence at all.

The participants in TARGET2 do not have independent credit ratings and the ratings of their owners – the member states themselves – act as a surrogate, because the government bonds of a member state are another form of central bank money, supposedly free of credit risk. A comparison of public credit ratings is sufficient to dispel the illusion contained in the Article of Faith.

The Article of Faith demands a belief that a holding of Italian government bonds – rated Baa3 by Moody's – carries the same credit risk as a holding of Netherlands government bonds – rated Aaa by Moody's.

The netting agreement itself

The netting agreement itself is thin to the point of emaciation.

Just as Article 6 of the 2012 TARGET Guideline ECB/2012/27 runs to only four paragraphs totaling 183 words, so the netting agreement is very short for a document dealing with such an important matter and such large amounts of money.

It even calls itself the wrong thing: Multilateral Netting is a system for handling inter-company invoices of multinationals e.g. sales between different subsidiaries of Ford Motor. The ultimate result of such a system must be 0 - because every receivable of one subsidiary is a payable of another.

The initial impression made by the document - 34 pages long – is of substance but this impression is soon dispelled as only three of the pages have any legal text:

Page number	Content
1	Title page
2-6	Lists of participants
7	Recitals
8-9	Agreement substance
10-34	One signature page each per participant

The substance is just two pages - pages 8 and 9.

The agreement is meant to achieve complicated matters between parties from different countries who are unrelated to one another and who are, presumably, subject to applicable laws in their own countries.

In the corporate banking world such an agreement would need to cover off numerous legal and regulatory issues, ensuring – inter alia – that:
- The parties had the legal powers to enter into such an agreement;
- That each party had authorized the entering into of the agreement in accordance with its own statutes;
- That there were no laws in their own country that could render their participation null and void, or confer on a third-party (such as a liquidator) the right to 'cherry-pick' the agreement.

Parties would normally be asked to present various documents as pre-conditions to the agreement coming into full force and effect such as:
- Copy of their own statutes demonstrating how the party makes a decision such as to sign the agreement;
- Copy of Board Minutes or of whatever body is needed to take the decision to sign the agreement, nominating the persons who are to sign, or an extract from the Trade Register listing the people and their powers to bind the company;
- Legal opinion positively confirming the validity of the pre-condition documents and the lack of blockers deriving from legal and regulatory issues.

None of this has been required and one can only speculate as to why not:
- The NCBs and the ECB are not subject to law in the same way in which every other natural and non-natural legal person in the EU is subject to law;
- The parties entered into the agreement in the knowledge that the agreement will never be tested, that a breach of the agreement will be handled at the time, by separate negotiation between the parties, and without the participation of any representatives of the public;
- The individuals who drafted, reviewed and signed the agreement have no knowledge of the way such services as Zero-Balancing and Notional Pooling are documented in the corporate banking world, nor of the legal and regulatory issues these services bring up.

As it is, the agreement is an extremely thin and unconvincing document upon which to anchor the treatment of such enormous amounts of money.

How to determine the invisible portion of the TARGET2 balances

The TARGET2 imbalances as documented by the ECB are very large, but even these figures are the result of two preceding stages of netting:
1. To net the balances of the two accounts that NCBs hold bilaterally;
2. To net the 25 positions that each NCB holds with the ECB as a result of the novation process with one another and with the balances on the nostro/vostro accounts each NCB has directly with the ECB.

The original unnetted figures at both of these preceding stages are unreported. However, we can offer one suggestion for what they are, based on the earlier discussion of reconciling the different balance sheets that the Eurosystem issues.

We noted that the 'Breakdown of Eurosystem aggregated balance sheet: December 2021' showed loans by the Eurosystem to Euro-area 'Monetary Financial Institutions' of €5.5 trillion at the time when the TLTRO balance was €2.2 trillion. The definition 'Monetary Financial Institutions' embraces credit institutions as well as members of the Eurosystem.

We noted that both the 'Disaggregated financial statement of the Eurosystem - Assets – December 2021' and the 'Consolidated balance sheet of the Eurosystem as at 31 December 2021' were consistent with the TLTRO figures: they both had a posting 5 of 'Lending to euro area credit institutions related to monetary policy operations denominated in euro' and the balance is €2.2 trillion, marked against Longer-term refinancing operations.

There was therefore an amount of €3.3 trillion of Eurosystem loans to 'Monetary Financial Institutions' that were either:

1. Made between 'Monetary Financial Institutions' that are not credit institutions but are still euro area residents: this can only be between Eurosystem members themselves;
2. Loans by Eurosystem members to euro area credit institutions that are related to payment operations denominated in euro, rather than monetary policy operations.

The gross TARGET2 positions should sit on an aggregated balance sheet, before the disaggregated and consolidated versions eliminate the offsets: the most telling offset is that loans between Euro-area 'Monetary Financial Institutions' reduce by €3.3 trillion between 'aggregated' and 'consolidated', inferring that the loans are between parties within the scope of consolidation: Eurosystem members.

This would infer that the full TARGET2 balances were:

In € billions	Amount
Loans between Euro-area 'Monetary Financial Institutions'	€5,527
Less loans to credit institutions - MRO/TLTRO	(€2,202)
Produces loans between Eurosystem members	€3,325
TARGET2 creditor NCBs	€1,792
TARGET2 debtor NCBs	€1,457
ECB balance	€335
Gross balances eliminated by netting (3,325 – 1,792)	€1,533

In other words a further €1.5 trillion of debts of one Eurosystem member to another are submerged.

The problem with this reading is that the NCBs vostro accounts with one another are supposed to have been zero-balanced into the vostro account of the ECB, and this should have happened during the end-of-day processes, only after which the Eurosystem and ECB balance sheets are determined. The result – at each of the 24 NCBs, 23 vostros of the other NCBs each with a zero balance and the ECB vostro holding its own balance combined with those of the 23 NCBs – should sit on the Eurosystem 'aggregated' balance sheet and be eliminated in the 'consolidated' one, because the business is between two Eurosystem members.

The 23 vostros being zero-balanced by each NCB into the ECB's vostro would logically have held some credit and some debit balances. Combining them on the ECB's vostro would have the effect of netting. If the €1.5 trillion is the balances of the ECB's vostros at the 24 NCBs after this process, the original balances would have been even higher.

Conclusions on TARGET2

The TARGET2 balances are a large and impenetrable subject, lacking transparency.

The usage of a single operational procedure – a zero-balancing of NCBs' accounts with one another into an ECB account – to cover all of the legal construct of Article 6 and the phases in the netting agreement introduces a mismatch which would be highly dangerous if applied in a corporate banking environment.

The documentational backing for the legal procedure is weak compared to what would be needed in the corporate banking world to achieve the same outcome, and actually the ECB does not have the correct documentation to account for the TARGET2 balances as it does, as if the NCBs were a Single Counterparty. The ECB should at least put all its Claims on NCBs as Assets on its balance sheet, and all its Obligations to NCBs as Liabilities. This would inflate the ECB's balance sheet by over €1.5 trillion.

The ECB's presentation of the figures is valid for 50 minutes per business day at most, given that the zero-balancing occurs in the TARGET2 end-of-day either at 18:15 or 18:45 CET, and it is reversed using the Cinderella function at around 19:05 CET when the books are opened for the following business day.

For the remaining 23+ hours of the business day, the NCBs have direct risk on one another, either without any netting if one believes that Article 6 fails to achieve it, or in the amount of their single, net bilateral obligation, whatever that is.

The credit risk is either a direct, unsecured risk on the NCB by virtue of maintaining a credit balance on a nostro account with it, or a secured risk through granting an overdraft to the NCB on its vostro account.

The security is likely to be securities issued by a public sector entity in the same country as the NCB, which represents 100% correlated security: since the debt of the NCB is guaranteed by the government of its Member State, securities issued by that same Member State or its agencies carries the same credit risk.

The quantum of credit risk being taken is unknown. It is certainly higher than what is shown in the ECB's accounts and monthly reports. If the correct figure is that €1.5 trillion difference between the Eurosystem 'aggregated' and 'consolidated' balance sheets, then that adds a further €1.5 trillion to the ECB's balance sheet. There is the possibility that this €1.5 trillion is itself a reduction of the gross balances, if this €1.5 trillion refers to the balances on the ECB's vostros after the NCBs' vostros have been zero-balanced into it.

It is a further important question whether it is a better result, from the credit risk point of view, for the NCBs to have overnight risk on the ECB than on one another. They have intraday risk on one another, and converting that to ECB risk for at most an hour is not necessarily a superior outcome. The ECB is unrated and thinly capitalised, and can only pay back the TARGET2 Obligations if it receives payment on the TARGET2 Assets.

The only benefit of the novation and netting to major TARGET2 creditors is that the ECB loss-sharing mechanism would serve to reduce their share of any loss from the amount that is owed to them by the NCBs direct, to a portion of the loss determined through their ECB capital key. The comfort derived from this may prove to be illusory as it is contingent upon other NCBs (and member states) being willing to accept a larger share of the loss than their direct exposure would indicate, and the loss share will naturally rise as the member state/NCB causing the loss will not be able to pay its share.

The situation is clouded further by the avenues open to member states and NCBs to 'cherry-pick' the arrangement in the ways that are open in the corporate banking world. Given that the underlying bank accounts are distributed around the NCBs and subject to their local laws, the avenues available for 'cherry-picking' are wider than is the case in a corporate banking set-up, which is customarily established in a single location and subject to a single governing law.

How matters would play out in practice if there were a major problem is a matter of conjecture. It cannot be held as certain that the incident would be handled in line with what is written in the agreements.

Indeed, given the questionable efficacy, the possibility of challenge and the likely need for swift remedial action, it is more likely that the TARGET2 imbalances will be formally converted into what they are latently: government-to-government loans from the solvent countries to a universe of ones requiring ongoing financing and in large amounts, concentrating on Italy, Spain, Portugal and Greece.

Appendix 5 – Recognised Agencies

Country	Agencies
Belgium	• Agence de Promotion Immobilière du Brabant wallon (APIBW) • Fonds Du Logement Des Familles Nombreuses De Wallonie Scrl (FLW) • Fonds régional bruxellois de refinancement des trésoreries communales (FRTC) • Infrabel SA • Société wallonne du crédit social SA (SWCS) • Société Wallonne du Logement SA (SWL)
Bulgaria	• None
Czech Rep	• None
Denmark	• None
Germany	• Bayerischen Landesbodenkreditanstalt (BayernLabo) Bremer Aufbau-Bank • Hamburgische Investitions- und Förderbank (IFB Hamburg) • Investitions und Strukturbank Rheinland-Pfalz • Investitionsbank Berlin (IBB) • Investitionsbank des Landes Brandenburg (ILB) • Investitionsbank Schleswig-Holstein (IB.SH) • Investitionsbank Sachsen-Anhalt • Kreditanstalt für Wiederaufbau (KfW) • Landesförderinstitut Mecklenburg-Vorpommern • Landeskreditbank Baden-Württemberg - Förderbank (L-Bank) • Landwirtschaftliche Rentenbank LfA • Förderbank Bayern • NBank • NRW.BANK • Saarländische Investitions-kreditbank AG • Sächsische Aufbaubank – Förderbank (SAB) • Thüringer Aufbaubank • Wirtschafts- und Infrastrukturbank Hessen (WIBank)
Estonia	• None
Ireland	• Housing Finance Agency plc (HFA)
Greece	• None
Spain	• ADIF-Alta Velocidad • Fondo de Amortización del Déficit Eléctrico, Fondo de Titulización de Activos (FADE) • Instituto Catalán De Finanzas (ICF) • Instituto de Crédito Oficial (ICO) • Instituto de Finanzas de Cantabria (ICAF)
France	• Agence Française de Développement (AFD) • Agence France Locale (AFL) • Assistance Publique-Hôpitaux de Paris (AP-HP) • Bpifrance Financement • Caisse d'Amortissement de la dette sociale (CADES) • Caisse des dépôts et consignations (CDC) • Action Logement Services (ALS) • Agence centrale des organismes de sécurité sociale (ACOSS) • Alliade Habitat • Batigère • Caisse Nationale des Autoroutes (CNA) • CDC Habitat • Clairsienne • Clesence • Grand Delta Habitat

Country	Agencies
France (continued)	• Groupement des Centres Hospitaliers Universitaires (CHU) / Centres Hospitaliers Régionaux (CHR) • Halpades Societe Anonyme HLM • Île-de-France Mobilités (previously STIF) • IN'LI • Maisons et cites Soginorpa • Néolia • SFIL S.A. • SNCF Réseau • Société du Grand Paris (SGP) • Unédic • Valloire Habitat • Vilogia
Croatia	• None
Italy	• Agenzia nazionale per l'attrazione degli investimenti e lo sviluppo d'impresa S.p.A. (Invitalia) • Cassa Depositi e prestiti S.p.A. (CDP) • Cassa del Trentino S.p.A. • Finlombarda S.p.A.
Cyprus	• None
Latvia	• Attistibas finanšu institucija Altum
Lithuania	• UAB Valstybės investicinis kapitalas (VIK)
Luxembourg	• None
Hungary	• None
Malta	• Malta Development Bank
Netherlands	• BNG Bank N.V. • Nederlandse Financierings-Maatschappij voor Ontwikkelingslanden N.V. (FMO) • Nederlandse Waterschapsbank N.V. (NWB Bank)
Austria	• Autobahnen- und Schnellstraßen-Finanzierungs-Aktiengesellschaft (ASFINAG) • ÖBB-Infrastruktur A.G. • Oesterreichische Kontrollbank A.G. (OeKB) • Wohnbau Burgenland GmbH
Poland	• None
Portugal	• Infraestruturas de Portugal S.A. (IP) • PARPÚBLICA - Participações Públicas S.A. (SGPS)
Romania	• None
Slovenia	• Družba za avtoceste v Republiki Sloveniji, d.d. (DARS) • SID – Slovenska izvozna in razvojna banka, d.d., Ljubljana (SID banka) • Slovenská záručná a rozvojová banka, a.s. (SZRB) Slovenski državni holding, d.d. (SDH)
Slovakia	• None
Finland	• Finnvera PLC • Kuntarahoitus Oyj/ Municipality Finance PLC (MuniFin) • Työllisyysrahasto (previously Työttömyysvakuutusrahasto (TVR))
Sweden	• None

Year	Project	EIB 'Project' Amount	EIB 'project' Details	EIF mentioned
2015	Montepio Loan for SMEs Midcaps & Other Priorities 3	€200 million	https://www.eib.org/en/press/all/2015-078-eib-and-montepio-sign-an-agreement-in-support-of-smes-and-midcaps	N
2015	EIB-IADB Joint Facility for SMEs & Midcaps PT	€30 million	https://www.eib.org/en/press/all/2015-079-first-tranche-of-the-eib-iadb-agreement-in-support-of-internationalisation-of-smes-signed-in-portugal	N
2015	BES Loan for Midcaps and Other Priorities III	€300 million	https://www.eib.org/en/press/all/2015-083-eib-lends-eur-300-million-to-novo-banco-for-financing-smes-and-midcaps-in-portugal	N
2015	Credito Agricola for SMEs and Other Priorities I	€50 million	https://www.eib.org/en/press/all/2015-081-eib-lends-eur-50-million-to-credito-agricola-for-financing-smes	N
2015	Banco Popular SMEs and Midcaps V	€500 million	https://www.eib.org/en/press/all/2015-111-bei-banco-popular-acuerdo-de-1-000-millones-de-eur-para-financiacion-de-pymes with Spain	N
2015	IHRU III – Rental Housing Rehabilitation	€25 million	https://www.eib.org/en/press/all/2015-158-eib-loan-for-rehabilitation-of-housing-in-portugal	N
2015	SAPEC Agro RDI	€25 million	https://www.eib.org/en/press/all/2015-161-eib-lends-eur-25-million-to-sapec-agro-and-tradecorp-international-for-rdi-programme	N
2015	Deutsche Bank KMU & Midcap Loan V	€250 million	https://www.eib.org/en/projects/all/20150005 Multicountry	N
2015	PF4EE Collateral Agreements	€55 million	https://www.eib.org/en/projects/all/20150420 Multicountry; Private Finance for Energy Efficiency	N
2015	BIAL Inovacao RDI II	€60 million	https://www.eib.org/en/press/all/2015-229-eib-lends-eur-60-million-to-bial-in-support-of-rdi	N
2015	BPI Loan for Agriculture SMEs & Midcaps	€50 million	https://www.eib.org/en/press/all/2015-273-bpi-receives-a-eur-50-million-eib-loan-for-smes-in-the-agriculture-sector	N
2015	BCP Loan for SMEs and Other Priorities 3	€500 million	https://www.eib.org/en/press/all/2015-275-eib-and-millennium-bcp-eur-500-million-to-facilitate-access-to-credit-for-smes-and-midcaps	N
2015	REN – Electricity System Upgrade III	€170 million	https://www.eib.org/en/press/all/2015-274-eib-lends-eur-80-million-to-ren-to-upgrade-the-portuguese-transmission-system	N
2015	BST Loan for SMEs Midcaps & Other Priorities IV	€500 million	https://www.eib.org/en/press/all/2016-362-eib-signs-a-eur-150-million-loan-with-banco-santander-totta-to-promote-economic-growth-and-employment-in-portugal	N
2016	Bankinter Loan for SMEs & Midcaps IV	€350 million	https://www.eib.org/en/press/all/2016-060-eur-350m-eib-bankinter-loan-agreement-for-smes with Spain	N
2016	Portucel Cacia Mill Optimisation	€25 million	https://www.eib.org/en/press/all/2016-167-eib-loan-to-support-the-navigator-company-cacia-pulp-mill-modernisation-and-expansion	N
2016	Growth Equity Fund Midcaps	€40 million	https://www.eib.org/en/press/all/2016-107-eib-group-provides-eur-100-million-for-new-private-equity-fund-investing-in-tech-and-industrial-firms with Spain	Y - EFSI
2016	Portugal Employment & Startups Programme	€300 million	https://www.eib.org/en/projects/all/20150353	N
2016	Wave Energy Device (FDP)	€10 million	https://www.eib.org/en/press/all/2016-175-finland-innovfin-european-support-for-innovation-in-finland with Finland	N
2016	EU Funds Co-Financing 2014-2020 (PT)	€250 million	https://www.eib.org/en/press/all/2016-192-eib-eur-750-million-to-support-priority-investments-in-portugal	N
2016	Midcap programme Loan Spain	€248 million	https://www.eib.org/en/projects/all/20160359 with Spain	N
Year	Project	EIB	EIB 'project' Details	EIF

		'Project' Amount		mentioned
2016	BST Employment & Startups Programme	€70 million	https://www.eib.org/en/projects/all/20160594	Y - EFSI
2016	BPI Employment & Startups Programme	€70 million	https://www.eib.org/en/projects/all/20160593	Y - EFSI
2016	BCP Employment & Startups Programme	€70 million	https://www.eib.org/en/projects/all/20160595	Y - EFSI
2016	CGD Employment & Startups Programme	€70 million	https://www.eib.org/en/press/all/2016-216-eib-supports-the-portuguese-economy-with-a-eur-300-million-programme-under-the-investment-plan-for-europe	Y - EFSI
2016	Montepio Employment & Startups Programme	€20 million	https://www.eib.org/en/press/all/2016-259-eu-supports-employment-and-innovation-in-portugal-with-a-eur-20-million-eib-loan-under-the-investment-plan-for-europe	Y - EFSI
2016	Lisbon Urban Regeneration Climate Housing FL	€160 million	https://www.eib.org/en/projects/all/20160209	N
2016	BPI Loan for SMEs and Other Priorities 5	€400 million	https://www.eib.org/en/press/all/2016-359-eib-signs-two-loans-with-bpi-for-a-total-eur-350-million-funding-to-support-smes-and-energy-efficiency-investments-in-portugal	N
2016	BPI Energy Efficiency FL PF4EE	€50 million	https://www.eib.org/en/press/all/2016-359-eib-signs-two-loans-with-bpi-for-a-total-eur-350-million-funding-to-support-smes-and-energy-efficiency-investments-in-portugal	N
2017	BCP Loan for SMEs and Other Priorities 4	€50 million	https://www.eib.org/en/press/all/2017-172-eib-signs-a-eur-250-million-loan-with-millennium-bcp-to-support-smes-and-midcaps-in-portugal	N
2017	CGD Loan for SMEs and Other Priorities III	€300 million	https://www.eib.org/en/press/all/2018-023-eu-bank-and-cgd-provide-eur-300-million-to-support-portuguese-smes	N
2017	Parenteral Solutions Industrial Project Portugal	€20 million	https://www.eib.org/en/press/all/2017-178-first-direct-loan-under-the-investment-plan-for-europe-to-a-portuguese-midcap	Y - EFSI
2017	Natural Gas Distribution Portugal 2016-2019	€29 million	https://www.eib.org/en/press/all/2017-174-juncker-plan-eur-29-million-eib-loan-to-finance-the-expansion-of-gas-distribution-in-portugal	Y - EFSI
2017	NOVA SBE Campus	€16 million	https://www.eib.org/en/press/all/2017-231-investment-plan-for-europe-eur-16-million-eib-loan-agreement-to-finance-construction-of-new-campus-for-the-nova-school-of-business-and-economics	Y - EFSI
2017	Usine du Futur & Innovation	€40 million	https://www.eib.org/en/press/all/2017-242-efsi-la-bei-finance-le-developpement-du-groupe-mecachrome-a-hauteur-de-40-meur with France	Y - EFSI
2017	Suma Capital Energy Efficiency	€20 million	https://www.eib.org/en/projects/all/20160551 with Spain	N
2017	IFRRU 2014-2020	€300 million	https://www.eib.org/en/press/all/2017-237-the-eib-supports-urban-rehabilitation-and-energy-efficiency-in-cities-of-portugal-with-a-eur-300-million-loan	N
2017	Portugal Water Supply & Sanitation	€420 million	https://www.eib.org/en/press/all/2017-235-eib-supports-the-modernisation-of-water-infrastructure-in-portugal-with-a-eur420-million-loan-under-the-investment-plan-for-europe	Y - EFSI
2017	Efficient Private Housing Programme PT	€70 million	https://www.eib.org/en/projects/all/20170127	N
2017	SCIENCE4YOU (EGFF)	€10 million	https://www.eib.org/en/press/all/2017-301-portuguese-toy-company-science4you-and-eib-sign-eur-10-million-loan-under-the-investment-plan-for-europe	Y - EFSI
2017	BPI Innovfin Mid-Cap Guarantee	€150 million	https://www.eib.org/en/press/all/2017-401-eib-and-bpi-join-forces-to-support-innovation-in-portugal-up-to-eur-300-million-provided-through-the-innovfin-midcap-guarantee-facility-for-smes-and-midcaps	N
Year	Project	EIB 'Project'	EIB 'project' Details	EIF mentioned

		Amount		
2017	Loan 4 SMEs & Midcaps Forest Fire Support	€75 million	https://www.eib.org/en/press/all/2018-019-eib-and-millennium-bcp-provide-eur-150m-to-finance-smes-and-midcaps-affected-by-forest-fires	N
2017	CGD Efficient Private Housing Programme	€30 million	https://www.eib.org/en/projects/all/20170842	N
2018	Instituição Financeira de Desenvolvimento IFD Loan for SMEs and Other Priorities	€250 million	https://www.eib.org/en/press/all/2018-022-eur-250-million-eib-credit-facility-to-ifd-first-eur-100-million-tranche-to-support-portuguese-smes-and-midcaps	N
2018	Plysa Forest Fire Extinction Fleet	€20 million	https://www.eib.org/en/projects/all/20170689 with Spain	N
2018	Portugal Irrigation Plan	€200 million	https://www.eib.org/en/press/all/2018-088-eib-and-ceb-provide-eur-280-million-to-finance-modernisation-and-expansion-of-irrigation-infrastructure-in-portugal	N
2018	Innovative Diagnostics Tools (MGF)	€17 million	https://www.eib.org/en/press/all/2015-279-eur-12-million-loan-under-innovfin-to-support-biosurfits-rdi-activities-in-medical-diagnostics	N
2018	Midcap Programme Loan Spain & Portugal 2	€400 million	https://www.eib.org/en/projects/all/20170871 with Spain	Y - EFSI
2018	BCP Efficient Private Housing Programme PT	€25 million	https://www.eib.org/en/projects/all/20170844	N
2018	Novobanco Efficient Private Housing Programme PT	€15 million	https://www.eib.org/en/projects/all/20170846	N
2018	Portuguese Ports Private Investment Plan 2017-19	€40 million	https://www.eib.org/en/projects/all/20170413	N
2018	Figueira Mill Optimisation	€40 million	https://www.eib.org/en/press/all/2018-266-eib-provides-eur-40-million-to-the-navigator-company-to-improve-production-and-energy-efficiency-at-figueira-da-foz-pulp-plant	N
2018	Tamega Iberdrola Hydropower & Storage Portugal	€650 million	https://www.eib.org/en/press/all/2018-198-major-investment-in-the-energy-sector-in-portugal-eib-finances-iberdrola-s-three-new-dams-and-hydropower-plants-on-the-tamega-and-torno-rivers	N
2018	CIE Automotive RDI & Convergence	€120 million	https://www.eib.org/en/press/all/2018-201-support-for-innovation-in-car-industry-eib-finances-cie-automotives-rdi-strategy-with-eur-80-million-loan-under-juncker-plan Multicountry	Y - EFSI
2018	Lisbon Climate Adaptation Drainage System	€65 million	https://www.eib.org/en/projects/all/20160412	N
2018	BPI Loan for SMEs and Other Priorities 6	€250 million	https://www.eib.org/en/press/all/2018-270-eib-and-bpi-join-forces-to-provide-eur-500-million-to-finance-small-and-medium-sized-portuguese-companies	N
2018	Credito Agricola Loan for SMEs and Other Priorities 2	€100 million	https://www.eib.org/en/press/all/2018-263-support-for-smes-in-portugal-eib-and-credito-agricola-provide-eur-200-million-to-finance-investments	N
2018	Windfloat Innovfin FDP	€60 million	https://www.eib.org/en/press/all/2018-259-eu-supports-breakthrough-wind-energy-technology-in-portugal-with-eur-60-million-loan-granted-by-the-eib-under-innovfin-to-windplus	N
2018	Bial Pharmceutical RDI	€n/a million	No information	Unknown
2018	Advanced Automotive Fabrics Project Portugal	€25 million	https://www.eib.org/en/press/all/2018-347-juncker-plan-eib-supports-portuguese-car-interiors-manufacturer-tmgs-growth-and-innovation-strategy	Y - EFSI
2018	IFD Restart & Modernise Programme	€100 million	https://www.eib.org/en/press/all/2018-346-eib-and-ifd-join-forces-to-finance-modernisation-of-portuguese-smes-and-mid-caps	N
2018	Energy & Environmental Sustainability Project	€55 million	https://www.eib.org/en/projects/all/20170480	N
2019	Fresh Vegetable Food Portugal	€35 million	https://www.eib.org/en/projects/all/20170902	N
Year	**Project**	**EIB 'Project'**	**EIB 'project' Details**	**EIF mentioned**

Year	Project	Amount		EIF mentioned
2019	BPI Loan for SMEs & Midcaps	€n/a million	No information	Unknown
2019	Madeira New Central Hospital	€159 million	https://www.eib.org/en/projects/all/20190108	N
2019	Wind Farms PT 1	€47 million	https://www.eib.org/en/projects/all/20180290	N
2019	Novo Banco Loan for SMEs & Midcaps	€225 million	https://www.eib.org/en/projects/all/20180197	N
2019	Portugal Solid Waste Investment Plan	€75 million	https://www.eib.org/en/projects/all/20180487	N
2019	BCP Innovative Midcap Linked Risk Sharing	€100 million	https://www.eib.org/en/projects/all/20180390	N
2019	Montepio Loan for SMEs Midcaps & Other Priorities 4	€300 million	https://www.eib.org/en/projects/all/20160864	N
2020	UCI Green Energy Mortgages MBIL SFSB	€100 million	https://www.eib.org/en/press/all/2020-128-eib-and-union-de-creditos-inmobiliarios-join-forces-to-boost-energy-efficiency-projects-in-spain-and-portugal with Spain	N
2020	Iberia Covid-19 Healthcare Programme Loan	€750 million	https://www.eib.org/en/projects/all/20200150 with Spain	N
2020	EV Charging Stations Iberia Programme Loan	€200 million	https://www.eib.org/en/projects/all/20190752 with Spain	N
2020	SCF Portugal Covid-19 Loan for SMEs and Midcaps	€434 million	https://www.eib.org/en/projects/all/20200142	N
2020	SCF Portugal Covid-19 ABS for SMEs and Midcaps	€55 million	https://www.eib.org/en/projects/all/20200298	N
2020	Figueira Environmental Enhancement	€28 million	https://www.eib.org/en/projects/all/20200029	N
2020	Elderly Care Investment in Portugal	€200 million	https://www.eib.org/en/press/all/2020-293-the-eib-and-ifd-provide-eur200-million-in-financing-to-upgrade-elderly-care-infrastructure-across-portugal	N
2020	Bizay (EGFF)	€20 million	https://www.eib.org/en/press/all/2020-335-web-summit-the-eib-provides-bizay-with-eur20-million-to-support-their-rd-programme-and-product-development-fostering-employment-in-portugal	Y - EFSI
2020	IFD Covid-19 Loan for SMEs and Midcaps	€340 million	https://www.eib.org/en/projects/all/20200300	N
2020	Portugal Irrigation Plan – Reguengos Subproject	€30 million	https://www.eib.org/en/projects/all/20190813	N
2020	Madeira Electricity Network Optimization	€65 million	https://www.eib.org/en/projects/all/20190873	N
2020	Global Shares (EGFF)	€n/a million	No information	Y – EFSI (through EGFF)
2020	Montepio Covid-19 Loans for SMEs and Midcaps	€158 million	https://www.eib.org/en/projects/all/20200351	N
2020	Montepio ABS Covid-19 Loans for SMEs and Midcaps	€71 million	https://www.eib.org/en/projects/all/20200352	N
2020	Portugal Water Distribution Optimization North	€28 million	https://www.eib.org/en/projects/all/20200073	N
2020	Icicle Wind Farm	€65 million	https://www.eib.org/en/press/all/2021-011-portugal-eib-and-bpi-provide-edp-renovaveis-with-eur112-million-to-construct-and-operate-two-wind-farms-with-a-total-capacity-of-125-mw	Y - EFSI
2021	Sugal Agro Sustainable Investment Programme	€40 million	https://www.eib.org/en/projects/all/20200438	N
2021	UCI Building Renovation MBIL	€50 million	https://www.eib.org/en/press/all/2021-158-eib-and-uci-join-forces-to-renovate-homes-in-spain-and-portugal-reducing-co2-emissions-by-up-to-10-269-tonnes-a-year with Spain	N
2021	CGD EGF Midcaps Risk Sharing	€113 million	https://www.eib.org/en/press/all/2021-217-portugal-eib-guarantee-of-eur113-million-to-cgd-to-support-faster-economic-recovery-of-portuguese-companies-from-covid-19	Y - EGF
2021	Midcap Programme Loan Spain & Portugal 3	€250 million	https://www.eib.org/en/projects/all/20210118 with Spain	N
Year	Project	EIB 'Project' Amount	EIB 'project' Details	EIF mentioned

2021	AFR-IX Medusa Submarine Cable System	€163 million	https://www.eib.org/en/projects/all/20210166 Multicountry	N
2021	Galp EV Sustainable Charging Network	€42 million	https://www.eib.org/en/press/all/2021-344-eib-to-provide-galp-with-eur732-million-to-promote-climate-action-and-social-cohesion-in-spain-and-portugal with Spain	N
2021	Alco Solar PV Green Energy Loan	€40 million	Same data as above	N
2021	NAV Portugal ATM Upgrade	€100 million	https://www.eib.org/en/projects/all/20200760	N
2021	Energy Efficient Refurbishments Spain & Portugal	€45 million	https://www.eib.org/en/projects/all/20210080 with Spain	N
2021	Unitranche Bridge Financings	€100 million	https://www.eib.org/en/press/all/2022-075-eib-to-provide-eur100-million-to-co-finance-solar-photovoltaic-and-wind-energy-projects-on-the-iberian-peninsula with Spain	N
2021	BCP EGF Midcaps Risk Sharing	€200 million	https://www.eib.org/en/projects/all/20200740	Y - EGF
2021	NB EGF Midcaps Risk Sharing	€100 million	https://www.eib.org/en/projects/all/20210678	Y - EGF
2021	Montepio EGF Midcaps Risk Sharing	€116 million	https://www.eib.org/en/projects/all/20210548	Y - EGF
2021	Medway Cargo Rolling Stock	€45 million	https://www.eib.org/en/projects/all/20200410	N

Bibliography

B Reynolds, D Blake and R Lyddon, *Managing Euro Risk: Saving Investors from Systemic Risk* (Politeia, 2020)

European Union – www.european-union.europa.eu

European Central Bank Annual Reports 2010-21 and further resources within the 'Statistics', 'Monetary Policy' and 'Payments and Markets' sections of the ECB website – www.ecb.europa.eu

European Investment Bank Annual Financial Reports 2010-21 – www.eib.org

European Investment Fund Annual Reports 2010-21 – www.eif.org

Euorpean Stability Mechanism and European Financial Stability Facility – www.esm.europa.eu

Eurostat statistical database – www.ecb.europa.eu/eurostat

EDP - Energias de Portugal SA Annual Report 2021 – www.edp.com

Bank for International Settlements – www.bis.org

Financial Stability Board – www.fsb.org

Monte dei Paschi di Siena Group – www.grupomps.it

Unicredit Group – www.unicreditgroup.eu

www.brugesgroup.com

Ingram Content Group UK Ltd.
Milton Keynes UK
UKHW050858050523
421284UK00012B/231